THE STORY OF JOHN TAYLOR

STORIES OF THE MODERN PROPHETS™

COURAGEOUS
_of_ DEFENDER
TRUTH

THE STORY OF JOHN TAYLOR

BLAINE M. YORGASON

The Living Scriptures®
Ogden, Utah

Published by The Living Scriptures®
Ogden, Utah

This book is a work of both fiction and nonfiction. Chapter beginning
narrative (printed in colored ink), which contains references to actual
historical characters, places, and incidents, is the product of the author's
creativity or is represented fictitiously. The majority of this book's content
(printed in black ink) is historical nonfiction based on the author's
research, containing endnotes and bibliography. The views expressed
herein are the responsibility of the author and do not necessarily
represent the position of Living Scriptures, Inc.

First Printing, 2002
Printed in the United States of America
10 9 8 7 6 5 4 3 2 1

ISBN 1-56473-177-4

In Appreciation:

For Jared and Margie Brown,
without whose courageous dream
this could not have been!

ℱOREWORD

When Jared F. Brown, President of Living Scriptures, first contacted me about writing *Stories of the Modern Prophets*™, I was troubled as well as excited. Excited, for I have held these men and their accomplishments in awe and reverence for nearly as long as I have memory. Yet troubled because the challenge of writing each book as Jared wanted seemed so formidable.

First, he wanted each manuscript to be written in an interesting story format that was *not* fictional and did not use fictional characters to carry the theme. Second, he wanted these books to be historical but not ponderous—the stories not of prophets, but of how the Lord turned boys and men into them. Third, he felt like each book should be advantageous to scholars without being burdened by footnotes or other types of documentation. Fourth, he wanted numerous photographs without turning the books into photo albums. And finally, he wanted each of these volumes to be so unique that it would stand alone, independent of other biographies and books about these great men.

As might be imagined, meeting these expectations proved more than challenging, yet I am confident we have found a way to accomplish it. First with *From Orphaned Boy to Prophet of God: The Story of Joseph F. Smith;* next with *Humble Servant, Spiritual Giant:*

The Story of Harold B. Lee; and now with *Courageous Defender of Truth: The Story of John Taylor,* each chapter begins with a historical *vignette*—a short, delicate literary sketch of some significant event in the life of that particular prophet. These are the story portions of the book—independent segments that can entertain young and old alike, bringing to literary life events that in any other format might seem like dry, historical details.

Following each *vignette* the historian in me takes over, and a chronological account is built of the historical facts surrounding the story. This portion is fully documented with sources consulted and/or quoted, although I use endnotes rather than footnotes to make the pages flow more easily.

Though I respect these men deeply, I have also chosen to use their first names throughout the texts, feeling that such usage gives the books a more intimate feel.

The photographs and illustrations, as before, are left up to the creative staff at Living Scriptures. In addition, Laurie Bonnell Stephens and her staff are already producing *The Modern Prophets*™ video documentaries on each of these great men.

Though difficult, it turns out that this is some of the most enjoyable writing I have ever done. Not only am I privileged to develop a more intimate understanding of our modern prophets and how the Lord prepared them for His work, but I have the opportunity to take significant moments from their lives and dramatize them in a way that shows their very human side. This satisfies both my training as a historian and my lifelong love of stories. I don't believe this format has ever been used, at least in this manner, and I am pleased to be a part of it.

Blaine M. Yorgason
February 2002

I

TRUE TO FAMILY AND FAITH

"Let me see, now." John Taylor was muttering under his breath as he leaned into the oars. "It'll be better if I avoid the dock, and if I use the alley I think I can get to the house without being seen. Leastwise, I hope so!"

The skiff he had borrowed was small. But at least, he was thinking with a slight smile, the leaking was minimal, and he didn't have to worry about bailing. Not that he wouldn't have bailed as well as rowed, had it come to that. Or anything else, he thought grimly—just so long as he could get over the river, accomplish his task, and get back again without being discovered.

The February night was cold and moonless. Floating chunks of ice were constantly knocking the small craft off course, and though his back was toward the distant but approaching shore, John remained as certain of where the skiff was headed as if he had been facing forward in broad daylight. For a fact, he had been rowing small boats in all sorts of weather since almost before he could remember. First in the backwaters of England's Morecambe Bay, and later on Lake Ullswater near Penrith, John had plied the waters in skiffs and every other sort of craft that might fall into the hands of a young boy. He had therefore become what might be considered a master oarsman—a skill which would stand him in good stead this lonely and dangerous night.

Though the wounds he had acquired in Carthage pained him constantly, he did his best to ignore them. But the missing flesh of his hip, though it was healed and scarred over, caused him particular agony when he sat for too long a time in one place—especially when the surface on which he sat was hard and without padding. But because he had never yet sat in a skiff with padded seats, he had expected to suffer during the mile-long crossing of the river. Such expectations made it no easier, however, and as he finally neared the eastern shore he was breathing in ragged gasps, his teeth set hard against the fiery agony.

"Remember, John," his mind forcefully reminded him as his oars dipped and pushed against the freezing water, "when you first entered upon Mormonism, you did it with your eyes open. You counted the cost. You looked upon it as a lifelong labor, and you considered that you were not only enlisted for time, but for eternity also. You do not wish to shrink now, no matter that you feel your incompetence. Add to that the fact that little Joseph James is counting on you."

With a quiet scrape the skiff pushed through the lip of ice and onto the gravel of the shore. Instantly shipping the oars, John stepped overboard, winced as the ice cracked and disintegrated beneath his weight, and then pulled the skiff further inland, into a stand of rushes. Reaching back aboard he took out his cane, turned, and limped upward through the snow-covered rushes, emerging within a dozen feet of where he had determined to enter the silent, darkened city of Nauvoo.

For a moment he paused, gazing intently at the snow-shrouded city, both looking and listening for any sign of life. Somewhere far off a dog barked and was answered by another, but near him there was nothing—neither light nor sound to intrude upon the senses. Still, John knew he had to be more than careful, for he was a marked and wanted man, and the enemies of the Saints would like nothing better than to capture him, beat him within an inch of his life, and then haul him before the leaders of the mob/militia who were systematically driving the Saints from their homes.

With a deep breath that became a cloud of steam he started forward once more, limping eastward over the frozen earth until he felt the rutted, uneven surface of Parley Street beneath his feet. Before him on his left loomed the Seventies Hall and blacksmith shop, and immediately after passing them he turned left and moved northward until he had limped past the now empty home of Brigham Young. At the ruts signifying Kimball Street he turned eastward again, but instead of staying in the road he soon drifted left onto a snowy path he had walked hundreds of times—a narrow path that led past his barn and now empty outbuildings, twisted through the small, skeletal-looking orchard he had so enjoyed in seasons of summer, and ended finally at the rear door to his own abandoned home.

Pulling his key from his pocket John inserted it into the lock and gently turned it, after which he turned the knob, pushed open the door, and crept stealthily inside. There he paused, his breath stilled as he strained to hear even the slightest of sounds. He had been gone only three days, John knew, yet he had no idea if someone had already taken possession of his home. But it was cold inside, the same as the out-of-doors; there was absolutely no sound anywhere; and intuitively he sensed that he was alone. Still he moved silently, without a light, wishing to create no effect that might warn another of his presence.

Through the kitchen he crept, into the parlor, and from there up the stairs and into the children's room where little Joseph James had slept. Inching through the inky blackness of the room he felt with his hands until he came to the far corner. Now, he thought with pounding heart, if it were only where he had left it when he had decided the wagon they had been loading at the time had no room for such a large child's toy…

Though Joseph James was ten going on eleven, for the entire two days since the Taylor family had crossed the Mississippi and gone into winter camp on Iowa's Sugar Creek, the boy had hardly stopped crying. Oh, he hadn't been wailing or anything like that; he was much too old for such outbursts. Rather, he had been almost constantly teary, with such a sad look on his face that John had finally sat him on a log and pleaded to know what was troubling him.

"It...it's my horse," Joseph James had responded quietly, "the one you made for me when I was tiny. I...I miss it, Father. I love that horse, and I keep feeling that I...I should have it with me." The boy took a deep breath. "I've been praying, too, asking the Lord to protect it until I can go back after it when I am grown a little older..."

Of course John had known instantly what his son was talking about—a small toy horse he had turned and carved and put on rockers shortly after they had settled in Nauvoo nearly six years before. He had even inserted a mane and tail made from hair taken from his own horse—a fact not lost on his small son, even then. From that day the boy had loved his rocking horse more than any other possession, rocking on it sometimes for hours on end. And even though he was now far too large to use it, John had suddenly realized the boy's emotional attachment was still there and needed to be honored. Moreover, he was feeling an interesting spiritual impression—

"You've been praying over it, Joseph James?"

"Is...that bad of me, Father?" The child was suddenly nervous. "I...I know it is only a toy..."

"Yes, but a very important toy. And what is important to us, no matter our age, is always important to our Heavenly Father. Would it make you happy, son, if we didn't wait for you to grow older? Instead, would you mind if I returned to Nauvoo and fetched it back for you?"

"You...would do that? Go all the way back across the river,

just for my horse?"

"Would you go, Joseph James, if you were the daddy and I was your brave son?"

Silently the boy had nodded.

"Then I shall do the same." Playfully John had tousled his son's hair.

"Run and tell your mother to pack me a little lunch. I shall leave as soon as my horse is saddled, and I hope to be back before morning."

Joyfully the boy had sped off to find Leonora, and John had walked to where his horse was tethered, his mind filled with the difficulties and dangers that had lain ahead of him. Yet he had also been praying about the impression of the Spirit that had led to his decision, and now as he stood in the darkened home in Nauvoo he smiled at the clarity of the impression—of the Lord's promise to him of safety and success. That prayer-given response alone, he knew, was what had given Leonora peace as he had kissed both her and Joseph James good-bye and ridden alone into the cold of the early evening.

Now, reaching down into the dark corner of the room, John's smile grew wider. The small wooden animal was exactly where he had left it something more than half a hundred hours before. If anyone had wandered through the home to loot it, they had missed the toy—another evidence of his small son's wonderful faith. After all, every other home he had heard anything of had already been either looted or occupied.

Taking the horse up in the hand that did not wield his cane, the still-smiling father turned and retraced his steps through and out of the silent, empty home. Yes, he was thinking as he closed the door and started back along the snowy path through his orchard and toward the frigid waters of the mighty Mississippi, he and his family might have been driven and deprived of all their worldly goods by the inhumane mobs. But the Lord was still mindful of them and was willing to bless them according to their faith—

Illustration by Robert T. Barrett

including that of a tenderhearted, ten-year-old boy! 1

John Taylor, third President of The Church of Jesus Christ of Latter-day Saints, loved and adored his large and widespread family. No sacrifice he could make for them was too great, no moment in his life so precious as those he could spend with them. Yet oftentimes those moments seemed rare, for in addition to his beloved family, John had given his heart and soul to the Lord. In fact, he had been close to the Spirit of the Lord since his earliest childhood and had never thought of his dedication to God as a conscious choice. For him the veil had always been remarkably thin, partially because it had been spiritually gifted to him, and partially because he was so thoroughly dedicated to obeying God and assisting in his work. He consistently endeavored to obey his own spiritual impressions and personal revelations, as well as the word of God revealed to the prophets both ancient and modern, and so throughout his life the Lord consistently stood beside him, blessing and protecting him in every way possible.

His lifelong ministry began while he was still a youth, as he labored first as an Exhorter for the Methodist faith, then served as a lay minister of that faith until his baptism as a young husband and father at the hands of Latter-day Saint apostle Parley P. Pratt. From then until the end of his life he preached the restored gospel relentlessly and fearlessly. Moreover, he so bravely stood against cruelty, injustice, and personal danger, that he earned from the adoring Saints the title "Champion of Truth and Right."

He was privileged to be in Carthage Jail with Joseph Smith, Joseph's brother Hyrum, and Willard Richards on the afternoon of June 27, 1844, when mobs attacked and martyred the two Smith brothers. Though Elder Richards escaped without a serious wound, John Taylor received five balls in his body—the same number of wounds received by both Joseph and Hyrum. Yet while they died, he lived, physically hampered from carrying the wounds (and one ball) with him for the remainder of his life. At his funeral in 1887, Elder F. D. Richards said:

> There were but very few men that attained the warm, personal relation that he attained to and maintained most successfully with the Prophet Joseph Smith till he died, and the story of that personal affection was consummated by the bullets he received in Carthage jail with the Prophet when he was slain. President Taylor was himself disabled. In the scene that he then passed through he experienced all that pertains to martyrdom. He never suffered greater pain, or more severe pain than he experienced in the jail with the Prophet Joseph. 2

For the next forty years John Taylor served the Latter-day Saints, showing forth "his magnanimity, his Priesthood and his fervor, and [being] a blessing to God's people in these valleys of the mountains." 3

"In person President Taylor was nearly six feet in height and of fine proportion, that combination which gives activity and strength. His head was large, the face oval and the features large, strong and finely chiseled. The forehead was high and massive, the eyes gray, deep-set, and of a mild, kindly expression, except when aroused, and then they were capable of reflecting all the feelings that moved his soul, whether of indignation, scorn or contempt. The nose was aquiline, the mouth well formed and expressive of firmness, the chin powerful and well rounded. In early life he was of a fair complexion, but with age the face grew swarthy, and even in middle life his abundant hair turned to a silvery whiteness, which but added beauty to his brow and made his appearance venerable.

"In his manner he was ever affable and polite, easy and gracious, yet princely in dignity. In his intercourse with others he was familiar but never vulgar. He was not a man whom a friend, however intimate, would slap familiarly on the back or turn and twist about

Courtesy of Church Archives, The Church of Jesus Christ of Latter-day Saints. ©Intellectual Reserve, Inc.

President John Taylor
1808–1887

CA. *mid-1880s*

when shaking hands; such proceedings with him would have been as much out of place as with the proudest crowned monarch in the presence-chamber. Yet there was no affectation in his deportment, no stiffness; his dignity was that with which nature clothes her noblest sons...

"He was deliberate in speech, almost slow, but not more so than the great principles he was wont to treat of required. His voice was clear, strong, resonant, and of wonderful compass; and whether it sank, as it often did, to the tender tones which give expression to the deep pathos that sometimes moved his soul, or calmly reasoned upon some heavenly doctrine, or was raised to its grandest swell or thunder tones to denounce injustice or oppression, no one could grow weary of listening to it.

"His eloquence was a majestic river full to the point of overflowing its banks, sweeping grandly through rich regions of thought. His discourse was mainly argumentative and abounding with occasional colloquialisms, not unfrequently *[sic]* of a humorous turn: for among his other qualities of mind he had a keen sense of the ridiculous. His gestures were few, but very significant. His manner was, in the main, calm and dispassionate, but when a train of thought more than ordinarily sublime stirred his emotions, he became more animated and impressive; ...the utterance was more rapid and the whole man was aglow with enthusiasm that it was impossible to resist.

"If, as it often chanced, his theme was the wrongs of the Saints, or if he spoke in defense of the broad principles of liberty and the rights of man, he then had a theme which called forth all his powers. His denunciations of injustice and tyranny were terrible. At such times his brow...grew dark as the coming storm approached. The form was drawn up to its full height, the gestures were majestic...the whole man, with the love of liberty burning like consuming fire in his bones, poured out impassioned utterances against tyranny in all its forms; and the demonstrations of the congregation as the climax was reached, is sufficient evidence that they were irresistibly borne along by that tempest of passion. Yet in these bursts of eloquence he never seemed to put forth all his strength. He always appeared to have still more force in reserve that he could have used had he so minded. Moreover, he had that rare faculty which in the very torrent, tempest and whirl-wind of passion exercised a temperance that gave it smoothness and never permitted it to become strained or incongruous.

"These qualities in him sprang from nature, not from training. There was nothing of the schools, nor of the studied elocutionist in his manner. His style of speaking was peculiarly his own and was well suited to the man, and to him alone…

"Of the deep religious convictions of President Taylor it is scarcely necessary to speak. His whole life demonstrates how deep was the religious soil in his nature, into which the seeds of truth were sown to bring forth an hundred fold. His devotion to his religion was not only sincere, it was without reserve. He gave himself and his whole life to it. His faith, his trust and confidence in God were complete." He would sometimes say:

I do not believe in a religion that cannot have all my affections, …but I believe in a religion that I can live for, or die for.

I would rather trust in the living God than in any other power on earth. I learned [while on missions] that I could go to God and He always relieved me. He always supplied my wants. I always had plenty to eat, drink and wear, and could ride on steam-boats or railroads, or anywhere I thought proper: God always opened my way, and so He will that of every man who will put his trust in Him.

I would rather have God for my friend than all other influences and powers outside. 4

Finally, when President Taylor passed away while in hiding from federal officials who were seeking his arrest because of polygamy, his two counselors, George Q. Cannon and Joseph F. Smith, declared boldly to the world: "Today...President John Taylor...occupies the place of a double martyr. [He] has been killed by the cruelty of officials who have, in this Territory, misrepresented the Government of the United States. There is no room to doubt that if he had been permitted to enjoy the comforts of home, the ministrations of his family, the exercise to which he had been accustomed, but of which he was deprived, he might have lived for many years yet. His blood stains the clothes of the men, who with insensate hate have offered rewards for his arrest and have hounded him to the grave."[5]

It is the story of this courageous, spiritually attuned martyr to the truth that we now present.

2

SEEKING A DEVOUT DESTINY

"I don't understand it, sir." Sixteen-year-old John Taylor was shaking his head in anguish. "Henry declared boldly that he would be part of my group, but he's stopped gathering with us, and now he won't even speak to me."

"This is Henry Hampton you're speaking of, John? The son of Widow Hampton?"

The young man nodded miserably. "Yes, sir. Henry Hampton it is."

"Well, that disappoints me, John. I'd have thought he was more religious minded than you have found him to be. And more committed to his word, I might add."

For a time the two rode in silence, John Taylor at the reins of the plodding draft horse. Casually the good master turner glanced at his youthful apprentice, once again taking stock. With his square jaw, piercing blue eyes, and thick shock of wavy dark hair, John Taylor was what the master turner's wife and daughters called handsome. But more, for a youth of sixteen he was strapping big, not only tall as a man but thick like a man in the arms, shoulders, and chest. He was strong as a man, too, able without difficulty to lift and move about the heavy planks from which the master turner crafted his prized furniture.

John Taylor was not only strong, but he was also quick-witted, studious, and of a sober mind. In only a few short months he had become a middling good hand at the lathe—something more than one of the turner's apprentices had failed to accomplish even after several years. He was also a reader, constantly borrowing books of his master by such authors as Fielding, Milton, Shakespeare, Scott, Spenser, Goldsmith, and even the local Lake poets such as William Wordsworth, Robert Southey, Samuel Taylor Coleridge, and, from across the Scottish border, prolific Sir Walter Scott. John had also discovered *Don Quixote* and *Gulliver's Travels* and seemed to have learned that the Bible was good literature as well as scripture.

Moreover, he had read these books and learned, for since the day before while the master and his apprentice had been traveling, taking a load of finely turned furniture to a family in Eastriggs on Solway Firth, John had kept up a lively conversation regarding first one book and then another, frequently surprising the master turner with his insights or questions. Now they were returning to home and shop, which were situated in Penrith, Cumberland, and the master turner was thinking with some regret that their journey was near an end.

"You say it is near this place where you take Henry and the other lads for prayer?" the master turner asked. At the moment the wagon was passing the giant megalith and surrounding circle of sixty-six huge stones known as Long Meg and her Daughters, which were easily visible in a nearby pasture.

John Taylor nodded. "That's right, sir. In that copse of wood off to the left of the old stone circle."

The master turner chuckled. "Well, lad, you couldn't have picked a more likely place for a prayer gathering, nor a more beautiful, either one. I say it's no wonder the ancient folk gathered to this valley, pagans though they were. Praying here feels like the natural thing to do. Why, with the river Eden running through, that same River Eden as turns my lathes and gives us livelihood, even those old pagan stone builders must have thought of our valley as the vale of Eden!

"Yes, sir, John," the older man enthused, warming to his subject, "take a look around, and you'll see what I mean! This is one of the most beautiful spots in all of England. Eastward there is the Pennine Range, which just here reach their loftiest altitude. Westward is the Cumbrian group, where the highest summits in England may be found—Mount Scawfell, and closer here to us is Mount Helvellyn, and then yonder is Skiddaw. And fifteen lakes nestled at their bases. I know Lake Windemere is the most often spoken of, and is closest to where you were born, but I'll take our Ullswater near Penrith and home. It hasn't the same beauty of some of the other lakes, but situated as it is at the foot of Mount Helvellyn gives it a rugged grandeur."

John Taylor nodded his agreement. "Aye," he declared softly, "'tis a beautiful land here, where one imagines he can see water nymphs playing with the clouds on mountaintops, frolicking with the snow and rain in rugged gorges, coquetting with the sun and dancing to the sheen of the moon. Truly, sir, it is a valley of surpassing beauty!"

Surprised, the good master cast his eye on his youthful apprentice. "There's a note of poetry in your speech, John. Have you read those words out of one of my books, or are they of your own creating?"

John Taylor's face flushed. "So far as I know, sir, they are from nothing I have read."

"Interesting. I had no idea you'd been so gifted."

"Oftentimes words seem to spring to my mouth without my even thinking of them," John Taylor admitted, feeling a little abashed. "Perhaps it is this land of lakes and mountains which brings it out in me. I don't know."

For a few moments more the two rode in silence, each lost in his own thoughts. Then, as a spitting little rain descended upon them, John Taylor spoke again. "Beautiful or not, this valley is far too damp for my tastes."

The good master laughed. "Rain and snow catchers these mountains are, John. On occasion the snow stays on the peaks eight months of the year. But look about you. Only a great deal of water could give us such beautiful greenery, which of course the good Lord knew when he placed our mountains where he did. Aye, John, if this isn't the very valley where the Lord planted the Garden of Eden and then placed Adam and Eve in the first place, it's enough like it to have fooled the old pagan Druids who did all this fool stone building!"

"I've wondered if our copse is too close to their pagan alters," John admitted quietly. "Perhaps that's why my group is not being blessed."

"Nonsense! You aren't worshipping idols and false gods, are you? Of course not! Jesus Christ is He whom you are endeavoring to worship, and pure Methodism is the religion that teaches Him best! Believe me, John, the Lord won't abandon you for that!"

"It isn't me I'm worried about, sir. I love the Lord and I love Methodism. It's those other fellows I've enticed to come to the wood and pray with me. At first they pray so fervently and make such solemn promises before the Lord, and then at the first wind of opposition they abandon their promises altogether. Surely that cannot be good for their eternal souls!"

"No, John, it cannot! On the other hand, not all boys are going to be as religious in nature as you have become."

"But I don't mean to be more religious than they are, sir! As an infant I was baptized into the Church of England like everyone else, and though my godparents vowed for me that I would renounce the devil and all his works, as well as the pomp and vanity of this wicked world and all the deceitful lusts of the flesh, not ever as I was growing up did it mean so much as a fig to me."

The youthful John Taylor thought guiltily of his sinful past in

Liverpool, where between the ages of thirteen and fourteen he had roamed the docks and frequented pubs on a nightly basis, where he had happily "spliced the main brace" with his unwholesome friends. He had been an apprentice then, too—to a cooper who cared not at all where John went at night, so long as he gave every ounce of his energy to his work during the day.

His favorite Liverpool pub had been the Lion and Crown, for there had held forth a worldly gentleman of some substance and breeding known as Mr. Winters. Night after night John had devoured the man's wit and wisdom, downing his own grog, which used up every farthing of his meager wages, and waiting upon the well-born gentleman. Here, he had thought, was the sort of person he'd like to become—except for one thing. Night after night the man had turned himself into a drunken fool, leaving it up to one or another of the lads in the pub to help him home.

One night John had been given this privilege, and at the door of the hovel where the man lived, he had been shocked to see the man's haggard wife and the hollow eyes of his ragged children. This was how the great Mr. Winters returned home every night to loved ones made destitute because of his weakness. This was where demon rum had led him—

"I'll take care of him, lad, and thank you for bringing him," the woman had stated quietly. Her hopeless resignation had stunned John, but not as much as her parting words, uttered after she had got her drunken husband in through the door. Looking back at John, she had said, "You're too young for this sort of thing, lad. Don't let it get hold of you."

John had never entered the Lion and Crown again.

"Not that I was highly disposed to do evil," he finally continued, shaking the tarnished image of his past from his mind, "but I am by nature vivacious and full of laughter and have felt little inclination toward the stiff creed propounded by the Church of England. However, whenever I read the Bible I feel a reverence for

God, and since a year or so past I've felt a terrible dread about offending Him."

"As all good Methodists must feel!"

John Taylor nodded. "Yes, sir! And that is why I accepted Methodism when I heard it preached that night in your home. There seemed substance to it—a living religion if you will—that asked of me that very thing which my heart seems yearning to give.

"You see, sir; I have seen things, heard things—"

"What do you mean?" The master turner was startled.

"I...I mean that often when alone, and sometimes even in company, I hear soft, sweet, melodious music, as if performed by angelic or supernatural beings. I've heard it since I was a wee child. Then, too, when but a small boy I saw in vision an angel in the heavens, holding a trumpet to his mouth and sounding a message to the nations. Now you see, sir, why I know that God is real and why I am so fearful of offending him."

"I do, John," the master replied thoughtfully, "and I see why the other boys you have endeavored to claim for the Lord might not be remaining with you. For a fact, what you have told me gives me great concern."

"It does?"

"Of course. You're not a prophet or apostle, John, but an apprentice turner, and you must remember that! Those holy men are dead and gone these many centuries; the Holy Writ is complete; and God isn't about to call others to those high and holy callings— not in our enlightened age!

"No, John, the less you speak of such fanciful things, the better off you'll be, for others will not understand or be as patient as I and will doubt wholeheartedly that you have any integrity in you at all. Do you understand me?"

"I...I think so. Only..."

"Good! Now, keep up your study of the Bible, John, and let your speech be confined to repeating the Lord's word as He has given it to the ancients. As I said, they're dead and gone these many centuries, and no one appreciates a young man who sets himself up to be the same as them. Instead, you be a missionary for those ancient, blessed men, John, just as you've been doing, but without your fanciful musings. That way your rewards will be great both here and hereafter, and you will in nowise offend either God or man.

"Now," and the good master smiled warmly as he spoke, "yonder is the gate, and the good woman of my house has it closed tight. If you'll hand me the reins and go unlatch it for us, John, then I'll put away the horse and wagon and give you the rest before sup."

"I'll do it, sir," John Taylor exclaimed, and with a determined expression he leaped from the wagon and sprinted for the gate. 1

Born November first, 1808, "at Bridge End farm in Stainton, near Milnthorpe, a small seaport" 2 near the head of Morecambe Bay and not far from Lake Windemere, the "'Queen of English Lakes,'" 3 John Taylor spent his youngest years in the county of Westmoreland, England. John's father's name was James Taylor, "whose forefathers for many generations had lived on an estate known as Craig Gate, in Ackenthwaite." 4 John Taylor's grandmother was the second wife of his grandfather, Edward Taylor. By his first wife, Edward Taylor had had two sons and three daughters, and by his second wife three daughters and one son, Edward himself dying before this youngest son, James, was born. Owing to the English laws of primogeniture, the eldest son took the estate and left the younger brothers and sisters, James included, to provide for themselves as best they could. Despite gaining nothing from his father's estate, James acquired a good education, "some proficiency in the Latin and Greek languages, and the higher branches of mathematics." 5

When he was of age, James married a young woman named Agnes Taylor, who was no relation. Agnes was a descendant

James and Agnes Taylor   *CA. 1868*

through her mother of the famous Richard Whittington, who in London during the latter part of the 1300s and early 1400s had served as high sheriff, three times as lord mayor, was elected to parliament, and had conferred upon him the honor of knighthood. Richard Whittington "was diligent and exceedingly prosperous in business, upright and liberal in character, 'a virtuous and godly man, full of good works, and those famous,' says an old chronicler. In many respects he was considerably in advance of his times and conferred a lustre on his family's name which will live forever in English story."6 Agnes Taylor was patterned in large measure after her illustrious ancestor.

> Agnes and James had ten children, eight sons and two daughters. The oldest son, Edward, died in his early twenties; two other sons, William and George, died during their first year; and their last two sons, George and Edward, died in boyhood. (They did not hesitate to name later sons after earlier ones who had died.) So Agnes and James ended up with a family of five—three boys and two girls [Elizabeth and Agnes]. Given the state of health and medicine at the time, this heavy mortality rate was not unusual. The first five children were born in the parish of Heversham, near Ackenthwaite. The second of these children was Agnes and James's most famous child—John Taylor.... The last five children [which included their two daughters] were born near Hale. 7

"Because of his education and the status of his family, James Taylor received a government appointment collecting customs duties, which led to his moving from place to place." 8 The family lived at Milnthorpe until 1814, then moved to Liverpool, where they resided until 1819. In that year, what James "had lost by an unjust law…was made up to him by the munificence of an uncle (on his mother's side), William T. Moon, who bequeathed to him a small estate in Hale, Westmoreland," 9 about one mile from Beetham.

The place of the estate is known today as Hale Green, but the contemporary term for it was Hale Grange, meaning an outlying farmhouse or group of buildings belonging to a manor where crops and tithes in kind were stored. 10

In 1819, when John was eleven years old, his father left government employ and removed with his family to the small estate. 11 After the move, for the next three years young John attended school at Beetham. He wrote in his early history:

> I well remember some of my boyish freaks [pranks, whimsies] as I wended my way with satchell to school. [At home] I got mixed up with ploughing, sowing, reaping, hay–making [and other farm work]…and have indelibly impressed on my mind some of my first mishaps in horsemanship in the shape of sundry curious evolutions between the horses' backs and terra firma. 12

At age fourteen John was bound as apprentice to a cooper, or barrel and cask maker, back in Liverpool. Though the cooper remained in business only a year before going bankrupt, it turned out to be a vital and pivotal year in the life of young John Taylor.

> Big for his age and looking older than his fourteen years, [John] roamed the docks with the swagger of a man, talking to sailors who had been to the ends of the earth, striking acquaintances with rough waterfront characters, eyeing painted street women, frequenting pubs with men of the world and drinking shoulder to shoulder with them.
>
> Though his wages were small they were free and clear; his keep came with the job, as well as a ration of grog. He came to look forward to [drinking]; before long every farthing of his wages, plus what he could pick up with odd jobs on the waterfront Sundays and evenings, went over

the bar at the Lion and Crown, where he was a man among men. He was particularly flattered to be accepted at the table where Mr. Winters presided. Mr. Winters, who had once been a gentleman of some substance, still maintained a degree of gentility, with the manners of one born well and the vocabulary of a former university professor. He was widely read, urbane, and possessed a good sense of humor and a broad outlook. Here, thought young John Taylor, was the sort of person he'd like to become, except for one thing. The one flaw in Mr. Winter's character was that every night he had just a drop too much and had to be helped home. 13

Then came the night when it became John's turn to support the man home, practically carrying him through the foggy streets while he admired and laughed at the man's drunken humor, until he came upon the man's haggard wife at the door, as portrayed in the *vignette* at the beginning of this chapter.

Not long after this, the cooperage went bankrupt, and a wiser John Taylor returned to the family estate in Hale.

Always a believer in things spiritual, from John's earliest childhood there had come regularly to his ears the soft and lovely sound of heavenly music. Also as a young boy he had seen, "in vision, an angel in the heavens, holding a trumpet to his mouth, sounding a message to the nations. The import of this vision he did not [then] understand."14

Following his sobering experience with Mr. Winters, John also became a seeker. He not only longed to understand God, but he fervently desired to know what place he himself had in the divine plan. Because the tradition-bound Church of England answered neither of these questions to his satisfaction, he turned to his own reading and study of the Bible, as well as the writings of other individuals who had addressed similar questions. Constantly he read and pondered; without any inner doubt he prayed; and quickly his spirit grew attuned to the eternal.

While apprenticed again—this time to a turner, or furniture maker, in the town of Penrith—at about age sixteen he heard the Methodist doctrine taught, "and as he perceived more spiritual light and force in their teachings than in the cold, set services of the Church of England, he became a Methodist. He was strictly sincere in his religious faith, and very zealous to learn what he then considered to be the truth. Believing that 'every good and perfect gift proceedeth from the Lord,' he prayed frequently in private. Most of his leisure hours were spent in reading the Bible, works on theology and in prayer. For the latter purpose he usually resorted to secluded places in the woods and fields."15 Now he began to experience further manifestations of the Holy Spirit. Not only did the Lord's spirit expand his mind to understand doctrines and principles, but he also had dreams and further visions. 16

> He prowled the dense forests of the mountains, once stumbling upon the bones of two bogus coiners, hanged in chains with the bodies left dangling as a warning. He swam the lakes, explored castle ruins, walked the roads bordered by hedgerows in the valley called the "Vale of Eden." And always he had the feeling that he wasn't alone. Not wanting to be branded one of the wild-eyed insane who roamed at will, he said nothing of the melodious music that came sweet and soft to him in this enchanted land. The feeling grew that he was set apart. The music played for him alone. But for what purpose? Toward what unknown sea did the river of life flow? 17

In actuality the young apprentice turner was seeking to understand the Lord's mostly hidden plan of salvation. Where in eternity had he come from? why was he there? and where, oh where in the Lord's grand scheme of things might he be headed?

At about this time the missionary spirit began to develop within him. To that end, John Taylor induced a number of boys about his own age to join with him in secret prayer, though none stayed with him long, and certainly he won no converts. Nevertheless, he persisted in his efforts, from time to time feeling compelled to share with others what he considered to be the good word of God.

> Living in the same neighborhood [in Penrith] was an old gentleman whom [John] greatly respected; he was a good man, a praying man, but he had a wife who did not want to pray, and also interfered with his devotions. She was restless and turbulent, a kind of thorn in his flesh. Under these circumstances he did not get along very well, but it used to drive him to the Lord. After a while she died, and he married again; this time to a very amiable lady. His wife was so pleasant and agreeable, that the change in his circumstances was very great. Being thus comfortably situated he became remiss in his religious duties; and among other things gave way to the temptations of liquor. Observing the course he was taking, young Taylor took up a labor with him. He felt a little abashed on account of his youth, but because of long friendship, and out of respect for the old gentleman's many good qualities, he felt it his duty to call his attention to his neglect of Christian precepts. He told him how he had seen him drunk a few days previously, and how it had hurt his feelings, as his course hitherto had been exemplary. The old gentleman appreciated the good feelings, the respect and courage of his young friend, deplored his weakness and promised amendment. 18

At age seventeen, because of his evident missionary zeal, John was appointed as a Methodist "exhorter," or local preacher. His first appointment was in a tiny village about seven miles from Penrith, probably Temple Sowerby, to which he, along with another from the Penrith church, walked early each Sabbath morning. On one of those occasions, when the sharp, clear morning air was silent save for the songs of distant birds, "he stopped suddenly, transfixed, as a voice sounded. After a few moments he said, 'I have a strong impression that I have to go to America to preach the gospel!' "19

As the months and years passed, "this impression remained with him: 'I could not shake it off.... I had some work to do which I did not then understand.' He repeated this experience to Agnes and James, and they accepted it as a legitimate whispering of the Spirit." 20

And so "now he knew his destiny; but there was a persistent doubt that kept nagging at him: Did he yet have the gospel he was to preach?"21

Though John knew little enough of America save what he had learned from the Liverpool docks' crusty sailors and his school geography lessons, the feeling that he was to go there continued to impress itself upon his mind as long as he remained in Penrith. Finally, at age twenty, having fully mastered the trade of turner, he returned to Hale where he started in business for himself under the auspices of his father. "Shortly after this, in 1830, his father [and mother, with their four younger children] emigrated to Upper Canada [present-day Ontario], leaving [John] to dispose of some unsold property and settle the affairs of the estate."22 And though he remained in England for another two years, acting as his father's agent, there continued in young John Taylor the unwavering presentiment that he had some vital work to perform in America that he did not yet fully understand.

With his father's work finally completed, in 1832 John followed his family to America. "While crossing the British channel the ship he sailed in encountered severe storms, which lasted a number of days. He saw several ships wrecked in that storm, and the captain and officers of his own ship expected hourly that she would go down. But not so with our young emigrant. The voice of the Spirit was still saying within him, 'You must yet go to America and preach the gospel.' 'So confident was I of my destiny,' he remarks, 'that I went on deck at midnight, and amidst the raging elements felt as calm as though I was sitting in a parlor at home. I believed I should reach America and perform my work.'"[23]

And so he did.

3

ℱINDING THE ᴀNCIENT ℭHURCH

"John, darling, are you certain?" Leonora Taylor stood with her hands clasped together over her apron. "Do you truly feel it right to send him away?"

Looking up from the lathe where he was finishing turning a leg for a new table, John Taylor noted the anxious expression on his wife's face. It was also noteworthy that she was interrupting him at work in his shop—something she rarely did. The depth of her concern was troubling.

"I hope," he said as he stepped away from his equipment and shook the wood shavings from his hands, "that you are not getting caught up in that man's delusions."

Looking stricken, Lenora turned away, and John immediately wished he could recall his words. After all, his wife was as much a seeker after truth as he and had every bit as much right to pray, to ponder, and even to come to her own conclusions. For him to judge either her or the subject of her investigations prematurely was completely unfair. Besides which, Lenora would never be guilty of such prejudice against him.

For a moment he stood silently, his eyes on his wife as he struggled to know the right thing to do—to say. Older than him by more than a decade, thirty-six-year-old Leonora had been reared on the

Isle of Man. She had come to Toronto as companion to the wife of a Mr. Mason, the private secretary of Lord Aylmer, Governor General of Canada. A devout Methodist, in Toronto she had associated with that church and so met John Taylor, who had become a class leader in the church.

Tall, slender, dark-haired, with classically beautiful features, Leonora was also mature, accomplished, charming, witty, and possessed all the attainments of a lady of culture. Immediately captivated, John had become an ardent suitor, and though Leonora had given him scant encouragement, he had persisted.

And well John knew how Leonora had felt about him. More than a dozen times he had proposed marriage to her, each time to be rejected, and each time she had very candidly explained her reasons for saying no. She thought him handsome but unpolished, a skilled furniture maker but no gentleman; he hadn't been to the right schools nor attended a university, and his intellectualism was filled with gaps common to the self-educated. Worst of all, though—and it had impressed John that Leonora was perceptive enough to see—there crouched beneath his charm and humor a tiger. It would turn out, she had told him, that he would be a man who would always be involved in fierce battles for principle. And truthfully, she did not know if she wished to live life associated with such a man.

Then had come to beautiful Leonora a dream, in response, John felt, to his fervent prayers. In the dream she had seen herself associated with him throughout his life. She felt strongly that it was a message from the Lord, had contacted him immediately, and forthwith had consented to his proposals. They had married on January 28, 1833, and between them now, following nearly three years of marriage, there existed a deep and abiding love, and John would not hurt her for the world. Yet in this instance, as regarding the stranger from the United States, he felt that Leonora was wrong. And somehow he had to help her see her error—

"What if he is a man of God?" Leonora pleaded.

"I believe him to be an impostor."

"He has performed a miracle, you know." Her statement was calm, matter-of-fact. "He has caused the blind to see."

"He what?" John did not even try to hide his surprise. "Someone we know?"

"Emily Herrick. At Mrs. Walton's urging he visited her last evening. There he placed his hands upon her head and in the name of Jesus commanded her eyes to be made well. When she removed her bandages she was instantly healed, her sight restored."

Now John's mind was racing. Emily Herrick, a young widow with four small children, had gone blind from an eye infection several months before. Prior to her blindness she had been a teacher at the Methodist school; since then she had been invalid, suffering great pain and living off the charity of the church society. But if she had actually been healed—

"Have you seen her?" he questioned.

"I have not. However, Mrs. Walton has assured me that she will be at her home tonight, to hear the stranger's doctrines." Now Leonora smiled disarmingly. "I should like very much to attend with them, John—in your company, of course. There, I am sure, you may question Emily at your leisure."

With a sigh John acquiesced, kissed his wife to say he was sorry for his harsh words, and, still feeling troubled, turned back to his lathe...

"How did the man heal your eyes?" The questioner was one of a large crowd that had gathered for the evening at the home of Mrs. Walton. "What did he do? Tell us exactly."

John Taylor, seated nearby, leaned forward with numerous others to hear how Emily Herrick would respond. There was no doubt she had been healed. She was absolutely radiant, her eyes sparkling bright, with no trace of the terrible infection he had seen only days before when he had sadly explained that beyond their prayers and their charity—which all had been offering already—there was nothing more that he or any other of her fellow Methodists could do.

"What did this man do?" a woman pressed before Emily could respond, pointing to where the stranger sat quietly in the corner. "How were your eyes opened and made well?"

"He laid his hands upon my head in the name of Jesus Christ," Emily finally responded. "He rebuked the inflammation and commanded my eyes to be made whole and restored to sight, and it was instantly done."

"Well, give God the glory," another stated, "for, as to this man, it is well known that he is an impostor, a follower of Joseph Smith, the false prophet."

Joseph Smith! With a sigh John Taylor shook his head. Why did this man, Parley Pratt, who seemed honest enough and sincere as an Easter sunrise, have to be a follower of the rascally Joe Smith, the Mormon impostor? All knew the ignominy of Smith and his fabled gold Bible. The subject was spoken of in mocking tones by almost all classes of people. Yet now Emily Herrick was claiming to have been healed by a Mormon who was claiming the full authority of the ancient apostleship. Who knew where it might all end!

As the grilling of Emily Herrick continued, John cast his mind back to the night before, when for the first time he had heard the preachments of Parley Parker Pratt. He, with Leonora and a few others, had been seated at this same table in Mrs. Walton's parlor, and as hostess, she had come right to the point.

"Mr. Pratt," she had declared, "we have for some years been anxiously looking for some providential event which would gather the sheep into one fold; build up the true church as in days of old, and prepare the humble followers of the Lamb, now scattered and divided, to receive their coming Lord when he shall descend to reign on the earth. As soon as Mrs. Taylor spoke of you I felt assured, as by a strange and unaccountable presentiment, that you were a messenger with important tidings on these subjects, and I was constrained to invite you here. Now we are all here anxiously waiting to hear your words."

"Well, Mrs. Walton," Parley Pratt had replied as he rose to his feet, "I will frankly relate to you and your friends the particulars of my message and the nature of my commission. A young man in the State of New York, whose name is Joseph Smith, was visited by an angel of God and, after several visions and much instruction, was enabled to obtain an ancient record, written by men of old on the American continent and containing the history, prophecies, and gospel in plainness, as revealed to them by Jesus and His messengers. This same Joseph Smith and others were also commissioned by the angels in these visions and ordained to the apostleship, with authority to organize the Church, to administer the ordinances, and to ordain others, and thus cause the full, plain gospel in its purity to be preached in all the world.

"By these apostles thus commissioned, I have also been ordained an apostle and sent forth by the word of prophecy to minister the baptism of repentance for remission of sins in the name of Jesus Christ and to administer the gift of the Holy Ghost, to heal the sick, to comfort the mourner, bind up the broken in heart, and proclaim the acceptable year of the Lord.

"I was also directed to this city by the Spirit of the Lord, with a promise that I should find a people here prepared to receive the gospel and that I should organize them in the same. But when I came and was rejected by all parties, I was about to leave the city, until the Lord sent you, as a widow, to receive me as I was about to depart; and thus I was provided for like Elijah of old. And now I bless your house, and all your family and kindred, in his name. Your sins shall be forgiven you; you shall understand and obey the gospel, and be filled with the Holy Ghost; for so great faith have I never seen in any of my country."

"Well, Mr. Pratt," the silly Mrs. Walton had exclaimed, her reason obviously departed in a fit of emotionalism, "this is precisely the message we were waiting for. We believe your words and are desirous to be baptized."

Then, for John Taylor at least, had come the first real surprise. "That is your duty and your privilege," Pratt had responded, "but wait yet a little while until I have an opportunity to teach others and invite them to partake with you of the same blessings."

Why had the man not jumped at the opportunity of making converts the night before? John had wondered. And now, as he watched the relentless grilling of Emily Herrick, he was still wondering, trying to decide how on earth the Mormon had managed to restore the blind woman's vision.

"Whether he be an impostor or not," Emily was saying to another questioner, "I know not; but this much I know, whereas I was blind, now I see! Can an impostor open the eyes of the blind?"

"It is Satan's counterfeit, to lure you from the true faith!"

"But my faith is in Jesus Christ, and it was in his holy name that I was healed. How can that be counterfeit?"

"Perhaps, then, you intend to be this man's disciple, to join the Mormons?"

Vehemently, Emily shook her head. "He said nothing to me about joining the Mormons, but taught me the gospel and bore testimony that God had restored its power to the earth." Now the young widow smiled. "Would you like to be partakers thereof? Or why do you inquire so earnestly about my eyes being healed?"

"Oh," a Methodist class leader replied, "we are John Wesley's disciples. We are the Christian church. We know John Wesley, but as to this man, we know not whence he is."

"How is it that you know not whence he is, and yet he has opened my eyes? Did John Wesley open the eyes of the blind? Can an impostor do it?"

"Ah," another church leader said belligerently, "we see how it is. You are determined to forsake the Christian church, the good old way, for the sake of these fools, these weak impostors—the Mormons. Well, farewell, Emily Herrick. But remember, you will have no more support from our society, no more encouragement of any kind. You shall not even teach a school for us! How then will you live?"

As these contentions and discouragements poured into the ears of the young mother, together with railings and probable lies, sophistry and slander, John could see the poor woman beginning to waver. Sickened by how his fellow church members were treating another human being, no matter her emotionalism or religious persuasions, John made the momentous decision that at least he would listen to Mr. Pratt. No matter what the others did, no matter what Emily Herrick or even his wife, Leonora, did, he, John Taylor, would thoroughly investigate the Mormon religion. For after all, under Pratt's ministering hands something had happened to the young widow's inflamed and sightless eyes! 1

John's voyage from Liverpool to America lasted several weeks, his ship landing at Ellis Island in New York harbor sometime in 1832. For several months he lingered in Brooklyn and then Albany, preaching and working to accumulate funds sufficient to carry him to his family in York (which was incorporated as Toronto in 1834)2, upper Canada. Upon his arrival in Toronto, John did two things: he established a house near his parents and attached a wood-turning shop so he might be gainfully employed, and he united himself with the Methodist church so he might continue his preaching of the gospel. It was among the Methodist faithful that he soon thereafter met Leonora Cannon, to whom he was instantly attracted.

"Leonora Cannon was a daughter of Captain George Cannon (grandfather of President George Q. Cannon) of Peel, Isle of Man. Captain Cannon died while Leonora was yet in her girlhood; the old homestead in Peel was rented to strangers, and she went to reside in England with a lady named Vail. Later she became an inmate of Governor Smelt's family, residing in Castle Rushen, Castletown, Isle of Man. Here she frequently met with many distinguished people from England. Finally in the capacity of companion to the wife of Mr. Mason, the private secretary of Lord Aylmer, Governor General of Canada, she went to Toronto, and being a devout Methodist, associated with that church and there met Mr. Taylor, who became her class leader."[3]

An ardent suitor, John proposed to Leonora and was promptly rejected. Yet he would not be dissuaded, for "Leonora was a refined, educated woman, witty, gifted with rare conversational powers, possessed of a deep religious nature and withal a fitting companion for John Taylor."[4] "She said no perhaps a dozen times before finally accepting for a reason valid in religious circles: a dream, accepted as guidance."[5] They were married January 28, 1833.

Frequently Leonora "accompanied her husband in filling his appointments to preach on the Sabbath, and he often alluded to the singular revelation he had received in his youth, about his having to preach the gospel in America.

"'Are you not now preaching the gospel in America?' Leonora would ask.

"'This is not the work; it is something of more importance,' he would answer."[6]

As a preacher in the Methodist church, both in England and Canada, [John] was very successful, and made many converts. "My object," he [remarked], "was to teach them what I then considered the leading doctrines of the Christian religion, rather than the peculiar dogmas of Methodism." His theological investigations had made him very much dissatisfied with existing creeds and churches, because of the wide difference between modern and primitive Christianity, in doctrine, in ordinances, in organization and above all, in spirit and power. [7]

John wrote:

> I often wondered…why the Christian religion was so
> changed from its primitive simplicity, and became con-
> vinced, before I dared acknowledge it, that we ought to
> have Apostles, Prophets, Pastors, Teachers and Evangelists
> —inspired men—as in former days.... [I was becoming
> more interested in teaching] the doctrines of the Christian
> religion, rather than the peculiar dogmas of Methodism. 8

Not alone in such feelings and conclusions, John and Leonora
began gathering with others, mostly men of John's same church
and calling. This group of seekers "called themselves the
'Dissenters,'"9 which obviously affected their standing in the
Methodist church and ultimately resulted in John losing his license
to preach. Meeting several times a week, they searched the scriptures and did their best to understand and interpret correctly the
ancient version or tenets of the Christian faith. Meanwhile, they
also fasted frequently and prayed fervently for the guidance of the
Holy Spirit and for "the Lord to send an authorized servant to
them with the truth."10 Though no authorized servant immediately
appeared, through such diligent efforts they were led, inexorably,
to the conclusion that all sects were in error and without authority
to preach the gospel or administer its ordinances.

"'If modern Christianity is true,' said they, 'then the Bible is
false,' and vice versa. Fortunately they clung to a firm belief in the
Bible; and further believed in a restoration of pure principles and a
true church."11

At about this same time, in Kirtland, Ohio, events were transpiring which would have a dramatic effect on certain of their
number. An authorized servant, Apostle Parley P. Pratt, was being
readied by the Lord to go among them. In his autobiography he
recorded:

It was now April [1836]; I had retired to rest one evening at an early hour, and was pondering my future course, when there came a knock at the door. I arose and opened it, when Elder Heber C. Kimball and others entered my house, and being filled with the spirit of prophecy, they blessed me and my wife, and prophesied as follows:

"Brother Parley, thy wife shall be healed from this hour, and shall bear a son, and his name shall be Parley; and he shall be a chosen instrument in the hands of the Lord to inherit the priesthood and to walk in the steps of his father. He shall do a great work in the earth in ministering the Word and teaching the children of men. Arise, therefore, and go forth in the ministry, nothing doubting. Take no thoughts for your debts, nor the necessaries of life, for the Lord will supply you with abundant means for all things.

"Thou shalt go to Upper Canada, even to the city of Toronto, the capital, and there thou shalt find a people prepared for the fulness of the gospel, and they shall receive thee, and thou shalt organize the Church among them, and it shall spread thence into the regions round about, and many shall be brought to the knowledge of the truth and shall be filled with joy; and from the things growing out of this mission, shall the fulness of the gospel spread into England, and cause a great work to be done in that land…"

This prophecy was the more marvelous, because being married near ten years we had never had any children; and for near six years my wife had been consumptive, and had been considered incurable. However, we called to mind the faith of Abraham of old, and judging Him faithful who had promised, we took courage. 12

Readying his affairs as best he could, within a few days Parley was on his way. After a long and tedious journey by coach he arrived in the city of Toronto, where through a series of divine interventions he arrived at the home of John and Leonora Taylor. Kindly received by Leonora, he was welcomed far less enthusiastically by John, who disdained the Mormons because of their reputation and who believed Joseph Smith to be a fraud.

After a short conversation, Parley went his way, only to spend the rest of the evening and all the next day in a futile search for a public place or house of worship where he might preach. When none was made available, the young apostle retired to the woods, bore testimony of his efforts and failure before the Lord, and returned to the home of John Taylor to bid him and his wife farewell. "'Rather an unpromising beginning,' Parley admitted wryly, 'considering the prophecies on my head concerning Toronto.'"13 For some reason, however, John delayed Parley in desultory conversation, and during the interim Leonora received her neighbor as a visitor.

"Mrs. Walton, I am glad to see you; there is a gentleman here from the United States who says the Lord sent him to this city to preach the gospel. He has applied in vain to the clergy and to the various authorities for opportunity to fulfill his mission, and is now about to leave the place. He may be a man of God; I am sorry to have him depart."

"Indeed!" said the lady; "well, I now understand the feelings and spirit which brought me to your house at this time. I have been busy over the wash tub and too weary to take a walk; but I felt impressed to walk out. I then thought I would make a call on my sister, the other side of town; but passing your door, the Spirit bade me go in; but I said to myself, I will go in when I return; but the Spirit said: go in now. I accordingly came in, and I am thankful that I did so. Tell the stranger he is welcome to my house.

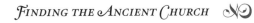

Portrait of Parley P. Pratt   CA. *early 1840s*

I am a widow; but I have a spare room and bed, and food in plenty. He shall have a home at my house, and two large rooms to preach in just when he pleases. Tell him I will send my son John over to pilot him to my house, while I go and gather my relatives and friends to come in this very evening and hear him talk; for I feel by the Spirit that he is a man sent by the Lord with a message which will do us good."14

Parley preached that evening to a small crowd of listeners, all of whom were accepting of his message except John Taylor, who considered the others silly for their gullibility. The next day, at Mrs. Walton's urging, Parley went to the home of a young widow named Emily Herrick who had gone blind some months before and whose eyes were still festering and causing her terrible pain. Laying his hands on her head, Parley rebuked the disease, whereupon "she threw off her bandages; opened her house to the light; dressed herself, and walking with open eyes, came to the meeting that same evening at sister Walton's, with eyes as well and bright as any other person's.... This remarkable miracle was soon noised abroad, and the poor woman's house was thronged from all parts of the city and country with visitors; all curious to witness for themselves, and to enquire of her how her eyes were healed."15

Amazed but still unconvinced, John Taylor worried that Leonora was "being infected by Mormonism...[even though h]is wife certainly wasn't an emotional, unstable type of person."16 During this second gathering at the Walton home, however, as John witnessed the attacks against Parley P. Pratt and Emily Herrick by his good Christian brethren and sisters as portrayed at the beginning of this chapter, he concluded with some embarrassment that perhaps he ought to investigate the Mormons further—even though the miraculously healed widow allowed herself to be coerced into rejecting Mormonism altogether.

The next day Parley was invited to meet with the "Dissenters" at the home of a man named Patrick. After the meeting was opened, John Taylor

> arose and read the New Testament account of Philip preaching at Samaria. There was great joy as the people heard the word and witnessed the casting out of devils, the healing of the sick and the lame, the conversion of the bewitched; many were baptized into the faith. When the apostles at Jerusalem heard that Samaria had accepted the gospel, they sent Peter and John to lay hands on believers that they might receive the Holy Ghost. "Now, where is our Philip?" John Taylor asked. "Where are the signs and the miracles? Where is our Peter and John? Where are our apostles? Where is our Holy Ghost by the laying on of hands?" If the present pattern of belief differed from that of the New Testament, "What claim have we to be considered the Church of Christ?"[17]

As John sat down the meeting opened up to a very candid discussion, with many of those present expressing their views for or against the possibilities that John's questions had raised. "Nothing definite was concluded on," Parley P. Pratt continues, "when the old preacher who invited me arose and said: " 'There is a stranger present who, perhaps, might wish to speak.' "

"The chairman observed that he was not aware of the presence of a stranger, but if such was the case he was at liberty, as were all persons in these meetings, to make remarks. I arose, and observed that I was a stranger from the United States; but not a stranger to the great principles under investigation in this meeting. I was prepared to speak on the subject at some length; but should not do so then, as the time had been well occupied and the people edified.

"My credentials were then presented to the meeting through the chairman, and a special appointment given out for me at evening.

"However they might differ as to the means of restoration of the Christian Church, certain it is that they appeared at the close to unite, with one voice, in acknowledgment of their destitution. 'O Lord,' said the chairman, in his closing prayer, 'we have neither apostles, visions, angels, revelations, gifts, tongues, ordinances, nor a Christian ministry; we acknowledge that we are destitute of everything like the pattern of the true Church, as laid down in thy holy Word, and we pray thee to send whom thou wilt.' At this all seemed to say Amen, while tears and sobs attested their sincerity."[18]

For the next three nights Parley preached in the Patrick home, addressing the issues John had spoken of and about which the Dissenters had prayed. By that time the crowds had grown so large, and the elderly minister so fearful for his flock, that Parley was not allowed to return. However, he simply retired to Mrs. Walton's home, and his preaching continued. "The truth was now plainly before this people," he wrote, "who had been in so wonderful a manner prepared for its reception, as predicted by [B]rother Kimball on my head before leaving home."[19]

"John Taylor was both shaken and excited by these meetings. He took detailed notes of eight sermons by Pratt and compared them with scripture. He studied the Book of Mormon and the Doctrine and Covenants. 'I made a regular business of it for three weeks,' he wrote, 'and followed Brother Parley from place to place.'"[20]

The result of his thorough investigation was conviction. By the time he made his decision, Leonora, too, was ready. "At length being perfectly satisfied of the truth of Mormonism, I was baptized by [Parley P. Pratt on May 9, 1836, and] my wife was also baptized at the same time. I have never doubted any principle of Mormonism since."[21]

"Now he knew the meaning of the angel with the trumpet; he understood the celestial music, and he was certain of the mission in America of which the voice had told him."22

"'I was almost immediately ordained an Elder and Brother Parley prophesied concerning me in a manner that almost made my hair stand on my head,' wrote John. What he was promised is not known, but [John] received valuable instruction as Elder Pratt was joined in his Canadian labors by his brother Orson and by Orson Hyde."23

John's first mission was to his parents, who were baptized by him "in May, 1836. Their enthusiastic reception of the gospel paved the way for the conversion of their daughters Elizabeth and Agnes and of their youngest living son, William."24

"Guided by the Spirit of the Lord, Elder Taylor and his more experienced companions were successful in teaching and baptizing 'a great many people,' and he watched as Elders Pratt and Hyde successfully debated ministers and exposed the errors of the ministers' theology. Elder Taylor himself enjoyed 'many manifestations from the Lord.' He witnessed the power of God in miraculous healings and in the utterance and fulfillment of many prophecies." And "when the brethren returned to Kirtland in the fall," it was John Taylor who "was set apart to preside over several branches of the Church in a newly formed district."25

4

OPPOSING APOSTASY

John Taylor was appalled! As he sat in the Kirtland Temple observing those who were gathering to the Sunday evening meeting, it was impossible not to see the anger, the actual darkness, on many of their faces. Truly the Lord's Church was being torn apart by apostasy, and whether by accident or divine design, the young wood turner from England found himself caught in the middle of it.

He had left Toronto early in March, 1837, his goal to meet the Prophet Joseph and to experience gospel-edified life in Kirtland. Joseph had turned out to be all he had hoped for and expected, a mild-mannered man full of excitement and enthusiasm for life. His thoughts and ideas were unique and profound, and he never opened his mouth but what eternal truths rolled out like the waters of a flood, enlightening John's mind and proving over and over again that Joseph Smith was indeed the Lord's mortal mouthpiece.

Kirtland, however, had been a severe disappointment. The community—and therefore the Church—was torn by dissension, and a bitter spirit of apostasy was destroying even the elect. A wild fever of speculation in city lots and other properties had collapsed in financial ruin, and many—including those high in the Church and close to Brother Joseph—were accusing the Prophet of fraud. The gathering of the Saints to Kirtland was seen as a scheme to sell real estate to incoming converts at inflated prices. The bank, or "safety society," started by some of the Kirtland leaders was on the brink of disaster; some claimed Joseph had prophesied it would never fail, and though he was on record as having said exactly the opposite, many were still calling him a fallen prophet.

Most heartbreaking of all to John Taylor, however, was that his dear friend Parley P. Pratt was numbered among the apostates. Parley's wife, Thankful, pregnant according to Heber C. Kimball's prophecy, had given birth to the promised son on March 24TH, with John and Parley waiting anxiously nearby. But whereas Elder Kimball had seemingly promised that Thankful would be cured, instead she had passed peacefully away within minutes of the baby's birth, a series of dreams having prepared her for that final event.

Immediately, Parley's heart had turned to stone. In anguish he had strode through the wooded hills, sobbing with grief and giving voice to his disillusionment. It was all a fraud, he had cried! His wife hadn't been healed at all; the bank Joseph had declared would become the greatest institution in the world was on the brink of failure; he had paid two thousand dollars for lots that hadn't cost Joseph a hundred, and now he couldn't get his money back! Not a single cent!

"Joseph and Sidney have led the people astray!" Parley had shouted as he strode forward, John trying to keep up. "False preaching and prophesying! I'm telling you, John, they've fallen, those two, and they are dragging the Church down to hell on their filthy coattails!"

For hours this had gone on, until John had felt he could hear no more and remain silent. Finally, when Parley paused in a clearing to rest, John had seized the moment.

"I am surprised to hear you speak so, Brother Parley," he had declared, his words made brisk and clipped by his British accent. "Before you left Canada you bore a strong testimony to Joseph Smith being a prophet of God, and to the truth of the work he has inaugurated; and you said you knew these things by revelation and the gift of the Holy Ghost. You gave to me a strict charge to the effect that though you or an angel from heaven was to declare anything else I was not to believe it. Now, Brother Parley, it is not man that I am following, but the Lord. The principles you taught me led me to Him, and I now have the same testimony that you then rejoiced in. If the work was true six months ago, it is true today; if Joseph Smith was then a prophet, he is now a prophet."

Apparently thunderstruck by his friend's testimony, Parley had said no more against Joseph Smith, at least in John's presence. Neither had he made any further effort to persuade John to his point of view. Still, he remained estranged, and John found himself worrying about his beloved missionary friend.

Now as he sat in the sacred temple of the Lord, he thought of his most recent visit to the grieving apostle. Already Parley had married again—an attractive widow named Mary Ann Frost Stearns, and she was doing a commendable job of caring for the baby. Facing financial ruin because of his speculations, he had also written a bitter letter to the Prophet, accusing Joseph of swindling him under the guise of religion.

On the other hand, and John found this amazing, Parley was also preparing to go on another mission, this time to New York, for he believed, still, in the truthfulness of the Church. "It is because of my belief," he had declared to John, "that it hurts me to see the Lord's prophets guilty of covetousness, extortion, and taking advantage of a brother in the gospel by undue religious influence."

"I am sorry, my dear friend," John had responded quietly. "But I cannot hold the Lord to a human scale of values, nor judge his prophets. God chooses whom he will. Prophets of ancient times— Abraham, Moses, David, Solomon—were guilty of sins and misdeeds, yet were divinely selected. Regardless of all accusations against Joseph, he remains the chosen instrument of God, and no aspersions on his character can cast a shadow on his position as the

Lord's mouthpiece."

Parley had not responded, but now, as John enjoyed the warmth from the nearby stove and waited for the temple to fill for the meeting, he prayed fervently that his beloved friend would emerge victorious from the dark cloud of doubt and confusion that had engulfed him.

Gradually the main assembly room of the temple was filling. Emma Smith and her three children, followed by spinster Eliza R. Snow, who was living in the Smith home, took seats in the box John had occupied. John stood, smiled a greeting, and then asked after Emma's husband. Joseph, the woman replied anxiously as she removed her wrap, had gone to Cleveland to raise money to cover the Church's debts and hopefully save the tottering bank. Brigham Young and Willard Richards had gone to New York for the same purpose.

More devotees to Mormonism filed by, some wearing friendly faces and others looking more guarded. Then there were the angry ones, militant apostates who were calling themselves "Reformers" and the "Old Standard." These, led by Joseph's former clerk Warren Parrish and apostle John F. Boynton, and including apostles Luke Johnson and Lyman Johnson and many others, took their places near the Melchizedek Priesthood pulpit at the west end of the hall. There they conversed in loud tones before turning to prowl about the room like so many ravenous wolves, conversing earnestly with anyone who would give them ear, seeking converts to their angry cause. Yet that cause, John had learned for himself during the past few weeks, hid under its pretended righteousness men who committed adultery and fornication, men who willingly perpetrated fraud, false accusation, false swearing, vexatious lawsuits, personal violence, and barefaced robbery.

Parrish, for instance, an admitted adulterer, was enraged that Joseph was blaming the bank failure, at least in part, on his defalcations of $20,000, which he was claiming as just wages. Boynton and Lyman Johnson had failed in their mercantile enterprise, promoted on a grand scale on credit, and this failure they were also blaming on Joseph Smith. It was a way, they had boasted openly, to avoid personal responsibility for the mercantile's debts. These and the others were men who had become wholly corrupted through giving themselves over to Satan through a host of different evils, and John found himself wondering that they were being allowed to pollute the Lord's holy house by their presence.

As a man moved along the aisles with a taper, lighting the lamps for the evening, John prayed for a return of the wondrous reverence that had inspired him and filled him with joy when he had first entered this holy edifice. John regretted still that he had not been present during the awe-inspiring day of the temple's dedication, when manifestations of heavenly power had been overwhelmingly evident. According to those who had been there, that day, and for several thereafter, hundreds of brethren and sisters had received the ministering of angels, had seen the light and personages of heavenly beings, had spoken in new tongues, and had even witnessed flaming tongues of fire and heard the mighty roaring wind as had occurred anciently on the day of Pentecost. Truly it had been a time when the heavens had been opened, when every man's mouth had been full of prophesying and every person's mind filled with the visions of eternity.

Yet now, John pondered sadly, just one short year later, the spiritual ecstasy of the Saints had crumbled into bitterness and apostasy. Through greed and worldliness they had given Satan power over them, and now he was running rampant in his effort to destroy the Lord's true Church before its work could hardly even begin. It was almost humorous, John thought—sad, but almost humorous. What had the Saints endured for their faith so far? Like the early Christians, they had been persecuted; in Missouri they had been mobbed and driven from their homes. Many had given up family, lands, wealth, and honor. All this—as well as hunger, misery, fatigue, and death—men would endure and suffer for their faith; then without so much as a second thought they would turn around and sell away that which they held so dear for a few pieces of silver.

Such were the sorry men who were again crowded beneath the Melchizedek Priesthood pulpit in the suddenly packed assembly room—

"My brothers and sisters in the Lord, let us begin this sacred service."

The man who now stood at the pulpit was Joseph Smith Sr., the Prophet's father. Tall and with a noble bearing at sixty-six, the patriarch of the Smith family led the congregation in prayer. Then, as John and the others listened attentively, he began to talk concerning the present troubles of the Saints, which he fearlessly attributed to weakness and lack of faith.

"You, Warren Parrish," he then declared, pointing downward at the apostate, "are an ordained Seventy in the Lord's true church and one of the seven presidents of the quorum. Yet there you sit, guilty of adultery and embezzlement, but having the effrontery to accuse my son, an innocent man if ever there was one—"

"I'll not listen to such slander!" Parrish shouted as he leaped to his feet with his clenched fist raised threateningly. "Shut your mouth, old man, or so help me, I'll—"

"You'll do nothing!" the senior Smith thundered wrathfully. "In the name of the Lord, I rebuke you, Warren Parrish! I rebuke you as well, John Boynton, and all the rest of you apostates! Sylvester Smith, Joseph Coe, Stephen Burnett, Luke and Lyman Johnson, Leonard Rich, Cyrus P. Smalling—"

Astounded at the rancorous, open bickering in the house of the Lord, John Taylor could do little more than stare. Beside him Eliza R. Snow's face was white, while Emma, worried that the shouting would frighten her children, was drawing them to her while murmuring that she shouldn't have come. John wondered the same about himself and for the first time considered that perhaps Parley had been right in staying away.

Now David Whitmer and Oliver Cowdery had joined the fray. From their seats in the pulpit they were also denouncing the Prophet, David shouting that Joseph was now receiving revelations without the seerstone and was changing the words of his previous revelations, while Oliver was on his feet screeching, as if he were at the legal bar, against Joseph's alleged affair with a girl named Fannie Alger.

"You keep silent about sacred things!" someone shouted at Oliver Cowdery from the rear of the room.

"Either that, or tell us a little about the plural wife you have taken!" another called out angrily.

Now Warren Parrish was standing on the bench, waving his hands at the congregation. "You fools! Can't you see that you are following a fallen prophet? These men are two of the Three Witnesses, for goodness sake! Listen to them!"

"Even the very elect can be deceived!" Father Smith shouted down from the pulpit. "You, Warren Parrish, are a liar and a man who loves a lie—"

"Liar and false swearer!" Parrish shrieked in return, and before anyone could stop him he had leaped the pews, vaulted onto the pulpit, and had begun wrestling with the aged patriarch.

"Oliver, help me," the elderly man cried as Parrish pummeled him with his fists, knocking him back against the pulpit. "William, my boy—"

While Oliver Cowdery sat silently and without moving, William Smith leaped to the aid of his father, grappling with the furious Parrish and pulling him off his attack. As John stared in amazement, the screams of the women and children adding to the din of the fighting men, John Boynton unsheathed his sword cane and flew to the pulpit, threatening to run William Smith through. As other men came to William's rescue, a number of apostates drew their weapons—bowie knives and pistols—and a grand mêlée began swirling around the high pulpit.

Heartsick at what was transpiring in the holy temple, John quickly helped Emma and the children into their wraps. Meanwhile men, women, and children were climbing out the temple's windows and crowding out the doors. Suddenly the stove was bumped by a fighting knot of men, the long stovepipe toppled over, and as smoke and soot billowed into the room, John found himself shoved into the thick of the fray.

Kicking a pistol from a man's hand and grabbing the arm of another who held a wicked-looking knife, John was filled with a desperate sense of fantasy as he fought with men he had revered as the Lord's chosen servants—and doing it here, of all places, in the house of the Lord!

Though violent, the struggle fortunately was brief. The apostate leaders were ejected, the stovepipe put back in place, and as brethren stood at the windows and doors, fanning to clear the air, Joseph Smith Sr. shakily made his way to the pulpit. Blood flowed from his nose, and a long red gash crossed his forehead. When he tried to speak, however, he could not, and so he stood helplessly—

"Father Smith," John heard himself saying as he moved to the trembling patriarch's side, "the majority of the Saints are still with us, and I should like very much to address them."

Numbly the elderly man nodded, clasped John's hand in gratitude, and without a word hobbled to his seat. Turning, John gazed down into the faces of the suddenly silent multitude.

With a silent prayer, he opened his remarks by referring to the ancient Israelites and to their murmurings against God and Moses. "From whence do we get our intelligence, and knowledge of the laws, ordinances, and doctrines of the kingdom of God?" he then asked the attentive congregation, his rich baritone voice ringing through the room. "Who understood even the first principles of the doctrines of Christ? Who in the Christian world taught them?

Illustration by Robert T. Barrett

If we, with our learning and intelligence, could not find out the first principles, which was the case with myself and millions of others, how can we find out the mysteries of the kingdom? It was Joseph Smith, under the guidance of the Almighty, who developed the first principles, and to him we must look for further instructions. If the spirit which he manifests does not bring blessings, I am very much afraid that the one manifested by those who have spoken against him will not be very likely to secure them either. The children of Israel, after seeing the power of God manifested in their midst, fell into rebellion and idolatry, and there is certainly very great danger of us doing the same thing."

In silence he descended to his seat, the meeting soon adjourned, and the next morning John began his journey back to Canada. While the apostates had been neither convinced nor silenced by his remarks, the faithful Saints had been strengthened and had seen in that fearless defender of the Prophet a champion of innocence and truth. While on his part, in commenting on this circumstance years later, John declared, "I was pained on the one hand to witness the hard feelings and severe expressions of apostates; while on the other, I rejoiced to see the firmness, faith, integrity and joy of the faithful."[1]

Through the winter of 1836–37, after the missionaries had disappeared across Lake Ontario bound for Kirtland, John Taylor found himself presiding over the various branches of the Church in and around Toronto. Constantly he was teaching, training new leaders, bearing witness of the Restoration, and baptizing. "He was now preaching the gospel in America in fulfillment of the revelation he [had] received in his youth."[2] Still the Spirit whispered that there was more, that he did not yet fully understand the heavenly message.

Leaving Leonora behind, in March of 1837 John paid a visit to Kirtland, headquarters of the Church. There he "met the Prophet Joseph Smith, who entertained him at his house and gave him many items of information pertaining to the work of the Lord in this dispensation."[3] He was also taken to the glorious new temple, sparkling in the sunlight from all the crockery crushed into the stucco—precious dinnerware donated by the faithful women of the Church.

Inside, he discovered that "the main assembly hall was a large rectangular room with a tier of four pulpits rising at each end—those at the west end being for the Melchizedek (higher priesthood) and at the east end for the Aaronic (lower priesthood). Flanking the pulpits were elevated pews for the choir. The congregation sat in stalls with movable pews, so that people could turn in either direction to face the pulpits. Curtains on rollers attached to the ceiling could be lowered to enclose each tier of pulpits and also to divide the room itself into four compartments for various services.

"The main hall was designed for meetings of the entire membership. Directly above it was a room of identical size used for meetings of…the priesthood…and an attic story which provided five rooms for school instruction and meetings by various priesthood quorums."[4]

In the temple John received what the Prophet was calling an endowment, a sacred ceremony set aside for faithful members of the Church. Joseph called the ceremony an endowment, he explained to John, because the Lord had revealed to him that through the ordinances so administered, John was receiving an endowment or gift of heavenly power that could be obtained nowhere else on earth. He had become a member of the holy order, with promises bestowed upon him that he might go forth "armed with the Lord's power, his welfare in the charge of angels. No weapon would be effective against him, and whomever should dig a pit for him would fall into it themselves. No combination of wickedness should prevail over him," for the Lord would rescue him and fight his battles. John cherished this endowment which would allow him and the rest of the Saints "to gather for the redemption of Zion" as the Kingdom of God rolled forth as the stone prophesied of by Daniel until it filled the entire world. 5

Thrilled to be so blessed, John also cherished his time in Kirtland with Brother Joseph. He was dismayed, however, to discover that both Kirtland itself and a great many of the Saints were filled with a bitter spirit of apostasy. "A number in the quorum of the Twelve were disaffected towards the Prophet, and the Church seemed on the point of disintegration."6

According to Lorenzo Snow:

> Singular as it may appear, this spirit of speculation pervaded the quorum of the Twelve Apostles and the quorum of the Seven Presidents of Seventies; indeed, there was not a quorum in the Church but was more or less touched with this spirit of speculation. As that spirit increased, disunion followed. Brethren and sisters began to slander and quarrel one with the other, because their interests were not in harmony...
>
> As President Woodruff stated here yesterday, one-half the quorum of the Apostles, in the days of Kirtland, fell beneath these evil influences. It was this speculation, this love of gold—the god of the world—which produced this doleful effect. 7

Among others, Parley P. Pratt was floundering in darkness. Coming to Elder Taylor, he told him of some things wherein he considered the Prophet Joseph in error. Parley records that "there were jarrings and discords in the Church at Kirtland, and many fell away and became enemies and apostates. There were also envyings, lyings, strifes and divisions, which caused much trouble and sorrow. By such spirits I was also accused, misrepresented and abused. And at one time, I also was overcome by the same spirit in a great measure, and it seemed as if the very powers of darkness which war against the Saints were let loose upon me."8

John responded with the testimony recorded at the beginning of this chapter. After pondering John's remarks for a time, Parley records:

> I went to brother Joseph Smith in tears, and, with a broken heart and contrite spirit, confessed wherein I had erred in spirit, murmured, or done or said amiss. He frankly forgave me, prayed for me and blessed me. Thus, by experience, I learned more fully to discern and to contrast the two spirits, and to resist the one and cleave to the other. And, being tempted in all points, even as others, I learned how to bear with, and excuse, and succor those who are tempted. 9

"'He with many others,'" John Taylor concluded, "'were passing under a dark cloud; he soon made all right with the Prophet Joseph, and was restored to full fellowship.'"10

The evening before he was scheduled to leave Kirtland for his return to Toronto, John attended one last meeting in the temple. As stated earlier, Joseph was in Cleveland, endeavoring to raise money to relieve the Church's debts, and in his absence the leaders of the apostate element "made a violent attack upon the character of the Prophet, which was warmly sustained by many of those present."11 It was at this time that the events portrayed in the *vignette* at the beginning of this chapter took place.

Departing for Canada in company with Isaac Russell and others the next morning, John had no idea that Parrish and the other apostates would bring charges of assault against the aged Joseph Smith Sr. and others who had fought against them. "The following day the apostate party issued formal charges against Father Smith and sixteen others, who then were bound over to the court to answer charges of assault, battery, and riot. Eliza R. Snow, who was present during the temple disturbance, was called as a witness. She had known Father Smith well for a number of years, and said she 'found the court scene as amusing as the Temple scene was appalling. The idea of such a man as Father Smith—so patriarchal in appearance—so circumspect in deportment and dignified in his manners, being guilty of riot, was at once ludicrous and farcical to all sane-minded persons.' Father Smith and his associates were all acquitted."12

By the following Sunday, John Taylor and his party had reached Queenstown, near Niagara Falls. Deciding to hold a public meeting, the men first retired to a secluded spot under a high cliff, just below the falls. While engaged in prayer, for the first time in his life John began speaking in tongues, in the midst of which the Spirit whispered a tremendous secret—that he would soon be called as one of the Twelve Apostles. Filled to bursting with this information, he led the party back into Queenstown, helped secure a place for a meeting, and delivered the sermon. The next day he and the others continued their journey and arrived in Toronto, from whence John immediately continued his labors.

> Leonora wasn't too sure she entirely liked what had happened to her husband. Since his conversion, he had neglected his business for his church work; and now, after returning from Kirtland, he was almost constantly out working in the branches under his supervision. The Canadian mission was proving a phenomenal success, as predicted by Heber C. Kimball. Two hundred wagons headed south toward Kirtland, filled with converts dedicated to the gathering of Zion. During the summer, John organized other groups which would follow. 13

In one of John's groups traveled a fellow Englishman named Joseph Fielding and his two unmarried sisters, Mary and Mercy Rachel, all of whom had been baptized in Black Creek by Parley P. Pratt the same day he had baptized John and Leonora. Through the Fieldings the future mission to England would open up—again as prophesied upon Parley P. Pratt's head by Heber C. Kimball.

Joseph Fielding would accompany the apostles on that mission; Mercy Rachel Fielding would marry Joseph Smith's new secretary, Robert Thompson, and would serve a mission with him to upper Canada; and Mary Fielding would become wife to Hyrum Smith upon the death of Hyrum's wife, Jerusha. Less than a year afterward, in far-off Missouri, Mary would bring into the world a child she would name Joseph Fielding Smith—a boy foreordained to become second counselor to John Taylor in the First Presidency of The Church of Jesus Christ of Latter-day Saints and later yet, sixth president of the Church. 14

Meanwhile, unhappy about John's defense of the Prophet Joseph in the temple, the apostates in Kirtland laid a plan to impede his effectiveness in Canada. Giving Doctor Sampson Avard, one of their number, a document of authority from his quorum, they sent him to upper Canada to take over John's assignment. Though John was away when Avard first arrived, the apostate immediately took over, boasting of his great power and what marvelous things he was about to accomplish. And though John had been cautioned by the apostles not to allow anyone to take over his calling without proper authorization, Avard's letter seemed real enough. Thus John gave up to the man his presidency and went into Whitby County to preach.

It was in August of that year, 1837, that the Prophet Joseph, accompanied by Sidney Rigdon and Thomas B. Marsh, then President of the Twelve Apostles, visited Canada. The course of the Prophet was in marked contrast with that of the self-sufficient high priest, Sampson Avard. The latter at once assumed the presidency of the churches, and commenced regulating affairs without consulting or even seeing Elder Taylor; the former, though acknowledged and sustained as the President of the Church in all the world, and Prophet, Seer and Revelator thereto, called for him, and would not move in any business concerning the churches in

Canada until he had seen him. Although Elder Taylor was some distance from Toronto, the Prophet sent for him, and patiently awaited his coming. On his arrival, to the great surprise of Elder Taylor, the Prophet began to counsel with him as to the best mode of procedure in relation to holding some conferences during their visit. Elder Taylor told the prophet that Elder Avard was presiding. It was Joseph's turn to be surprised now. Avard had never been sent to preside in Canada by his consent. Elder Taylor told him of the credentials that Avard had presented from the high priests' quorum. Joseph insisted that there must be some mistake; an imposition had been practiced, at which he was much annoyed.

Obtaining a carriage, Elder Taylor accompanied the Prophet and his associates in visiting the churches. "This was as great a treat to me as I ever enjoyed," he remarks. "I had daily opportunity of conversing with them, of listening to their instructions, and in participating in the rich stores of intelligence that flowed continually from the Prophet Joseph."

A conference was held in…Scarboro…. Doctor Avard was present, and the Prophet reproved him severely for coming to that place with fictitious papers. He also censured Elder Taylor for yielding up his office on so flimsy a pretext; but palliated it on account of his youth and inexperience. He gave him a strict charge never again, on any account, to give up any office or calling unless he received orders from a legitimate source that could be relied upon; otherwise he would be held responsible for any evil that might accrue from it...

Before the Prophet and his companions left Canada, they ordained Elder Taylor a High Priest, on the 21st of August, 1837, and reappointed him to preside over the Churches. 15

At this same time, at the request of Joseph Fielding, John wrote a letter to Fielding's brother in Preston, England, "giving an account of the restoration of the gospel through the ministration of angels to the Prophet Joseph Smith. This was doubtless the first announcement of these things in England, by an authorized servant of God."16 Later in the fall, after Fielding's brother had responded positively to John's letter, Joseph Fielding accompanied Elders Heber C. Kimball and Orson Hyde on a mission to England, thus fulfilling Elder Kimball's own prophecy. As it turned out, it was in Fielding's brother's chapel in Preston that Elder Kimball preached the first gospel sermon of this dispensation in that land.

It was also in the fall of 1837 that John "received word from the Prophet Joseph that he would be chosen to fill one of the vacancies in the quorum of Apostles."17 Knowing that this would necessitate a move to Kirtland, he broached the subject with Leonora. But she "was appalled. They were settled at Toronto, established in business, among their own people. She was dubious about moving to the States, particularly to Kirtland, a hotbed of apostasy and dissent.

"All the more reason for the faithful to gather, [John] pointed out. And, besides, the collapse of land values had made investment in Kirtland property a rare bargain. He and a friend, Henry Humphrey, had planned on opening a furniture-making shop at Kirtland. Humphrey had located a five-acre farm for them, with good house and barn, at a bargain price.

"Nothing could stop John; his mind was made up. Leonora could only wonder at his complete faith as he liquidated his Toronto assets to put everything, including their savings, into Kirtland property."18

As winter closed in upon them, Leonora, her belly swollen with child, grew more and more worried. Practically penniless, John had no teams, no wagon, and no provisions. Yet he had set the date for their departure and was already going about the branches of the Church, bidding them farewell. Even John's parents, Agnes and James, along with three of their younger children, were preparing to start south with him. 19 Such faith was hard for her to understand, yet all she could do was wait and watch.

Finally Leonora pressed her husband, pleading that he present her with some definite plan. In response, John reminded her of Joseph Smith's letter and the important call he was about to receive. He then explained that "the work seemed great, the duties arduous and responsible. I felt my own weakness and littleness; but I felt determined, the Lord being my helper, to endeavor to magnify it. When I first entered upon Mormonism, I did it with my eyes open. I counted the cost. I looked upon it as a life-long labor, and I considered that I was not only enlisted for time, but for eternity also, and did not wish to shrink now, although I felt my incompetency."20 Therefore, he concluded, he intended to put his trust in the Lord.

Then came another letter, indicating that the Prophet had been forced to flee from Kirtland to a place called Far West, in Missouri, and requesting that John join him there. Stunned, for this would mean he would lose everything he had invested in Kirtland and would in actual fact be penniless, John informed Leonora of the change in plans.

"But how are you going to perform a journey of thirteen or fourteen hundred miles by land, and to a wilderness country without means?"

"I don't know; but the Lord will open out the way."

"Everywhere [John] went, he told the Saints about the time he expected to leave for Far West, but still no visible prospect of getting there was yet in sight. Three or four days before the time appointed for his departure, he called upon a Brother John Mills, who had previously talked of going with him to Kirtland when the time came that he could leave Canada. Elder Taylor now told him that he would have to give up going to Kirtland as he had received word from the Prophet to go to Far West.

"Well, I'll go to Far West too," said Brother Mills, "won't you go with me, Brother Taylor, I have plenty of teams?"

ELDER TAYLOR.—"Brother Mills, I have nothing to pay you with for taking me."

BROTHER MILLS.—"That makes no difference."

ELDER TAYLOR.—"But I have no money to pay my expenses."

BROTHER MILLS.—"I have plenty, and it is at your service."

ELDER TAYLOR.—"That is very kind of you, but I object to getting into debt without the prospect of being able to pay."

BROTHER MILLS.—"But you need not pay."

ELDER TAYLOR.—"Well, if you'll clear me of all responsibility in the matter, and take the Lord for your paymaster, I'll go with you."

BROTHER MILLS.— "Oh, I am quite willing to agree to that."

And so it was arranged right then that they would travel together to Far West. Before the day of their departure had come, the Saints sent to Elder Taylor plenty of supplies, flour, cakes and hams; and as it was the winter season, and such things would keep, they furnished him enough roasted geese, ducks, and other cooked provisions to last himself and several other families hundreds of miles on the journey. Others sent him money and clothing, so that he had an abundance of everything; and as Brother Mills had supplied the necessary conveyance for the journey, it would appear that he had not trusted in the Lord in vain. 21

Traveling southward around Lake Ontario, the caravan of sleighs and wagons at length arrived in Kirtland. By then spring was in the air and the roads were turning to slush, so the sleighs had to be traded for wagons in order for the journey to be continued. Meanwhile, John could not help but notice that Kirtland was "no longer Zion. Joseph and Sidney, hectored by writs, judgments, warrants, and lawsuits, had fled Kirtland in January, pursued more than two hundred miles by enemies, 'armed with pistols and guns,' the prophet reported, 'seeking our lives.' The church printing office had been attached by the sheriff, but before he could take possession someone put the torch to it. To meet a legal judgment, the temple on which the Saints had lavished such sacrifice and hard work was auctioned off for $150."22 John recorded:

> Distress, ruin and poverty...seemed to prevail. Apostates and corrupt men were prowling about as so many wolves seeking whom they might devour. They were oppressive, cruel, heartless; devising every pretext that the most satanic malignity could invent to harass the Saints. Fraud, false accusation and false swearing, vexatious law suits, personal violence, and bare-faced robbery abounded. They were truly afflicted, persecuted and tormented. 23

Abandoning Kirtland to whatever fate awaited it, John and the Canadian Saints continued southward. Soon, however, the roads being literally impassable, they halted at a small village to await drier conditions. During the wait John became acquainted with a number of the local inhabitants, who at length desired to hear him preach. When the local minister refused them his church, John held forth in a cabinetmaker's shop. "He proved the Bible true, and then taught them its principles. He proved The Book of Mormon true, and then preached from that. They were highly delighted with his lectures; and when the time came that he had to leave them, they deeply regretted his departure."24

Later on their journey, near Columbus, Ohio, another community arranged to hear John preach—this time in the open air. As the time for the service approached, a number of the Saints came to John with news that in the community were a group of ruffians who were boasting that if John attempted to preach, they would dress him with tar and feathers and send him on his way. After a moment's reflection, John thanked them for the information and informed them that he intended to preach just the same. The brethren pleaded with him to reconsider—to no avail. They could go with him or not, he told them, but he intended to go and preach.

As John arrived, he saw that the assembly was extremely large. Going to the front, he informed them that "he had lately come from Canada—a land under monarchical rule"—and "that standing as he then did on free soil, among free men," brought forth in him some remarkably peculiar sensations. He continued:

> Gentlemen, I now stand among men whose fathers fought for and obtained one of the greatest blessings ever conferred upon the human family—the right to think, to speak, to write; the right to say who shall govern them, and the right to worship God according to the dictates of their own consciences—all of them sacred, human rights, and now guaranteed by the American Constitution. I see around me the sons of those noble sires, who, rather than bow to the behests of a tyrant, pledged their lives, fortunes and sacred honors to burst those fetters, enjoy freedom themselves, bequeath it to their posterity, or die in the attempt.
>
> They nobly fought and nobly conquered; and now the cap of liberty is elevated on the tops of your liberty poles throughout the land, and the flag of freedom waves from Wisconsin to Louisiana—from Maine to Missouri. Not only so, but your vessels—foremost in the world—sail over

oceans, seas and bays; visiting every nation, and wherever those vessels go your flag flutters in the breeze, a hope is inspired among the downtrodden millions, that they, perchance, if they cannot find liberty in their own land, may find it with you. Gentlemen, with you liberty is more than a name; it is incorporated in your system; it is proclaimed by your senators; thundered by your cannon; lisped by your infants; taught to your school-boys; it echoes from mountain to mountain; reverberates through your valleys, and is whispered by every breeze. Is it any wonder, gentlemen, under these circumstances—having lately emerged from a monarchical government, that I should experience peculiar sensations in rising to address you?

But, by the by, I have been informed that you purpose to tar and feather me, for my religious opinions. Is this the boon you have inherited from your fathers? Is this the blessing they purchased with their dearest hearts' blood—this your liberty? If so, you now have a victim, and we will have an offering to the goddess of liberty." Here he tore open his vest and said: "Gentlemen come on with your tar and feathers, your victim is ready; and ye shades of the venerable patriots, gaze upon the deeds of your degenerate sons! Come on, gentlemen! Come on, I say, I am ready!"

"No one moved, no one spoke. He stood there drawn to his full height, calm but defiant—the master of the situation.

"After a pause of some moments he continued his remarks and preached with great boldness and power for some three hours."25

The tedious journey continued on to Indianapolis where, at the house of a Brother Miller, on June 8, 1838, Leonora gave birth to their second son and third child, whom they named Joseph James. George John, born January 31, 1834, and Mary Anne, born January 23, 1836, had both been born in Canada. In Indianapolis, while Leonora spent two months recuperating, John made himself a carriage, turned furniture for hire at a local shop, and did enough preaching to raise up a small branch of the Church.

With Brother Mills deciding to stay in Indianapolis to continue his employment, in August John and Leonora and their three children parted from him and continued their journey. On into September they traveled westward, at last crossing the mighty Mississippi by flatboat and continuing into Missouri.

As they were approaching DeWitt, in Carroll County, Missouri—the first Mormon community the Taylors had seen since leaving Kirtland early in the spring—the deeply rutted road started the wagon lurching and swaying. As Leonora clutched the baby and the older children held to whatever they could, John was jolted almost off the seat. As his foot slipped off the brake, the teams lunged again, and John was pulled over the dash and under the oncoming wheels of the wagon. Before he could move, the crushing front wheel rolled over his arm, numbing it. Again he tried to move, couldn't, and then the iron tire of the rear wheel crushed across his arm again.

"He was struggling to arise, green sick, when Leonora ran into view up the hill. Was he all right? His arm! Everyone was safe; she'd seized the reins and got the team under control; George was tending the horses, and Mary Anne had the baby. She insisted that he lie down, while with his penknife she slit his sleeve, examining the arm. It was severely bruised, but no bones broken."26

At DeWitt John's old friend Henry Humphrey welcomed him to his home, insisting that he stay there until he was fully recovered. The next morning at breakfast Henry mentioned that new trouble with the Missouri mobs was brewing. As if confirming this, a rider galloped into town moments later with the disturbing news that two preachers, Sashiel Woods and Abbott Hancock, were coming with a mob to drive the Saints from DeWitt. John wrote:

This was the first mob I had ever seen, ...and the whole affair was new to me, especially when I considered the kind of officers they had. I had heretofore looked upon gospel ministers as messengers of peace; here they came not only in a war-like capacity, but as the leaders of an armed mob— a gang of marauders and free-booters, with the avowed object of driving peaceful citizens—men, women and children—from their homes. 27

Although John thought of himself as a peace-loving follower of Christ, he also believed in self-defense and in his responsibility to defend his family against such lawlessness—this in spite of the fact that there were twenty-four Mormons as opposed to about a hundred and fifty amongst the mob. He continued:

I had no arms,...and heretofore considered that I needed none in a Christian civilized land; but I found I had been laboring under a mistake. The civilization here was of a very low order, and the Christianity of a very questionable character. I therefore threw off the sling and bandages from my lame arm, suppressed my repugnance to fighting, borrowed a gun, bought a brace of pistols, and prepared myself at least for defensive measures....

These reverend gentlemen...concluded that it was best to have a parley, and by a little strategy throw us off our guard. Having captured a stray Saint, they sent by him a message informing us that they would like three or four of our leaders to come and treat with them. To this we returned answer that they had come in the capacity of banditti, to interfere with our rights when in the peaceful prosecution of our daily avocations; that we could have no confidence in men occupying so questionable a position; that their ruse to divide us would not work; and though inferior to them in numbers, if they attempted to molest us, we should protect ourselves as best we could. 28

Following some further discussion the mob retreated, warning John and the others that if they were not gone in ten days' time, they would return with increased forces; kill every man, woman, and child; and throw their goods into the Missouri.

Next morning Taylor headed north toward Far West, rifle across his knees as he drove the team, pistols in his waistband, alert for ambush. A new and strange emotion possessed him, until he paid scant attention to his throbbing arm; his senses were quickened as he watched for signs of the enemy at every thicket and bend of the road.

When he reached Far West, three days later, he met the church leaders—Joseph, Sidney, Brigham Young, Heber C. Kimball, Thomas B. Marsh, Orson Hyde, Parley Pratt, Lyman Wight, Hyrum Smith—and they, also, had changed. They were all armed now, and the talk was of strategy, plans for defense and attack.

Taylor had always considered himself a minister of the gospel, carrying God's word to the unsaved. Now he realized that he also was a soldier. A war was going on.... These men were spiritual leaders, but they also had become military commanders, directing the forces of the Kingdom of God against the mobbers.

Joseph, speaking to the group, said, "O ye Twelve, and all Saints, profit by this important key, that in all your trials, troubles, and temptations, afflictions, bonds, imprisonment, and death, see to it that you do not betray heaven, that you do not betray Jesus Christ, that you do not betray your brethren.... Whatever you do, do not betray your friends."

This became Taylor's creed. Until the end of his life he was to be at war, fighting one battle after another for the faith. There could be no compromise, no quarter; for him it would be the Kingdom of God, or nothing; all or none. 29

But at least, John thought as he surveyed the rough frontier town of Far West, Missouri, he was finally gathered with the Saints and could here begin his service as an apostle of the Lord Jesus Christ. He had come to America—and he had come to preach.

5

WIELDING THE PEN AS A SWORD

"Well, John, I dare say you never expected this when you started for Missouri."

Considered a tall man, John Taylor still had to look up to meet the gaze of Joseph Smith. He was never sure if that was because he was actually shorter or because he considered the Prophet in every way superior—to himself as well as to every other man on earth. But it didn't matter, not really. What mattered was that he was privileged to actually be there, standing next to the Lord's earthly mouthpiece, enjoying his presence, rejoicing in the heavenly wisdom that flowed like living water from the man's lips. Joseph Smith was mortal like himself and filled with the frailties of mortality, and was quick to admit it. Still, Joseph had been called by God as a prophet, seer, and revelator; John knew it as truth by personal revelation of his own, and he could never get past the feeling of honor and even awe that overwhelmed him whenever Joseph came near.

Even, he thought wryly, under circumstances such as these—

"You shall see," Joseph continued, sounding almost as if he were filled with good humor rather than dour foreboding, "that you have landed in Zion in the middle of the climatic battle between the Saints and the Missourians. You mark my words, Brother Taylor, for you will see that I am right. What happens in the next few hours, days, or perhaps weeks and months, will decide our fate on this sacred land the Lord has given for our inheritance."

"Is there a chance we might not triumph, Brother Joseph?"

"Man always has his agency," the Prophet replied quietly. "I'd say it will depend on how a few of us exercise it." The Prophet immediately brightened. "But don't let that discourage you, John. The Lord has given me the promise that the Saints will yet overcome. I do not know how or when, but I know they will!"

"So we go forward in faith, leaving the Lord to work out the miracle?"

Joseph smiled. "Exactly right, dear brother. The miracle, and the timing of it. Now, here comes our dear Colonel Hinckle, who has been off treating with the enemy in our behalf. Shall we go and meet him, brethren, and see what advantages the mobbers wish us to give up this go-round?"

As Joseph and the others strode toward the advancing Colonel George M. Hinckle, leader of the Mormon forces and the highest ranking militia officer in Caldwell County, John couldn't help but think of Joseph's words and of the fact that this conflict with the Missourians was indeed a war—a war that had already been in progress for several years!

The Book of Mormon taught that in the last days, the Saints were to build a holy city, the "New Jerusalem," or "Zion," on the American continent. In July, 1831, the Lord had revealed the place where the city should be located and a temple built. That place was Independence, near the western boundary of Missouri, and here the Saints were commanded to gather, purchase the land, and dedicate it unto the Lord. As they did so, it wasn't long before the newcomers began clashing with the old settlers.

The old settlers came mainly from the slave states of the South. Most of the early Saints had come from the free states in the north—many of them from New England. The old settlers lived like frontiersmen and seemed to care little about developing their lands, leaving the rich prairie land uncultivated for want of plows that would break the tough sod. The Saints tended to work as a group; industrious and frugal, they were eager to establish good homes and farms, to develop and beautify the country on the way to making it the Zion of God. Furthermore, there was little common ground to be found between the two in their choices of amusements, as the Missourians struck the Saints as habitual Sabbath breakers who loved horse racing, cockfighting, and gambling, accompanied by drunkenness and blasphemy. Not only religion, but upbringing kept the Saints and the old settlers apart on these matters.

All of this, coupled with mistrust amongst the old settlers that stemmed from early efforts of the Saints to proselyte among the Indians along the frontier, fed the tensions between the two parties. As more Saints poured into the county, it was easy for the old settlers to see how they would eventually be supplanted by the newcomers, and what started as suspicion became conviction—there would be no room left for "Gentiles" in the Mormon Zion if something wasn't done.

Although some of the Saints had been unwise in much of their talk of how this land was their promised inheritance, as Joseph admitted candidly, they had been guilty of no overt act against the peace; and aside from a little Christian exhortation, perhaps, the Saints had not interfered with their neighbors. There was no real cause for violence—except for jealousy, fear, and the general opposition of the adversary to the work of God.

Lacking a real cause, the local inhabitants brought all manner of false accusations against the Saints, including claims that the Mormons were promoting insurrection amongst slaves and had designs to possess the land by force. And there was always religion, "Mormonism," with its "gold Bible" and its Joe Smith. It was denounced as blasphemy—"derogatory of God and religion, and subversive of human reason."

And so the old settlers determined to be rid of the Saints, "peaceably if they could, forcibly if they must," pledging to the cause their "bodily power, their lives, fortunes and sacred honors." Then they organized the mobs that had driven some twelve hundred Saints from Jackson County, stolen their goods, burned their homes, and taken their lands.

That had been five years ago, in December, 1833.

The exiles had found a temporary resting place in Clay and surrounding counties, where they had remained until 1836, when, at the request of the citizens of Clay County, they had moved northward to largely uninhabited lands and petitioned the state to form a new county. Their petition was granted, and the new county had been called Caldwell, with the county seat at Far West.

Unfortunately, the rapid growth in both population and prosperity in the new county had again stirred up jealousy and distrust amongst the surrounding citizens. The Saints had been despoiled and driven once with relative impunity; in fact some of those who had taken a prominent part in expelling the Saints from Jackson County currently held high positions in the state. The time seemed ripe to once again reap what the Saints had sown.

Finally, as a match to the fuse, there had been the recent troubles at the election in Gallatin, Daviess County, which adjoined Caldwell on the north.

One more fear harbored by the Missourians was the Saints' growing political power. The Saints, as a united people, often voted as a block, and with their increasing numbers, the old inhabitants feared losing power in their own state. A number of Saints, all qualified to vote, had determined to cast their ballots during the recent election at Gallatin, where some of the old settlers had tried to prevent them. On this matter, the brethren refused to quietly submit, and a disturbance had broken out. Using that as their pretext, the mob had commenced open hostilities.

Thus, "the clouds which had been gathering hatred and jealousy for so long, burst almost without warning upon the unprotected heads of the Saints."

Now, as John followed the long-striding prophet toward the approaching Colonel Hinckle, he found himself shaking his own head in disgust. Mob violence such as he had helped temporarily forestall in DeWitt had become an almost daily occurrence; property was being destroyed; men were frequently tied up and beaten until blood streamed down their backs; the chastity of women and even young girls was being forcibly outraged; the wanton shooting of cattle and hogs was common; houses were being burned in the presence of their owners; fields of grain were being trampled, burned, and otherwise destroyed—try as he would, John could think of no better description for the carnage the Saints were experiencing than war!

And now it had come to Far West, where more than four thousand Saints—many of them refugees who had been burned, pillaged, and driven from other communities—were suddenly surrounded by between three thousand and thirty-five hundred heavily armed men, ostensibly of the state militia. In reality, they were the very mobbers who had been sacking and driving the Saints all along, every last one of them dedicated to the destruction rather than the protection of God's people. As Joseph liked to put it, the whole dark and blackening affair was enough to make hell itself shudder, to stand aghast and pale, and the hands of the very devil to tremble and palsy.

In response, the Prophet had called John to serve on a committee of nine men, including Edward Partridge, Brigham Young, and Heber C. Kimball, whose purpose was to draft a report to the Missouri state legislature regarding the persecution of the Mormons. John had already written out a rough draft of the outrages, and others of the committee were now adding to it. May God grant, he prayed fervently as he followed Joseph to the rendezvous, that this would be one of those occasions when the pen would prove mightier than the sword!

"Well, Colonel," Joseph Smith began without preamble, "what do the mobbers wish of us this time?"

Standing in front of Joseph Smith, George Hinckle squared his shoulders. "They are not mobbers, Brother Joseph," he replied stiffly, "but state militia under command of Generals Lucas, Doniphan, and Parks, sent under authority of Governor Boggs to quell any disturbance that might arise, no matter from what quarter."

"Very well," Joseph responded with a disarming smile, "since the Saints here in Far West are engaged only in the peaceful pursuit of their daily affairs, and since our peace is well-enough protected by our own Caldwell County boys, of which you are commander, Colonel, why have they come here?"

Colonel Hinckle appeared exasperated. "I told you—to protect the citizenry from any illegal uprising."

"Colonel," Joseph declared, his eyes boring into those of the rigidly standing officer, "there will be no such uprising on the part of our people! Nevertheless, we cannot stand by and see our wives and our children butchered the way the mobs butchered those innocents at Haun's Mill! Those men formed against us yonder are not militia but mobocrats, sir; you know that, and their hearts are filled with the spirit of murder, tyranny, and oppression. I tell you, Colonel Hinckle, they are our enemies, and their every intention is to attack and destroy us before nightfall!"

"They intend nothing of the sort!" Colonel Hinckle remonstrated haughtily. "They have asked that we order our militia to retreat, after which they will enter into negotiations—"

"Retreat!" Joseph thundered, cutting the suddenly cowering man off in midsentence. "Why, where in the name of God shall we go?"

Abruptly ignoring the trembling Colonel Hinckle, Joseph turned toward the scattered line of men who made up the Caldwell County militia. "Boys," he shouted, his words ringing with power such as John had never heard, "follow me!" And without a backward glance he raised his sword and strode across the open prairie toward the assembling mob.

To John's amazement about two hundred men raised their weapons and followed the Prophet, their battle cries rending the still evening air. Two hundred against upwards of three thousand, all heavily armed, he thought as he joined in. Certainly they would all be slaughtered—

"All right, men," Joseph's voice thundered as he halted less than a hundred yards from the gathered enemy, "take positions and prepare to fire! And do not be afraid, brethren. In the name of Israel's God I promise that not one of you will be slain, while they shall fall by the hundreds and even thousands!

"Ready! Aim!"

"Joseph," someone called, "there's a flag of truce coming toward us! It looks like General Doniphan and his aides."

Turning, John was astounded to see a small group of mounted men coming forward under a flag of truce. They had heard the Prophet's words, apparently, and were surrendering—

"Brother Rich," Joseph asked after watching the approaching men for an instant, "will you go and treat with them?"

Instantly, young Charles C. Rich lowered his weapon, nodded, and strode forward. For perhaps five minutes he and the mounted men parleyed, and then Brother Rich separated from them and walked back to where Joseph, John, and a few of the others, were waiting.

"Well?" Joseph asked.

"General Doniphan says that our Colonel Hinckle is lying, that Lucas and Parks intend to destroy Far West this very night, Brother Joseph. First, though, they wish us to surrender our arms and liberate Adam Lightner and John Cleminson, both non-members, and John Cleminson's wife, who is a member."

"Does anyone know these people?"

"I know them," a man responded.

"Very well. Go and make them the offer. Tell them they are free to go."

As the man sped off, John looked to see that though General Doniphan had left the field, his aides had remained behind, apparently waiting under their flag of truce for an answer.

"What is happening here?" Colonel Hinckle belatedly demanded as he strode up.

"Colonel," Joseph declared, his eyes boring into those of the wrathful officer, "I have taken command for the moment, and everything is under control."

"But, you can't do that—"

"I already have, Colonel. By the by, did you perchance forget to tell us that the mob intend to attack us as soon as their friends are liberated and they have our weapons?"

Dumfounded, Colonel Hinckle was still stammering after a reply when the runner came loping back.

"Where are the supposed hostages?" Joseph questioned.

"They don't want to be liberated," the man replied with a grin. "They said to tell the mob that they have always been treated with consideration by the Mormons, and they intend to stay with us."

As those nearby chuckled, Joseph nodded. "Very well. Brother Rich, would you mind awfully much if I delivered this message in person?"

"Not at all."

"Good. Brother Taylor, would you like to accompany me?"

Silently, John fell in beside the Prophet, and together they strode to where the aides to General Doniphan were waiting There, without any blustering or braggadocio, Joseph delivered the message. Then, as he and John were turning, both men noticed a troop of cavalry, about two hundred strong, approaching on a fast lope.

"Are those Neil Gilliam's boys?" Joseph demanded of the aides. Neil Gilliam, John knew, was leader of one of the most notorious and bloodthirsty mobs then roaming the country. Usually they dressed as Indians, painted bodies and all, and prided themselves that their atrocities were every bit as fierce as those of actual savages.

"Yes, sir," one of the aides replied as he observed the approaching men. "That looks like Gilliam's boys, all right."

"Very well. You know that I am Joseph Smith, the prophet. Go tell your general for me, sir, that if he does not immediately withdraw those men, I will send them all to hell!"

Stunned, the aides took only an instant to stare at the unruffled leader of the Saints. Then they whipped their mounts about and flew away, two toward the approaching mob of Neil Gilliam and the other toward the waiting General Doniphan.

Moments later, as John watched in amazement, the two hundred or so men of Gilliam's mob stampeded to a halt, milled for a moment around the excited aides, and then as one they turned and beat a hasty and inglorious retreat toward a distant stand of trees.

"Well, Brother Taylor," Joseph declared quietly, "sufficient unto the day is the evil thereof. I would say they've had enough excitement for now. As for tomorrow, who knows? But for tonight, our people can rest in peace. Shall we rejoin the brethren?"

And with a bright smile, the Prophet took John Taylor by the arm and led him back toward the besieged and frightened community of Far West. 1

When John, Leonora, and their three children arrived in Far West in September, 1838, "the city was not quite two years old—yet already it was a thriving metropolis of some three thousand inhabitants, the largest town in the state north of the Missouri River. Joseph had laid out the city on a plat containing four sections—two miles square—with wide streets forming blocks of four acres and each acre divided into four lots. The large public square in the center of the city was atop the highest knoll of the surrounding prairie, and from it [John] could see for miles in all directions—the cultivated fields of the Saints, the endless sweep of the rolling prairie dotted with Gentile villages, their white church spires gleaming in the sunlight. In the public square was the temple site, an excavation one hundred and ten feet by eighty, marked by large stones rolled into place at each corner. But work on the basement had been suspended due to trouble with mobs."2

In fact, John and Leonora did indeed find themselves in the midst of the climactic battle of what the Missourians called the Mormon War. Apparently the Lord did not wish John to fight with the use of powder and ball, however, for shortly after his arrival in Far West, Joseph called him to fight with the power of his pen. John "was appointed to a committee which would draft a report to the Missouri state legislature on the persecution of the Mormons. …While the committee as a whole would conceive and shape the report, the nitty-gritty of getting it down on paper would largely be a collaboration of [John] Taylor and [Bishop] Partridge." 3

For three months the men labored on the report, Bishop Partridge providing an eye-witness account of the persecution that had raged in Jackson, Clay, Caldwell, Carroll, and Daviess Counties. John also interviewed a host of others; he had seen for himself in DeWitt the rabid anti-Mormon bias of two ministers, Abbot Hancock and Sashiel Woods; and he was well aware of the uncompromising hatred of such men as Colonel William Peniston, the leader of the state militia. More, "a visit to any tavern or grocery where Gentiles gathered was sufficient to encounter first-hand hostility…[while] a balanced Gentile viewpoint was available from Joseph's lawyer, Alexander Doniphan, who was also a general of the state militia." 4

John was very much affected by the pain and suffering he encountered and the seemingly endless accounts of robbery, rapine, and murder. More than thirty years later, he declared:

> My mind wanders back upwardly of thirty years ago,... when in the state of Missouri, Mr. McBride, a gray-haired, venerable veteran of the Revolution, with feeble frame and tottering steps, cried to a Missouri patriot: "Spare my life, I am a revolutionary soldier, I fought for liberty, would you murder me? What is my offense, I believe in God and revelation?" This frenzied disciple of a misplaced faith said, "Take that you God d____d Mormon," and with the butt of his gun he dashed his brains out, and he lay quivering there, his white locks clotted with his own brains and gore, on the soil that he had heretofore shed his blood to redeem—a sacrifice at the shrine of liberty! 5

"After three months the report 'To the Honorable Legislature of the State of Missouri' was presented to that body by a Mormon member of it, John Corrill."6 By then Governor Lilburn W. Boggs had issued to the militia his infamous extermination order, declaring that the Mormons either be exterminated or driven from the state, and that same militia under Generals Lucas and Parks had surrounded Far West. It was then that the incident portrayed at the beginning of this chapter occurred.

Though the initial plot had been foiled, by the next afternoon the duplicitous Colonel George M. Hinckle had betrayed Joseph, Hyrum, Sidney, Parley P. Pratt, Lyman Wight, George Robinson, and several others into the mobbers' hands. That night General Lucas ordered that the brethren be shot the next morning in the square at Far West. But General Doniphan, who had been ordered to perform the execution, flatly refused, declaring it to be cold-blooded murder. Stymied, Lucas then hauled the brethren, under constantly repeated threats of death by hanging, to Richmond, where they were tried by a mock court and then imprisoned on charges of high treason, murder, burglary, arson, robbery, and larceny. Meanwhile, the Saints remaining at Far West had been disarmed and then ordered to pay for the cost of the "war" by allowing the mobbers to seize their real property, which they did, robbing, raping, and plundering the Saints and their possessions at will. Finally, though it was by then the dead of winter, the destitute Saints were ordered on pain of certain death to be out of the state before spring.

> The result of these outrages was that some four hundred of the Saints were either murdered outright or died from exposure and hardship inflicted upon them in this unhallowed persecution; from twelve to fifteen thousand citizens of the United States were expelled from the state of Missouri—from the lands they had purchased of the general government; while their homes were destroyed, and their stock and much other property were confiscated. 7

John and his family were witnesses to these cruel and illegal proceedings and suffered through many of them.

Such tragic results indicate that the report to the state legislature made by John and the rest of the committee accomplished nothing except, perhaps, to provide the majority of the legislators with a little base merriment.

> With fine irony, historian B. H. Roberts notes that the Missouri legislature, "while the petition of the Saints for a redress of their wrongs was lying before it, appropriated two hundred thousand dollars to defray the expenses incurred in driving the 'Mormons' from the State, and dispossessing them of their property!" 8

While the legislature was thus mocking the Mormons and the exodus of the hungry, freezing Saints was beginning, John Taylor, on December 19, 1838, was appointed by Brigham Young and Heber C. Kimball to redraft, with Bishop Partridge, the Saints' petition of grievances against Missouri and send it on to the federal government. In that same meeting Elders Kimball and Young also ordained John an apostle of the Lord Jesus Christ. 9 At last he was ready to begin the work for which the Lord had been preparing him since the earliest days of his youth.

> Brigham Young was in charge of the exodus of Mormons from Missouri. The Saints, harassed by mobs, forced to leave behind what wagons wouldn't carry, were required to travel across the entire width of the state, ill-equipped for winter storms, seeking a new Zion at a place as yet unknown. It was Brigham's first opportunity to exercise his administrative ability, and he displayed a most remarkable talent in organizing a defeated people, infusing courage, making the retreat to Illinois in mid-winter a heroic endeavor rather than a rout. [John's] role was to act as liaison between the Saints and the state militia. 10

During the course of the winter, many of the Saints took the opportunity to visit the Church's First Presidency in their pitiful cell in Liberty, Clay County, Missouri. Prior to his family's exodus from the state, John also traveled to Liberty. Just north of the town square he found a solid stone building with mere slits for windows and an inner shell of squared oak logs to make it escape proof. The jail had two cells, one up and one down; the lower cell was called the dungeon, and it was here that Joseph, Hyrum, and Sidney, as well as stalwart supporters Lyman Wight, Caleb Baldwin, and Alexander McRae, were usually kept.

After lubricating the guards' desires to help with large portions of Leonora's apple pie, John and his hamper of food for the prisoners were finally admitted to the dungeon. "The plump guard, John Hogarth…quickly [shut] the door [behind John] to avoid the fetid air that almost made Taylor's stomach turn over. The [fourteen-foot-square] room was heavy with smoke; the tiny stove, whose flue connected with the one of the cell above, had little draft. Beds were mounds of moldy straw on the floor; sanitary facilities consisted of pitcher, basin and reeking [bucket] commode." 11

After serving up Leonora's hamper of food to the emaciated men and reporting on the condition of the Saints as they were making their exodus, John described the petition he and Bishop Partridge were preparing to send to Washington. He then received instructions from Joseph relative to the petition as well as a possible future jailbreak. Assuring the brethren that they had not been forgotten, John left the jail and started for his wagon.

Nearby he was met by Sheriff Samuel Hadley, who informed him quietly that a movement was afoot to grant the prisoners a change of venue, and then, because the whole situation had become an embarrassment to the state, see that they were assassinated en route.

John "looked at the sheriff steadily. There was only one reason why the man would be telling him this. Hadley rubbed the fingers of his right hand significantly against the thumb. Taylor nodded agreement. It was a matter of money. It might be possible, the sheriff suggested, that the prisoners would escape while being transferred. And if he made a deal with the prophet, he wanted to be sure that somebody would stand behind it.

"Taylor gave his personal guarantee that the bribe would be paid, then he climbed into the rig and drove away." 12

March found John and Leonora with their children in Quincy, Illinois—a Mississippi River city that had offered the buffeted Saints a temporary haven. "Several of the Apostles who met there held a consultation in respect to the revelation which had been given the July previous, commanding their quorum to take leave of the Saints in the city of Far West, on the 26TH day of April, 1839, at the building spot of the Lord's house, previous to crossing the Atlantic on a mission to foreign lands. It had been the constant boast of the mob from the time the revelation was made known, that this was one of 'Joe Smith's' revelations that should fail of fulfillment if no other did. But the several Apostles who took part in the above mentioned consultation, among whom was Elder Taylor, were determined that the revelation should not fail, and agreed to return to Far West by different routes, and meet at the temple site on the day appointed." 13

The apostles (those who had not fallen away or were not in prison) departed from Quincy on April 18, 1839, and by care and stealth began to make their way back across Missouri. On a slippery hillside deep in Missouri, four days later, they came upon Elder John E. Page trying to right his overturned wagon. John Taylor was overjoyed to see him, for they were close friends with much in common. Page had made a remarkable record as a missionary in Canada, personally converting more than six hundred souls. He had also arrived in DeWitt at the same time as John, leading one of the companies of Canadian Saints. And finally, both men had been ordained apostles on the same day back in December. 14

Though Elder Page had now lost his wife and two of his children to the persecution, after a few moments to say farewell, he left his remaining children with friends and joined the apostles, determined with them to see that Joseph's revelation would be fulfilled.

For three more days they traveled, the last day feeling unusually protected as they passed wagon after wagon of Saints fleeing in the opposite direction. Yet they continued unmolested, brethren gathering from one wagon after another to accompany them, until by nightfall of April 25, numbering more than thirty members, they arrived at the abandoned city.

There was a bright moon, and Taylor was filled with a consuming rage at the sight of the devastated city; chimneys standing stark among burned ruins, piles of brick and timber marking the sites of demolished business and church buildings, fences down, homes unroofed, weeds tall in the wide streets.

The men put up in vacant houses; the apostles camped in the residence of Morris Phelps, who was in jail at Richmond with Parley Pratt and others. They were making supper when the back door opened and a bald, powerfully built man slipped inside. It was Heber C. Kimball, with news that he had passed the word around the countryside, and the faithful still in the vicinity would gather at the temple site soon after midnight.

Then, eyes sparkling, Heber gave the big news—Joseph and the brethren at Liberty jail had escaped! Even now they were riding on fast horses toward Quincy. Heber had verified this report and had paid $400 to a man who presented an order drawn by the prophet for purchase of the horses used in the escape.

Taylor was filled to bursting with joy as he spread his bedroll on the floor. Through the grace of God the prophet had been spared.15

Shortly after midnight the apostles, now five in number, held a meeting during which Wilford Woodruff and George A. Smith, having been previously called and sustained, were ordained to the apostleship, thus giving the assembled apostles a majority of the quorum. Next, thirty-one people were cut off from the Church—including John's Canadian friends "Isabella Walton, the widow whose home had been the birthplace of the church there, along with members of her family; her daughter, Mary, was on the list, together with her husband and Taylor's old friend, Isaac Russell." 16

Following this meeting the apostles gathered to the moonlit hole in the ground that had been dug to hold the foundations of the temple.

In the chill darkness they sang an opening hymn, after which prayer was offered up by each of the apostles in the order of their standing, or place of seniority, in the quorum. Then "Elder Alpheus Cutler, the master workman of the Lord's House, laid the south-east corner stone in its position, and stated that in consequence of the peculiar situation of the Saints it was deemed prudent to discontinue further labor on the house until the Lord should open the way for its completion." 17 All then sang the hymn "Adam-ondi-Ahman," 18 composed by William W. Phelps, after which the apostles took leave of the Saints who were present and started on their way to fill their missions beyond the Atlantic.

As the route toward the ocean lay through Quincy, the brethren paused there to assist their families and conclude certain matters of business having to do with deteriorating relationships between the Saints and the heretofore friendly citizens of Quincy. Feeling that the problems stemmed from the Saints being blamed for things they were not guilty of, on May 1, the date of his return from Far West, John penned the following lines to the editor of the *Quincy Argus*:

> Sir,—We warn the citizens of Quincy against individuals, who may pretend to belong to our community...who never did belong to our church, and others who once did but for various reasons have been expelled from our fellowship. 19

Two days later, as the apostles visited with the Prophet, he heartily approved of their actions in Far West, blessed them to be successful during their missionary labors in Europe, and then assigned John to "write an account of Mormon difficulties in Missouri, which had been requested by the editor of the *St. Louis Gazette....*

However, when [John] sent in the article [some two months later], the editor evidently found the facts too strong a dish for the Missouri table and rejected it. Taylor wasn't surprised. He put the article in his luggage as he packed up for England, trusting that the Lord would open the way for its publication." 20

Meanwhile, the Saints had begun leaving Quincy and gathering to a spot on the Mississippi River called Commerce. Located upriver from Quincy, the unhealthy location soon swelled into a rough-hewn community known as Nauvoo. Unable to do better because there was nothing else available, John settled Leonora and the children in an abandoned log military barracks in Montrose, Iowa, across the river from Nauvoo. His parents, James and Agnes, with their children, "moved on to a wilderness area thirty miles north of Nauvoo, to a place called Oquawka, the county seat of Henderson County." 21

Malaria was more than prevalent on both sides of the river; the Saints were highly susceptible at least partially because their strength had been so decimated during the previous year. Leonora and the children quickly fell victim to the wretched effects of this disease, though John seemed to remain healthy.

It was the 8TH of August when he left Montrose to fill his mission. He dedicated his wife and family to the care of the Lord and blessed them in His name. In explanation of his mixed feelings at the time, John wrote:

> The thought of the hardships they had just endured,... the uncertainty of their continuing in the house they then occupied—and that only a solitary room—the prevalence of disease, the poverty of the brethren, their insecurity from mobs, together with the uncertainty of what might take place during my absence, produced feelings of no ordinary character. These solicitations, paternal and conjugal, were enhanced also by the time and distance that

was to separate us. But the thought of going forth at the command of the God of Israel to revisit my native land, to unfold the principles of eternal truth and make known the things that God had revealed for the salvation of the world, overcame every other feeling. 22

6

WITHOUT PURSE OR SCRIP

"Tell us again about Brother Taylor, Mother; when Father brought him to your home on the Isle of Man when he was a missionary."

Ann Hughlings Pitchforth smiled patiently at her three daughters, for though she was trying to pretty her hair in preparation for meeting Brother Taylor up at the temple, she knew the girls—and even the older Samuel, her only living son—had a sense that something unusual was going on and wanted to know as much as they could. "You love to hear about Brother Taylor, don't you?"

All three girls nodded silently.

It was January 30, 1846, and outside Ann's home the frigid winds from off the northern Great Plains were again buffeting the bustling city of Nauvoo and all who were sheltered within it. Yet the potbellied stove in the corner kept Ann's parlor room toasty, a high stack of firewood chopped by John and his son lined an entire wall, and along another wall her precious piano—obtained for her by Brother Taylor—stayed nicely in tune for her numerous pianoforte students. Surely she was blessed beyond measure; and now to receive this amazing added blessing—

"Very well," she smiled again. "It was a lovely day in Douglas; Brother Taylor had just come in by boat from Morecambe and Liverpool, and he was standing on a corner holding a street meeting when Solomon first noticed him."

"What was it that brought him to our island?"

"The Spirit of the Lord, he told me. Of course his wife, Sister Leonora Cannon Taylor, is also from the Isle of Man, and so he had been thinking of going there to introduce the gospel for some time. But when he chose to go, it was because he suddenly could not get the idea to depart from his mind."

"Was Brother Taylor singing when Father found him, Mother?"

"He was, Annie. Brother Taylor loves to sing. He has one of the finest deep baritone voices I have ever heard. His voice was what caught your father's ear, and then his message—that God had restored to Earth his ancient gospel—captured Solomon's interest, and so he brought him to our home."

"Brother Taylor is a handsome man, isn't he, Mother?"

Ann smiled and hoped she was covering her blush. "Both Solomon and I agreed that our new lodger was altogether as fascinating a young man as we had ever met. And from a woman's point of view, Mercy, I don't believe an evangelist as tall, handsome, and charming as John Taylor has ever visited the Isle of Man. He was a welcome relief from our usual long-faced sin-stompers."

The girls giggled. "Is that what Father called preachers?" Sarah asked.

"It is," Ann responded with both sadness and resignation. "He had little patience with them and thought them boring. However, no one ever went to sleep during Brother Taylor's sermons."

"To the best of my knowledge, none of us ever missed any of his meetings," Samuel, added quietly. "Except perhaps for Father. I felt from the first that Brother Taylor was speaking the absolute truth about our Lord and Savior and his one true church, and my heart yearned to follow him into the waters of baptism."

"As did we all," Ann smiled. "For years I had been secretly studying the New Testament, coming to know our Lord, and it took no time to discover that Brother Taylor's religion embodied all I had come to believe. Still, Sammy, you had the courage to lead the way—the first to be baptized on the Isle of Man in this last dispensation! I was so very proud of you then, and you have been such a fine example to us ever since. I pray that you will ever hold true!"

"I will, Mother. Don't fret yourself about that. All of us will hold true, no matter what may happen."

"Thank you, Sammy. No doubt there will be more trials and persecutions, just as Brother Taylor experienced while he lived in our home—"

"And drove the Saints from Missouri!"

"And killed our dear prophet and his brother here in Nauvoo this past spring!"

"And made Brother Taylor a living martyr with them," Ann concluded quietly as sudden tears filled her eyes. "But he is such a fine and brave man! Never a word of complaint, no matter how terrible his wounds. And he fears nothing! I recollect once when one of his lectures on the Isle of Man was rudely interrupted by a disorderly party of Methodist preachers. They were so furious at him, the newspaper, the *Manx Liberal*, reported that they seemed ready to fight. The man in charge of the hall proposed that if they believed Brother Taylor had said anything contrary to the word of God, they should agree to a public debate with him. The rowdies readily accepted the idea, and the next day one of their number, a minister named Thomas Hamilton, challenged him to a debate, charging him with misquoting, mutilating, taking from and adding to the Bible.

"Brother Taylor accepted the challenge, he told me, not because he felt he could teach Hamilton anything, but merely to remove public prejudice and to let it be known that he courted publicity and light and was not afraid of bringing his principles to the touchstone of truth.

"The debate generated tremendous excitement. Everyone I knew in Douglas was talking about it, and all wanted to be in attendance. Each side was given an hour to present its case before the noisy hall, and then each had another half hour for final responses. Speaking first, Hamilton conducted himself so poorly that the *Manx Liberal* described him as a mere braggadocio, possessing no qualifications save ignorance and presumption.

"Feeling that the man had given him nothing to refute, Brother Taylor spent his hour presenting his regular missionary message. During the rebuttal period Hamilton did little more than repeat his nonsense of the first hour, whereupon Brother Taylor, as the *Liberal* described it, inflicted deserved chastisement on the arrogant simpleton who had given the challenge without being able to utter a single sentence against his opponent. This he did right well, for there sat poor Mr. Hamilton, biting his lips and shaking his head, every muscle of his distorted countenance seeming to implore the mercy of the meeting. As he finished his remarks, Brother Taylor affectionately urged Mr. Hamilton to repent and be baptized for the remission of his sins.

"At the end of the three hours allotted, and when the meeting was ready to vote on the proposition that Hamilton had proved none of his charges, more excitement erupted. Of course the vote would have gone overwhelmingly against him, but suddenly some of Hamilton's boisterous supporters began again to make charges against Brother Taylor and demand time to prove them. The audience, however, hissed, groaned, and shouted them down. Finally Brother Taylor himself gave the doxology and a closing prayer, and the meeting was over. His description of it later, as Sammy and I drove him home in our carriage, was that of all the lame attempts to oppose the truth that ever he had heard, he thought Hamilton's was the weakest and the worst, and that was why the people were so disgusted with him.

"Now, girls, I am almost late for my meeting with Brother Taylor and Brother Brigham Young at the temple, so we simply must stop chattering!"

"Is that why you are making yourself so pretty, Mother? Because you are going to the temple?"

"No, silly," Sarah scorned as if she were the font of all knowledge. "To the Lord, righteous people are always pretty. I think Mother's making all this fuss because she's going to be meeting her 'handsome' Brother Taylor."

"Sarah!" Not even a little upset, Ann knew that once again she was blushing. But how in the world, she wondered, was she supposed to hide the fact that within a matter of hours, Elder Young would have sealed her, in an incredibly sacred but highly secret ceremony, as the tenth wife of her dearly beloved missionary and apostle of the Lord, John Taylor? There was simply no earthly way— 1

After leaving Leonora and his three children sick in bed, racked with chills and fever, and having taken courage from Leonora's whispered, "God bless you, John, till we meet again," John Taylor started for England on his first mission by crossing the Mississippi by ferry to Nauvoo. There he called at the home of Joseph Smith. "It was August, the worst period of the sickly season. The marsh miasma was taking a dreadful toll of the Saints; finding enough able-bodied men to dig graves was a problem.... The earth was spongy underfoot from the many springs oozing from the bluff rising on the east. A few men were digging at a drainage ditch, but progress was slow with so many felled with ague and so much other work to be done.... As [John] picked his way among the tents and wagons, clouds of insects rose up before him, drawn by the fetid stench of diarrhea and vomit." 2

From the Prophet, John learned that his missionary companion,

Portrait of John Taylor   *N.D.*

Wilford Woodruff, was waiting for him at the blockhouse near the upper landing. Walking together to the site, the two men found Elder Woodruff lying deathly sick on a side of leather in the shade of the building.

"Well, Brother Woodruff, " Joseph said, "you have started on your mission."

"Yes; but I feel and look more like a subject for the dissecting room," Woodruff admitted.

"What did you say that for?" the prophet demanded. "Get up and go along! All will be right with you," he promised. 3

Taking Joseph at his word, Elder Woodruff struggled to his feet with John's assistance. At that moment a wagon came along, and the driver offered the missionaries a ride as far as he was going. Quickly Joseph gave each of the men blessings and counseled them to preach only faith, repentance, baptism, and the reception of the Holy Ghost and to leave alone all other information relative to the Restoration. Then they were in the back of the wagon and it was rattling toward the outskirts of Nauvoo.

A short time later the companions came upon two other apostles, Parley P. Pratt and Heber C. Kimball, who were hewing logs for building cabins. When Parley offered Elder Woodruff all he had—an empty purse—Heber then handed the missionaries his last dollar to put in it. With a hearty cheer the two then sent John and Elder Woodruff on their way—no longer traveling completely without purse or scrip!

The several-month journey that followed must have seemed like a nightmare to both missionaries. At Macomb, Illinois, they stopped with Don Carlos Smith, and both men preached in a grove of trees. Elder Woodruff was too weak to preach much, so John took over and delivered a powerful sermon. Afterwards George Miller came forward and requested baptism—thus becoming the first convert of the mission. Brother Miller later became Presiding Bishop of the Church. 4

Traveling in the wagon of longtime Church member Zebedee Coltrin, the missionaries at length departed Macomb for Cleveland, Ohio, having first obtained donations totaling nine dollars and a horse. John was still healthy, Elder Woodruff terribly ill. In Springfield they halted for several more days, holding meetings and selling the horse to finance the publication of John's once-rejected article on the Missouri persecutions. His first publication, this eight-page pamphlet established John's reputation among the Saints as an able defender of the faith.

Near Terre Haute, Indiana, John "became suddenly and violently sick. Coltrin reined the team to allow him to relieve himself, but as Taylor climbed out he fell as if shot. The other two lifted him into the wagon, and as it rattled along both missionaries lay upon the jostling wagon-bed, Taylor fainting several times. For days Taylor seemed to get sicker by the mile. After spending a bad night with a 'bilious fever' at Germantown, he insisted on holding a meeting the next day. It was Sunday, and he was on a mission to carry the gospel to the Gentiles. 'He wished me to speak, and I did so,' Woodruff recorded, 'dwelling upon the first principles of the gospel. He followed me, and spoke until he was exhausted.' At the verge of collapse, both men spent another bad night." 5

With daylight both Zebedee Coltrin and Elder Woodruff agreed that John was about to breathe his last mortal breath. Committing him to the Lord by the laying on of hands, the two continued their journey, leaving John at an inn to die in peace. There, John declared,

> among strangers, a distance of several hundreds of miles from my home.... I was brought down to the gates of death several times....

The people in this neighborhood treated me with the greatest kindness, and as there was a chapel close to the inn where I stayed, at their request I preached to them, but I was so weak that I had to sit down and preach. After staying here about five weeks I was so far recovered as to be able to proceed. 6

Before his departure, however, John received an unexpected blessing. The Gentiles to whom he had been preaching were much surprised that

although he was a long distance from his home and friends, and had been prostrate with sickness among strangers, and on expenses, he never alluded to these things or begged for assistance. What a contrast between this servant of God and the sectarian priests of the day! Had one of their number been similarly situated, what a tale of woe would have been told of his heroic suffering for the gospel's sake, and what pathetic appeals would have been made to the generous who loved the Lord, for assistance! But this Apostle of Jesus Christ bore all patiently, more anxious to deliver the message he bore than secure his own comfort. At last a gentleman waited upon him, and asking to be excused for the liberty he was about to take, referred to the above matters in the following manner:

"Mr. Taylor, you do not act as most preachers do; you have said nothing about your circumstances or money, yet you have been here some time sick; your doctor's, hotel and other bills must be heavy. Some friends and myself have talked these matters over and would like to assist you, though we do not wish to give any offense."

In replying to this Elder Taylor thanked the gentleman, and said:

"I preach without purse or scrip, leaving the Lord to manage those matters you speak of in His own way; and as you have been prompted by the Lord and your own generous impulses, I shall thankfully receive whatever assistance you are disposed to render me."

The gentleman then presented him a small sum of money, which, with what he had, was sufficient to settle all his bills and enable him to pursue his journey.

Commenting upon the above incident, Elder Taylor says: "I would rather put my trust in the Lord than in any of the kings of the earth."[7]

Due to relapses in his health that seemed to coincide with his preaching engagements, John lost additional weeks in Dayton and again in Kirtland. Through amazing perseverance he continued on toward New York, however, doing his best to comply with the requirement of God to preach the gospel in his native land. Finally arriving at the house of Parley P. Pratt, whom John "had left in Nauvoo a few months before, putting up a log house; but who was now presiding over a large branch of the Church in the metropolis of the United States,"[8] John could only shake his head in wonder.

Wilford Woodruff, who had been in New York for some time, was anxious to be on his way to England. Unfortunately he had no money with which to purchase the fare. John, who had seen the Lord miraculously provide for him throughout his tedious journey, but who had arrived at Elder Pratt's home with but one cent in his pocket, let it be known on inquiry into his financial circumstances that he had plenty of money. Hearing that, Elder Pratt approached him as follows:

ELDER PRATT: "Brother Taylor, I hear you have plenty of money?"

ELDER TAYLOR: "Yes, Brother Pratt, that's true."

ELDER PRATT: "Well, I am about to publish my 'Voice of

Warning' and 'Millennial Poems,' I am very much in need of money, and if you could furnish me two or three hundred dollars I should be very much obliged."

ELDER TAYLOR: "Well, Brother Parley, you are welcome to anything I have, if it will be of service to you."

ELDER PRATT: "I never saw the time when means would be more acceptable."

ELDER TAYLOR: "Then you are welcome to all I have." And putting his hand into his pocket Elder Taylor gave him his copper cent. A laugh followed.

"But I thought you gave it out that you had plenty of money," said Parley.

"Yes, and so I have," replied Elder Taylor. "I am well clothed, you furnish me plenty to eat and drink and good lodging; with all these things and a penny over, as I owe nothing, is not that plenty?" 9

That night in a meeting of the apostles and others, Elder Pratt urged the brethren to assist John with the means to pay his passage to England. John objected to this, telling the brethren instead to assist Elder Pratt, as Parley had both a family to support as well as his publishing endeavors. After the meeting Wilford Woodruff expressed discomfort at John's words, as he had been waiting to accompany John to England and had already secured his own passage on the packet ship Oxford.

ELDER TAYLOR: "Well, Brother Woodruff, if you think it best for me to go, I will accompany you."

ELDER WOODRUFF: "But where will you get the money?"

ELDER TAYLOR: "Oh, there will be no difficulty about that. Go and take a passage for me on your vessel, and I will furnish you the means."

A Brother Theodore Turley, hearing the above conversation, and thinking that Elder Taylor had resources unknown to himself or Brother Woodruff, said: "I wish I could go with you, I would do your cooking and wait on you."

The passage to be secured was in the steerage—these missionaries were not going on flowery beds of ease—hence the necessity of such service as Brother Turley proposed rendering. In answer to this appeal, Elder Taylor told Brother Woodruff to take a passage for Brother Turley also.

At the time of making these arrangements Elder Taylor had no money, but the Spirit had whispered him that means would be forthcoming, and when had that still, small voice failed him! In that he trusted, and he did not trust in vain. Although he did not ask for a penny of anyone, from various persons in voluntary donations he received money enough to meet his engagements for the passage of himself and Brother Turley, but no more. [10]

The journey from New York to Liverpool, which commenced on December 10, 1839, was miserable, with storms and seasickness plaguing the missionaries most of the way. The *Oxford*, of the Black Ball Line, carried fifteen passengers with cabin passage; the rest, the apostles and Elder Turley included, traveled steerage, which cost much less but which required them to bunk two to a berth and bring their own food, bedding, and cooking utensils. Though the steerage was "'crowded and unhealthy,' reeking with vomit and overrun with cockroaches and rats,"[11] it was a full two weeks before John made it onto the deck for reasons other than to be violently ill. But it was a calm morning, so he, Wilford Woodruff, and Theodore Turley sat on an anchor discussing the almost wholesale apostasy of the English mission since the apostles had departed hardly more than a year before. All felt that it would indeed be a time of testing for the British Saints.

Upon their arrival in England the three missionaries called a meeting of the priesthood at Preston, where it was decided that John would commence his labors in Liverpool, where he had lived as a boy. There he would work with his former Canadian associate, Joseph Fielding, who had been presiding over the branch in Preston.

John's first order of business in Liverpool was to look up his wife's brother, George Cannon, who immediately invited John to make the Cannon home his headquarters. John accepted and within days had baptized George; his wife, Ann Quayle; and their three eldest children. One of these, twelve-year-old George Quayle Cannon, would later become John's counselor in the First Presidency of the Church. Three months later, when Brigham Young, Heber C. Kimball, and the Pratt brothers finally arrived, John and Joseph Fielding had baptized twenty-seven people.

It happened that Brigham Young's group of apostles and others arrived in England on April 6, 1840, the tenth birthday of the Church. They were all exhausted, still sick with fevers picked up in Nauvoo months before, and their journey over the ocean had been exceptionally rough. After meeting up with John and Elder Fielding on the 11TH, the brethren traveled to Preston by railway, stopping at the home of Willard Richards. "So emaciated was President Young at this time from his long sickness, and journey, that when Elder Richards returned home...from a mission to Clitheroe, and found him in his room, he did not know him." 12

On the 14TH of April "a council of the Twelve, namely, Brigham Young, Heber C. Kimball, Parley P. Pratt, Orson Pratt, Wilford Woodruff, George A. Smith and John Taylor, was held at the house of Elder Willard Richards, in Preston, England, when the latter was ordained to the Apostleship,—agreeably to the revelation,— by President Young, under the hands of the quorum present." 13 That brought to eight the number of the Quorum then in England.

In a report sent to the Prophet Joseph, Brigham Young declared:

The work of the Lord is progressing here.... According to the account that the Elders give of their labors, there have been about eight or nine hundred persons baptized since they left. The Gospel is spreading, the devils are roaring. As nigh as I can learn, the priests are howling, the tares are binding up, the wheat is gathering, nations are trembling, and kingdoms tottering; "men's hearts failing them for fear, and for looking for those things that are coming on the earth." The poor among men are rejoicing in the Lord, and the meek do increase their joy. The hearts of the wicked do wax worse and worse, deceiving and being deceived. 14

Other business transacted by the apostles included the decision to republish, there in England, the Book of Mormon, to publish a hymn book, and to begin publication of a new periodical to be called the *Latter-day Saints' Millennial Star*. John was appointed one of a committee of three to select the hymns for the hymnal. It was also determined that he and Joseph Fielding should continue their already successful missionary labors in and around Liverpool.

[John's] proselyting method was simple and direct. Instead of trying to till the stony soil among the fallen—the drunks, prostitutes, and riffraff of the waterfront grog shops—Taylor worked the vineyard among people already interested in religion, at their own churches. On his first Sunday in Liverpool, he and Joseph Fielding...made the rounds of churches, requesting the privilege of speaking. When this was granted, he startled both pastor and flock by informing them they were in darkness, without authority to baptize, bestow the Holy Ghost, or act in the name of God, and warning them to prepare for the great and dreadful day of the Lord's return.

During the week, "We visited many of the leading ministers in Liverpool," Taylor reported, "but found them generally so bigoted and wrapped up in sectarianism that there was very little room for the truth in their hearts." They were "too holy to be righteous, too good to be pure, and had too much religion to enter into the kingdom of heaven." 15

Still, John's success was phenomenal. At the congregation of a Mr. Matthews, a brother-in-law to Joseph Fielding, John arose after listening to a very devout young man (not Mr. Matthews, who was away) lament about the sad spiritual state of the church. Requesting permission to speak, John was asked by the pastor to refrain and go to the vestry, where the congregation's class leaders and elders would hear him out. There John declared the following to about twenty men who had gathered to hear him out:

> Gentlemen, friends and brethren; I have listened with deep interest to the things that I have heard this morning. I have observed with peculiar emotions the deep anxiety, the fervent prayer and the strong solicitude manifested by you in relation to obtaining the Holy Ghost. I have been pleased with the correct views you entertain in regard to the situation of the world. We believe in those things as you do. We hear that you believe in baptism and the laying on of hands, so also do we. Brethren and friends, we are the humble followers of Jesus Christ and are from America. I lately arrived in this place, and have come five thousand miles without purse or scrip, and I testify to you, my brethren, that the Lord has revealed Himself from heaven and put us in possession of these things you are so anxiously looking for and praying that you may receive. ("Glory be to God," was shouted by many present, and great emotion manifested.)

That thing has taken place which is spoken of by John in the Revelations, where he says: "I saw another angel fly in the midst of heaven, having the everlasting gospel to preach unto them that dwell upon the earth, and to every nation and kindred and tongue and people, saying with a loud voice, Fear God and give glory to him, for the hour of his judgment is come." Brethren, we the servants of God are come to this place to warn the inhabitants of their approaching danger, and to call upon them to repent and be baptized in the name of Jesus Christ, and they shall receive the gift of the Holy Ghost.

I feel an anxious desire to deliver this testimony. I feel the word of the Lord like fire in my bones and am desirous to have an opportunity of proclaiming to you those blessings that you are looking for, that you may rejoice with us in those glorious things which God has revealed for the salvation of the world in the last days. 16

"This speech filled many with exceeding great rejoicing, some even wept for joy, while others were equally filled with zealous rage. The class so affected demanded to know if they were not Mormons. 'No,' replied Elder Taylor, 'we belong to the Church of Jesus Christ of Latter-day Saints, called by our enemies the "Mormon Church."'" 17

By the second week of such bold activities John had stirred up enough interest that a crowd of three hundred attended his sermon in a hall he had rented for the purpose. After ten of those three hundred requested and were given baptism and confirmation, John took out a year's contract on a music hall in Bold Street, which had a capacity of 1,500 persons. He then announced a series of lectures in that location and was soon filling the hall on a regular basis.

Following one of his sermons John was introduced to a man from Ireland, with whom he held a lively debate. When the Irishman's friend expressed dismay over the rancorous way the debate had gone, John reassured him by prophesying that the man would be the first person in this dispensation to be baptized in Ireland. Not many days later John was in Ireland and performed the baptism himself, thus opening the work on the Emerald Isle. [18]

One day John called upon a Mr. Radcliff, who was agent for the Bible Society and superintendent of the School of Arts. Though John and Mr. Radcliff agreed on many things John was preaching, there was a woman present, a Miss Brannan, who did not. From the Isle of Man and a former acquaintance of John's wife, Leonora, she expressed a fear of John's religion and even censured him for condemning others. After being ably defended before the woman by Mr. Radcliff, who informed the woman that John was merely calling them ignorant rather than condemning them, John remarked that he was thinking of going to the Isle of Man and would be pleased to call upon her. Miss Brannan replied that

she would be glad to see him, but not as a religious teacher. Or if he was like other preachers, she would be pleased to receive him. To this the Elder replied that he should visit the Isle of Man whether she desired him to or not; that there were others there who would receive the gospel if she rejected it, and as to the matter of being like other ministers, it reminded him of the story of the Prophet Micah, who was told to speak as the other prophets of king Ahab had spoken, and it would be well with him; but Micah replied: "As the Lord liveth, even what my God saith, that will I speak." So, likewise, he could only declare that which God had revealed; if that came in conflict with the doctrines and practices of men, so much the worse for their doctrines and practices. [19]

Whether or not John ever saw Miss Brannan again, he did make his way to the Isle of Man, which he opened for missionary work. On September 16, 1840, accompanied by Hiram Clark and William Mitchell, he sailed from Liverpool, arriving in Douglas on the following day.

"As he set foot on the Isle of Man, John Taylor's lonesomeness for Leonora came flooding back, for it was here, he knew, that she had spent her youth. He allowed himself to think also of her privations and suffering and the ordeal of separation they both endured." 20 At his first opportunity he recorded:

> Thou hast passed through trials, Nora, but thou shalt rejoice! Thou hast been driven from thy home for the truth's sake, but thou and thy children shall have a home in the Kingdom of God! Thou hast suffered the bereavement of thy husband—the tender association has been severed—that others may be made partakers of endless life; but thou and thy husband shall yet reign together in the celestial kingdom of God. A few more struggles and the battle will be fought, the victory will be ours, and with the redeemed out of every nation we will sing, "Glory, and honor, and power, and might, and majesty, and dominion be ascribed to Him that sitteth upon the throne, and to the Lamb, forever and ever [!]" 21

John accompanied his companions partway to the town of Ramsey; they stopped at an out-of-the-way place and sang, prayed, blessed each other and spoke in tongues. John then sent them on their way and returned alone to Douglas, where he began work by contacting some of Leonora's girlhood friends, visiting a local Primitive Methodist preacher, and hiring the largest hall in town, the Wellington Rooms, capable of holding a thousand people. Immediately he set about filling the hall by preaching on the street corners, doing his best to generate interest in his message.

One who paused to listen on a street corner that first day was a wealthy Jewish businessman named Solomon Pitchforth. Intrigued by both the man and his message, Solomon offered to provide John with housing and board and immediately took him home to meet his wife, Ann, as well as their children.

Ann Hughlings Pitchforth had been born in Grantham, Lincolnshire, England, the fourth child of John and Ann Williams Hughlings. Her father was a wealthy wool manufacturer and collector of the king's revenues. When she was nine, Ann was given a piano and instruction, and in time she became an accomplished pianist, performing frequently in public gatherings. She married Solomon Pitchforth, and they became the parents of six children, including two boys who died at birth. The Pitchforths had moved several times before settling in Douglas on the Isle of Man.

Within days of John's arrival, Ann "agreed that their lodger was altogether as fascinating a young man as they had ever met. And from a woman's point of view, Ann pointed out, it was small wonder that the fair sex thronged to his meetings; she couldn't remember when an evangelist as handsome and charming as John Taylor had visited the Isle of Man. Yes, her husband agreed, and a welcome relief to long-faced sin-stompers. Taylor had the rare combination of deep spirituality with a lively sense of humor. Nobody went to sleep during his sermons." 22

Besides, "being Jewish, [they] could view Taylor's missionary activities dispassionately, as entertainment; and, they agreed, certainly no theatrical event had aroused more interest nor provided half the show as did John Taylor's introduction of Mormonism to the Isle of Man." 23

One such show was his encounter with the disorderly party of Primitive Methodist preachers and others that led to his debate with Thomas Hamiliton, as described in the *vignette* at the beginning of this chapter. As John reported to the editor of the new British publication, the *Latter-day Saints' Millennial Star:*

Mr. Hamilton was so well acquainted with history that he could declare that in some countries where there was no water they baptized with oil! about which opinion I had the hardihood to be a little sceptical *[sic]* despite of his great proficiency in historical lore; for I was foolish enough to wonder (as any old woman would do who did not possess the same knowledge of history as himself,) what they made use of as a beverage in that country! as oil would not be very palatable to drink at all times, and also what they cooked their victuals with. It was the same individual, sir, who on being asked his authority to preach answered "I sent myself," I was led to tell him that I was of that opinion before, but that he had confirmed my impressions; that I had thought from the beginning that God had nothing to do with sending him out. Yet foolish, ignorant, and untaught as he was, there are those, sir, who had it not been for this exposure, might have mistaken him for a wise man, and have thought that he was called of God. 24

As the Pitchforths continued to listen and observe, John kept up a relentless pace. "He replied in print to a series of newspaper articles against the Mormons by a Mr. J. Curran, and to each of three pamphlets published by the Reverend Robert Heys, a Wesleyan minister. So important was his battle with Heys, in fact, that he missed the October conference in Liverpool because of it. On October 2, 1840, he wrote Brigham Young: 'A methodist publication has come out in opposition to [the gospel] & the fire is begenning *[sic]* to rage & I do not wish to leave the field untill *[sic]* my enemies & the enemies of God lay down their arms or till there is a sufficient army to contend with theirs.' Four days later Taylor reported to Young that he had 'got into the wars' and that as 'I have got into the scrape I shall have to fight through.' His fellow apostles followed his war of words with delight. 'Elder Taylor's letters in the *Manx Liberal* are superlative, Methodist Priests stand no chance at all,' exulted Orson Pratt to Wilford Woodruff and George A. Smith, and later he laughed that 'Taylor [in his 2ND address] has cut Hey into fine fodder.... Taylor understands weilding the weapons of truth to a very good advantage & he has a very good...opportunity of doing it. I presume we could do more good in Edinburgh & London if we could bring the enemy into open combat.'" 25

Ann Pitchforth "had never seen such religious excitement on the Isle of Man. But while crowds flocked to the Market Hall to hear Taylor, the churches of Douglas were virtually empty on Sundays. With glee, Taylor told her that the priests were complaining bitterly. One minister went to the high bailiff and demanded that something be done to put the Mormons down.... 'My whole congregation was there,' he complained....

"The high bailiff, however, pointed out that England provided freedom of worship. And very probably, Ann surmised, he felt that the ministers of established faiths had earned their comeuppance." 26

One evening two of Ann's friends came into Douglas to hear John preach. Afterward they invited him to hold a "chimney corner" meeting at their home. Ann and her children accompanied John to this meeting, where he "sat in a chimney corner talking to a few neighbors who came into the house where he was, and baptized and confirmed eight people the same night. They simply would not wait until morning." 27

Another one of these chimney-corner meetings was held in the "home of Charles Cowley, who lived near the village of Kirk German and who, according to his own account, had been 'seeking and praying for correct information concerning the Will of God.' He and his wife, Ann, read in the newspaper about the minister from America who was to preach in Douglas, and Ann's brother-in-law, John Quayle, went to hear him. Deeply impressed, he brought

Elder Taylor to Cowley's farmhouse where, in the course of the evening, Quayle and his wife, Catherine, along with the Cowleys, were convinced that the apostle's message was the truth." 28

Finally, when the persecution from the priests and others opposing the work became too severe, John and his followers abandoned the hall and traveled into the farm fields west of Douglas, to a place called Hillberry, for their meetings. While Solomon Pitchforth may not have attended all of these gatherings, Ann and her children did, and they were growing more and more interested in John's message. They were also overwhelmed by what were quite obviously miracles performed by the Lord in John's behalf. For instance, the costs of publishing the three pamphlets written in response to the Reverend Robert Heys, mentioned above, were defrayed "after a stranger and a fish vendor delivered the exact money needed for printing to [John's] door in answer to his fervent prayers." 29

> Ann Pitchforth didn't realize what was happening to her until the day John Taylor looked directly into her eyes and asked, "Are you ready for baptism?"
>
> She answered, "Yes."
>
> Ann Pitchforth discovered that she would pay a stiff price for her new faith. Solomon tried hard to reconcile himself to his family becoming Christians and Mormons; but when his only [living] son was called to be a missionary, it was too much. The marriage broke up. Ann moved with the children to the home of her father; Solomon went to Australia. 30

John organized a branch of the Church in Douglas before he left in mid-November, 1840, to return to Liverpool. He spent the rest of his mission mostly in the Liverpool area, preaching, working with publications, and helping to organize the emigration program. He also visited Manchester, Birmingham, Sheffield, and several other cities and briefly returned to the Isle of Man in March, 1841.

"Prior to leaving England [John] published a report of his labors in the *Millennial Star,* part of which follows:

> I feel to rejoice before God that He has blessed my humble endeavors to promote His cause and Kingdom and for all the blessings I have received from this island; for although I have traveled 5,000 miles without purse or scrip, besides traveling so far in this country on railroads, coaches, steamboats, wagons, on horseback, and almost every way, and been amongst strangers and in strange lands, I have never for once been at a loss for either money, clothes, friends or a home, from that day until now; neither have I ever asked a person for a farthing. Thus I have proved the Lord, and I know that He is according to His word. And now as I am going away, I bear testimony that this work is of God—that He has spoken from the heavens—that Joseph Smith is a Prophet of the Lord— that the Book of Mormon is true; and I know that this work will roll on until "the kingdoms of this world become the Kingdoms of our God and His Christ." 31

"When John Taylor and fellow apostles sailed on the *Rochester* [in April of 1841], some eight thousand souls in Great Britain had been brought to the faith. An agency was established to help converts gather in Zion, and they were embarking by the shipload.... The Book of Mormon and the hymn book were in print, the *Millennial Star* launched, with Parley Pratt staying in England as editor." 32 For more than a year, John had raised his voice in defense of the Church in his native land while, as Brigham had said, the gospel spread and the devils roared. Now it was time to return home where, as the Saints gathered and prepared to raise a temple to their God, the devils were beginning to roar around Nauvoo.

7

THE CONSPIRING MOBS OF NAUVOO

"My goodness, John, where are you going in such a rush?"

Glancing at Leonora, John Taylor didn't even take time for a smile. It was the morning of Sunday, June 23, 1844, and he had just been given some disturbing news. "Joseph and Hyrum left during the night," he responded as he leaned over to pull on his boots. "Sister Thompson just now apprised me of it."

Knowing that he was speaking of Mercy Rachel Thompson, the widowed sister of Joseph Fielding and Mary Fielding Smith, Leonora nodded. "How did she find out?"

"Apparently Hyrum bid her farewell as he was leaving. The thing is, I was with him and Joseph until after midnight, and I only came home to sleep because I thought no decision would be made before this morning."

"Do you suppose something else happened during the night— some new urgency that impelled the Prophet to leave?"

John's look was bleak. "I can imagine nothing else! There is such a spirit of hatred and murder being manifest toward Joseph and Hyrum by enemies both within and without the Church, it is no small wonder they have fled! What I don't understand is, why would they depart without me?"

"You...you would have left without bidding the children

and I farewell?"

Rising to his feet, John took his beloved Leonora by the hand. When they had married he had been twenty-three and she thirty-six, and she had seemed to him the most beautifully mature woman in the world. But now that he was thirty-four and she forty-seven, her face creased with wrinkles and her hair mostly gray, he could not get used to the fact that his sweet companion had somehow turned old. It did not change his love for her, but it was for him a fierce reminder of how brief and transitory their mortal experience could be.

"My dear," he softly replied as he embraced her, "I would hope you know me better than that. Had I left during the night, I would most certainly have called upon you for a fond farewell—even if it had meant waking you in the wee hours of the morning."

"Yes, John, dear, I know you would have done that for me." Tenderly Leonora lay her head against her husband's shoulder. "You have always been more than thoughtful, and I love you the more for it. I am sorry I sounded as though I doubted. But I must ask, darling; do…do you go now, to travel into hiding with the Prophet?"

"I can not," John replied quietly, his voice sounding full of despair. "Save that he crossed the river, I have no idea which way he has gone."

"But surely that was discussed."

"It was." John turned from his wife and stood at the window, gazing out at the early morning activities in Nauvoo. "Joseph favored going to the far West, to Oregon or upper California, and scouting out a country where the Saints might dwell in peace. Others favored he and Hyrum traveling downriver to the Ohio and then east, perhaps to Pennsylvania or Massachusetts. There they could lobby safely for our cause until such time as the government realized how shamefully our people are being treated. When I left them, they had not decided which would be the best course to follow."

Leonora nodded. "Joseph has prophesied that the Saints would one day go to the Rocky Mountains and would there become a favored people. I have heard he even saw in vision the country where we would settle."

John smiled but remained at the window. "Yes, he rehearsed those very things to us last evening. There is no doubt that is where he would like to go. Yet other voices were raised in opposition, and so I don't know what he will do."

"They did not consider staying, seeing the thing through?"

Sighing, John turned back to the room. "Leonora, dear, Governor Ford demands their presence in Carthage—which as you well know is the very seat of all the satanic hatred being leveled against them. I felt lucky yesterday morning to escape from Carthage with my life; Dr. Bernhisel felt the same, and we were not even the ones the mob wants. Hyrum's sentiment last evening was that he and Joseph should go to Carthage and throw themselves on the mercy of Governor Ford, allowing him to bear the burden of their safety. Joseph declared, however, that if they should ever go to Carthage their lives would be forfeit, and I agree! I both saw and heard the devilish rantings and railings of that mob, Leonora! They want nothing less than Joseph's and Hyrum's deaths! At all costs, therefore, our Prophet and his brother must flee from this country, and the fewer who know their whereabouts or destination, the better!"

"Then what about you, John? Where will you go?"

Again John turned to the window and looked out, his gaze distant. "In the past few moments, Nora, it has come to me that I could make a run to upper Canada. We have many friends in Toronto who would house me, and I could accomplish much good under the protection of a foreign flag."

"That is a journey of fifteen hundred miles, darling. I hope you would not be traveling alone."

"No, my dear, I would not go alone. Brother Cyrus Wheelock is an active, enterprising man, and I believe I shall ask him to accompany me. I shall also remove from the printing office the account books, the type, and the stereotype plates of the Book of Mormon and Doctrine and Covenants. I will either take those things with me or see that they are shipped east to the other brethren of the Twelve. Perhaps a publication of them in the East would provide some necessary monies for our cause."

"Oh, John, please do be careful!"

John chuckled. "My dear Nora, I intend nothing less. In fact I shall disguise myself so thoroughly that even our own faithful brethren won't recognize me. Now, if you would be so good as to gather the children? I must send some trusted individuals on errands, and then I will bid all of you a last farewell—"1

John Taylor and the other apostles arrived from England to their homes in Nauvoo on July 1, 1841, and their immediate reception was all any of them could have hoped for. Heber C. Kimball recorded that " 'when we struck the dock, I think there were about 300 Saints there to meet us, and a greater manifestation of love and gladness I never saw before. President Smith was the first one that caught us by the hand. I never saw him feel better in my life than he does at this time; this is the case with the Saints in general.... We found our families well, except Sister Taylor who was quite low." 2

In fact, Leonora was very nearly dead, still dwelling in the ramshackle old log barracks in Montrose, Iowa, where John had left her two years before. As John's eyes adjusted to the gloom and he saw her lying on the bed, he was shocked to see how she had aged. "He sat beside the bed, holding her hand, while in a weak voice she poured out her travails. The old barrack was so dilapidated that a skunk came in every night. Twice she'd found a huge snake in the room. On a night when the children were sick, drunken Indians had come to the door, trying to get in. And in all the months that he'd been away, not a single one of his relatives had put a nose in the door to offer help."3 Quite literally, "the hardships in Missouri, the separation from her husband,— on whose strong arm and steadfast courage she was wont to lean,— and the consequent increase of care in watching over her family, had at last broken down [Leonora's] strength; and hence [John] found her pale and wan, and death clutching at her precious life. He called in twenty Elders, who prayed for her; she was anointed with oil, hands were laid upon her, and, in fulfillment of God's promise, the prayer of faith healed the sick—the Lord raised her up."4

Within days John was at work building his family a new home on the corner of Parley and Granger Streets in Nauvoo, his property adjoining Brother Brigham's at the rear.5 He also became immediately active in all the affairs of the Church and community. He was elected to the city council; in August he was elected a regent of the University of Nauvoo; he was chosen Judge Advocate with the rank of colonel in the Nauvoo Legion; in October he was assigned to again petition the government for redress of wrongs sustained in Missouri; and besides all this he labored tirelessly writing letters and epistles for his brethren of the Twelve, including an official denunciation of thieves who were infesting Nauvoo and whose villainy was being charged to the Saints. He also spent many hours with the Prophet Joseph Smith, and between the two there formed an ever closer friendship.6 No doubt that is what led to Joseph choosing to hide from his Missouri enemies with John's parents:

> In 1842 an attempt was made on the life of Governor Lilburn W. Boggs of Missouri. Enemies of the Church in Missouri determined to extradite Joseph Smith to the state to stand trial for that and other crimes of which he was accused. Certain that he would not receive a fair trial

in Missouri, which had earlier expelled the Saints, the Prophet sought to avoid arrest. He had also received word that some persons were determined to return him to Missouri, dead or alive, and, indeed, in September 1842 his home was searched. He managed to elude the kidnapping party, which had come without legal documents permitting an arrest. On October 7, 1842, the Prophet's diary, as kept by Willard Richards, states: "From the situation and appearance of things abroad, I concluded to leave home for a short season, until there should be some change in the proceedings of my enemies. Accordingly, at twenty minutes after eight o'clock in the evening, I started away in company with Brothers John Taylor, Wilson Law, and John D. Parker, and traveled through the night and part of the next day; and, after a tedious journey, arrived at Father James Taylor's [feeling] well and in good spirits."

The Prophet remained with Agnes and James for two weeks, went back to Nauvoo to be with his family for one apprehensive night, then returned to the Taylors for still another week. He obviously enjoyed Agnes's twinkling eyes and respectful and helpful attitude. We can be sure that he liked her potato pie and roast lamb smothered with her special Cumbrian sauce.

Agnes often expressed her pleasure at this three-week visit of the Prophet. As one of her friends wrote at the time of her death: "She highly appreciated the confidence which he [Joseph Smith] reposed in the integrity of her partner and herself in selecting their residence as a place of retreat at a time when he was menaced by great danger. His friendship and the teachings which she received from him during those days were among the most pleasing recollections of her subsequent life."[7]

In February, 1842, John was chosen as associate editor of the *Times and Seasons*, the Prophet Joseph being editor-in-chief. "This appointment introduced him into a field of labor for which he was admirably adapted, and in which, during his lifetime—notwithstanding his labors in that sphere were frequently interrupted by the drivings of the Church and calls to other kinds of employments—he accomplished much good, and became well known as a powerful writer.

"He occupied the position of associate editor on the *Times and Seasons* for about a year, when the Prophet's increasing cares made it necessary for him to resign his place as editor-in-chief. Elder Taylor was appointed to take his place. He continued to edit and publish that periodical [as well as the *Nauvoo Neighbor,* a large imperial weekly] until the Church was driven out of Nauvoo in the spring of 1846." 8

"On the 1st of November, 1842, [John] celebrated his 34TH birthday. With his wife and four small children favorably located; with his standing in the Church as an Apostle, with a growing and profitable business, John looked forward to a life of happiness, peace and prosperity." 9

Still, the gospel had new demands to make of him. Not long after his return from England, Joseph had made known to John and the other members of the Twelve the doctrine of celestial marriage—"marriage that is to endure for time and for eternity, the ceremony being performed by one holding that power which binds on earth and binds in heaven. Celestial marriage also [included] a plurality of wives.

"This system of marriage had been revealed to the Prophet a number of years before, but he had kept the matter in his own heart. The time had come, however, when the principles of this marriage system must be made known to [a select group of] others and the practice thereof entered into by the faithful in the Priesthood....

"The plurality of wives included in this system of marriage is what gave rise to grave concern in the minds of the faithful men to whom it was revealed. The world never made a greater mistake than when it supposed that plural marriage was hailed with delight by the Elders who were commanded of the Lord to introduce its practice in this generation. They saw clearly that it would bring additional reproach upon them from the world; that it would run counter to the traditions and prejudices of society, as, indeed, it was contrary to their own traditions; that their motives would be misunderstood or misconstrued. All this they saw, and naturally shrank from the undertaking required of them by the revelation of God." 10 Of his own experience, John wrote:

> Joseph Smith told the Twelve that if this law was not practiced, if they would not enter into this covenant, then the Kingdom of God could not go one step further. Now, we did not feel like preventing the Kingdom of God from going forward. We professed to be the Apostles of the Lord, and did not feel like putting ourselves in a position to retard the progress of the Kingdom of God. The revelation says that "All those who have this law revealed unto them must obey the same." Now, that is not my word. I did not make it. It was the Prophet of God who revealed that to us in Nauvoo, and I bear witness of this solemn fact before God, that He did reveal this sacred principle to me and others of the Twelve, and in this revelation it is stated that it is the will and law of God that "all those who have this law revealed unto them must obey the same."
>
> I had always entertained strict ideas of virtue, and I felt as a married man that this was to me, outside of this principle, an appalling thing to do. The idea of going and asking a young lady to be married to me when I had already

a wife! It was a thing calculated to stir up feelings from the innermost depths of the human soul. I had always entertained the strictest regard of chastity. I had never in my life seen the time when I have known of a man deceiving a woman—and it is often done in the world, where, notwithstanding the crime, the man is received into society and the poor woman is looked upon as a pariah and an outcast—I have always looked upon such a thing as infamous, and upon such a man as a villain.... Hence, with the feelings I had entertained, nothing but a knowledge of God, and the revelations of God, and the truth of them, could have induced me to embrace such a principle as this.

We [the Twelve] seemed to put off, as far as we could, what might be termed the evil day.

Some time after these things were made known unto us, I was riding out of Nauvoo on horseback, and met Joseph Smith coming in, he, too, being on horseback.... I bowed to Joseph, and having done the same to me, he said: "Stop"; and he looked at me very intently. "Look here," said he, "those things that have been spoken of must be fulfilled, and if they are not entered into right away the keys will be turned."

Well, what did I do? Did I feel to stand in the way of this great, eternal principle, and treat lightly the things of God? No. I replied: "Brother Joseph, I will try and carry these things out." 11

John meant exactly what he said.

That evening when the children were in bed, he told Leonora that he must discuss a serious matter. She surprised him by saying yes, she already knew—the wives of the Twelve had been talking about it. It was difficult for her to believe that the restoration of the true gospel of ancient

times would require the family life of the old prophets—
the taking of wives and concubines. Knowing the nature
of men, it was much easier to believe that Joseph was
rationalizing his own lusts.

To believe that, Taylor said, was to accuse Joseph
of being a fallen prophet.

Leonora made a defeated sigh. She realized this,
she said, and that is why she must accept the Principle.
Joseph had made it an issue on which the entire gospel
depended.

Then, turning sharply on him, she asked if he'd picked
out his plural? She'd warn him right now that she wouldn't
be a sister in the Principle with some baby-faced tease
young enough to be her daughter and without a brain in
her silly head.

No, that wasn't the type of wife he wanted, Taylor said.
He admired women of mature culture and refinement;
that's why he had fallen in love with her at Toronto. During
the time since Joseph had spoken, he'd been looking
around and had decided there was a young lady at Nauvoo
who would make an excellent wife and also could be
a sister in the Principle to Leonora.

Leonora asked if she knew the girl.

Taylor nodded. "Your cousin—Elizabeth Kaighin." 12

Immediately Leonora was satisfied. Thirty years of age, tall,
willowy, aristocratic and culturally refined, Elizabeth Kaighin
was also from the Isle of Man. Like John and Leonora, she had
emigrated to Canada, had investigated the Church along with
them, and had been baptized by Parley P. Pratt the same afternoon
they had been. Since that time she had remained a close friend
to Leonora, and Leonora knew she would fit nicely into her
household.

"Whatever reservations Elizabeth might have had at [John's] proposal were swept away. It was the Lord's command, and she had always admired Leonora's handsome husband. Through fasting and prayer she received a testimony to the Principle; in a private ceremony she was joined to John Taylor in the new and everlasting covenant, her name entered in the Book of the Law of the Lord."13 That sealing took place on December 12, 1843. 14

By then, Nauvoo had grown from an infested swamp to a respectable community of nearly 5,000 inhabitants—the largest city at the time in Illinois. It was divided into four wards, a glorious temple and other public buildings were under construction, both a periodical and a weekly were being published, and there seemed every possibility that the city would become a commercial and manufacturing center as well as headquarters for the Church. Yet all was not well in the city beautiful, and very quickly John was caught in the thick of the troubles.

Just as the Saints had experienced difficulty with their neighbors in New York; Kirtland, Ohio; Jackson County and Far West, Missouri; and Quincy, Illinois; so was the same pattern developing again. In their weakness the Saints had not been seen as a threat, but as they gathered together they gained strength, both economically and socially, and that strength was viewed with terrible suspicion. Add to that the animosity of religious leaders who were constantly losing members of their flocks to this new and unique religion; stir in the political power that came with the growing body of Saints in Illinois; and finally toss into the mix the hatred of apostates and others who had chosen iniquitous lifestyles (many of whom were busy justifying themselves or trying to strengthen their own positions by seeking the overthrow of those Church leaders who had exposed and humiliated them), and it can be understood why the Church and its leaders attracted such enmity.

In describing these conditions, John Taylor started with those who struck from closest to home, the apostates:

There were a number of wicked and corrupt men living in Nauvoo and its vicinity, who had belonged to the church, but whose conduct was incompatible with the gospel; they were accordingly dealt with by the church and severed from its communion. Some of these had been prominent members, and held official stations, either in the city or church. Among these were John C. Bennett, formerly mayor; William Law, counselor to Joseph Smith; Wilson Law, his natural brother, and general in the Nauvoo Legion; Dr. R. D. Foster, a man of some property, but with a very bad reputation; Francis and Chauncey Higbee, the latter a young lawyer, and both sons of a respectable and honored man in the church, known as Judge Elias Higbee, who died about twelve months before.

Besides these, there were a great many apostates, both in the city and county, of less notoriety, who for their delinquencies, had been expelled from the church. John C. Bennett and Francis and Chauncey Higbee were cut off from the church; the former was also cashiered from his generalship for the most flagrant acts of seduction and adultery; and the developments in their cases were so scandalous that the high council, before whom they were tried, had to sit with closed doors.

William Law, although counselor to Joseph, was found to be his most bitter foe and malinger, and to hold intercourse [it was alleged], contrary to all law, in his own house, with a young lady resident with him; and it was afterwards proved that he had conspired with some Missourians, to take Joseph Smith's life, and [the Prophet] was only saved by Josiah Arnold and Daniel Garn, who, being on guard at his house, prevented the assassins from seeing him. Yet, although having murder in his heart, his manners were generally courteous and mild, and he was well calculated to deceive.

General Wilson Law was cut off from the church for seduction, falsehood, and defamation; both the above were also court-martialed by the Nauvoo Legion and expelled. Foster was also cut off I believe, for dishonesty, fraud, and falsehood. I know he was eminently guilty of the whole, but whether these were the specific charges or not, I don't know, but I do know that he was a notoriously wicked and corrupt man. 15

Problems with other religionists arose as they had in Missouri, as other Christian sects viewed the Saints with a perplexity that became maddening enough to turn many to violence. The Saints fit no typical Christian mold, used an almost alien religious language, found support in obscure scriptures that could not be argued, proclaimed their own new scriptures, prospered wherever they went, and smugly proclaimed themselves the Lord's only true church on the earth. Worst of all, they actively sought converts among their neighbors—and many joined with them.

On the political front, at this time there were two American parties, the Whigs and the Democrats, and the Saints could not vote for one without offending the other. To make matters worse, candidates for office would often make opposition to the Saints part of their platform. This left the Saints compelled, in self-defense, to vote against them, which often resulted in victory for the candidate's opponent. The result was more enemies, and though the loser and his party's downfall had been of their own making, still they looked to take their rage out on the Saints.

The last group John and the Saints had to contend with composed the local criminal element, which was a loosely organized band or group of bands that infested the whole of the western country at that time. There was a combination of horse thieves extending through the whole northwest corner of the state. There were counterfeiters in most of the cities and villages, and in some districts the judges, sheriffs, constables, jailers, and professional men were more or less associated with them, along with the more usual criminal element on hand to do the more usual dirty work. Their object in persecuting the Saints was threefold: to cover their own evil, to prevent the Saints from exposing and prosecuting them, and, especially, to plunder—if the Saints were driven out as they had been in Missouri, the city they had built and its spoils would be there for the taking. In some districts the influence of these lawless individuals was so great as to control important state and county offices.

John Taylor continues:

This conglomeration of apostate "Mormons," religious bigots, political fanatics, and blacklegs, all united their forces against the "Mormons," and [in 1842] organized themselves into a party, denominated "anti-Mormons." Some of them, we have reason to believe, joined the church in order to cover their nefarious practices, and when they were expelled for their unrighteousness only raged with greater violence. They circulated every kind of falsehood that they could collect or manufacture against the "Mormons." They also had a paper to assist them in their infamous designs, called the *Warsaw Signal,* edited by a Mr. Thomas Sharp, a violent and unprincipled man, who shrunk not from any enormity. The anti-"Mormons" had public meetings, which were very numerously attended, where they passed resolutions of the most violent and inflammatory kind, threatening to drive, expel and exterminate the "Mormons" from the state, at the same time accusing them of every evil in the vocabulary of crime.

They appointed their meetings in various parts of Hancock, McDonough, and other counties, which soon resulted in the organization of armed mobs, under the direction of officers who reported to their headquarters, and the reports of which were published in the anti-"Mormon paper," and circulated through the adjoining counties. We also published in the *Times and Seasons* and the *Nauvoo Neighbor* (two papers published and edited by me at that time), an account, not only of their proceedings, but our own. But such was the hostile feeling, so well arranged their plans, and so desperate and lawless their measures, that it was with the greatest difficulty that we could get our papers circulated; they were destroyed by postmasters and others, and scarcely ever arrived at the place of their destination, so that a great many of the people, who would have been otherwise peaceable, were excited by their misrepresentations, and instigated to join their hostile or predatory bands. 16

The events thus described continued, with more or less intrigue and general success, from 1842 until mid 1844. And no matter how diligently Church leaders tried to alter course or set things right, matters only grew worse.

In February 1844, to "remove the Prophet out of the filthy slough of party politics.... Elder Taylor urged the Prophet's nomination for the presidency of the United States...

"In a long editorial in the *Neighbor,* in which he nominates the Prophet for President, [John] represents that as Henry Clay— then one of the prominent candidates for President—inclined strongly to the old school of federalists, his political principles were diametrically opposed to those entertained by the people of

Nauvoo, and hence they could not conscientiously vote for him; and they had even stronger objections to Mr. Van Buren, who, when the Saints appealed to him to redress the outrages put upon them in Missouri, admitted the justice of their cause, but claimed that he was powerless to assist them; he also held that Congress was powerless to redress their grievances....

"Then, after enlarging upon the fitness of the Prophet for the high office of President of the United States, [John] adds:

> One great reason that we have for pursuing our present course is that at every election we have been made a political target for the filthy demagogues in the country to shoot their loathsome arrows at. And every story has been put into circulation to blast our fame.... The journals have teemed with this filthy trash, and even men who ought to have more respect for themselves—men contending for the gubernatorial chair—have made use of terms so degrading, so mean, so humiliating, that a Billingsgate fisherwoman would have considered herself disgraced with. We refuse any longer to be thus bedaubed for either party; we tell all such to let their filth flow in its own legitimate channel, for we are sick of the loathsome smell.... Under existing circumstances we have no other alternative [than that of withdrawing from both political parties,] and if we can accomplish our object, well; if not we shall have the satisfaction of knowing we have acted conscientiously and have used our best judgment; and if we have to throw away our votes, we had better do so upon a worthy, rather than upon an unworthy individual, who might make use of the weapon we put in his hand to destroy us. 17

And so the Prophet Joseph was put before the country for President of the United States. He published his views on the powers and policy of the government and called upon his friends to support him. All the Twelve but two—John Taylor and Willard Richards—were immediately dispatched for the East, where they were assigned to campaign vigorously in behalf of Joseph Smith for President of the United States. Joseph directed that John and Elder Richards remain in Nauvoo, Elder Richards to continue as Joseph's personal secretary and John to continue his significant editorial work in Nauvoo's two papers.

So the spring of 1844 passed away, with the Brethren doing all they could, the Church members growing more and more concerned and even frightened, and the Church's enemies growing daily in numbers and in power. All the scheming of these groups came to a head in May, when they issued their own newspaper, a rabid anti-Mormon sheet they called the *Nauvoo Expositor.*

John writes of it as follows:

Emboldened by the acts of those outside, the apostate "Mormons," associated with others, commenced the publication of a libelous paper in Nauvoo, called the *Nauvoo Expositor.* This paper not only reprinted from the others, but put in circulation the most libelous, false, and infamous reports concerning the citizens of Nauvoo, and especially the ladies. It was, however, no sooner put in circulation, than the indignation of the whole community was aroused; so much so, that they threatened its annihilation; and I do not believe that in any other city in the United States, if the same charges had been made against the citizens, it would have been permitted to remain one day. As it was among us, under these circumstances, it was thought best to convene the city council to take into consideration the adoption of some measures for its removal, as it was deemed better that this should be done legally than illegally. Joseph Smith, therefore, who was mayor, convened the city council for that purpose; the paper was introduced and read, and the subject examined. All, or nearly all present, expressed their indignation at the course taken by the *Expositor,* which was owned by some of the aforesaid apostates, associated with one or two others. Wilson Law, Dr. Foster, Charles Ivins and the Higbees before referred to, some lawyers, storekeepers, and others in Nauvoo who were not "Mormons," together with the anti-"Mormons" outside of the city, sustained it. The calculation was, by false statements, to unsettle the minds of many in the city, and to form combinations there similar to the anti-"Mormon" associations outside of the city. Various attempts had heretofore been made by the party to annoy and irritate the citizens of Nauvoo; false accusations had been made, vexatious lawsuits instituted, threats made, and various devices resorted to, to influence the public mind, and, if possible, to provoke us to the commission of some overt act that might make us amenable to the law. With a perfect knowledge, therefore, of the designs of these infernal scoundrels who were in our midst, as well of those who surrounded us, the city council entered upon an investigation of the matter. They felt that they were in a critical position, and that any move made for the abating of that press would be looked upon, or at least represented, as a direct attack upon the liberty of speech, and that, so far from displeasing our enemies, it would be looked upon by them as one of the best circumstances that could transpire to assist them in the nefarious and bloody designs. Being a member of the city council, I well remember the feeling of responsibility that seemed to rest upon all present; nor shall I soon forget the bold, manly, independent expressions of Joseph Smith on that occasion in relation to this matter. He exhibited in glowing colors the meanness, corruption and ultimate designs of the anti-"Mormons"; their despicable characters and ungodly influences, especially of those who were in our midst. He told of the responsibility that rested upon us, as guardians of the public interest, to stand up in the defense of the injured and oppressed, to stem the current of corruption, and as men and saints, to put a stop to this flagrant outrage upon this people's rights....

The subject was discussed in various forms, and after the remarks made by the mayor, every one seemed to be waiting for some one else to speak.

After a considerable pause, I arose and expressed my feelings frankly, as Joseph had done, and numbers of others followed in the same strain; and I think, but am not certain, that I made a motion for the removal of that press as a nuisance. This motion was finally put, and carried by all but one; and he conceded that the measure was just, but abstained through fear.

Several of the members of the city council were not in the church....

After the passage of the bill, the marshal, John P. Greene was ordered to abate or remove, which he forthwith proceeded to do by summoning a posse of men for that purpose. The press was removed or broken, I don't remember which, by the marshal, and the types scattered in the street....

This, as was foreseen, was the very course our enemies wished us to pursue, as it afforded them an opportunity of circulating a very plausible story about the "Mormons" being opposed to the liberty of the press and of free speech, which they were not slow to avail themselves of. Stories were fabricated, and facts perverted; false statements were made, and this act brought in as an example to sustain the whole of their fabrications; and, as if inspired by satan, they labored with an energy and zeal worthy of a better cause.... The anti-"Mormon" paper, the *Warsaw Signal,* was filled with inflammatory articles and misrepresentations in relation to us, and especially to this act of destroying the press. We were represented as a horde of lawless ruffians and brigands, anti-American and anti-republican, steeped in crime and iniquity, opposed to freedom of speech and of the press, and all the rights and immunities of a free and enlightened people; that neither person nor property was secure, that we had designs upon the citizens of Illinois and of the United States, and the people were called upon to rise en masse, and put us down, drive us away, or exterminate us as a pest to society, and alike dangerous to our neighbors, the state, and the commonwealth. 18

It didn't take long for these reports to be circulated by other newspapers throughout the United States. John published a true assessment of the situation in both the *Times and Seasons* and the *Nauvoo Neighbor,* but the Saints found it impossible to circulate them in the immediate counties, as they were destroyed at the post offices or elsewhere by those with anti-Mormon sympathies. Mail that was to go abroad was sent thirty or forty miles from Nauvoo, or sometimes all the way to St. Louis, and still their enemies saw to it that half or more of the Mormon's papers never reached their destination.

The false reports stirred up the populace of west-central Illinois, and the ranks of the anti-Mormons swelled as people held meetings, passed resolutions, and committed both "men and means" to the cause of getting rid of the Mormons.

John's account continues:

In the meantime legal proceedings were instituted against the members of the city council of Nauvoo. A writ...was issued upon the affidavit of the Laws, Fosters, Higbees, and Ivins, by Mr. Morrison, a justice of the peace in Carthage, and the county seat of Hancock, and put into the hands of one David Bettisworth, a constable of the same place....

The council did not refuse to attend to the legal proceedings in the case, but as the law of Illinois made it the privilege of the persons accused to go "or appear before the issuer of the writ, or any other justice of peace," they requested to be taken before another magistrate, either in the city of Nauvoo or at any reasonable distance out of it.

This the constable, who was a mobocrat, refused to do, and as this was our legal privilege, we refused to be dragged, contrary to law, a distance of eighteen miles, when at the same time we had reason to believe that an organized band of mobocrats were assembled for the purpose of extermination or murder, and among whom it would not be safe to go without a superior force of armed men. A writ of habeas corpus was called for, and issued by the municipal court of Nauvoo, taking us out of the hands of Bettisworth, and placing us in the charge of the city marshal. We went before the municipal court, and were dismissed. Our refusal to obey this illegal proceeding was by them construed into a refusal to submit to law, and circulated as such, and the people either did believe, or professed to believe, that we were in open rebellion against the laws and the authorities of the state. Hence mobs began to assemble, among which all through the country inflammatory speeches were made, exciting them to mobocracy and violence. Soon they commenced their depredations in our outside settlements, kidnaping some, and whipping and otherwise abusing others.

The persons thus abused fled to Nauvoo…and related their injuries to Joseph Smith, then mayor of the city, and lieutenant-general of the Nauvoo Legion. They also went before magistrates, and made affidavits of what they had suffered, seen, and heard. These affidavits, in connection with a copy of all our proceedings, were forwarded by Joseph Smith to [Thomas] Ford, then governor of Illinois, with an expression of our desire to abide law, and a request that the governor would instruct him how to proceed in the case of arrival of an armed mob against the city. The governor sent back instructions to Joseph Smith that, as he was lieutenant-general of the Nauvoo Legion, it was his duty to protect the city and surrounding country, and issued orders to that effect. Upon the reception of these orders Joseph Smith assembled the people of the city, and laid before them the governor's instructions; he also convened the officers of the Nauvoo Legion for the purpose of conferring in relation to the best mode of defense. He also issued orders to the men to hold themselves in readiness in case of being called upon. 19

Meanwhile the Saints' enemies continued to gather in mobs and commit depredations against any Latter-day Saint they happened upon. An account of their acts was forwarded to Governor Ford almost daily, accompanied by affidavits from eyewitnesses. Church leaders also responded by sending spokespersons to outlying communities to give an account of the true state of affairs in an attempt to quell the anxiety. They had some success in the more distant counties, but closer to home, they could not overcome the anti-Mormons' influence. Guards were stationed around Nauvoo and pickets out on the prairie. As opposing forces drew nearer, parties were sent out to reconnoiter, and the city was placed under martial law. People passing through the city were questioned, and passes were issued to show the guards.

John's account explains that Joseph continued sending messengers to the governor, but the weather was so wet, with the rivers swollen and the bridges sometimes washed away, that communication became difficult. Meanwhile, at the suggestion of Judge Thomas, judge of the judicial district that included Nauvoo, Joseph and members of the city council appeared before Esquire Daniel H. Wells, a non-Mormon, to have a second hearing over the *Expositor* matter. This was done in order to satisfy even the anti-Mormons and would, according to Judge Thomas, put the matter to rest. After this second full hearing, the case was again dismissed.

At the same time, the mobs had at last attracted Governor Ford's attention; he came to Carthage, and made it his headquarters. Carthage was the county seat of Hancock County but also a hotbed for the mobs. Along the way, the governor collected forces to quell any uprising that might occur. Unfortunately, many of his ranks were mobbers who were simply eager to join an entity that might go after the Saints.

John Taylor continues:

> After [the governor's] arrival at Carthage, he sent two gentlemen…to Nauvoo as a committee to wait upon General Joseph Smith,…with a request that General Smith would send out a committee to wait upon the governor and represent to him the state of affairs in relation to the difficulties that then existed in the county….
>
> Dr. J. M. Bernhisel and myself were appointed as a committee by General Smith to wait upon the governor. Previous to going, however, we were furnished with affidavits and documents in relation both to our proceedings and those of the mob…. We started from Nauvoo in company with the aforesaid gentlemen at about seven o'clock on the evening of the 21ST of June, and

arrived at Carthage about 11 P.M. We put up at the same
hotel with the governor, kept by a Mr. Hamilton. On our
arrival we found the governor in bed, but not so with the
other inhabitants. The town was filled with a perfect set of
rabble and rowdies, who, under the influence of bacchus,
seemed to be holding a grand saturnalia, whooping, yelling
and vociferating, as if bedlam had broken loose....

That night I lay awake with my pistols under my pillow,
waiting for any emergency.... In the morning [Saturday,
June 22] we arose early, and after breakfast sought an
interview with the governor, and were told that we could
have an audience, I think, at ten o'clock. 20

When John and Dr. Bernhisel were finally admitted to see the governor, they found him surrounded by twenty or so of the Church's
worst enemies. Utterly disgusted, they proceeded with their
assignment, handing Ford the documents they had brought to
Carthage. John continues:

During our conversation and explanations with the
governor we were frequently rudely and impudently
contradicted by the fellows he had around him, and of
whom he seemed to take no notice.

He opened and read a number of the documents himself,
and as he proceeded, he was frequently interrupted by
"That's a lie!" "That's a G__ d____d lie!" "That's an infernal
falsehood!" "That's a blasted lie!" etc.

These men evidently winced at an exposure of their
acts, and thus vulgarly, impudently, and falsely repudiated
them.... During the conversation, the governor expressed
a desire that Joseph Smith, and all parties concerned in
passing or executing the city law, in relation to the press,
had better come to Carthage; that, however repugnant
it might be to our feelings, he thought it would have

a tendency to allay public excitement, and prove to the people what we professed, that we wished to be governed by law. We represented to him the course we had taken in relation to this matter, and our willingness to go before another magistrate other than the municipal court; the illegal refusal of our request by the constable; our dismissal by the municipal court, a legally constituted tribunal; our subsequent trial before Squire Wells at the instance of Judge Thomas, the circuit judge, and our dismissal by him; that we had fulfilled the law in every particular; that it was our enemies who were breaking the law, and, having murderous designs, were only making use of this as a pretext to get us into their power. The governor stated that the people viewed it differently, and that, notwithstanding our opinions, he would recommend that the people should be satisfied. We then remarked to him that, should Joseph Smith comply with his request, it would be extremely unsafe, in the present excited state of the country, to come without an armed force; that we had a sufficiency of men, and were competent to defend ourselves, but there might be danger of collision should our forces and [those] of our enemies be brought into such close proximity. He strenuously advised us not to bring any arms, and pledged his faith as governor, and the faith of the state, that we should be protected, and that he would guarantee our perfect safety....

About five o'clock in the afternoon we took our departure with not the most pleasant feelings. The associations of the governor, the spirit that he manifested to compromise with these scoundrels, the length of time that he had kept us waiting, and his general deportment, together with the infernal spirit that we saw exhibited by those whom he had admitted to his councils, made the prospect anything but promising.

We returned on horseback, and arrived at Nauvoo, I think, at about eight or nine o'clock at night.... We went directly to Brother Joseph's.... A council was called, consisting of Joseph's brother Hyrum, Dr. Richards, Dr. Bernhisel, myself, and one or two others.

We then gave a detail of our interview with the governor. Brother Joseph was very much dissatisfied with the governor's letter, and with his general deportment, and so were the council, and it became a serious question as to the course we should pursue. Various projects were discussed, but nothing definitely decided upon for some time....

As it was now between two and three o'clock in the morning, and I had had no rest on the previous night, I was fatigued, and thinking that Brother Joseph might not return [from visiting with two gentlemen who had requested an interview], I left for home and rest. 21

With John at home asleep, Joseph returned to the informal council meeting in the Mansion. While gone, he told them, he had received an impression to go west, not east, and all would be well:

The way is open. It is clear to my mind what to do. All they want is Hyrum and myself; then tell everybody to go about their business, and not collect in groups, but scatter about. There is no danger; they will come here and search for us. Let them search; they will not harm you in person or in property, and not even a hair of your head. We will cross the river tonight and go away to the West. 22

John continues:

Being very much fatigued, I slept soundly, and was

somewhat surprised in the morning by Mrs. Thompson entering my room about seven o'clock, [Sunday, June 23] and exclaiming in surprise, "What, you here? the brethren have crossed the river some time since."

"What brethren?" I asked.

"Brother Joseph, and Hyrum, and Brother Richards," she answered. 23

Startled, for he had not expected Joseph and Hyrum to leave without him, and completely unaware of the Prophet's middle-of-the-night prophecy, John dressed and told Leonora of Joseph's decision to go into hiding. He also told her that he thought he should also go into hiding—by traveling to Canada, where he could labor in behalf of the Church without concern for the mobs. Tearfully they bid each other farewell, John bid adieu to his children, and then he set his hastily made plans into motion.

John quickly gathered together the type, stereotype plates of the Book of Mormon and Doctrine and Covenants, account books, and other valuable things from the printing office. These he had determined to take with him in order to protect them from the mobs. He then disguised himself and climbed into the boat in which he was to be rowed across the river. Then occurred an incident which John later described as laughable:

> [H]aving bid adieu to my family, I went to a house adjoining the river, owned by Brother Eddy. There I disguised myself so as not to be known, and so effectually was the transformation that those who had come after me with a boat did not know me. I went down to the boat and sat in it. Brother Bell, thinking it was a stranger, watched my moves for some time very impatiently, and then said to Brother Wheelock, "I wish that old gentleman would go away; he has been pottering around the boat for some time, and I am afraid Elder Taylor will be coming."

When he discovered his mistake, he was not a little amused. 24

By the evening of Sunday, June 23RD, John was across the river and ready to depart. As he was preparing to climb into his saddle, however, Elias Smith appeared with word not only that he had found Joseph and the others, but that they had changed their minds and were returning to Nauvoo so they could appear in Carthage as the governor had requested. Furthermore, they wished John to go with them.

John says:

I must confess that I felt a good deal disappointed at this news, but I immediately made preparations to go....

On meeting the brethren I learned that it was not Brother Joseph's desire to return, but that he came back by request of some of the brethren, and that it coincided more with Brother Hyrum's feelings than those of Brother Joseph. In fact, after his return, Brother Hyrum expressed himself as perfectly satisfied with the course taken, and said that he felt much more at ease in his mind than he did before. On our return the calculation was to throw ourselves under the immediate protection of the governor, and to trust to his word and faith for our preservation....

In the morning [Monday, June 24] Brother Joseph had an interview with the officers of the Legion, with the leading members of the city council, and with the principal men of the city. The officers were instructed to dismiss their men, but to have them in a state of readiness to be called upon in any emergency that might occur.

About half past six o'clock [in the evening] the members of the city council, the marshal, Brothers Joseph and Hyrum, and a number of others started for Carthage, on horseback. We were instructed by Brother Joseph

Smith not to take any arms, and we consequently left them behind....

We arrived [in Carthage] late in the night. A great deal of excitement prevailed on and after our arrival. The governor had received into his company all of the companies that had been in the mob; these fellows were riotous and disorderly, hallooing, yelling, and whooping about the streets like Indians, many of them intoxicated; the whole presented a scene of rowdyism and low-bred ruffianism only found among mobocrats and desperadoes, and entirely revolting to the best feelings of humanity. The governor made a speech to them to the effect that he would show Joseph and Hyrum Smith to them in the morning....

[The next morning, Tuesday, June 25TH,] the companies with the governor were drawn up in line, and General Deming, I think, took Joseph by the arm and Hyrum... and as he passed through between the ranks, the governor leading in front, very politely introduced them as General Joseph Smith and General Hyrum Smith.

All were orderly and courteous except one company of mobocrats—the Carthage Greys—who seemed to find fault on account of too much honor being paid to the Mormons. There was afterward a row between the companies, and they came pretty near having a fight; the more orderly not feeling disposed to endorse or submit to the rowdyism of the mobocrats. The result was that General Deming, who was very much of a gentleman, ordered the Carthage Greys, a company under the command of Captain [Robert F.] Smith, a magistrate in Carthage, and a most violent mobocrat, under arrest. This matter, however, was shortly afterward adjusted, and the difficulty settled between them.

The mayor [Joseph Smith], aldermen, councilors, as well as the marshal of the city of Nauvoo, together with some persons who had assisted the marshal in removing the press in Nauvoo, appeared before Justice Smith, the aforesaid captain and mobocrat, to again answer the charge of destroying the press; but as there was so much excitement, and as the man was an unprincipled villain before whom we were to have our hearing, we thought it most prudent to give bail, and consequently became security for each other in $500 bonds each, to appear before the county court at its next session. We had engaged as counsel a lawyer by the name of Wood, of Burlington, Iowa; and Reed, I think, of Madison, Iowa. After some little discussion the bonds were signed, and we were all dismissed. 25

Before the brethren had time, even, to make plans to return to Nauvoo, two of the mobbers, Augustine Spencer and a man named Norton—who were well known as liars and thieves, and the first of whom had recently been before Joseph in Nauvoo for mistreating a lame brother—swore out affidavits that Joseph and Hyrum Smith were guilty of treason. A writ was issued for their arrest, and Constable Bettisworth, another of the mobbers, wanted to rush them to prison without a hearing.

John explains what followed:

[T]he proceedings in this case were altogether illegal. Providing the court was sincere, which it was not, and providing these men's oaths were true, and that Joseph and Hyrum were guilty of treason, still the whole course was illegal.

The magistrate made out a mittimus, and committed them to prison without a hearing, which he had no right legally to do. The statute of Illinois expressly provides that "all men shall have a hearing before a magistrate before they shall be committed to prison"; and Mr. Robert F. Smith, the magistrate, had made out a mittimus committing them to prison contrary to law without such hearing. As I was informed of this illegal proceeding, I went immediately to the governor and informed him of it. Whether he was apprised of it before or not, I do not know; but my opinion is that he was.

I represented to him the characters of the parties who had made oath, the outrageous nature of the charge, the indignity offered to men in the position which they occupied, and declared to him that he knew very well it was a vexatious proceeding, and that the accused were not guilty of any such crime. The governor replied, he was very sorry that the thing had occurred; that he did not believe the charges, but that he thought the best thing to be done was to let the law take its course. I then reminded him that we had come out there at his insistance, not to satisfy the law, which we had done before, but the prejudices of the people, in relation to the affair of the press; that at his instance we had given bonds, which we could not by law be required to do to satisfy the people, and that it was asking too much to require gentlemen in their position in life to suffer the degradation of being immured in a jail at the instance of such worthless scoundrels as those who had made this affidavit. The governor replied that it was an unpleasant affair, and looked very hard; but that it was a matter over which he had no control, as it belonged to the judiciary; that he, as the executive, could not interfere with their proceedings, and that he had no doubt but that they would immediately be dismissed. I told him that we had looked to him for protection from such insults, and that I thought we had a right to do so from the solemn promises which he had

made to me and to Dr. Bernhisel in relation to our coming
without guard or arms; that we had relied upon his faith,
and had a right to expect him to fulfill his engagements
after we had placed ourselves implicitly under his care, and
complied with all his requests, although extra-judicial.

He replied that he would detail a guard, if we required
it, and see us protected, but that he could not interfere
with the judiciary. I expressed my dissatisfaction at the
course taken, and told him that if we were to be subject to
mob rule, and to be dragged, contrary to law, into prison at
the instance of every infernal scoundrel whose oaths could
be bought for a dram of whiskey, his protection availed
very little, and we had miscalculated his promises.

Seeing there was no prospect of redress from the
governor, I returned to the room, and found the Constable
Bettisworth very urgent to hurry Brothers Joseph and
Hyrum to prison, whilst the brethren were remonstrating
with him. At the same time a great rabble was gathered in
the streets and around the door, and from the rowdyism
manifested I was afraid there was a design to murder the
prisoners on the way to the jail.

Without conferring with any person, my next feelings
were to procure a guard, and, seeing a man habited as
a soldier in the room, I went to him and said, "I am afraid
there is a design against the lives of the Messrs. Smith; will
you go immediately and bring your captain; and, if not
convenient, any other captain of a company, and I will pay
you well for your trouble?" He said he would, and departed
forthwith, and soon returned with his captain, whose
name I have forgotten, and introduced him to me. I told
him of my fears, and requested him immediately to fetch
his company.

He departed forthwith, and arrived at the door with

them just at the time when the constable was hurrying the brethren downstairs. A number of the brethren went along, together with one or two strangers; and all of us safely lodged in prison, remained there during the night. 26

MESSENGER OF MERCY AT CARTHAGE

"Doc...tor R...Richards," John Taylor gasped, pleading, "stop! Please! D...don't leave me...not in this pl...ace!"

It had been warm in the upper room of the jail before the mob came—almost stifling. Even with both windows in the room wide open, no stray crosscurrent of breeze had seemed able to give the inmates any measure of relief. For two days it had rained sporadically, tuning the air muggy and humid, and none of them had been wearing their coats. Now though, as he lay suffering and bleeding on the floor beneath the bed, John found himself chilling and wishing for some covering.

"Doctor," he gasped again, "please...take me with you—"

Turning, and looking almost as if he had heard a ghost, Willard Richards stared across the room to where John lay under the bed. "Brother Taylor," he whispered in disbelief, "you...you're alive?"

"I...I must be. But you mustn't lea...leave me...here—"

Nodding silently, Willard Richards turned and stepped from the room, crossed the narrow landing, and tried the metal door that led into the cell for criminals. Finding it loose he opened it, hurried back to John's hiding place, and with seemingly little effort reached under the bed and pulled John into the open.

"I'm sorry if this is painful," he whispered as he lifted John by grasping him beneath the arms, "but we have no time to waste!"

Stifling a cry, John allowed himself to be dragged on his heels across the chamber, passing Hyrum Smith's lifeless body as they went. Though there was a red haze before his eyes, and he thought he might be dying or at the very least passing out from the pain and severity of his wounds, still he looked but could see no sign of Joseph—no sign of their beloved Prophet. Perhaps, he found himself thinking, Brother Joseph has escaped! Perhaps the Lord has accomplished another miracle—

"Oh, Brother Taylor," Doctor Richards exclaimed as he backed his way across the upper landing, "is it possible they have killed both Brother Hyrum and Joseph? It surely cannot be, and yet I saw them shoot both of them!"

As the big man wormed himself and his nearly lifeless burden through the narrow door of the criminal cell, John was finding it difficult to breathe. Joseph dead? But…how could that be? How could the Lord allow His prophet to be slain? And if it were true, then what on earth would the Church ever do without him—

Inside the cell Doctor Richards dumped John unceremoniously upon a moldering pile of straw that had broken free of a worn and dirty mattress. "I am sorry I cannot do better for you," he whispered anxiously. "This is a hard case to lay you on the floor, but if your wounds are not fatal, I want you to live to tell the story." Then, working feverishly, he pulled some straw and another filthy old mattress over the torn and bloody body of his friend and fellow apostle. "That may hide you, and you may yet live to tell the tale, but I expect they will kill me in a few moments."

For a few seconds the doctor stared toward the door. Then, elevating his hands as Joseph had once taught them, he exclaimed, "O Lord, my God, spare Thy servants!"

As Doctor Richards completed his prayer, both he and John were startled to hear some of the mob come rushing back up the stairs. Freezing in position, the doctor signaled John to be still, though his eyes betrayed clearly that he thought all was now lost.

Suddenly, however, someone shrieked, "The Mormons are coming!" As quickly as that, the frightened mob tumbled back the way they had come, and again John and Doctor Richards found themselves alone.

Sighing deeply and giving John a silent nod, the doctor turned and hurried out through the metal door, closed it behind him, and then John could hear no more.

In agony the wounded apostle lay in the silent room, his body awash with the unbelievable pain of his wounds while his soul suffered the exquisite torment of fearing that his beloved Joseph had been slain. Finally forcing such thoughts from his mind as best he could, John considered instead his wounds, taking mental evaluation of how seriously he had been hurt. The first bullet had struck him in the thigh just as he had reached the window in an attempt to escape, totally immobilizing him. Unable to stop himself, he had begun to fall outside, when some force had suddenly thrown him back onto the floor, at the same time restoring his mobility. Instantly he had begun to crawl toward the bed to hide beneath it, receiving three more wounds in the meantime—a ball below the left knee, another in his left arm that passed down and into his hand, and a third that had torn away a portion of his left hip as large as a man's hand, dashing the mangled fragments of his blood and flesh against the wall behind him.

Meanwhile, the pandemonium of shouting, screaming men mingled with gunfire had been deafening; and that, combined with the dense and acrid gun smoke that was roiling in the room, had made it impossible for John to tell what was happening. That Hyrum was dead appeared obvious, for he lay in plain view only feet away from John's hiding place. As for Joseph and Doctor Richards, however, he had been able to ascertain nothing. Yet, he had thought, with so much firing into the small room, how could either of them possibly have survived—

"He's leaped from the window!" someone had suddenly shouted, and within seconds the gunfire had ended and the horde of painted-faced mobbers had been pounding down the stairs and out the door of the jail. Already at the window, Doctor Richards, miraculously unscathed, had pulled his head back in. Turning then, he had started toward the door, which is when John had called out for him to stop—

A sudden creaking of hinges warned John, and as he stilled himself the metal door opened and Doctor Richards stepped through, then hurried to where John lay hidden. "The mob has fled," the doctor reported as he leaned down and pulled the straw away from John's face. But his look was bleak and stricken, and John knew that he had not delivered the worst news.

"Joseph?" he gasped as a terrible fear seized his heart. "Wh...at of Joseph?"

"He is most assuredly dead," Willard Richards replied woodenly as he slumped onto the floor beside his fellow apostle. "I have been down to his body, Brother Taylor. There is suddenly not a soul left around, mobber or otherwise! But Joseph is surely gone, and so is his dear brother Hyrum!"

In a strangling stupor of thought John closed his eyes, trying to imagine the scope of the terrible news Doctor Richards had delivered. But he could not grasp it, for it seemed as though there was a void in the great field of human existence, and a dark gloomy chasm in the Kingdom of God. All seemed hopeless, for truly they had been left alone—1

On Wednesday, June 26, 1844, at about 9:30 in the morning, Governor Ford, in company with Colonel Thomas Geddes, arrived at the Carthage Jail to meet as promised with Joseph and Hyrum Smith. At the governor's request, Joseph rehearsed for him all that had transpired in relation to the Saints' difficulties, the excited state of the surrounding country, "the tumultuous mobocratic movements of [their] enemies, the precautionary measures used by himself (Joseph Smith), the acts of the city council, the destruction of the press, and the moves of the mob and [the Saints] up to that time." 2

John Taylor, who was present in the room, reported on the conversation that followed, which lasted for about forty-five minutes. At its conclusion, at a quarter past ten o'clock in the morning, the governor rose to his feet, signaling an end to the conference. "'I am in hopes that you will be acquitted,'" he said to Joseph and Hyrum while Colonel Geddes squirmed with discomfort, "'and if I go [to Nauvoo] I will certainly take you along. I do not, however, apprehend danger. I think you are perfectly safe either here or anywhere else. I can not, however, interfere with the law. I am placed in peculiar circumstances, and seem to be blamed by all parties.'"

Now Joseph also arose, his dignified frame towering over that of the governor. "'Governor Ford, I ask nothing but what is legal; I have a right to expect protection, at least from you; for, independent of law, you have pledged your faith and that of the state for my protection, and I wish to go to Nauvoo.'"

"'And you shall have protection, General Smith.'" With a note of finality the governor shrugged into his coat. "'I did not make this promise without consulting my officers, who all pledged their honor to its fulfillment. I do not know that I shall go tomorrow to Nauvoo, but if I do I will take you along.'" 3

And with that, the duplicitous governor and troubled Colonel Geddes turned and made their way down the steep stairs and out of the jail.

Following Governor Ford's departure, Joseph dictated to Dr. Willard Richards specific orders for Marshal John P. Green and Major-General Dunham at Nauvoo. Then, turning to John Taylor, he remarked, "'I have had a good deal of anxiety about my safety since I left Nauvoo, which I never had before when I was under arrest. I could not help those feelings, and they have depressed me.'" 4

For the next few hours, while Dan Jones and Stephen Markham whittled on the ill-fitting door with a penknife in order to close it tightly and thus give them a little more security, Joseph, Hyrum, John, and Elder Richards took turns teaching various elements of the gospel to the guards. Some of them, convinced by the preaching, were relieved of their duties and sent home.

Hyrum, concerned by Joseph's sober attitude, pleaded with him to think more positively. Joseph replied, "Could my brother, Hyrum but be liberated, it would not matter so much about me. Poor Rigdon, I am glad he is gone to Pittsburgh out of the way; were he to preside he would lead the Church to destruction in less than five years." 5

Joseph then dictated more letters to Elder Richards, meanwhile encouraging John to sing several hymns and songs. Joseph also related to the brethren a dream he had been given about William and Wilson Law and another dream about trying to save a steamboat in a storm.

Shortly thereafter several men came to the jail for Joseph and Hyrum, intending to take them for examination on the charge of treason. Their lawyer, Esquire Reid, refused to allow the illegal examination to be conducted. At about 2:30 Constable Bettisworth appeared with a company of the Carthage Greys and presented an order to the jailor, Mr. Stigall, for the prisoners to be taken for examination. Joseph sent Dr. Bernhisel to the governor with this news and then sent John Taylor to Esquire Reid with the same. The two men had hardly returned when Bettisworth was back with the soldiers, determined to haul Joseph and Hyrum off to be illegally examined.

"Joseph, seeing the mob gathering and assuming a threatening aspect, concluded it best to go with them then, and putting on his hat, walked boldly into the midst of a hollow square of the Carthage Greys; yet evidently expecting to be massacred in the streets before arriving at the Court House, politely locked arms with the worst mobocrat he could see, and Hyrum locked arms with Joseph, followed by Dr. Richards, and escorted by a guard. Elders Taylor, Jones, Markham, and Fullmer followed, outside the hollow square, and accompanied them to the court room." 6

> On arraignment before the justice, counsel for the accused asked for a continuation until the next day to procure witnesses. This was granted; a new mittimus was made out and they were again committed to prison. After the departure of the accused, and without consulting them or their counsel, the time for the hearing of the case was further postponed until the 29TH. 7

The next morning, Thursday, June 27TH, after Dan Jones had over-heard several threats that Joseph and Hyrum and the others were to be killed that day, Joseph sent him with the information to the governor. Ford reassured Brother Jones that the prisoners would not be harmed and sent him back, but the guard would not allow him into the jail. Again he went to the governor, hearing more threats right in the governor's presence, and again he was pacified and told to stop worrying. Moments later Jones's own life was threatened, and then in the street he ran into Chauncey L. Higbee, who declared, "We are determined to kill Joe and Hyrum, and you had better go away to save yourself." 8

After breakfast Joseph dictated a letter to his wife Emma, which he closed by saying:

> P.S.—Dear Emma, I am very much resigned to my lot, knowing I am justified, and have done the best that could be done. Give my love to the children and all my friends,

Mr. Brewer, and all who inquire after me; and as for treason, I know that I have not committed any, and they cannot prove anything of the kind, so you need not have any fears that anything can happen to us on that account. May God bless you all. Amen. 9

A little later, Cyrus H. Wheelock spoke to Governor Ford, who was then preparing to start for Nauvoo. Brother Wheelock declared:

> Sir you must be aware by this time that the prisoners have no fears in relation to any lawful demands made against them, but you have heard sufficient to justify you in the belief that their enemies would destroy them if they had them in their power; and now, sir, I am about to leave for Nauvoo, and I fear for those men; they are safe as regards the law, but they are not safe from the hands of traitors, and midnight assassins who thirst for their blood and have determined to spill it; and under these circumstances I leave with a heavy heart.
>
> Ford replied: "I was never in such a dilemma in my life; but your friends shall be protected, and have a fair trial by the law; in this pledge I am not alone; I have obtained the pledge of the whole of the army to sustain me." 10

Returning to the prison, Brother Wheelock gave a pistol to Joseph, who then handed another pistol he had been given by John Fullmer to his brother Hyrum. Wheelock, Stephen Markham, and John Fullmer then left the jail, all intending to go to Nauvoo to obtain help for the prisoners.

> At this point we pick up John Taylor's account:
> Sometime after dinner we sent for some wine. It has been reported by some that this was taken as a sacrament. It was no such thing; our spirits were generally dull and

heavy, and it was for to revive us. I think it was Captain Jones who went after it, but they would not suffer him to return. I believe we all drank of the wine, and gave some to one or two of the prison guards. We all of us felt unusually dull and languid, with a remarkable depression of spirits. In consonance with those feelings I sang…[a] song, that had lately been introduced into Nauvoo, entitled, "A Poor Wayfaring Man of Grief," etc.

The song is pathetic, and the tune quite plaintive, and was very much in accordance with our feelings at the time for our spirits were all depressed, dull and gloomy and surcharged with indefinite ominous forebodings. After a lapse of some time, Brother Hyrum requested me again to sing that song. I replied, "Brother Hyrum, I do not feel like singing"; when he remarked, "Oh! never mind; commence singing, and you will get the spirit of it." At his request I did so....

Soon afterwards I was sitting at one of the front windows of the jail, when I saw a number of men, with painted faces, coming around the corner of the jail, and aiming towards the stairs. The other brethren had seen the same, for, as I went to the door, I found Brother Hyrum Smith and Dr. Richards already leaning against it. They both pressed against the door with their shoulders to prevent its being opened, as the lock and latch were comparatively useless. While in this position, the mob, who had come upstairs, and tried to open the door, probably thought it was locked, and fired a ball through the keyhole; at this Dr. Richards and Brother Hyrum leaped back from the door, with their faces towards it; almost instantly another ball passed through the panel of the door, and struck Brother Hyrum on the left side of the nose, entering his face and head. At the same instant, another ball from the outside entered his back, passing through his body and striking his watch. 11

In part to demonstrate that the Carthage Greys were involved in the murder, John notes that the second ball to strike Hyrum came from the back, through the window opposite the door. Based on its trajectory, according to John's analysis, it must have been fired by one of the Carthage Greys, who had been placed some distance from the jail to "protect" the brethren, as the balls from weapons fired near the building would have entered the ceiling of the second-story room and could not have struck Hyrum where he was then standing. Neither was there a later time when Hyrum could have received the second wound, for immediately after the first ball had struck him he fell to his back, crying, "I am a dead man!" He did not move again. 12

John's account continues:

I shall never forget the feeling of deep sympathy and regard manifested in the countenance of Brother Joseph as he drew nigh to Hyrum, and, leaning over him, exclaimed, "Oh! my poor, dear brother Hyrum!" He, however, instantly arose, and with a firm, quick step, and a determined expression of countenance, approached the door, and pulling the six-shooter left by Brother Wheelock from his pocket, opened the door slightly and snapped the pistol six successive times; only three of the barrels, however, were discharged. I afterwards understood that two or three were wounded by these discharges, two of whom, I am informed, died. I had in my hands a large, strong hickory stick brought there by Brother Markham, and left by him, which I had seized as soon as I saw the mob approach; and while Brother Joseph was firing the pistol, I stood close behind him. As soon as he had discharged it he stepped back, and I immediately took his place next to the door, while he occupied the one I had done while he was shooting. Brother Richards, at this time, had a knotty walking-stick in his hands belonging to me, and stood next to Brother Joseph, a little farther from the door, in an oblique direction, apparently to avoid the rake of the fire from the door. The firing of Brother Joseph made our assailants pause for a moment; very soon after, however, they pushed the door some distance open, and protruded and discharged their guns into the room, when I parried them off with my stick, giving another direction to the balls.

It certainly was a terrible scene: streams of fire as thick as my arm passed by me as these men fired, and, unarmed as we were, it looked like certain death. I remember feeling as though my time had come, but I do not know when, in any critical position, I was more calm, unruffled, and energetic, and acted with more promptness and decision. It certainly was far from pleasant to be so near the muzzles of those firearms as they belched forth their liquid flame and deadly balls. While I was engaged in parrying the guns, Brother Joseph said, "That's right, Brother Taylor, parry them off as well as you can." These were the last words I ever heard him speak on earth.

Every moment the crowd at the door became more dense, as they were unquestionably pressed on by those in the rear ascending the stairs, until the whole entrance at the door was literally crowded with muskets and rifles, which, with the swearing, shouting, and demoniacal expressions of those outside the door and on the stairs, and the firing of the guns, mingled with their horrid oaths and execrations, made it look like pandemonium let loose, and was, indeed, a fit representation of the horrid deed in which they were engaged.

After parrying the guns for some time, which now protruded thicker and farther into the room, and seeing no hope of escape or protection there, as we were now unarmed, it occurred to me that we might have some friends outside, and that there might be some chance of escape in that direction, but here there seemed to be none. As I expected them every moment to rush into the room—nothing but extreme cowardice having kept them out—as the tumult and pressure increased, without any other hope, I made a spring for the window which was right in front of the jail door, where the mob was standing, and also exposed to the fire of the Carthage Greys, who were stationed some ten or twelve rods off. The weather was hot, we all of us had our coats off, and the window was raised to admit air. As I reached the window, and was on the point of leaping out, I was struck by a ball from the door about midway of my thigh, which struck the bone, and flattened out almost to the size of a quarter of a dollar, and then passed on through the fleshy part to within about half an inch of the outside. I think some prominent nerve must have been severed or injured for, as soon as the ball struck me, I fell like a bird when shot, or an ox when struck by a butcher, and lost entirely and instantaneously all power of action or locomotion. I fell upon the windowsill, and cried out, "I am shot!" Not possessing any power to move, I felt myself falling outside of the window, but immediately I fell inside, from some, at that time, unknown cause. When I struck the floor my animation seemed restored, as I have seen it sometimes in squirrels and birds after being shot. As soon as I felt the power of motion I crawled under the bed, which was in a corner of the room, not far from the window where I received my wound. While on the way and under the bed I was wounded in three other places; one ball entered a little below the left knee, and never was extracted; another entered the forepart of my left arm, a little above the wrist, and, passing down by the joint, lodged in the fleshy part of my hand, about midway, a little above the upper joint of my little finger; another struck me on the fleshy part of my left hip, and tore away the flesh as large as my hand, dashing the mangled fragments of flesh and blood against the wall.

My wounds were painful, and the sensation produced was as though a ball had passed through and down the whole length of my leg. I very well remember my reflections at the time. I had a very painful idea of becoming lame and decrepid [sic], and being an object of pity, and I felt as though I would rather die than be placed in such circumstances. 13

Almost immediately after John had crawled under the bed, Joseph stepped to the same window, which was fifteen or twenty feet above the ground. As he leaned out, "two balls pierced him from the door, and one entered his right breast from without, and he fell outward, exclaiming, 'Oh Lord, My God!' As his feet went out of the window [Elder Richards's] head went in, the balls whistling all around. He fell on his left side a dead man.

"At this instant the cry was raised, 'He's leaped the window!' and the mob on the stairs and in the entry ran out." 14

As Willard Richards turned from the window toward the door, John called out to him from beneath the bed, pleading to be taken along. What followed is as was related at the beginning of the chapter, up to Doctor Richards's confirmation to John of Joseph's death.

John continues his narrative:

I felt a dull, lonely, sickening sensation at the news. When I reflected that our noble chieftain, the Prophet of the living God, had fallen, and that I had seen his brother in the cold embrace of death, it seemed as though there was a void or vacuum in the great field of human existence to me, and a dark gloomy chasm in the kingdom, and that we were left alone. Oh, how lonely was the feeling! How cold, barren and desolate! In the midst of difficulties he was always the first in motion; in critical positions his counsel was always sought. As our Prophet he approached our God, and obtained for us his will; but now our Prophet, our counselor, our general, our leader, was gone, and amid the fiery ordeal that we then had to pass through, we were left alone without his aid, and as our future guide for things spiritual or temporal, and for all things pertaining to this world, or the next, he had spoken for the last time on earth.

These reflections and a thousand others flashed upon my mind. I thought, why must the good perish, and the virtuous be destroyed? Why must God's nobility, the salt of the earth, the most exalted of the human family, and the most perfect types of all excellence, fall victims to the cruel, fiendish hate of incarnate devils?

The poignancy of my grief, I presume, however, was somewhat allayed by the extreme suffering that I endured from my wounds. 15

In the silence of the afternoon Doctor Richards moved John again, dragging him from the cell to the top of the stairs, evidently with the intention of taking him to some place of greater safety. There he was again left, with Hyrum's body in full view, while Richards started down the stairs.

John continues:

There [Hyrum] lay as I had left him; he had not moved a limb; he lay placid and calm, a monument of greatness

(clockwise from upper left):
Joseph Smith, Hyrum Smith,
Willard Richards and John Taylor

CA. 1840S

even in death; but his noble spirit had left its tenement, and was gone to dwell in regions more congenial to its exalted nature. Poor Hyrum! He was a great and good man, and my soul was cemented to his. If ever there was an exemplary, honest, and virtuous man, an embodiment of all that is noble in the human form, Hyrum Smith was its representative.

While I lay there a number of persons came around, among whom was a physician. The doctor, on seeing a ball lodged in my left hand, took a penknife from his pocket and made an incision in it for the purpose of extracting the ball therefrom, and having obtained a pair of carpenter's compasses, made use of them to draw or pry out the ball, alternately using the penknife and compasses. After sawing for some time with a dull penknife, and prying and pulling with the compasses, he ultimately succeeded in extracting the ball, which weighed about half an ounce. Some time afterwards he remarked to a friend of mine, that I had "nerves like the devil" to stand what I did in its extraction. I really thought I had need of nerves to stand such surgical butchery, and that, whatever my nerves may be, his practice was devilish.

The party then wanted to move John to a hotel owned by a Mr. Hamilton, where the brethren had stayed before they were committed to jail. John told them that he did not think it would be safe, and he did not want to go. The group protested, arguing that he could be better cared for at the hotel, and the move they counseled was for his own good.

I replied, "I don't know you. Whom am I among? I am surrounded by assassins and murderers; witness your deeds. Don't talk to me of kindness or comfort; look at your murdered victims. Look at me! I want none of your counsel nor comfort. There may be some safety here; I can be assured of none anywhere," etc.

They…made the most solemn asseverations, and swore by God and the devil, and everything else that they could think of, that they would stand by me to death and protect me. In half an hour every one of them had fled from the town.

Soon after a coroner's jury were assembled in the room over the body of Hyrum. Among the jurors was Captain Smith of the "Carthage Greys," who had assisted in the murder, and the same justice before whom we had been tried. I learned of Francis Higbee as being in the neighborhood. On hearing his name mentioned, I immediately rose and said, "Captain Smith, you are a justice of the peace; I have heard his name mentioned; I want to swear my life against him." I was informed that word was immediately sent to him to leave the place, which he did.

Brother Richards, meanwhile, had been busy with the coroner's inquest and making arrangements for Joseph and Hyrum's bodies to be taken to Nauvoo. When he was able to return to John's aid, only then was John taken to Mr. Hamilton's hotel, though they had a difficult time securing enough people to help carry John there, "for immediately after the murder a great fear fell upon all the people, and men, and children fled with great precipitation, leaving nothing nor anybody in the town but two or three women and children and one or two sick persons." Mr. Hamilton himself was reluctant to stay with John at his tavern, agreeing only after Elder Richards promised that he and his family would be protected—the Hamiltons looked at John as something of a hostage who guaranteed their own safety from reprisals by the Mormons.

The whole community knew that a dreadful outrage had been perpetrated by those villains, and fearing lest the citizens of Nauvoo, as they possessed the power, might have a disposition to visit them with a terrible vengeance, they fled in the wildest confusion. And, indeed, it was with very great difficulty that the citizens of Nauvoo could be restrained. A horrid, barbarous murder had been committed, the most solemn pledge violated, and that, too, while the victims were, contrary to the requirements of the law, putting themselves into the hands of the governor to pacify a popular excitement. This outrage was enhanced by the reflection that our people were able to protect themselves against not only all the mob, but against three times their number and that of the governor's troops put together....

The whole events were so faithless, so dastardly, so mean, cowardly, and contemptible, without one extenuating circumstance, that it would not have been surprising if the citizens of Nauvoo had arisen *en masse*, and blotted the wretches out of existence. The citizens of Carthage knew they would have done so under such circumstances, and, judging us by themselves, they were all panic-stricken, and fled.... Fearing that when the people heard that their Prophet and Patriarch had been murdered under the above circumstances they might act rashly, and knowing that, if they once got roused, like a mighty avalanche, they would lay the country waste before them and take a terrible vengeance—as none of the Twelve were in Nauvoo, and no one, perhaps, with sufficient influence to control the people, Dr. Richards, after consulting me, wrote the following note, fearing that my family might be seriously affected by the news. I told him to insert that I was slightly wounded....

Carthage Jail, 8 o'clock 5 min. p.m., June 27th, 1844.

> Joseph and Hyrum are dead. Taylor wounded, not very badly. I am well. Our guard was forced, as we believe, by a band of Missourians from 100 to 200. The job was done in an instant, and the party fled towards Nauvoo instantly. This is as I believe it. The citizens here are afraid of the "Mormons" attacking them; I promise them, no!
> [Signed] W. Richards.

> N.B.—The citizens promise us protection; alarm guns have been fired.
> [Signed] John Taylor.

> I remember signing my name as quickly as possible, lest the tremor of my hand should be noticed, and the fears of my family excited. 16

Willard Richards then dispatched a messenger, George D. Grant, with the note, but Grant was intercepted out in the countryside by the governor who, on hearing a cannon fired at Carthage, which was to be the signal for the murder, had immediately fled with his company. Obviously fearing that the citizens of Nauvoo, when apprised of the horrible outrage, would immediately rise and pursue, he turned Grant back to Carthage. A second messenger was sent who was also turned back. Not until a third attempt could the news be got to Nauvoo.

Though the identities of the last two messengers are unknown, it is possible that one of them was Samuel H. Smith, brother to Joseph and Hyrum, who that evening finally reached the brethren in Carthage. He lived nearby at the time and had been on his way to Carthage to see his brothers when he was met by some of the mob who had been dismissed by the governor and were on their way home. On learning that he was Joseph Smith's brother they had sought his life also, but he fled into the woods, where he was chased for some time before he escaped and made his way to Carthage. He arrived at Hamilton's on horseback, not only fatigued from the chase, but also upset by the death of his brothers. These stresses apparently contributed to a fever, which led to Samuel's death July 30, 1844. Thus, John notes, a third Smith brother fell victim, indirectly, to the mob.

It was almost five o'clock the next morning before John's wounds were properly dressed, with Brother Richards attending to other details and other nursing help from the citizens of Carthage being in short supply. Leonora started her journey from Nauvoo the next day with a Dr. Samuel Bennet. John's parents, who lived near Oquakie, arrived shortly after Leonora.

John's narrative continues:

I was called upon by several gentlemen of Quincy and other places, among whom was Judge Ralston, as well as by our own people, and a medical man extracted a ball from my left thigh that was giving me much pain; it lay about half an inch deep, and my thigh was considerably swollen. The doctor asked me if I would be tied during the operation; I told him no; that I could endure the cutting associated with the operation as well without, and I did so; indeed, so great was the pain I endured that the cutting was rather a relief than otherwise.

A very laughable incident occurred at the time; my wife, Leonora, went into an adjoining room to pray for me, that I might be sustained during the operation. While on her knees at prayer, a Mrs. Bedell, an old lady of the Methodist association, entered, and, patting Mrs. Taylor on her back with her hand, said, "There's a good lady, pray for God to forgive your sins; pray that you may be converted, and the Lord may have mercy on your soul."

The scene was so ludicrous that Mrs. Taylor knew not

whether to laugh or be angry. Mrs. Taylor informed me that Mr. Hamilton, the father of the Hamilton who kept the house, rejoiced at the murder, and said in company that it was done up in the best possible style, and showed good generalship, and she farther believed that the other branches of the family sanctioned it. These were the associates of the old lady referred to, and yet she could talk of conversion and saving souls in the midst of blood and murder: such is man and such consistency!...

The governor passed on, staying at Carthage only a few minutes, and he did not stop until he got fifty miles from Nauvoo.17

While he remained in Carthage, prior to his wife Leonora's arrival, John was attended to by what he described as "a pretty good sort of a man, who was lame of a leg." Afterward he was cared for by Leonora, his mother, his sister Elizabeth, and others. He was also visited by a good number of friends and local brethren from Macedonia and La Harpe. Besides these, many non-Mormons from Quincy came to visit, some of whom expressed their indignation over the mob and sympathy for John. Alexander Williams, another member, told John of his suspicion that the people of Carthage had evil intentions in keeping him there and stated that he had, at a given point in some woods, fifty men, and if John would say the word he would raise another fifty and take the apostle out of there.

Though John refused the offer, his life must indeed have been in danger. A Colonel Jones left him two loaded pistols in case he was attacked. And some time after his return to Nauvoo, when John had recovered and was publishing an account of the affair, a lawyer, Mr. Backman, reported that he had prevented a man named Jackson, who had tried to wed Hyrum's daughter, from ascending the stairs of the jail with a design to murder John—and that Backman regretted he had not let Jackson do the deed.

Others also publicly declared that John "ought to be killed, and they would do it, but that it was too damned cowardly to shoot a wounded man; and thus, by the chivalry of murderers, [John] was prevented from being a second time mutilated or killed. Many of the mob came around and treated [him] with apparent respect, and the officers and people generally looked upon [him] as a hostage, and feared that [his] removal would be the signal for the rising of the 'Mormons.'" 18

John concludes his account with the story of his homecoming:

I do not remember the time that I stayed at Carthage, but I think three or four days after the murder, when Brother Marks with a carriage, Brother James Allred with a wagon, Dr. Ells, and a number of others on horseback, came for the purpose of taking me to Nauvoo. I was very weak at the time, occasioned by the loss of blood and the great discharge of my wounds, so when my wife asked me if I could talk I could barely whisper no. Quite a discussion arose as to the propriety of my removal, the physicians and people of Carthage protesting that it would be my death, while my friends were anxious for my removal if possible.

I suppose the former were actuated by the above-named desire to keep me. Colonel Jones was, I believe, sincere; he had acted as a friend all the time, and he told Mrs. Taylor she ought to persuade me not to go, for he did not believe I had strength enough to reach Nauvoo. It was finally agreed, however, that I should go; but as it was thought that I could not stand riding in a wagon or carriage, they prepared a litter for me; I was carried downstairs and put upon it. A number of men assisted to carry me, some of whom had been engaged in the mob. As soon as I got downstairs, I felt much better and strengthened, so that I could talk; I suppose the effect of the fresh air.

When [we] had got near the outside of the town, I remembered some woods that we had to go through, and telling a person near to call for Dr. Ells, who was riding a very good horse, I said, "Doctor, I perceive that the people are getting fatigued with carrying me; a number of 'Mormons' live about two or three miles from here, near our route; will you ride to their settlement as quick as possible, and have them come and meet us!" He started off on a gallop immediately. My object in this was to obtain protection in case of an attack, rather than to obtain help to carry me.

Very soon after the men from Carthage made one excuse after another, until they had all left, and I felt glad to get rid of them. I found that the tramping of those carrying me produced violent pain, and a sleigh was produced and attached to the hind end of Brother James Allred's wagon, a bed placed upon it, and I propped up on the bed. Mrs. Taylor rode with me, applying ice water to my wounds. As the sleigh was dragged over the grass on the prairie, which was quite tall, it moved very easily and gave me very little pain.

When I got within five or six miles of Nauvoo the brethren commenced to meet me from the city, and they increased in number as we drew nearer, until there was a very large company of people of all ages and both sexes, principally, however, men.

For some time there had been almost incessant rain, so that in many low places on the prairie it was from one to three feet deep in water, and at such places the brethren whom we met took hold of the sleigh, lifted it, and carried it over the water, and when we arrived in the neighborhood of the city, where the roads were excessively muddy and bad, the brethren tore down the fences, and we passed through the fields.

Never shall I forget the differences of feeling that I experienced between the place that I had left and the one that I had now arrived at. I had left a lot of reckless, bloodthirsty murderers, and had come to the City of the Saints, the people of the Living God; friends of truth and righteousness, thousands of whom stood there with warm, true hearts to offer their friendship and services, and to welcome my return. It is true it was a painful scene, and brought sorrowful remembrance to my mind, but to me it caused a thrill of joy to find myself once more in the bosom of my friends, and to meet with the cordial welcome of true, honest hearts. What was very remarkable, I found myself very much better after my arrival at Nauvoo than I was when I started on my journey, although I had traveled eighteen miles.19

This leaves only John's fabled watch, which he sent for the next day. John had instructed Willard Richards to take his purse and watch with him when he left Carthage, fearing that they would be stolen. Brother Richards put the watch and purse into John's pants pocket, cut the pocket out of the pants, and tied the bundle securely with a string. It was this bundle, still tied up, that John's family retrieved for him.

My family, however, were not a little startled to find that my watch had been struck with a ball. I sent for my vest, and, upon examination, it was found that there was a cut as if with a knife, in the vest pocket which had contained my watch. In the pocket the fragments of the glass were found literally ground to powder. It then occurred to me that a ball had struck me at the time I felt myself falling

John Taylor's pocket watch

*CA. 1898
(date image taken
by Johnson Studio, SLC)*

out of the window, and that it was this force that threw me inside. I had often remarked to Mrs. Taylor the singular fact of finding myself inside the room, when I felt a moment before, after being shot, that I was falling out, and I never could account for it until then; but here the thing was fully elucidated, and was rendered plain to my mind. I was indeed falling out, when some villain aimed at my heart. The ball struck my watch, and forced me back; if I had fallen out I should assuredly have been killed, if not by the fall, by those around, and this ball, intended to dispatch me, was turned by an overruling Providence into a messenger of mercy, and saved my life. I shall never forget the feelings of gratitude that I then experienced towards my heavenly Father; the whole scene was vividly portrayed before me, and my heart melted before the Lord. I felt that the Lord had preserved me by a special act of mercy; that my time had not yet come, and that I had still a work to perform upon the earth.

(Signed) John Taylor. 20

No Peace After the Martyrdom

As he glanced out the window, John Taylor could see the gathering darkness of the December storm clouds. They had come boiling southeastward out of Iowa, crossing the Mississippi and enveloping Nauvoo and the country round about in a gloom that was certain to turn any minute into what the local citizenry called a swash-stompin' gully washer—a horrific rainstorm that would flood streets and homes and most likely turn to snow by morning. At least, he thought gloomily, the locals told the truth about something!

There was something else causing him to think of the impending storm, something that he knew would be with him for the remainder of his life. His finally healed wounds were aching— the wounds he had received a year and a half before when he had fallen before a hail of bullets in the Carthage jail. Now, whenever a storm approached, his hip, wrist, and knee throbbed terrifically, and whenever he rose to his feet to walk he found himself hobbling like an old man.

Stretching his leg out from the chair and massaging it softly, John sighed with weariness. Would things never change? Would Satan and his minions never stop tormenting and driving the people of God?

Around him sat several members of the Twelve: Brigham Young, Parley and Orson Pratt, Orson Hyde, Heber C. Kimball, Willard Richards, George A. Smith, and Wilford Woodruff. They had been summoned together by this sorry specimen of a man called Major Warren, who had supposedly come with writs to arrest the bunch of them. Well, John thought grimly, he was certainly welcome to try—

Without effort his mind slipped back to the hectic days following the martyrdom, when he had been recovering and the Twelve had been returning from their missions, and all decisions had been made by him and Elder Richards. Parley had been the first to get back to Nauvoo, followed quickly by Sidney Rigdon, who had begun to make his play for leadership of the Church. But he had moved too slowly, and by the time he had felt ready to force the Saints into a decision, Brigham and the rest of the apostles had gathered.

After Sidney had left for Pittsburgh, the Twelve had carried on, determined to see Israel gathered and the Church grow in the way Joseph had taught that it should. To that end they had also continued Nauvoo's extensive building campaign: the temple was now almost completed, the Mansion was finished, and a trades union and numerous industries were bidding fair to succeed, thus providing the Saints with all they needed to sustain, and even enjoy, life.

Unfortunately, as the Saints grew in Nauvoo, their opposition grew as well. Not only had the murderers at Carthage been allowed to wholly escape the consequences of their crime, but virtually no one was being punished for any of the continued illegalities being fostered against the Saints. Now the Saints themselves, along with the city council of Nauvoo, were being accused of sheltering criminals and blamed for an alleged increase in thievery, counterfeiting, and all manner of crimes in Hancock Country, when the Saints and citizens themselves were the victims.

And conditions were going from bad to worse.

The anti-Mormons had used a mock attack on one of their own meetings as provocation for burning houses and grain belonging to the Saints in Morley settlement, near where the conspirators had been plotting, and now the citizens of Quincy had decided that the Mormons must leave the state. Weary from the continual harassment and violence, John had joined with the rest of the Brethren in agreeing to leave in the spring—but some of the mobocrats, apparently, couldn't wait. Despite the Saints' making active and extensive preparations to leave, and despite their allowing the military to supersede civil authority when this Major Warren was sent into Hancock County with a company of militia to keep the peace, there had been no peace! Illegal writs were regularly being issued for the arrest of the Twelve, and house-burning and even murder continued on Major Warren's watch. At last, taxed beyond his limits, John had written an editorial declaring that he would submit no longer "to the injustice being heaped upon himself and the people." President Young had made a similar declaration, which had also appeared in print. And so Major Warren, in late November, had sought his first interview with the Church authorities to upbraid them for declaring their "resistance to law." Incensed by the man's attack, John had finally risen to his feet.

"Major Warren," he had declared, his voice filled with righteous wrath, "I stand before you as a man who has received deep injury from the citizens of this state, and consequently have some feelings. You talk, sir, about 'the majesty of the law, and maintaining the law.' Why, sir, the law to us is a mere farce. For years past the law has been made use of only as an engine of oppression. We have received no protection from it. I have suffered under its cruel influence. You talk about your troops being efficient, supporting law and preserving peace. This tale may do to tell some, but we have seen too much! It fails to charm us. I stand before you as a victim of such protection. I went from this place some time ago in a time of difficulty like the present, as one of a committee by the special request of Governor Ford, who solemnly pledged his honor for my protection; but how was I protected? I was shot nearly to pieces, and two of the best men in the world were shot dead at my side. This is a specimen of your protection!"

Sitting there massaging his aching leg, John almost laughed as he remembered the man's response. No doubt Warren knew what was coming, as he had interrupted to say that he did not wish to discuss the Carthage shooting, but wished to keep the conversation relative to the present troubles.

"I am sorry," John had declared fiercely, "but what happened in Carthage is relevant to today, sir, and I will point out that relevance momentarily. You may think the outrage in Carthage was an outbreak—a sudden ebullition of feeling that the governor could not control; but who was it that did the horrid deed? The governor's troops, sir, were among the foremost of that bloody gang. And where, sir—tell me where is our redress? You talk about the majesty of the law! What has become of those murder-ers? Have they been hung or shot, or in any way punished? No, sir, you know they have not. With their hands yet reeking in blood, having become hardened in their deeds of infamy, knowing that they will not be punished, they are now applying the torch to the houses of those they have already so deeply injured. What has been done to them under your administration? Have they been brought to justice, have they been punished for their infamous proceed-ings? No, sir; not one of them! They are still burning houses under your supervision; and you have either been unwilling or unable to stop them. Houses have been burned since your arrival here; men have been kidnapped, cattle stolen, our brethren abused and robbed when going after their own corn. Are we to stand still and let marauders and house-burners come into our city under the real or assumed name of 'governor's troops,' and yet offer no resistance to their nefarious deeds? Are we to be held still by you, sir, while they thrust the hot iron into us? I tell you plainly for one—I will not do it! I speak now on my own responsibility, and I tell you, sir, I will not stand it! I care nothing for your decrees, your martial law or any other law, I mean to protect myself; and if my brethren are to be insulted and abused in going after their own corn, and pursuing their lawful business—if nobody else will go to protect them, I will! They shall not be abused under pretext of law or anything else; and there is not a patriot in the world but what would bear me out in it."

John had then paused, his clear eyes glaring fiercely at the major. "Where is the spirit of '76?" he had then continued. "Where is the fire that burned in the bosoms of those who fought and bled for liberty? Is there no one who will stand up in defense of the oppressed? If a man had the least spark of humanity burning in his bosom—if he were not hardened and desperate, he would be ashamed to oppress a people already goaded by a yoke too intolerable to be borne, and that, too, in a boasted land of liberty. Talk about law! Sir, I stand before you as a victim of law. I feel warm on this subject—who would not? I have seen my best friends shot down while under legal protection. Where is our governor? These scenes have been enacted under his supervision. Where are our generals and judges? They have aided in these matters. If an honorable jury is legally selected, then a house-burner or perhaps a murderer makes affidavit that he has reason to believe they are partial, and immediately the judge will order a mobocratic sheriff and jury for the purpose of acquitting the guilty and condemning the innocent! What are all these legal men but a pack of scoundrels? And you will talk to us of law and order, and threaten us with punishment for disobeying your commands and protecting our rights! What are we? Are we beasts? I tell you for one, sir, I shall protect myself, law or no law, judge or no judge, governor or no governor. I will not stand such infernal rascality, and if I have to fight it out, I will sell my life as dearly as I can."

Major Warren had left with an earful, John knew, but with no determination to change. Now he was back in Nauvoo again, having ridden in smartly at the head of his troops, apparently to show the greatness of his power and glory. It was reported that he also had writs for the Twelve, but he had sent word that he wanted a second interview with them and pledged that no writs would be served. Of course they all knew the man's word meant nothing—

Still the Twelve had gathered; the major had opened by reading a letter from Mr. Brayman, attorney general of the state pro tem, asking if the statements made "by Mr. Young and Mr. Taylor, to the effect that they would not be subject to any law and would resist all civil process, was to be looked upon as sincere."

Instantly on his feet, Brigham Young had denied having made such a statement. Their grievances lay not with the law, but with maladministration and illegal prosecution. The Saints had always been subject to law and would continue to be so! Then without further comment, the President of the Twelve had retaken his seat.

His anger and emotions churning within him, John now pushed thoughts of his throbbing leg from his mind and pulled himself to his feet. "Excuse me," he said as he positioned himself to lean on his now-necessary walking stick, "but I wish to make a few remarks concerning my own individual feelings."

"Yes, Mr. Taylor, you may speak, but take care for the things you say."

Caring naught for Major Warren and his men, but feeling certain that what he was about to say would create for himself nothing but trouble with Brigham Young and the other members of the Quorum, who were understandably seeking peace, John nevertheless pushed ahead. It was time and long past when truth should be spoken to these scoundrels; it was certainly past time for him to make a stand!

"Major Warren," he declared as his eyes flashed, "I have endured as much as I feel willing to endure under this government! I feel myself oppressed and wronged! I have never violated any law in the United States, and to be vexed and annoyed continually with vexatious lawsuits and illegal prosecutions, I do not feel disposed tamely to submit to. If it is not enough for me to be deprived of my rights and my liberty; if it is not enough for me to sacrifice my property and to become an exile; if I cannot have the short space of six months to dispose of my effects and to leave the state—then let the governor tell me, and I will leave now! But I cannot and will not endure a continuation of these wrongs! I do not mean to be taken by any unjust requisition and thrust into prison; if I am, I must go there dead; for they shall not take me there alive. I have no personal feelings against you, Major Warren, but I will not longer put up with these accumulated wrongs!"

As John remained standing, his manner calm but resolute, the silence in the room grew oppressive. Finally Major Warren, obviously afraid to serve his writs in the face of John's strong resistance, rose slowly to his feet. He would not—apparently could not—look John in the eye! Instead, he either glared at the others or stared at the floor, and he seemed just as unable to speak or to respond. Finally, he angrily thrust his hat on his head, turned, and with haughty step led his men out the door and to their horses.

Only after the troop was riding down Mulholland Street and out of Nauvoo did the members of the Twelve begin to stir.

"Well, the *Warsaw Signal* will make hay out of this one," Parley P. Pratt declared sarcastically.

"Let them," Brigham Young breathed, instantly stopping further speculation with his surprising support of Elder Taylor. "John was right, and I feel to second every thing he has said!" Turning then, he grinned up at the much taller apostle. "By thunder, Brother Taylor, it is no wonder folks are calling you Defender of Truth and Right! No man could have said it better!"

John smiled a bit sheepishly. "I felt surprised myself at the manner in which I spoke," he admitted as he put on his own hat, buttoned up his coat, and limped toward the door, "but I have no doubt that I was directed by the Spirit of the Lord." 1

After the wounded John Taylor's return to Nauvoo, he spent the next several months convalescing. Because he and Willard Richards were the only members of the Twelve in Nauvoo, the rest being away on missions, the two met daily in John's bedroom to plan the future course of the Church. Within a few days Parley P. Pratt arrived and united with his brethren, and for the next several weeks the three continued to meet in John's home as they sought the Lord's will in directing the Church's affairs.

The anti-Mormon mobbers and murderers, cowed by the enormity of their crime in Carthage, crawled back into their holes to await further developments. If nothing else, their cowardice gave Nauvoo and its people a short breather—time in which to work out the quandary into which their prophets' deaths had thrown them. In the short history of the Church no prophet had ever died—Joseph had always been there to tell them what to do next. But now he was gone, and it was left to the Saints to work out the meaning of the instructions he had left them.

Into that vacuum stepped Sidney Rigdon and others— men with grandiose and self-serving ideas about the future of themselves and the Restored Church. Some of the Twelve and other important leaders in Nauvoo, including stake president William Marks, were deceived by these people; so, too, were a good number of the Saints. Yet the majority of the Twelve knew with certainty that their calling as apostles gave them, as a quorum, authority equal to that of the First Presidency. That, the Lord had declared to Joseph by revelation. 2 Further, in one of his last meetings with the Twelve, after performing certain sacred ordinances, Joseph had told them that the burden of the Kingdom, with its keys of authority which they had just been given, had now been rolled off his shoulders and onto theirs. 3

It was with this understanding that Brigham Young, as senior member of the Twelve, gave Sidney Rigdon full opportunity to bid for the leadership of the Church. "Afraid to put in a claim to be made President outright, he sought to be appointed 'guardian' to the Church, to build it up to Joseph. He held secret meetings among those favorable to his plans, circulated wonderful 'revelations' among them, and ordained men to offices heretofore unheard of in the Church; and at last appointed a day for the Church to assemble and select a 'guardian.' The day appointed was the 8TH of August." 4 As it turned out, Brigham Young returned on the 6TH.

After Sidney's several-hour harangue and diatribe, Brigham stood, with full approval of the majority of his quorum, and explained to the assembled Saints what Joseph had said and done. Then he bore his testimony regarding the position and authority of the Quorum of the Twelve Apostles in the latter-day work and gave the people their freedom to choose.

With few exceptions the Saints rejected Sidney's claims and sustained Brigham and the Twelve. "The Twelve being sustained as the presiding authority, they took the direction of affairs and issued a general epistle to the Church, in which they expressed a determination to carry on the work so well begun by the Prophet Joseph. Nauvoo must be enlarged, the temple completed and the gathering of Israel go on. 'The gospel in its fullness must now roll forth,' said they, 'through every neighborhood of this wide-spread country, and to all the world...until the kingdoms of this world become the kingdom of our Lord and of His Christ.'

"Capitalists were invited to Nauvoo to establish manufactories, and were assured that the people there had sufficient skill and ingenuity among them to carry on nearly all kinds of industry. Elder Taylor took a prominent part in these temporal affairs as well as in things spiritual. On his recommendation and under his supervision a 'Trades Union' was formed, an organization having for its object the establishment of industries that would produce, as far as possible, everything needed by the people of Nauvoo, and a surplus for exportation."5

As John Taylor and others kept written pressure on the governor to bring to justice the murderers of Joseph and Hyrum, a trial was begun in October, 1844, with bills of indictment being brought against Levi Williams, Thomas Sharp, Mark Aldrich, Jacob Davis, William Grover, John Allen, William Willis, and William Gallaher. Unfortunately, numerous friends of the indicted raised such a row in and around Carthage that the judge, Jesse Thomas, urged John Taylor and the other witnesses to return to Nauvoo for their own safety. He then postponed the trial until May 19, 1845.

When the trial finally commenced, more than a thousand armed men had assembled to keep the Mormons and their friends out of the courthouse, and the jury was selected almost entirely from among this number. Many witnesses for the prosecution were intimidated by the presence of these armed and noisy men and became too terrified to tell the truth. Some had gone so far as to threaten Governor Ford and said that "if he insisted on pushing the investigation they would make him an accessory to the crime."6 Governor Ford described the court's dilemma as follows:

> During the progress of these trials, the judge was compelled to permit the courthouse to be filled and surrounded by armed bands, who attended court to browbeat and over-awe the administration of justice. The judge himself was in a duress, and informed me that he did not consider his life secure any part of the time. The consequence was, that the crowd had everything their own way.... And truly there can be no government in a free country where the people do not voluntarily obey the laws. 7

One member of the mob who had killed Joseph, William M. Daniels, had become convinced that Joseph was a prophet when he saw him die. He testified, but his testimony was thrown out because he spoke so adamantly in favor of Joseph Smith.

> Attorney Lamborn [Attorney General of Illinois] prosecuted clearly to the jury and every bystander the certainty of the guilt of the defendants. Frank Worrell, lieutenant in the Carthage Greys and in charge of the guards at the jail, was asked by the prosecuting attorney if the guards had had their guns loaded with blanks, and he refused to answer on the grounds that he could not without incriminating himself. Defense Attorney Warren said that if the prisoners were guilty of murder, he himself was guilty, alleging that public opinion acquiesced the murder of the Smiths. According to John Hayes, "There was not a man on the jury, in the court, in the county, that did not know the defendants had done the murder. But it was not proven, and the verdict of Not Guilty was right in law." 8

When news of the verdict reached Nauvoo, the *Nauvoo Neighbor* mentioned a vote by the city council the previous year to refer the case to God for a righteous judgment if "the law failed to atone" for Hyrum and Joseph, 9 and then the city and the Saints got on about their business of building and sustaining the Kingdom of God.

In January 1845 the state of Illinois revoked the Nauvoo City Charter, leaving the Saints with no legal government and no provisions for preventing lawlessness or anarchy. Nevertheless, the Saints were prepared to go on as usual, and did. "Ward bishops were directed to set apart deacons 'to attend to all things needful and especially to watch that the peace and good order hitherto sustained by the city might still be preserved.' The deacons proved very efficient in maintaining order. President Young wrote in his journal with apparent satisfaction:

> The deacons have become very efficient looking after the welfare of the Saints; every part of the city is watched with the strictest care, and whatever time of night the streets are traveled at the corner of every block a deacon is found attending to his duty.

"For troublemakers there were other means of control such as the 'whistling and whittling brigade.' Mosiah Hancock, a member of the brigade, said, 'We kept a good watch and were directed to keep an eye on the 'Black Ducks' [individuals of the known criminal element then abounding in Nauvoo]. We really tried to do our duty and we succeeded in bagging some game.'" [10]

One of the primary needs of the Saints, according to the various members of the Twelve who spoke on the subject, was receiving their endowment. To that end the apostles urged the Saints to hurry with completion of the temple. "Heber C. Kimball referred to Joseph's endowing the Twelve with all the power of the priesthood and to Joseph's instructions that the Twelve should endow the Saints. But he added, 'You cannot obtain these things until that house (the Temple) is built.' 'The first thing we have got to do is to build the Temple,' said John Taylor, 'where we can receive those blessings which we so much desire. Never mind mobocrats, but let us do what God has commanded us.'" [11]

By March of 1845 "the trumpet stones on the capitals atop the pilasters were set," and on May 24 Brigham Young laid the capstone while the congregation gave the Hosanna Shout. Work proceeded through the summer as crews labored while other men stood at arms to protect them from the increasing activity of the mobs, and the sacred edifice was sufficiently completed by October, 1845, that general conference—the last to be held in Nauvoo—was convened in the grand hall on the ground floor. At that time, "'about five thousand saints had the inexpressible joy and great gratification to meet for the first time in the House of the Lord in the City of Joseph.'" 12

On December 10, 1845, endowment work commenced for the Saints living in and near the newly renamed "City of Joseph." "Rooms set apart for the endowment ceremonies were used day and night, wherein hundreds of Saints received their temple blessings. Brigham Young devoted himself entirely to the work," 13 as did John Taylor and the other members of the Twelve. "By February 7, 1846, at last 5,615 endowments had been given," but many others were forced to wait until a temple could be built for them in the West. 14

Other ordinances, including baptisms for the dead and sealings, were also performed. One of these ordinances was the sealing of Ann Hughlings Pitchforth to John Taylor as a plural wife. Following her husband's departure for Australia after he had refused to accept the gospel, Ann and her children had immigrated to Nauvoo, arriving in 1845. With a piano procured for her by John Taylor and the allowance her father regularly sent from the Isle of Man, Ann lived comfortably during her brief time in the city. Her musical talents were appreciated, and she was soon engaged to teach piano to many Nauvoo residents.

Industrial growth, the temple, prosperous farms—these and a host of other things gave mute evidence to people throughout Hancock County and Illinois that Nauvoo and the Church had not only remained intact following Joseph's and Hyrum's deaths, but had in fact become more prosperous than anyone had thought possible. Immigration of new converts had rapidly enlarged the population and increased the work force. Industries had sprung into existence, and their diversity had made the exchange of local productions not only possible but profitable!

Unfortunately, as it had ever done, this prosperity raised the ire of the unpunished mobs and murderers who had believed that with Joseph's and Hyrum's deaths the Church would collapse and

Nauvoo would be abandoned. Incensed that the opposite had occurred, the murderers and their supporters once again began going about the country, charging the Saints with thievery and every other sort of crime evil imagination could conceive. This worked so well that by early fall of 1845, Illinois had not only forgotten "her shame in permitting the prophets of God to be murdered, but...[was] applauding the deed." 15

Made bold by the impunity with which [these] scoundrels had preyed upon the Saints, there was a further gathering of thieves, blacklegs and counterfeiters into Hancock County, and all their desperate crimes were credited to the Mormon people, together with many which had no existence, except as they were coined by the lying tongues of men bent on the destruction of the Saints. The city council of Nauvoo took up the matter, investigated it, and defied the world to substantiate a single instance where they had screened criminals from the law. The citizens in mass meeting assembled denied the slanderous allegations; the deputy sheriff of Hancock County denied them over his signature; Governor Ford investigated them, and in his annual message to the legislature, said: "I have investigated the charge of promiscuous stealing and find it to be greatly exaggerated. I could not ascertain that there were a greater proportion of thieves in that community than in any other of the same number of inhabitants, and perhaps if the city of Nauvoo were compared with St. Louis, or any other western city, the proportion would not be so great."

Regardless of these denials the charges of thieving, counterfeiting and shielding criminals were repeated until popular prejudice was thoroughly aroused against the inhabitants of Nauvoo, and [even honorable citizens of Illinois] began to demand their extermination. Made utterly reckless by the success of their misrepresentations, the anti-Mormons held a meeting to devise means for getting rid of the Saints. A number of their own crowd fired upon the house where the meeting was being held. This was charged to the Mormons, and made a pretext for burning the houses and stacks of grain belonging to the Saints in Morley settlement, near which the aforesaid meeting was held.

This outrage was not avenged by the citizens of Nauvoo, though their means of doing so were ample. 16

As the frightened citizens of Morley settlement fled to Nauvoo, the gathering mobs spread their activities to other outlying settlements of the Saints, burning houses and stacks of grain and driving the citizens, including the aged and infirm, onto the open prairie. And as had been the case in Ohio and Missouri, a disproportionate number of the leading instigators in Hancock County were "men of the cloth," good pastors, reverends, and ministers who saw the Saints not only as stealers of their own flocks, but as perverters of that which was Christian and true. Hence they piously preached against them in their sermons on the Sabbath and during the rest of the week led many in their congregations out to burn, rape, pillage, and murder in the name of God—thus ridding their country of "evil."

Concerned by the increasing lawlessness in Hancock County, Sheriff Backenstos, who was not a member of the Church, called for a posse of law-abiding non-Mormon citizens to help him quell the illegalities. To his surprise and dismay, not a single individual volunteered, and so house-burning and other acts of depredation continued. 17 Eventually, after mobs began threatening his own family, Sheriff Backenstos took an armed Mormon posse to rescue his own family from Carthage and brought them back safely to Nauvoo. He then rode after another mob that had been committing depredations at a settlement near Nauvoo. Upon his arrival the mob fled, he and his posse pursued them for some distance, and at his order to fire, two of the mob fell dead and several others were wounded. 18 Sheriff Backenstos then declared martial law in Hancock County.

> In the midst of these exciting scenes a mass meeting in Quincy resolved that the only hope for peace was in the removal of the Mormons from the state, and they appointed a committee to wait upon the Church authorities to lay these conclusions before them, and request them to leave. Weary with being continually harassed with illegal prosecutions and mob violence, the Saints agreed to leave the state in the spring, providing the citizens in Hancock and surrounding counties would use their influence in assisting them to rent or sell their property, that they might have means with which to remove; and further that they would cease vexatious lawsuits against them, as they had violated no law. This proposition was accepted by the people of Quincy and also by the anti-Mormons in Hancock County. The civil authorities were largely superceded by the military, Major Warren being sent into Hancock County with a company of militia to keep the peace. 19

However, far too many of the mob looked upon the Saints' departure as an almost unparalleled economic opportunity; their beautiful homes and farms, as well as their rapidly developing industries, were too much to be ignored. Greedy beyond imagination for these things, and egged on by their religious leaders and others who could not wait to see ruin come to the Church, members of the mob broke the non-Mormon side of the treaty daily. Illegal writs were constantly served against John Taylor and others of the Twelve; house-burnings and other acts of depredation continued unabated;

and murder again became part of the mob's litany.

In an editorial in the *Times and Seasons*, John Taylor, who by then was exasperated beyond endurance, declared that he would no longer submit to the injustices being heaped upon himself and the Saints. Brigham Young made similar remarks. Troubled by the Saints' "resistance to law," Major Warren made two appointments late in the year to visit with the brethren of the Twelve. There he upbraided them severely and was himself chastised by John Taylor in particular. It is these two encounters between John Taylor and Major Warren that are dealt with in the *vignette* at the beginning of this chapter.

Meanwhile, John and the Twelve faced the daunting task of getting an entire people prepared to abandon Nauvoo early the following spring. "All through the winter of 1845–6 the Saints in Nauvoo were busy making their preparations for the contemplated exodus. Early dawn and the latest twilight saw them hurrying to and fro gathering together provisions, cattle, carriages, wagons, seeds, farming implements—everything that was likely to be of service to them in the new homes they were going to make somewhere in the wilderness. Nor did their labors end with the light of day. Often it happened that the dingy smithies were illuminated through the night by the blazing forge, and the stillness of midnight was broken by the merry ring of anvils, while others sat in council devising the best methods of traveling and organizing into companies those whose arrangements were nearing completion." [20]

There was approximately one blacksmith shop for every one hundred Latter-day Saint families in the area, and every shop was buzzing.

Companies were organized so that each one had cabinetmakers, wheelwrights, carpenters, and wagonmakers; and all were kept constantly at work. People were making tents and wagon covers out of anything.

"Green timber was prepared for the spokes and felloes, some kiln-dried, and some boiled in salt and water.... Iron was brought from different parts of the country, and blacksmiths were at work night and day."

Instead of using the large, heavy conestoga wagons generally known as prairie schooners, the Saints were building their own wagons to specifications that would more nearly fit their needs, except for some wagons that were purchased from Louis Epenschield. Also, the money saved from making their own would help to provide the supplies that every person was to have with him when he left. Parley P. Pratt had reckoned that a family of five persons should take the following:

"1 good wagon, 3 yoke cattle, 2 cows, 2 beef cattle, 3 sheep, 1,000 lbs. flour, 20 lbs. sugar, 1 rifle and ammunition, a tent and tent-poles, from 10 to 20 lbs. seed to a family, from 25 to 100 lbs. tools for farming, and a few other items." 21

"Meanwhile the Twelve and other leaders studied possible destinations in the West. Maps and travelers' accounts about California and Oregon and particularly John C. Fremont's journal compiled during his 1842 exploration were perused. Fremont's journal contained an extensive description of Salt Lake Valley. Preparations for the exodus continued. Governor Ford wrote: 'All houses in Nauvoo, and even the temple, were converted into work-shops; and before spring twelve thousand wagons were in readiness.' Captains of fifties and tens reported to the council on January 13, 1846, that 140 horses and seventy wagons were ready for immediate service.... By the end of January, 1846, 2,000 persons were prepared to leave Nauvoo. President Young met with the Twelve and other leaders on February 2 and agreed that it was imperative that they start west as soon as possible."[22]

This midwinter departure was not a condition of the treaty the Saints had signed, but was designed to settle all doubts that the Church was indeed leaving the United States and heading west. Such a desperate action, it was hoped, would forestall further mobbings and depredations by their persecutors, thus giving those Saints who remained behind a short period of peace in which to finish their preparations.

On February 4, 1846, Charles Shumway led the first covered wagons loaded with Saints and supplies onto flatboats and ferries, and they began crossing the mile-wide Mississippi River. "When it became clear that the Saints would have to leave Illinois, as they had left Missouri, Agnes and James [Taylor, John's parents,] moved to Nauvoo…and prepared for the journey west."[23]

Elder Taylor and his family crossed the river on the 16TH of February, and joined the Camp of Israel in the wilderness of the Territory of Iowa. For his own family and those who had lived with him in Nauvoo, he had eight wagons and a carriage, with the necessary force of teams. Snow was on the ground when he left Nauvoo, and shortly after crossing the river a thaw set in, which made traveling difficult. An encampment was made at a place where wood was plentiful, and there the exiles made themselves as comfortable as possible, until traveling should become less disagreeable.

There they lay, exposed to the inclement season, while only a short distance away—almost in view—were their comfortable houses, their beautiful city and magnificent temple! These homes which they had left, and that city were still theirs, for so hurried had been their departure that they had no time to dispose of property.

Elder Taylor had left a large, two-story brick house well

furnished, with a brick store on one side and a new brick building that he had erected for a printing office on the other, and a large barn in the rear. This lot and the buildings were worth $10,000. In addition to this property, a short distance east of Nauvoo he had a farm of 106 acres of unimproved land, another of 80 acres, 40 of which was under cultivation and the remaining 40 timber. He also had a corner lot 101 x 85 feet on Main and Water street, opposite the Nauvoo Mansion. All this—to say nothing of breaking up his printing and book-binding establishment—he had been compelled to leave with but small hope of ever receiving anything for it; while he himself was driven forth an exile to wander, perhaps to perish, in the wilderness, a victim of religious intolerance.

This was in an age of boasted enlightenment—in the 19TH century! In the great American Republic— the vaunted asylum of the oppressed! 24

By February 25 the weather had turned so cold that caravans of wagons crossed the river on the ice, and this unusual condition continued for the next several days. For the Latter-day Saints, as well as for John and his growing family, their destiny lay westward, somewhere beyond the snow-covered and windswept plains of Iowa, and so in that direction they pointed their shaggy coated teams and already-breaking-down wagons.

10

LONGING FOR SWEET MUSIC IN THE WEST

"Oh, Mother dear, how I wish we'd never come to this awful country!"

Ann Pitchforth, forty-five years old but feeling like an achy old woman, looked up at her middle daughter. "Now, Sarah, that's no proper way for you to talk, and you know it."

"I don't know it," the eleven-year-old girl flounced angrily. "All it ever does is rain! Day and night, rain, rain, rain! There's mud everywhere, and I…well, I hate it! I hate always being dirty! I just wish we'd stayed in England! Or gone to Australia with Father! I'll bet it's warm and dry where he is!"

"Sarah," her older sister Mercy remonstrated quietly as she worked beside her sister-in-law over the small fire, "you really mustn't say such things. Mother isn't well, you know, and your complaining only upsets her the more."

Sarah, who was Ann Pitchforth's thinker as well as complainer, grew silent, and Ann smiled gratefully up at Mercy. Almost fourteen, Mercy was rapidly developing into a woman. But her spirit had always seemed old to Ann, or at least more mature than her years, for she could see through issues that others found overwhelming, and the consequences of her and others' actions never seemed to catch her by surprise.

"Well, Sarah's sure enough right about one thing," Samuel Pitchforth stated quietly as he pulled a leather strip through a torn harness strap. "The rain this fall seems to be nonstop, and I'm getting more than middling tired of it!"

Sam's speech ended in a fit of coughing, his thin body being racked by spasms, and Ann watched as her son's young wife reached over and rubbed her hand on his bony back. Mary Mitchell was indeed precious, and constantly Ann blessed the moment Sammy had been introduced to her. A proper English girl, Mary had been born in Herefordshire and had gathered to Nauvoo with her family. There she and Sammy had met and wed, and Ann found herself thinking wistfully of the day when the two would give her a first grandchild. If only she could live long enough to see it—

A new fit of coughing racked her own thin and emaciated body, and Ann turned her head from her children to hide the blood that was now discoloring her spittle. She was seriously ill—so ill that each time she awakened she was surprised that she had not passed on. She was also terribly cold, as if she had never been warm in her life and could never hope to be warm again. It was now October of 1846. They had finally crossed the Missouri River and were with the Saints in Council Bluffs, but she couldn't remember really feeling well since she had left Nauvoo in Brother Taylor's company the previous February.

At their first camp on Sugar Creek the storms had come, the shrieking wind blowing down tents and tearing off wagon covers. Then the temperature had dropped like a lead ball, until all were so terribly numb and frostbitten that it was a wonder any had survived. On the worst night of all, Ann recalled, she had not slept a wink, for Patty Sessions had needed help with the nine babies born between darkness and dawn, and she had joyfully offered herself for that purpose.

So the winter had passed, with her wading through the powdered snow of frigid temperatures or the slush of warmer days, gathering twigs and bark for the teams, cooking for her family over an open fire in zero-degree weather, and huddling alone so many nights in the wagon as the frost crept silently through her bedclothes and seeped into her very bones. Skin had peeled from her frostbitten nose, ears, and fingers, while her joints had swelled gnarled and red, causing her to wish many times she had brought the cookstove instead of her cherished piano.

Yet along the march of the Camp of Israel there had been happy times, memorable for the hours and even precious moments she had been able to spend with Brother Taylor and the rest of the Lord's Saints. Sugar Creek, Lick Creek, Chariton River, Richardson's Point, Evans' Camp—no banquet could compare to wild game cooked at a great fire following a hard day's march, especially when it was followed by a talk by one of the Lord's chosen apostles, or better yet, a few moments spent in private conversation with her beloved husband, Brother Taylor. One night when the camp had sung together, accompanied by Captain William Pitt's brass band, she had crawled into her wagon, thrown the quilt back from the piano, and played along with them. And on that night, standing outside the wagon where she played, Elder Taylor had lifted his rich baritone voice until surely he had outsung even the angels who seemed daily to accompany them.

Oh, her mind cried out in silent sorrow, if only she hadn't grown so ill after that night in the rain near Locust Creek, holding a quilt while Patty Sessions had delivered another two babies. The other sisters assisting them had not taken cold, but she had, and it had been aggravated a day later when her piano had torn loose during a climb up a steep and muddy hillside, overturning the wagon and burying not only itself but both her and her daughter-in-law, Mary, in the mud at the bottom of the hill.

How well she remembered Brother Taylor's booming laugh as he had pulled her out, set her on his knee, and wiped the mud from her face. Of course he had not been laughing at her, she knew, but at the completely destroyed piano, which she had vowed to everyone would accompany her all the way to the Pacific sea—and would there be of far greater worth than the cookstove she had chosen to leave behind. Now, though, there would be no piano—

Of course Ann had cleaned up as best she could after the upset, but her clothing had soaked through and could not then be changed, the rain had continued its downpour through the freshly torn cover of the righted wagon, and by the time she had reached Garden Grove she had been so weakened and chilled that Brother Taylor had counseled her to stay for a time and recuperate.

She had agreed; he had left her to return to Nauvoo for the secret dedication of the temple, and upon his return she had still looked so drawn that he had been unwilling to have her accompany him further west. Thus they had parted, she assuring him that she would catch up with him shortly, and he assuring her that once in upper California he would procure for her the finest piano in the country, to which she had lovingly responded that she looked forward to again accompanying him as he sang for her and the Saints the glorious hymns of Zion—

Only—somehow she had never managed to catch up with him! Yet with hope springing ever in her breast—for she truly loved Brother Taylor and yearned to be at his side as befitted a dutiful wife—she had somehow endured the seemingly endless journey, telling herself that she would rest up and regain her strength at Mount Pisgah and perhaps even meet up with Brother Taylor if he perchance had lingered there. But he had not; the hot weather had brought the sickly season, and in her weakened condition Ann had contracted what was called the ague, or malaria. Still suffering from the chills and fever, at Mount Pisgah she and the children had also received the disappointing word that Brother Taylor had been sent, in company with Elders Pratt and Hyde, to put down a serious apostasy among the Church leaders in England.

Devastated, for she knew well the rigors and dangers of such a journey, Ann had nevertheless pressed steadily if slowly forward, praying at all times for Brother Taylor and his families and giving thanks for Sammy and his sweet bride, who took over running the camp whenever the chills and fever put her down. Yes, and many were the nights when her secret tears of loneliness wet her pillow, for now it would be another year before she saw Brother Taylor again, if she ever saw him again at all—

In early September, just as they had departed from Mount Pisgah, she had developed scurvy, or the black canker, which swelled and discolored her legs and caused some of her teeth to fall out of swollen gums. It was now October 26, 1846; they had arrived in Winter Quarters that very day to be with the Saints, and again it was raining. No wonder poor Sarah was so tired of it. Worse for Ann, however, the black canker had caused almost constant bleeding in her mucous membranes, and Ann knew the disease had progressed to a most serious stage. But Tom Speirs, whom Brother Taylor had asked to watch out for them upon their arrival, had said there were a few potatoes scattered about Winter Quarters, and in the morning he was going to take Sammy to a nearby abandoned fort where some horseradish could be found. Either might be sufficient to pull her through, she thought, but she would have to get them soon—

"Mother, are you feeling better now?"

Doing her best to smile, Ann reached out and caressed the cheek of little Annie, who at a precocious five was almost always the camp pet. Hardly more than a baby when they had emigrated from England's Isle of Man, Annie had no recollections of England or of her father, Solomon Pitchforth, either one. Ann and the older children were all heartbroken when Solomon had determined to break up the family rather than accept the Lord's gospel, thus forcing them to gather to Nauvoo without him.

Thank the Lord that tiny Annie had been spared those painful memories.

"Are you well now, Mother?" Annie pressed. "At least we're out of the rain now, and being dry makes me feel better!"

"Yes, Annie dear, I'm feeling much better than I was, thank you. This is a nice, warm straw bed we have here on the ground, and Brother Speirs was awfully good to prepare such a fine shelter for us."

"He told me Elder Taylor instructed him to do it," Sam said.

"Yes, Sammy, I know. It seems that Brother Taylor has watched out for us since the very first day Solomon brought him to our home at Hanover Street on the North Quay, though at the time I thought it was us doing the looking out for him."

For a moment Ann was silent, remembering. Outside the shelter—a deep dugout in a cut bank half a mile back from the Missouri River—the rain continued to fall in torrents, turning all of Winter Quarters into a quagmire. But in the dugout it was dry, the small fire was spreading warmth, and even the occasional drips from overhead were hardly noticed.

"Are you still thankful that you chose to be baptized, Mother?" It was Mercy who asked.

"Yes, Mother," Sarah chimed in. "Don't you wish, after suffering through this horrid journey and your terrible illnesses, that you had remained Jewish with Father?"

"Not for one second have I regretted my decision! When Brother Taylor asked if I was ready for baptism, I could only answer with the truth. I was ready, for the Lord had made it known unto me." Ann gazed up at her two eldest daughters. "Remember, Mercy and Sarah, I was no enthusiastic girl in her teens. I was accustomed to being extremely cautious and weighing all circumstances ere I jumped to a conclusion. From my childhood I had studied the scriptures, and in secret I had poured out my heart to the Lord. When Brother Taylor came to our house on the

North Quay and boarded with us, in spite of my unbelieving heart, I could not deny baptism and at the same time believe the New Testament. However, I was so resolved not to be deluded, that I thought I would just get baptized and then only go so far as I could see was right. Ever slow and cautious, I received the truth; many such as Sammy ran before me, while I crept slowly along. I soon felt a spirit of gathering pervading my bosom, however, and a strong desire to be enabled to visit Nauvoo, to see and judge for myself. The rest you know, for you have lived it with me."

Ann suddenly grew more animated. "But know this, my children, and remember it to your graves. I rejoice that ever I came to this land and received an endowment in the temple of the Lord. I am well satisfied that I have followed no cunningly devised fable. I can rejoice in the Lord all the day long and smile at the taunts of the ignorant, crying, delusion! delusion! I do not bow to educational prejudice, sectarian bigotry, nor popular opinion. I dare not barter my eternal peace for man's opinion, nor set of men; I dare to think and judge for myself. Facts are stubborn things, they cannot be beat down nor be annihilated by clamor. Truth cannot be destroyed by persecution. I daily see living witnesses who testify that Joseph Smith was a prophet of the Lord; testimony upon testimony proves it, anecdote upon anecdote, with first one friend and then another who bespeak of the love he had for the Saints and of the love they yet have for him.

"Remember, my dear ones, not all the powers of earth and hell combined can break this chain of love and union that cements Joseph Smith and the Saints to the Lord Jesus Christ. Devils and persecuting Christians may hate, being of one and the same spirit, but the Saints of the latter days will triumph by love. This is a power above our tormentors; they cannot cope with it; they may, in accordance with the spirit that dwells in them, murder, burn houses, drive into exile, but no further. Can they chain the heart or bind the pure free spirit? No! With love and union we go to the wild regions of the far West, and soon the wilderness shall rejoice and blossom as the rose. Polished society shall grace the desert. The cities and temples of the Saints shall arise; the stone cut out of the mountain without hands has begun to roll on, and soon the wicked will be confounded. Brother Joseph declared these things to the apostles; our dear Brother Taylor has shared them with me on numerous occasions, and I know of myself that they are true!"

"Brother Taylor is a wonderful missionary, isn't he?" her oldest daughter said, the first to break the silence after Ann's sudden speech.

"Yes, Mercy, he is. Of course, as one of the Lord's apostles, he holds the keys to missionary work in all of the earth. That is why the devil cannot stand before him."

"Is that why you became his plural wife back in Nauvoo, Mother? So the devil would leave us alone?"

Ann smiled patiently. "No, Annie, it isn't. I was sealed to Brother Taylor because I love him with all my heart and soul and wish always to be near him. After all, he has brought such eternal joy and happiness to you, my dear ones—"

"When he returns from England, Mother, will Brother Taylor be our father?"

"Your father is Solomon Pitchforth," Ann replied with a sigh. "But you may rest assured that Brother Taylor will always watch over you as if he were your father."

"That's right, Annie." Samuel reached out and tousled his youngest sister's hair. "That's why, before he departed for England, he asked Brother Speirs to assist us. Now, Mother is tired, so we must allow her to rest—"

Except for a cup of warm tea, Ann couldn't bring herself to eat the supper Mercy and Mary had prepared. Still, the small fire and dry straw were helping her to feel warm, and the hot drink seemed to spread to her legs and chest. She no longer coughed, the pain departed from her limbs, and even her gums stopped feeling tender. Despite the storm outside, she felt warm and cozy—

Lying there, in her mind, Ann was with Brother Taylor again on that last evening before the exodus from Nauvoo—before he had been called to return to England. He had written a song for the trail, and as she had accompanied him on her precious piano— the piano now lost to the trail—he had sung in his strong baritone:

> The Upper California, O! That's the land for me,
> It lies between the mountains and the great Pacific sea;
> The Saints can be supported there,
> And taste the sweets of liberty.
> In Upper California—O! That's the land for me.

John Taylor's sweet voice now seemed to fill the dugout as he sang of the promised land, where "Our towers and temples there shall rise, Along the great Pacific Sea." Ann would meet her beloved John Taylor there, she knew, as her heavy eyes closed in peace; she would meet him at the final gathering, when they would dwell together in eternal, celestial glory— 1

Once John Taylor's company, composed of eight wagons and a carriage, was lined out on Main Street in Nauvoo, he no doubt made one final pass of inspection. The entire caravan stretched "from the *Times and Seasons* office past [his] house and up the block beyond the gunsmith shop of John Browning. Taylor moved from wagon to wagon, checking the yoked ox teams, the loads, the conditions of the wagons. George, now twelve, was teamster of the first wagon. Leonora sat between him and ten-year-old Mary Ann. [John] gave the signal, and George headed the line of wagons toward the lower river landing. Leonora looked straight ahead as the oxen plodded past the red brick mansion that had been her home. She never looked back." 2

Massaging his leg where one of the assassin's bullets had

torn through the flesh, Elder Taylor "climbed into his carriage and nodded to Joseph James. The seven-year-old slapped the reins on the rumps of the horses. Taylor told the boy there were several calls he had to make before joining the company at the river landing. He didn't explain that he wanted to say farewell to four of the ten women he had married who wouldn't be leaving with him."3

While John was attending to this final parting, his mind was no doubt considering the eventful nineteen months since the martyrdom—that and wondering exactly what he might expect for the future. Of course it really didn't matter, for John knew by the witness of the Holy Spirit that Joseph had given him and the others the eternal truth—God's pure and holy gospel—and whatever he was called upon to pass through because of that would ultimately be worth it.

For that reason he had delayed his departure for two weeks to work day and night in the temple in order that more of the Saints might have their endowments before the approaching journey. The other brethren of the Twelve had done the same, but now all were leaving, Brigham Young and Heber C. Kimball having gone the afternoon before. Now it was his turn, and so he hastened to the lower landing to check with his parents and supervise the loading of the company's teams and wagons onto the fleet of flatboats and ferries that were daily plying the river.

Taylor crossed to a covered wagon to exchange a few words with a young couple, Sam and Mary Pitchforth, then he ducked under the canvas to say hello to Ann Pitchforth, Sam's mother and Taylor's tenth wife. A lady of quality and accomplishment, Ann had a special place in Taylor's affections. The middle-aged Jewish convert had given recitals and taught the pianoforte at Nauvoo, though protesting that in the entire city she hadn't yet found an instrument in tune. Taylor, who admired her refusal to lower standards because of circumstance, had secured the best piano in Nauvoo for her use and had instructed departing missionaries to seek out a piano tuner, take the gospel to him, and bring him to Zion.

The piano, covered with a quilt, stood tall in the wagon. With a smile he reminded Ann that it still wasn't too late to exchange it for the cook stove. She returned the smile without changing her mind. Man cannot live by bread alone, she reminded him. If members of Capt. William Pitt's band could bring their instruments along, why couldn't she take her piano? 4

The crossing went without incident until John was nearing the end of his third trip in a small skiff. Behind him on a flatboat a teamster spat a stream of tobacco juice into the eye of one of the oxen; the animal recoiled in pain; and within a moment the flatboat had overturned and was sinking. The wagon on board was already at the bottom, and men, women, and children were floundering amongst the animals and debris in the ice-choked river. One of those children was John's own Joseph James. 5

Rowing quickly to the site, John pulled his bedraggled son into the skiff, assisted in the rescue of others, and then made for the Iowa shore where an anxious Leonora was waiting to change the seven-year-old into dry clothes and warm him at a nearby fire. As it turned out, two oxen died in the mishap; a young man dived with a rope to the sunken wagon and secured it so it could be pulled out; and from then on no teamsters were allowed to chew while working near the animals.

Pushing westward from the river, John and his company traveled through the slush and mud to a spot on Sugar Creek where wood for fires was plentiful, and there they made themselves as comfortable as possible while they waited for the weather to moderate. It didn't, but only grew colder, the temperature dropping so low that by February 25 the river was frozen over from shore to shore. As soon as it was determined that the ice was thick enough to support wagons and teams, the Saints began streaming by the hundreds and then thousands across the frozen river, hoping not to be left behind by Brigham Young and the other apostles.

> Advice had been given for every family to have eighteen months of supplies on hand, but when loyal Church members saw their leaders leaving, many of them did not wait until they could comply with this requirement. Instead they hurried on to be with the heads of the Church....
>
> In fact, they hastened so fast that by the end of February about five thousand people had crossed the river on their way west, including eight hundred leaders of families who reported at Sugar Creek with not more than two weeks' provisions for themselves and their teams. The lead camp had moved approximately only 150 miles from Nauvoo when the supplies of Brigham Young and the other apostles ran out because of their sharing with those in need. 6

To make traveling easier, the Twelve had organized the people into "companies of from seventy to a hundred wagons; but these companies followed each other so closely that they formed an almost unbroken procession across the Territory of Iowa." 7

B. H. Roberts, John Taylor's biographer, has written graphically of the Saints' journey across Iowa:

> To tell in detail the story of that journey from Nauvoo to Council Bluffs—how the Saints struggled on through trackless prairies converted into vast bogs by the spring thaws and rain and sleet which seemed to fall continuously;

how the bleak winds from the pitiless northwest were more cruel than the sharpest frosts; how the young and strong left the main companies to go into Missouri and districts in Iowa remote from their line of march to exchange household furniture for corn or flour; how those who had merely enough provisions for themselves—no one had a surplus—divided with those who had none; how heroically they struggled against weakness and disease brought on through exposure; how they laid away their dead in nameless graves—to tell all this would fill a volume of itself, and belongs rather to a history of the whole people than to this biography. 8

A year later, as John wrote to the Saints in Great Britain, he spoke somewhat of his own experiences during the journey to the West. One of his themes was that mobs and persecution really had nothing to do with the Saints heading for the valleys of the mountains. "Many living witnesses…can testify that we proposed moving to California, leaving the land of our oppression, preaching the gospel to the Lamanites, building up other temples to the living God, establishing ourselves in the far distant West. The cruel and perfidious persecutions that we endured, tended to hasten our departure, but did not dictate it. It jeopardized our lives, property and liberty, but was not the cause of our removal.

"Many a time…have I listened to the voice of our beloved Prophet [Joseph Smith], while in council, dwell on this subject [the removal of the Saints to the Rocky Mountains] with delight; his eyes sparkling with animation, and his soul fired with the inspiration of the Spirit of the living God. It was a theme that caused the bosoms of all who were privileged to listen, to thrill with delight; intimately connected with this, were themes upon which prophets, patriarchs, priests and kings dwelt with pleasure and delight: of them they prophesied, sung, wrote, spoke and desired to see, but died without the sight. My spirit glows with sacred fire while I reflect upon these scenes, and I say, O Lord, hasten the day! Let Zion be established! Let the mountain of the Lord's house be established in the tops of the mountains!"9

John then prophesied that even though the Saints had suffered great losses and had sacrificed tremendously, it would soon be evident that they were better off than if they had remained in Nauvoo.

John also discussed the sufferings of the Saints occasioned by the furious winter storms that had buffeted them almost mercilessly, yet not once forgetting to vindicate God, who had drawn near his people during those darkest hours. He continued: "We sustained no injury therefrom; our health and our lives were preserved—we outlived the trying scene—we felt contented and happy—the songs of Zion resounded from wagon to wagon—from tent to tent; the sound reverberated through the woods, and its echo was returned from the distant hills; peace, harmony, and contentment reigned in the habitations of the Saints...

"It is true that in our sojourning we do not possess all the luxuries and delicacies of old established countries and cities, but we have an abundance of the staple commodities, such as flour, meal, beef, mutton, pork, milk, butter and in some instances cheese, sugar,...etc., etc. We feel contented and happy in the wilderness. The God of Israel is with us—union and peace prevail; and as we journey, as did Abraham of old, with our flocks and herds to a distant land, we feel that like him, we are doing the will of our Heavenly Father and relying upon His word and promises; and having His blessing, we feel that we are children of the same promise and hope, and that the great Jehovah is our God."10

Two views of the Mormon exodus across Iowa, both by non-Mormons, are also worthy of note. Colonel Thomas L. Kane wrote of the Saints' winter travels:

Under the most favorable circumstances, an expedition of this sort, undertaken at such a season of the year, could scarcely fail to be disastrous. But the pioneer company had set out in haste, and were very imperfectly supplied with necessities. The cold was intense. They moved in the teeth of the keen-edged northwest winds, such as sweep down the Iowa peninsula from the ice-bound regions of the timber-shaded Slave Lake and Lake of the Woods; on the Bald Prairie there, nothing above the dead grass breaks their free course over the hard rolled hills. Even along the scattered water-courses, where they broke the thick ice to give their cattle drink, the annual autumn fires had left little wood of value. The party, therefore, often wanted for good camp-fires, the first luxury of all travelers; but to men insufficiently furnished with tents and other appliances of shelter, almost an essential to life. After days of fatigue, their nights were often freezing. Their stock of food, also, proved inadequate; and as their systems became impoverished, their suffering from the cold increased. 11

And with a somewhat different point of view, Hubert Howe Bancroft wrote:

Without attempting long distances in a single day, they made camp rather early, and after the usual manner of emigrants, the wagons in a circle or semi-circle round the camp-fire, placed so as best to shield them from the wind and wild beasts and Indians, with the animals at a convenient distance, some staked, and some running loose, but all carefully guarded. The country through which they passed was much of it well wooded; the land was fertile and afforded abundant pastures, the grass in summer being from one to ten feet high. Provisions were cheap: corn twelve cents and wheat twenty-five to thirty cents a bushel, beef two cents a pound, and all payable in labor at what was then considered good wages, say forty or fifty cents a day. 12

And back again to Thomas L. Kane:

The spring came at last. It overtook them in the Sac and Fox country, still on the naked prairie, not yet half way over the trail they were following between the Mississippi and Missouri Rivers. But it brought its own share of troubles with it. The months with which it opened proved nearly as trying as the worst of winter.

The snow and sleet and rain which fell, as it appeared to them, without intermission, made the road over the rich prairie soil as impassable as one vast bog of heavy black mud. Sometimes they would fasten the horses and oxen of four or five wagons to one, and attempt to get ahead in this way, taking turns; but at the close of a day of hard toil for themselves and their cattle, they would find themselves a quarter or half a mile from the place they had left in the morning. The heavy rains raised all water-courses; the most trifling streams were impassable. Wood fit for bridging was often not to be had, and in such cases the only recourse was to halt for freshets to subside—a matter in the case of the headwaters of the Chariton, for instance, of over three weeks' delay. 13

It was May when John and his company arrived at Garden Grove. There word arrived that the temple back in Nauvoo was finally completed and ready for dedication. As he prepared for his return to the City of Joseph, John counseled Ann Pitchforth to halt with "this 'traveling stake of Zion'" until she could regain her strength. He then departed in his carriage, promising to check up on her upon his return. At Garden Grove "the Saints began breaking sod and planting 715 acres to supply the exodus. Sam [Pitchforth] was one of 359 men reporting for work duty: 100 needed to split rails; 10 to build fences; 48 to make houses; 12 to dig wells; 10 to build bridges; and the remainder to clear land, plow, and plant." 14

During John's return from Nauvoo following the temple dedication, he passed "'eight hundred teams' moving across Iowa, 'together with cattle and sheep in abundance.'" 15 At Garden Grove, John "found that Ann Pitchforth had recovered from her cold; but she looked drawn. The rigors of the march were particularly difficult for a lady of middle age who never before in her life had done physical labor. They said farewell here, and Taylor went on with his company, without knowing that they never would see each other again on this earth." 16

"The 5TH of June found Elder Taylor with his company at Mount Pisgah, in Iowa, about one hundred and sixty miles from Nauvoo, where the companies under Brigham Young and Heber C. Kimball had encamped and were putting in crops for those who would come on later to harvest.

"From Mount Pisgah to the 'Bluffs' he met numerous squads of Pottawattamie Indians, all of whom he treated kindly, and generally distributed tobacco among them, a thing with which they were highly pleased. These Indians had been removed from their lands east of the Mississippi some years before, and were themselves exiles. Perhaps it was that fact which led them to treat kindly the exiled Saints. At any rate they gave them permission to pass through their reservation, and finally permitted them to settle for a time upon their lands and use what timber they needed to build temporary abodes.

"Elder Taylor brought his company up to the main encampment at Council Bluffs on the 17TH of June. Soon afterwards he was busily engaged with his brethren in raising a company of pioneers to go to the Rocky Mountains in advance of the main body of the people. He was going as one of this company and began putting his wagons in order." 17

The encampment at Winter Quarters was described by Colonel Thomas L. Kane, who visited it shortly after the arrival of the Taylor company:

> They were collected a little distance above the Pottawattamie Agency. The hills of the high prairie crowding in upon the river at this point and overhanging it, appear of an unusual and commanding elevation. They are called the "Council Bluffs.". . . To the south of them, a rich alluvial flat of considerable width follows down the Missouri some eight miles, to where it is lost from view by a turn, which forms the site of an Indian town of Point aux Poules. Across the river from this spot the hills recur again, but are skirted at their base by as much low ground as suffices for a landing. This landing, and the large flat or bottom on the east side of the river, were covered with covered carts and wagons; and each one of the Council Bluff hills opposite was crowded with its own great camp, gay with bright white canvas, and alive with the busy stir of swarming occupants. In the clear blue morning air the smoke streamed up from more than a thousand cooking fires. Countless roads and by-paths checkered all manner of geometric figures on the hill-sides. Herd boys were dozing upon the slopes; sheep and horses, cows and oxen were feeding round them, and other herds in the luxuriant meadows of the then swollen river. From a single point I counted four thousand head of cattle in view at one time. As I approached, it seemed to me the children there were to prove still more numerous. 18

The Brethren's plans to send an advance party of four hundred men to the Rocky Mountains were shelved by the arrival of a Captain James Allen at Mount Pisgah on June 26, who in the name of the United States called upon the refugees for five hundred volunteers to march to California to aid in the war with Mexico. This call to arms having been previously arranged during meetings between U.S. President James Polk and Elder Jesse Little, president of the Eastern and Middle States Missions, Brigham Young and other Church leaders determined to look upon it as an opportunity rather than an imposition. 19 "For this purpose meetings were called and the proposition of enlistment made to the brethren. It was not at first received with much enthusiasm by the people. Perhaps they could not forget that the general government had witnessed without protest their expatriation and expulsion from the confines of the United States. They also remembered that their repeated appeals for justice had been met with repeated and increasing indifference, and it required no small amount of persuasion at the first to induce men to enlist." 20

As the brethren of the Twelve fanned out to drum up support for the Battalion in the various camps, none was more earnest than John Taylor. At a meeting called in the camp of George A. Smith, for instance, he declared:

> Many have felt something like rebelling against the government of the United States. I have myself felt swearing mad at the government for the treatment we have received at the hands of those in authority, although I don't know that I ever swore much. We have had cause to feel as we have, and any man having a spark of the love of liberty in him would have felt likewise. We are now something like Abraham was, wandering about we know not whither, but fleeing from a land of tyranny and oppression.

"He then explained that it was the present intention to settle in some part of California, which at that time belonged to Mexico; but to go there they must have a legal pretext else they would be regarded as interlopers. As the United States was at war with Mexico, they had a right, according to the law of nations, to invade her territory; and if they enlisted in the service of the United States they would have a right to go there; and as the stipulations offered by the government provided for their being disbanded in California, they would be at or near the place of their proposed destination, with a right to remain. There they would be the 'old settlers,' and bringing in some thirty thousand people, there was a prospect of obtaining a state or territorial government, where they could live in peace. Their children could boast, too, that their fathers had fought and bled for their country. 'Although,' [he added] 'I do not think you will have much fighting to do. Still, I do not say this to encourage cowards to go on this expedition.' "

> A great many seem to distrust the government…and are afraid they will not be carried to California, but be sent to Texas or somewhere else. They will not be—they need not fear. Who cannot trust the United States? Her flag floats over every ocean, and her ministry are in every nation. I know it is a great journey for a man to undertake and leave his family; but Captain Allen says he will give absolute permission for the families to remain here. He has also obtained a writing from the Pottawattamie sub-agency, signed by the chiefs and braves to that effect, so that everything is straightforward.

"He concluded by making a motion that a body of five hundred men be raised, and make Captain Allen Lieutenant-Colonel, a promotion he had been promised providing he raised the battalion. That motion was carried." 21

By July 16TH the number of men had been raised, and the Battalion was ready to depart for Fort Leavenworth, where they were to be paid in advance and outfitted for their march to California. John, meanwhile, was enduring another trial of his own faith. The men of his company whom he had sent out to trade for corn and flour and to swap horses for cattle returned without having any success. John declared:

> I now found myself in the wilderness without the means of procuring the necessary provisions for a year and a half.... Twelve months prior to this time, I had ten thousand dollars' worth of property at my disposal! 22

The very next day, however, John was visited by a brother named Stewart who was seeking counsel. Before leaving, he loaned John enough money to relieve him of his embarrassments, and John wrote joyfully, "'I felt thankful to the Lord that He had opened my way, as He always does in time of need.'" 23

Meanwhile the brethren of the Twelve had received word from England of wild financial schemes, fraud, transgression, and chicanery among the highest leaders of the Church in Great Britain—Reuben Hedlock, Thomas Ward, and John Banks. These reports were confirmed to Brigham Young through the impressions of the Spirit, after which he assigned John Taylor, Orson Hyde, and Parley P. Pratt to make a hurried journey to England to correct the abuses and set the affairs of the Church in order.

It was also at this time that a new plague struck the Camp of Israel. John had seen nothing like it since that first dreadful summer in Nauvoo. Called "congestive fever" or simply "the fever," the disease was malaria, and it seemed to have come in conjunction with another deadly malady called "black canker" but which was in reality scurvy. Again we turn to Thomas L. Kane, who himself was struck down with the fever, for a description of the camp's suffering:

> I found, as early as the 31ST of July, that 37 per cent of its inhabitants were down with the Fever and a sort of

strange scorbutic disease, frequently fatal, which they named the Black Canker. The camps...on the eastern side of the Missouri were yet worse fated.

In some of these, the fever prevailed to such an extent that hardly any escaped it. They let their cows go unmilked. They wanted for voices to raise the Psalm of Sundays. The few who were able to keep their feet, went about among the tents and wagons with food and water, like nurses through the wards of an Infirmary. Here at one time the digging got behind hand: burials were slow; and you might see women sitting in the open tents keeping the flies off their dead children, sometimes after decomposition had set in....24

Unable to do anything about the spreading disease, and having been called to go immediately to England, the three apostles bid their loved ones farewell and took passage down the Missouri River in an open flatboat owned by a party of Presbyterian missionaries who were returning to St. Joseph after laboring among the Pawnee Indians. John had no way of knowing that Ann Pitchforth had been stricken by the fever, would soon contract black canker, and was already failing rapidly in her general health.

The journey down the Missouri must have been amicable, for "at St. Joseph the brethren purchased the boat [from the Presbyterian missionaries] and continued their journey, rowing all day and tying up the boat and sleeping on shore at night. They reached Fort Leavenworth before the departure of the Battalion for the West and from those brethren—just then drawing their bounty of forty dollars each from the government—received some assistance to help them on their journey. The brethren of the Battalion were also desirous of sending some means to their families in the wilderness, and Parley P. Pratt was chosen to carry it to them. While he returned to the encampment of the Saints, Elder Taylor and Orson Hyde continued their journey to England, arriving in Liverpool on the 3RD of October." 25

Acting immediately, the brethren divided responsibilities, Elder Hyde taking over the *Star* while John delved into the apostasy. However, a sample of John's droll humor surfaced in a notice he slipped into the next issue of the *Star,* which dealt with the English custom of dropping and adding the letter *h,* making it difficult for them to comprehend the spelling of "Orson Hyde." The notice reads:

> Persons procuring post-office orders to send to us are requested to be particular in giving out our name correctly. Some orders have come payable to "Horse and Hyde," some to "Horson Ide." To avoid giving an incorrect pronunciation of our name, the person wishing to procure an order for us had better write our name on a paper, in a plain legible hand, and present it to the Post Master issuing the order. This will save us trouble. Remember that our name is—ORSON HYDE. 26

John, meanwhile, issued a circular denouncing the activities of Hedlock and his counselors and calling a conference for October 17. By then Elder Pratt had arrived, and the chief offenders, excluding Hedlock, had been disfellowshipped until they could appear before the authorities of the Camp of Israel. Hedlock himself would not meet with the three apostles, but fled to London where he lived out his life in obscurity in company with a prostitute. He was excommunicated at once, after which John wrote the following reflections:

> Elder Hedlock might have occupied a high and exalted situation in the Church, both in time and in eternity; but he has cast from his head the crown—he has dashed from him the cup of mercy, and has bartered the hope of eternal life with crowns, principalities, powers, thrones

and dominions, for the gratification of his own sensual appetite; to feed on husks and straw—to wallow in filth and mire! 27

From October until mid-January 1847 the three brethren labored among the British Saints day and night, everywhere being received with joy as confidence in the Church was restored. Many of the members were rebaptized; new members were added daily; and it was a general time of refreshing made possible through the Spirit of the Lord.

It was during these labors that John received word from Winter Quarters of the passing on October 26 of his sweet wife Ann Pitchforth Taylor. John had loved the woman deeply and sorrowed greatly over her loss. In coming years he remained close to the Pitchforth children and did all in his power to assist them as they matured to adulthood and remained active in the Church for which their mother had sacrificed her life. 28

Near the end of January, after numerous hasty good-byes, John departed from Liverpool in company with Elder Pratt and fourteen emigrating Saints on the ship *America,* though he admitted to having strange presentiments of danger or a shipwreck. Interestingly, before they were hardly out into the Irish Sea they met with a terrible gale which prevented them for nine days from even reaching the Atlantic. Finally returning to Liverpool, a second start was made on February 7TH. During the pleasant voyage of thirty-six days, John was pleased to renew acquaintance with one of his converts from his first mission to England—twenty-two-year-old Sophia Whitaker. She was emigrating to join the Saints with her two sisters, and immediately she and John were drawn to each other. Before the ship made port at New Orleans, John and Sophia were sealed to each other by Elder Parley P. Pratt—Sophia becoming John's twelfth wife. 29

Sophia Whitaker Taylor

CA. 1880

In New Orleans John wrote a letter to the editor of the *Star*, probably still Orson Hyde, giving an account of his recent experiences in the British Isles. He wrote:

As I had no time before I left England, I now wish to say a few words to the Saints. When I was there, in consequence of having so many places to visit, and to travel so extensively, my stay was necessarily short at the various branches; and it made it impossible for me to visit so many places, to form so extensive an acquaintance with the Saints as I should gladly have done had time permitted. If my stay had been longer, I should gladly have spent two, three, or six months more, in order to have visited all the branches and seen the Saints at their homes, for I love the people of God, and delight in the habitations of the righteous. There peace reigns—there reigns the spirit of God—and there is my home. And here I wish to say, that although very much pressed and hurried, I have seldom enjoyed myself better than I did on my late visit to the British churches. I saw an honesty and simplicity which I admired. The Saints seemed to vie with each other in many little acts of kindness and charity which were duly appreciated by me, and which I have taken pleasure in acknowledging. They were esteemed not so much on account of their intrinsic value as for the feelings of those who administered them....

Our arrival in England was very opportune.... Before we left [Council Bluffs], it was revealed to the authorities that the presidency in England was in transgression, and that it was necessary that some of the Twelve should proceed immediately to England.... When Elder Hyde and myself were in New York, and Elder Pratt in Boston, we thought it expedient, rather than to wait two or three days for him, to proceed immediately to Liverpool. We found on our arrival that we had not come any too soon. The teachers of the people were under transgression; they were corrupt: they were acting dishonorably, and dishonestly; stripping the poor of their last pittance, and yet those wanton profligates professed that they were doing the will of God, while they, under a cloak of religion, were reveling in debauchery, drunkenness and fraud! But they have their reward.

Many of the Elders were at a loss what to do. They saw that things were out of order, but how to regulate them they knew not.... They felt a disposition to hope for the best, but it seemed to be hoping against hope; in fact the whole head was sick and the whole heart faint; and had it not been that the Saints were in possession of the eternal principles of truth, and had the testimony of the Spirit, giving them assurance of the truth and verity of this work, they might all have made ship-wreck of faith.

As Elder Pratt and myself journeyed among the churches, we found them generally doing well, rejoiced to see us, and expressing a willingness to follow our advice in all things.... I would here say a word or two to the Saints by way of caution. Because you have been deceived by your former leaders, do not mistrust those you have now, but let them have your confidence and your prayers.... I say again have confidence in your presidency; neither condemn one man for what another has done, neither be afraid of him. Give all good men your confidence; if they betray it, judge them according to that which they have done—not what they may or may not do. It is a devilish principle to be jealous of men who have done no wrong, and to withhold our confidence from those who ought to have our support, merely because it is possible they may abuse it....

Now brethren, as I had not time before I left, I must take the liberty from this side of the ocean, of saying farewell—farewell! and God bless you for ever and ever, worlds without end. Amen. It is a long distance to salute you from, as I am now six thousand miles from you, but I know it will be welcome, for I came more than six thousand miles to see you, and I had to salute my family from your homes. We have yet two thousand miles to go to see our families, and part of that through mobbers, black-legs and murderers, who would gladly take our lives, but we trust in the God of Israel, that He will take us safely through, and that we shall arrive in the camp of Israel in peace, and rejoice in once more meeting our families and friends.

I left the camp in company with my brethren, July 3RD, 1846, and when I return shall have traveled upwards of seventeen thousand miles, three thousand of this was in England, Scotland and Wales. I now feel well in health and spirits, am thankful that so much of my mission is completed, and I bless the name of the God of Israel. 30

From New Orleans the two brethren and the accompanying Saints traveled by the steamship *Patrick Henry* to St. Louis, arriving on March 25, 1847. Elder Pratt parted from them at this point to travel across country to Winter Quarters, while John and the emigrating Saints continued by steamship up the Missouri toward the same destination. At St. Joseph, however, John also took carriage, feeling anxious to reach the camp with some scientific instruments he had purchased in England before the start of the pioneering party for the West. These instruments consisted of two sextants, two barometers, two artificial horizons, one circular reflector, several thermometers and a telescope—to be used by Orson Pratt a few months later as he surveyed and laid out Great

Salt Lake City.

Missing the pioneer camp by just two days, John found them on the Elkhorn, some thirty miles from Winter Quarters, and there he delivered the instruments as well as some money donated by the British Saints. The labors of John and his companions were highly approved by Brigham Young, who heartily welcomed them back to the camp and their families, where—after a detour of seventeen thousand miles—John would again take up the journey westward.

11

TRIALS ON THE TRAIL

"What is that you have dug up, Brother Taylor?"

Glancing up at the precocious Annie Pitchforth, John palmed the small round objects in question. "These, Annie," he responded quietly as he rubbed the dirt from them with the fingers of the same hand that held them, "are potatoes."

"Potatoes?" It was obvious that Annie was finding John's answer difficult to believe. "They look more like the marbles the boys in Nauvoo played with. Or peas, perhaps."

John chuckled. "You're quite right, child. They do look more like peas than potatoes. The trouble is, with the tops of the vines blackened as they are by frost, these will be the largest potatoes we'll be getting."

"Will they taste the same as real potatoes, Father?" his son Joseph James asked.

Slowly John raised to his feet, his eyes surveying the acreage put to crops by Brigham Young's pioneering party. "I hope so," John replied. "I truly do!"

It was now the sixth of October, 1847; he and Parley Pratt had entered the valley with their lead companies the day before, and now the two brethren, with little Annie Pitchforth and John's son in tow, were taking stock of what they had with which to face the coming winter. And part of the problem, John knew, was that despite the evidence of an early frost, absolutely no one knew what sort of a winter the gathering assemblage of Saints might expect.

"Is that corn over there?" Joseph James then asked, pointing to a nearby field that appeared to be mostly stubble.

"Well, son, I'd say that's what it was supposed to be."

"Come on, Annie," Joseph James urged, not noticing his father's discouragement, "I'll race you to the corn!"

With squeals of innocent joy the two children were off across the field as fast as they could run. Parley was already off inspecting another of the carefully platted fields, and so John took his shovel and moved to the split-rail fence that surrounded the entire field, where he perched himself on the top rail.

It had truly been a difficult summer, he thought, as the hot October sun beat down upon him. Yet all in the large company of Saints had willingly endured the rigors of the journey from Winter Quarters because they had expected something better at the end. But instead they had found this—

In the distance Annie squealed shrilly over something or other that Joseph James was doing, and John couldn't help but recall the evening on the trail near the confluence of the South and North Forks of the Platte when the child had turned up missing. John had joined with others in a desperate search, all of them knowing that any number of things might have happened to her. She might have had an accident, slipped into the river, been kidnapped by Pawnees, simply wandered away and gotten lost on the endless prairie—

Fervently John had prayed as he searched, pleading that the Lord spare the child and direct him or another of the searchers to her before it grew full dark—

As the sun set he had been prowling a brushy area at the foot of some sandy bluffs and was crossing a dry wash when the warning whirr of a rattlesnake brought him to an instant halt.

Moving only his eyes he sought the location of the snake—and felt his heart practically stop as he discovered not only the large reptile but little Annie as well, crouching by a bush in the bottom of the wash, poking the big snake with a stick.

In anger the snake's massive body—as big around as John's muscled forearm—curled into a threatening coil, its head moving back and forth as it regarded its small tormentor. Then, before John could even react, the snake had struck! Its mouth yawed wide and the white fangs lashed out—to fall inches short of their intended victim. Annie had giggled and prodded at the snake again, giggling more as it recoiled for another vicious strike.

Kicking sand at the snake, John had grabbed Annie up and stepped back, then watched as the reptile slithered away into the brush. Hurrying back to camp, he had come close to scolding the child, asking if she didn't know that one bite from such a snake could easily kill her.

Annie drew back to gaze at John—she looked so much like her mother, he realized. Wide eyed, she asked in childhood innocence, "It's not a bad thing to die, is it? I'd be with my mommy then. She said she was going to wonderful place where she would be sure to wait for us. She said that's what dying was."

His own heart suddenly breaking, not only because of Annie's sorrow but because so many that he loved were being called upon to suffer so much, John had buried his face in the surprised child's neck and wept.

"I...put flowers on your mother's grave," he had said brokenly when he was finally able to speak.

"I know," Annie had replied matter-of-factly. "Sammy saw you do it and told us he saw you cry. He cried, too, when he told us. Are you our daddy now, Brother Taylor?"

"I am, if you want me to be," John had responded.

"We do. Even Sammy, and he's already full growed—"

"Grown, Annie. Full grown."

"Yes, that's what I meant to say. Sammy and Mary want you for their daddy, too. And I'll always do as you say—"

Now, as John sat on the split-rail fence watching the frail little girl at play with Joseph James, he found himself grieving anew— not just for Ann and Annie but for himself, for Sammy, Mary, Mercy, and Sarah Pitchforth; for Leonora and her children; for Parley and his loved ones—for every one of the fifteen hundred and fifty-three souls who had followed the two apostles west to the valley. They had come in faith, all thousand and a half of them, with their six hundred wagons, more than two thousand oxen, horses, almost a thousand cows (many of which of necessity had seen service under the yoke as oxen had died or been stolen by the Indians), plus sheep, scores of chickens, and goodness only knew how many pigs, as they had been multiplying all along the way. Yet willingly they had all come westward, not to explore and plant and leave again as had Brigham's pioneers had planned to, but to settle, to establish homes, and to begin to build up this desolate valley as a Zion unto their God!

It had been a difficult journey, too, with conflicts arising over leadership of the huge throng that had only been settled, strangely enough, when he and Parley had captured, broken, and finally ridden back to camp two stray and half-wild mares. More strange, that had occurred earlier on the same day that little Annie had attacked her rattlesnake. Dubbed the "cowboy apostles" because of their exploits, his and Parley's surprising actions had brought grudging respect from the recalcitrants, and from that day forward there had been no further questioning of their leadership.

Of course there had still been plenty of questions—where to camp, what to eat, where to find fuel and water, who to do what tasks, when to sleep, when to arise, which trails to follow, how to treat the Indians—the questions, and therefore the decisions to be made, had never seemed to end and neither had the tortuous trail. From their staging area on the Elkhorn, they had plodded westward along the north side of the Platte and the Loupe Fork to Grand Island, then on to the confluence with the South Fork and still onward along the North Platte to Chimney Rock and beyond to Fort Laramie. Northwest then they had traveled to the Mormon-built ferry at the last crossing of the North Platte, then past Devil's Gate and along the Sweetwater to South Pass. From there the passage had been dry until they had reached the Big Sandy, which they had followed to its confluence with the Green; then onward still to Church Butte and old Fort Bridger, on down Echo Canyon to the Weber, then up and over Hogs Back Ridge to Camp Clayton and Mormon Flat; on up again over Big Mountain and down to Birch Spring and Camp Grant; then up one last time over Little Mountain to Last Camp and then down past Donner Hill and through Emigration Canyon into the Valley of the Great Salt Lake.

The impossibly large company had begun their journey on the 21ST and 22ND of June and had traveled in anything but a leisurely fashion throughout the entire summer and fall, putting up with all the normal and abnormal rigors of the trail, holding regular religious services every Sabbath, attending to their prayers morning and evening at the sound of the Nauvoo Bell, assisting and sharing willingly as individual supplies had run low, and all of them daily looking forward to their arrival in the valley. There, they had been told by their leaders, they would find peace; and there, they had also been told, they would find crops ready for the harvest and homes ready for habitation against the snows and cold of a high-mountain winter.

And some of what they had been told, John had to admit, had turned out to be true. Orson Pratt, using the instruments John had brought from England the previous spring, had surveyed the future city, dividing it into ten-acre blocks separated by enormously wide streets. The pioneers had also partially completed a ten-acre stockade, with houses of adobe and log forming a continuous wall around its perimeter. Though nowhere near large enough, both John and Parley had approved of it, as had the members of their camp. There also seemed to be plenty of peace, though who knew what dangers might be lurking in the surrounding hills? It was the condition of the planted crops in the nearby fenced field, however, that all of them had found most troubling—that were not as they had been told they would be.

Silently many of the Saints had already walked through cornfields that hadn't had time before the frost to come into tassel, their stubby stalks stripped bare of leaves by huge, black crickets with strange-looking tails. Neither had any of the other vegetables planted by the Pioneers had time to mature. Beans, squash, peas, melons, carrots, cabbage, turnips—all were complete failures! Clouds of the voracious crickets had dispersed before the Saints from a stripped field of buckwheat that had never even come to head. Everywhere the people looked seemed as desolation, and now both apostles knew without speaking that the rapidly coming winter would find their thousand and a half trusting Saints once again barely subsisting off their already depleted, two-year-old stores, perhaps dying of starvation, and certainly doing their level best to fight off the black canker with whatever bit of nourishment these tiny pellets of new potatoes such as he held in his hand might provide.

Well, John thought wryly as he dropped them onto the hard-packed earth, slapped the dirt on his hands against his trousers, and then ran his somewhat clean fingers through his very unwashed hair, if he and the Saints couldn't eat, they could at least get started on the additional twenty acres of stockade and cabins they were going to need.

With a sigh of resignation, John replaced his bedraggled hat and slid wearily off the mostly useless fence. Parley and the two children were calling him, and well he knew there was no longer time to sit on a fence dreaming—1

The biggest dilemma John Taylor and Parley P. Pratt faced once they had returned from their mission to England was deciding how to explain to the people the changes that had occurred in the plans for continued westward movement. "When Taylor left for England, everything had been arranged: An advance party under Bishop George Miller would winter at Grand Island, 250 miles along the way, plant crops next spring for emigrants to harvest, then the Miller company would push on to the Great Basin. Another company would try to cross the Rockies that fall, but, if unable to, would winter at Fort Laramie, plant crops there in the spring, and move on. With the way 'now prepared,' Taylor reported in the *Millennial Star,* emigrant companies who followed would find

> the roads, bridges and ferry boats made; there are stopping places also on the way, where they can rest, obtain vegetables and corn, and when they arrive at the far end, instead of finding a wild waste, they will meet with friends, provisions, and a home. 2

Instead, the two apostles were stunned to discover that the advance parties had been recalled to Winter Quarters. Regardless of the reasons, this meant there were no crops being planted at Fort Laramie or Grand Island or in the Great Basin; no roads, bridges, or ferries being built; and no houses or provisions awaiting the westward-moving Saints once they arrived in the Great Basin. Everything now depended on the pioneering party of Brigham Young—144 young men and three women who had been hand-picked to make a dash to the mountains where they could make necessary preparations for those, under John, Parley P. Pratt, and others, who would follow.

The difficulty with this was that Brigham had chosen the slowest route, choosing to blaze a new trail along the rugged north side of the Platte River instead of taking the already established, relatively easy trail along the south side. Additionally, while the Indians on the south side were friendly and at peace, those on the north side of the Platte—the Pawnee—were still wild and warlike and had to be watched constantly. Already, in fact, they had slain one brother, and according to reports, much livestock had also been stolen.

Of course, Brigham had his reasons, but the journey that all thought could be accomplished in thirty-five days was already stretching out; the reports coming back to Winter Quarters indicated that it would now take twice that long just to reach Fort Laramie.

Still, John and Parley had it to do, so with characteristic enthusiasm they began organizing the company, sending all those who qualified as being prepared on to the Elkhorn to await departure.

The plan of organization for traveling was to divide the people into companies of one hundred wagons, subdivided into companies of fifty wagons, and ten wagons, with captains over each division, the captains of fifties being subordinate to captains of hundreds, and captains of tens being subordinate to captains of fifties—all being subject to the direction of the Apostles. Each fifty had a blacksmith with tools for repairing wagons and shoeing animals. Three hundred pounds of breadstuff were required for each person. Every man had to have a gun with one hundred rounds of ammunition; and each family was expected to take along its proportion of seed grain and agricultural implements. 3

Gradually six hundred wagons gathered together, ready to start. There were 1553 individuals in the company, 2213 oxen, 124 horses, 887 cows, 358 sheep, 716 chickens, and a number of pigs.

On the 21ST and 22ND of June this large company began its journey. It was late in the season for starting on such an expedition. It was too late for them to put in crops that season, even if they stopped far short of the eastern base of the Rocky Mountains. They barely had provisions to last them a year and a half, and if their first crop failed, starvation must follow, for they would be from ten to fifteen hundred miles from the nearest point where food could be obtained, and no swifter means of transportation than horse or ox teams!

It was a bold undertaking, this moving over fifteen hundred souls—more than half of whom were women and children—into an unknown country, through hostile tribes of savages. Had it not been for the assurance of the support and protection of Jehovah, it would have been not only a bold but a reckless movement—the action of madmen. But as it was, the undertaking was a sublime evidence of their faith in God and their leaders.

This company differed from the pioneers. The latter was made up of able-bodied men, excepting three women—none were helpless. They had the best of teams, and if they failed in finding a place of settlement they could return to the place of starting. Meantime their families were not endangered. They were secure at Winter Quarters. Not so with the Pratt and Taylor company. They had their all upon the altar, including their wives and children, who must share their hardships and their fate. They knew not their destination, they entrusted all on a single venture, from which there was no chance of retreat. If they should fail to find a suitable location and raise a crop the first season, there was no getting provisions to them, nor them to provisions. They must succeed, or perish in the wilderness to which they had started. With a faith that has never been surpassed, they placed themselves under the guidance and protection of their God, and we shall see...that they trusted not in vain. 4

For the next nearly four months, though there were at least 1553 individual and even memorable experiences each and every day— experiences such as little Annie Pitchforth's encounter with the rattlesnake—not a great deal happened to the camp as a whole that was worthy of note. One night several companies were nearly run under by stampeding cattle startled into running by a herd boy in another company, and all, including John and Parley, helped to re-gather most of them, though forty-five of the oxen vanished forever. On another occasion, as mentioned in the beginning of the chapter, John and Parley, who had both been without a saddle horse the entire journey, managed to rope and then ride back to camp two stray mares that had grown wild and unruly. Amazed by the apostles' cowboying skills, the incident had the effect of quieting a great deal of grumbling among certain of the brethren who thought others were more qualified to lead.

One other incident worthy of note occurred on what was known as the Upper Crossing of the Sweetwater, east of South Pass, between three and four hundred miles east of the Salt Lake Valley. There, on a morning in early September when it had snowed three inches and was threatening more, causing all sorts of worry throughout the company over what sort of climate they were heading into, John Taylor's company encountered Brigham Young and the returning pioneers on the road back to Winter Quarters.

That band of men had entered the Salt Lake Valley, selected a site for a city, commenced the erection of a fort, plowed several acres of land and planted late crops; and having left a few of their number with some members of the Mormon Battalion who had joined them there to continue the work, they were now on their way back to Winter Quarters with the glad news that a gathering place had been selected for Israel. 5

As John, Parley, and others from both groups gathered in council, to Parley's surprise he was chastised rather severely by the president of his quorum. He details the matter as follows:

> A council was called, in which I was highly censured and chastened by President Young and others. This arose in part from some defect in the organization under my superintendence at the Elk Horn, and in part from other misunderstandings on the road. I was charged with neglecting to observe the order of organization entered into under the superintendence of the President before he left the camps at Winter Quarters; and of variously interfering with previous arrangements. In short, I was severely reproved and chastened. I no doubt deserved this chastisement; and I humbled myself, acknowledged my faults and errors, and asked forgiveness. I was frankly forgiven, and, bidding each other farewell, each company passed on their way. This school of experience made me more humble and careful in the future, and I think it was the means of making me a wiser and better man ever after. 6

It is not known whether John received the same sort of chastisement. Meanwhile, during the council and as the weather had cleared and become warm and sunny, the sisters of John's company had been curiously active. "There was a nervous activity in the camp, mysterious movements among the sisters. Trunks that had been undisturbed on the journey were opened, their contents investigated and certain articles hurriedly conveyed to a beautiful, natural lawn enclosed by a dense growth of bushes. Several improvised tables of uncommon length, covered with snow-white linen, and fast being burdened with glittering tableware, gave evidence that a surprise was in store for the weary pioneers. The 'fatted calf' was killed; game and fish were prepared in abundance; fruits, jellies and relishes reserved for special occasions were brought out until truly it was a royal feast.

"Moreover, though the place selected for the spread was adjacent to the camp, it was successful as a surprise. The pioneers knew nothing of what had taken place until they were led by Elder Taylor through a natural opening in the bushes fringing the enclosure, and the grand feast burst upon their astonished vision.

"One hundred and thirty sat down at the supper; and if for a moment rising emotions at this manifestation of love choked their utterance and threatened to blunt the edge of appetite, the danger soon passed under the genial influence of the sisters who waited upon the tables and pressed their guests to eat: in the end they paid a full and hearty compliment to the culinary skill of the sisters.

"Supper over and cleared away, preparations were made for dancing; and soon was added to the sweet confusion of laughter and cheerful conversation the merry strains of the violin, and the strong, clear voice of the prompter directing the dancers through the mazes of quadrilles, Scotch-reels, French-fours and other figures of harmless dances suitable to the guileless manners and the religious character of the participants. Dancing was interspersed with songs and recitations. 'We felt mutually edified and blessed,' writes Elder Taylor, 'we praised the Lord and blessed one another.' So closed a pleasant day, though the morning with its clouds and snow [had] looked very unpromising."[7]

With morning the pioneer company departed eastward, while the Pratt-Taylor company continued west, finally knowing with certainty their ultimate destination. Parley P. Pratt described the remainder of their journey as follows:

After bidding farewell to the President and pioneers, and

to my own brother, Orson Pratt, who was one of them, we continued our journey; and after many toils, vexations and trials, such as breaking wagons, losing cattle, upsetting, etc., we arrived in the Valley of Great Salt Lake.... Here we found a fort commenced and partly built by the pioneers, consisting of an enclosure of a block of ten acres with a wall, or in part of buildings of adobes or logs. We also found a city laid out and a public square dedicated for a Temple of God. We found also much ground planted in late crops, which, however, did not mature, being planted late in July; although there were obtained for seed a few small potatoes, from the size of a pea upward to that of half an inch in diameter. These being sound and planted another year produced some very fine potatoes, and, finally, con- tributed mainly in seeding the territory with that almost indispensable article of food.

After we had arrived on the ground of Great Salt Lake City we pitched our tents by the side of a spring of water; and, after resting a little, I devoted my time chiefly to building temporary houses, putting in crops, and obtaining fuel from the mountains. 8

One assumes that John Taylor did the same.

12

PETITIONING POWER FROM HEAVEN

"It isn't right, John, and you know it!" Leonora Taylor was standing at the tailgate of one of the wagons, grinding bran and shorts for another of their seemingly endless meals of gruel. "A woman's body needs more than gruel and stringy beef, particularly when she's expecting a child!"

John grunted to himself but continued without comment to shape a beam for use in one of the three apartment-homes he was building for his families. Those homes were a project, too, taking up ninety feet of one wall of the new fort. All morning he'd spent in the bottom of the saw pit, whipsawing logs into lumber with young George Whitaker. And though he'd worn a net against the sawdust, still the finer dust had sifted through and into his eyes, nose, and mouth, choking off his breathing and causing him to go about half blind. This work, though, was a little better, for he was seated, there was no sawdust, and he was working his adze to square the beam for a better fit. Of course, young George had stayed fresh throughout the morning, but then he hadn't been in the bottom of the pit or forty years old, either one—

"John, I asked you a question!"

"No you didn't, Nora. You made a comment." This time John smiled up at his wife, hoping that she would see that he was only

teasing. "But of course you are right. That was a stringy old cow."
Now John chuckled. "For a fact, when I was butchering her she was
so pitifully without fat that I thought I would be forced to grease
the saw and knife."

"That wasn't a bit funny!"

"Of course it wasn't," John continued in fun. "It was the gospel's
own truth is what it was."

Pausing for a breather from his work on the beam, John
surveyed from his perch the new addition to the stockade the
pioneers had started. Three times the size of the first ten-acre fort,
this one, tacked onto the south end of the old one, enclosed a full
thirty acres. Of course that was more than enough for the sixteen
hundred people now in the valley. The thing was, with spring thousands more would be leaving Winter Quarters, and by fall they, too,
would need secure homes and space for their children.

The stockade was a good design, too, he thought as he
stretched the tired, aching muscles of his body, taking care not to
strain his still-tender hip and thigh where the Carthage mob's bullet had torn away so much flesh. The back walls of houses formed
the outer walls of the stockade, all of them built either of adobe
brick or notched logs. The only openings in those outer walls were
loopholes for defense, for as yet no one knew the true disposition
of the local Lamanites. Of course young George Bean and some of
the others were already communicating by sign with a few, and
George was even picking up their language—a sign that the Lord
had gifted him for it. George and the others swore that the small,
dark-skinned people were peaceful, and they might just be right.
But what about the others some had seen in the mountains while
cutting wood—taller, more commanding in appearance, and
mounted on fine looking horses? Were they also friendly?

Of course, John didn't know, but neither was it worth the risk
of finding out the hard way. Better to be prepared, he thought, with
a solid stockade inside which they could all be protected.

So, the back walls of the houses lined the outside, their roofs all sloping down toward the center of the stockade. And on the inner walls were the doors and only windows, for all side walls were merely partitions between one house and the next. That didn't do much for complete privacy, John knew, but for now it was the best that any of them could do.

His three homes would even have doors between the partitions so the family could go back and forth without having to go outside to do it. He had whipsawed four-inch beams from the center of each of his logs, and these beams formed the framework of his homes. The outer slabs would be laid up as the exterior walls, and the planks cut from around the center beams would form the inner walls and floors—a rare luxury which he thought well worth the extra effort. He was also going to plaster the inner walls with a fine white clay one of the brethren had located nearby, and this would make his homes among the finest in the fort—

"John," Leonora pressed, "what are you going to do about Sophia and Jane? Both of them are big with child, you know. They need greens, vegetables, fresh food. Sophia, in particular, is filled with cravings—a certain sign that she isn't getting enough of what her baby needs."

Leonora was speaking of Sophia Whitaker, George's younger sister, and Jane Ballantyne, his plural wife Ann Ballantyne's sister. Both of these young women were also John's plural wives, and both would be delivering John's children before the next spring. He was also courting Sophia's sister, Harriet, though no decision had yet been made about whether she would be joining his large family. Of course all his plural wives, as they became pregnant, adopted the fiction of being married to absent missionaries, though among the Saints pretty much everyone was coming to understand the truth. And both Jane and Sophia wanted the houses done before they gave birth, though John was of the firm opinion that it wouldn't matter all that much. Besides, their children one day would likely boast of having been born in a covered wagon—

"My goodness, John, where is your mind today?" Leonora was clearly exasperated, and immediately John felt badly that he had brought her to this. "Are you like most other men," his agitated wife continued, "caring only about getting a baby started and then leaving everything else to the woman? Your wives have desperate needs, John, and you're responsible for doing something about it!"

"Nora," John finally breathed, holding his voice down but looking directly at his wife, "what you say is true, all of it, and the situation haunts me day and night. The thought of one or both of those babies being born defective in mind or body—well, I couldn't bear to be the cause of it. The trouble is, I have no idea what to do for the girls—them or any of the other expectant mothers in the camp."

"Have you inquired of the Lord?" Leonora's voice was now much softer and more tender.

"I have," John replied bleakly. "The fact is, all of us—men, women, and especially children—need fresh food of some sort, at least if we're to avoid the scurvy this winter. Parl' and I have even discussed sending an express over the mountains to California, our best and only chance at buying up fresh food. The trouble with that idea is that the Battalion boys here in camp barely got over the Sierras ahead of the snows, and they swear there's no way to get back across before snow-melt in the spring."

"What does the Lord tell you?" Leonora, a woman of great faith, seemed adamant that only therein lay the answer. "Have you and Elder Pratt approached him together?"

"We have, Nora. Just yesterday, in fact. We rode to the top of that round hill yonder, the one some folks are calling Ensign Peak. There we clothed ourselves in the robes of the priesthood and sought the Lord, just as Brother Joseph taught us back in Nauvoo. The tops of the mountains, he told us, are temples to the Lord God when his people are in poverty, and that we were to use them as such."

Instantly Leonora's eyes filled with tears. "Oh, John, dear, I had no idea! I...I'm sorry I have been troubling you so—"

"You've no reason to apologize, darling, and every reason in the world to be concerned. The thing is, I feel very ambivalent about the answer we were given."

"But...why?"

John shook his head. "Because all we could get through the whisperings of the Spirit, Nora, was to be at peace. The Lord seemed to be telling us that since He brought us here, the problem was His, and He would take care of it in His own way."

"Well, with all my heart I hope He hurries!"

"So do I," John breathed fervently. "So do I—"1

As one studies the life of this humble servant of God, one is struck by the number of times when the Lord did open doors and provide directions and/or blessings in accordance with his prayerful requests. Such an answer came as a result of the desperate need of the Saints for fresh vegetables and nutrients. Not long after the Saints' arrival in the valley, George Bean approached John in company with an elderly Indian whom Bean declared to be a Goshute medicine man. According to Bean, "the Goshutes were camped at the hot springs at the north end of the valley, where they were being ravaged by measles. This white man's disease, for which they had no immunity, was killing them by the dozens. The skills of the medicine man were ineffective, the waters of the hot springs didn't help, and he had come seeking stronger medicine. Yellow Bird, twelve-year-old son of Chief Little Face and his father's favorite child, was deathly sick. The Lamanites had heard of miraculous cures effected by the Mormonites with the laying on of hands. Would Brother Taylor cure the sick boy?

"Taylor agreed to try. He went out for a horse and found...

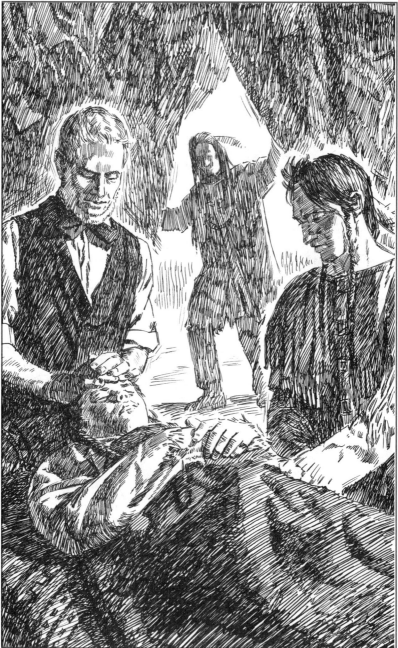

Illustration by Robert T. Barrett

George Whitaker.... When Taylor asked if he'd like to help administer to Yellow Bird, Whitaker was dubious. Did Brother John realize the responsibility? If the child died, he'd be blamed, and there could be Indian trouble. However, Whitaker said, he'd come along and assist if Brother John wished.

"Taylor advised him to keep on with [his other tasks]. Faith healing depended upon faith, and he didn't want anyone to assist with reservations. Young Bean could help with the ordinance.

At the Lamanite encampment, sick Indians were soaking in the hot springs, while about thirty corpses with their dogs lay about the pools; except for killing their dogs, the Indians had been too overwhelmed by the epidemic to take care of their dead. Taylor told Bean to get a detail of men to attend to the burial, as soon as they got back to the fort.

The medicine man took them to the wickiup of Chief Little Face. As he opened the flap the shaft of light caused a cry of pain from the sick boy within. The chief and two squaws sat by Yellow Bird, whose eyes were red-rimmed and body splotched with patches of ugly rash. His quick breathing came in wheezing gasps, broken by a dry cough.

Bean anointed the boy's head with consecrated oil, then both men laid hands on the fever-flushed head while Taylor administered a healing blessing. The following morning Bean took a detail of men to bury the dead Lamanites, and on returning reported that Yellow Bird was considerably better. Several days later Chief Little Face and Yellow Bird arrived with several braves to offer gifts of appreciation—deerskin moccasins and gloves, together with sego lily and camus bulbs, thistle roots, sunflower seeds, pine nuts, wild honey, and a bag of meal which had the rich flavor of cracklings. Taylor accompanied them to the places where the bulbs and thistle roots could be dug up; and he returned with the comfortable knowledge that it needn't be a winter of famine after all. The Saints could live off the land, just as the Indians did. Their vegetables grew wild; their meat was to be had for the hunting. 2

It is interesting to note that while the Indian food—particularly the meal—lasted, the pregnant women in John's family did quite well. When it was gone they were "once again... gnawed by persistent yearning." John and George Bean returned to the Goshute camp to learn the secret of the meal. Willingly the chief took them to where a harvest was being conducted—a wheat field planted by the pioneers that hadn't matured. With lighted torches the Indians encircled the field, then set the dried grain afire. As it burned, "millions of crickets leaped up and fell back into the flames. The Indians moved across the blackened ground, collecting the roasted crickets in baskets. Then at their village the squaws ground the insects into meal with stones and mixed it with honey for the delicious cakes.

"[John] took some of the fresh meal home for his pregnant wives. While he knew that John the Baptist had lived on locusts and honey, he found his own appetite for the fare gone. However, if Sophia and Jane craved it, what they didn't know wouldn't hurt them." 3

With the failure of that first year's crops, the needs of the Pratt-Taylor company were in some ways simplified. With nothing but tiny potatoes to harvest for the next year's seed, and wild bulbs to dig once they learned the need and the knack, all their energies could be put to planting winter crops for the next spring and enlarging the fort and building habitations in preparation for the winter that was upon them. John wrote of his experiences:

Our houses... were built on the outside line [of the fort] in shanty form, with the highest wall outside, the roof sloping towards the interior. The windows and doors were placed on the side facing the enclosure, the outside being left solid, excepting loop holes—for protection. Our corrals, hay-stacks and stables were some distance behind and outside the fort.

About Christmas, I had put up, enclosed and covered about ninety feet of building made of split logs, out of which was taken a four-inch plank. The plank was used for partitions, etc.,…. In addition to this, I had built corrals and stables behind, and enclosed a garden spot in front, with a board-rail fence. I assisted in all this labor of sawing, building, hauling, etc.,—enough for one fall. 4

Neither did John and his brethren neglect their ecclesiastical duties. Before they departed for Winter Quarters, Brigham Young and the other apostles then present had organized a stake of Zion, calling John Smith, the Prophet Joseph's uncle, as stake president. Because they had, as yet, no place to worship, services on the Sabbath, and even occasionally on weekday evenings, were held in the private residences of the leading elders. "All through that winter Elder Taylor was diligent in that labor, going from house to house to instruct the Saints. Meetings for his own family were frequently called, and there he taught them how to live in peace, to be courteous, kind and considerate of each other's feelings." 5

On November 28, President Smith, with the approval of the presiding apostles, called for a day when the Saints were to repent of any past sins and to renew their covenants through re-baptism. Both John and Elder Pratt stepped forth to set the example, most of the rest of the Saints responded to this call, and it was reported that the Spirit of God rested upon the people in great power. 6

Immediately after this, John, Elder Pratt, and some other brethren went on a fishing and exploring expedition to the south. John with his wood-turning skills had constructed the boat, and his wives had labored together spinning a hundred-foot seine, or net, to be used on the lake. 7 Elder Pratt records:

> Some time in December, having finished sowing wheat and rye, I started, in company with a Brother Higby and others, for Utah Lake with a boat and fish net. We travelled some thirty miles with our boat, etc., on an ox wagon, while some of us rode on horseback. This distance brought us to the foot of Utah Lake, a beautiful sheet of fresh water, some thirty-six miles long by fifteen broad. Here we launched our boat and tried our net, being probably the first boat and net ever used on this sheet of water in modern times.
>
> We sailed up and down the lake shore on its western side for many miles, but had only poor success in fishing. We, however, caught a few samples of mountain trout and other fish.
>
> After exploring the lake and valley for a day or two the company returned home, and a Brother Summers and myself struck westward from the foot of the lake on horseback, on an exploring tour. On this tour we discovered and partly explored Cedar Valley, and there crossed over the west mountain range and discovered a valley beyond; passing through which we crossed a range of hills northward, and entered Tooele Valley. Passing still northward, we camped one night on a bold mountain stream, and the next day we came to the southern extreme of Great Salt Lake, and passing round between it and the west mountain we journeyed in an eastern course, and, crossing the Jordan, arrived in Salt Lake City—having devoted nearly one week to our fishing, hunting and exploring expedition. During all this time we had fine weather and warm days; but the night we arrived home was a cold one, with a severe snow

storm. And thus closed the year 1847. 8

Like Elder Pratt, John said little about that first Christmas, but as the New Year approached, he was faced with a dilemma. It seems that while on the trail to the valley, the members of the camp had covenanted not to hold any dances until after their first harvest. In their society and community, because there were no others, such covenants were considered to be law. Of course they had not known there would be no harvest that fall, but there hadn't been, and now their covenant presented a legal difficulty. On New Year's Day, 1848, John recorded how he and his family had solved the problem—revealing not only his wisdom but his respect for the Lord's revealed lines of authority. He writes:

> As today was New Year's Day, several of my family spoke to me about having a party as usual upon that day. The plan they proposed getting it up on was that every one should bring his own provisions. The principle itself was repugnant to me, but still under the circumstances, if we had a party, this must be the principle we must have it on, as I could not possibly spare provisions for so large a company as we must necessarily have; and upon this plan there was one gotten up. We had an excellent supper, sixty-nine sat down and we enjoyed ourselves very much. I gave the presidency to Brother Sherwood. I sat at the head of one table, Brother Hunter at another, Brother Horne and Shurtliff at others. After the tables were cleared, the order was given for dancing. My reasons for indulging in this recreation were that Brother Shurtliff went up and saw Uncle John Smith...and told him that we had made calculations upon having a dance; but when I heard there was a law against it, I was resolved not to have any unless Uncle John should say I was justified in doing it. He said if he was me he would have the dance as it had been arranged for.

I sent to Uncle John to see about this, not because I thought there was any harm in dancing, but because I did not wish to encourage law-breaking by my example in this thing. There was an intermission in the dancing when we had some singing and a comic sermon from Brother Sherwood, after which dancing was resumed and continued until a little after eleven o'clock. Brother Sherwood called the house to order and told them the time had come to separate; but before parting he had a few remarks to make. He spoke on a variety of principles and made some very good remarks. Upon his concluding I arose and made some remarks upon the object of our meeting, my object in having dancing, on the principles of power existing in the kingdom, and the active part we are destined to take in the affairs of kingdoms. 9

Perhaps by chance, that first winter in the valley was unusually dry and warm. Though it stormed in the mountains all around them, the valley was usually clear of snow, and as the days warmed in late February and early March, the brethren assumed that the climate was wonderful and went to planting their spring gardens. Then— and it turned out that this was typical—the warm weather turned to rain and then to snow, which fell more than a foot deep before the temperatures dropped and turned everything back to winter. Stunned and dismayed, the Saints did what they could to endure severely leaking roofs, vermin by the thousands that also sought the indoors, and the worsening shortage of food. John even proposed a tax on those who had food, to be administered by the High Council, to help those who were in need—with the High Council to decide who got taxed and who got helped.

Weeks later, when the real spring finally arrived, everyone replanted. But now, of course, the harvest would be delayed, and the anxious Saints continued to subsist on what little food they had available. It became a season of starvation for many. Parley P. Pratt, whose experiences were common to John Taylor and most of the others, wrote:

We had to struggle against great difficulties in trying to mature a first crop. We had not only the difficulties and inexperience incidental to an unknown and untried climate, but also swarms of insects equal to the locusts of Egypt, and also a terrible drought, while we were entirely inexperienced in the art of irrigation; still we struggled on, trusting in God.

During this spring and summer my family and myself, in common with many of the camp, suffered much for want of food. This was the more severe on me and my family because we had lost nearly all our cows, and the few which were spared to us were dry, and, therefore, we had no milk to help out our provisions. I had ploughed and subdued land to the amount of near forty acres, and had cultivated the same in grain and vegetables. In this labor every woman and child in my family, so far as they were of sufficient age and strength, had joined to help me, and had toiled incessantly in the field, suffering every hardship which human nature could well endure. Myself and some of them were compelled to go with bare feet for several months, reserving our Indian moccasins for extra occasions. We toiled hard and lived on a few greens and on thistle and other roots. We had some-times a little flour and some cheese, and sometimes we were able to procure from our neighbors a little sour skimmed milk or buttermilk.

In this way we lived and raised our first crop in these valleys. And how great was our joy in partaking of the first fruits of our industry. 10

In August the Saints held a harvest feast to celebrate the fact that they had not only survived their first year, but prospered. That they had, and would continue to do so, was attested to by a General Wilson who came to the valley during the fall of 1849 to entreat the Saints to join with California in forming a large state which they could then subdivide at a later date. John, Charles C. Rich, and Orson Spencer met with the general and agreed to the idea, which would have saved them terrible troubles with the government in later years. Except their letter of agreement, sent to California, was detained by a snowstorm, and in the meantime California had made other plans which excluded the Saints and their territory, stopping statehood in its tracks.

Meanwhile, General Wilson had written Senator Truman Smith of Connecticut regarding the Saints' marvelous accomplishments. That worthy, in a speech delivered in the U.S. Senate on July 8, 1850, read excerpts from the general's letter; to wit:

A more orderly, earnest, industrious and civil people, I have never been among than these, and it is incredible how much they have done here in the wilderness in so short a time. In this city which contains about from four to five thousand inhabitants, I have not met in a citizen a single idler, or any person who looks like a loafer. Their prospects for crops are fair, and there is a spirit and energy in all that you see that cannot be equaled in any city of any size that I have ever been in, and I will add, not even in old Connecticut. 11

The winter of 1848–49, with Brigham Young and approximately five thousand additional Saints in the valley, was roughly the same as the first one. Times remained difficult, and on many occasions the majority of the people subsisted on the food that for untold generations had fed the Indians. Yet the city was indeed growing, and the foundation which John and Elder Pratt and their company had helped to lay was beginning to support a great commonwealth.

13

FAILURE IN A SWEET ENDEAVOR

"Yes, Brother John, this is it. The factory building that Brother Truman Angell designed to house your sugar machinery."

In wonder John Taylor gazed at the large building. He recalled having once asked Brigham for a building like the carpenter shop on Temple Square—a much smaller building than the one he was looking at—and Brigham's sharp retort: that he might as well take the whole territory. Yet here was this facility built at Brigham's direction, and still the project had failed. It was located on the Church farm southeast of the city, and despite having never manufactured an ounce of sugar, the people were already calling the place Sugar House—a name he supposed was going to stick.

Ahh, the vagaries of life—

"Well, Phillip," he said with a wry smile, "if building size had anything to do with it, our sugar business should have been a resounding success."

Phillip De LaMare nodded soberly. "It should have been a resounding success for many reasons," he responded quietly. "I still find myself wondering that it wasn't. Do you recollect that night on the trail, Brother John? When I was engaged in hauling the sugar machinery to the valley in those forty Santa Fe wagons, and you stopped to stay the night with me? You intimated at that time that it seemed there were forces opposed to us that we were not aware of. Do you still feel that way?"

"More than ever, Phillip. I have pondered much over our resounding failure at making sugar, and I can lay it to no other source: Satan, or those who serve him in this world, was behind our struggles, and I believe I understand why."

"How did you get involved with the sugar industry in the first place, Father?" George Taylor, John's eldest son, who had just returned from New York with his father, had until then sat his horse quietly listening. "And what sorts of opposition did you encounter? I recall your announcement in conference following your return from France that we would soon have sugar in the territory, and yet none has ever been produced."

"In fact," De LaMare added quietly, "there won't be any, for Brother Brigham has already dismantled the machinery and taken parts away for use in other manufacturing ventures."

John chuckled. "Interesting, isn't it." Calmly he turned his horse and with the others began the slow ride back to the city. "But therein, George, lies a tale, which if you would like, Phillip and I will relate."

"I should like that very much, Father."

"It began, I suppose, in a meeting of the Twelve and the First Presidency before I went on my mission to France; 1849, I believe it was. We were discussing the atrocious cost of things imported into the valley and how to set up home manufacturing for such things. It was brought up by someone—Brother Brigham, I believe—that the freight alone on the sugar the Saints in Zion needed annually was $45,000. That figure stuck with me. Then while I was laboring in France I received several communications from the President asking me to keep my eyes open for industries that might be imported and established in the valley.

"One day a brother came into the office and announced that he was a sugar maker and desired to emigrate to Zion. Believing his appearance to be providential, I immediately launched an investigation into the feasibility of reproducing the vaunted sugar beet industry of Europe in Utah."

"I was already acquainted with you father, as I had donated a portion of my means to see the Book of Mormon translated and published in French and German," Phillip interjected. "I offered to assist Brother John in his investigation."

"We were also assisted by your Uncle Mollenhauer," John added, "because he had labored for a time in a sugar manufacturing plant in England."

"Yes, and Curtis Bolton, one of the missionaries."

"Ahh," John sighed, "poor Brother Bolton. I fear that I nearly ran his legs off during our investigation. I am certain that I wore out his boots, and I know he went to bed for a week when I finally allowed it.

"Still, George, we learned what we could," John went on, addressing his son. "We visited the sugar-making plant at Arras, after which both Phillip and Mollenhauer remained there to learn the business while I went to Germany to gather up the German translation of the Book of Mormon I had arranged to have done there."

"The French manufacturers at Arras appeared most cooperative," Phillip added as they continued their horses at a walk toward the city. "They gave us every specification and plan for building our own sugar manufacturing plant here in the valley."

"After returning to Arras," John continued, "I took these two brethren with me to England, where we established a joint stock company to fund the purchase and shipment of machinery we would need to manufacture sugar here in the valley."

"We named it the Deseret Manufacturing Company," Phillip added quietly. "The DMC. I now call it the Damn Miserable Company."

"Yes," John nodded, "that seems an appropriate title, all right. I subscribed for $10,000 of stock; Phillip here for $5,000; Captain Joseph Russell, a ship-builder who had built Sam Brannan's *Brooklyn*, took $45,000; and Brothers Coward and Collinson each took $5,000. We then contracted with a machinery manufacturing company in Liverpool—Fawcett-Preston & Company—to build our machinery, for which we paid them $12,500 in cash."

"That seems a great deal of money!"

"It was, George, and it was only the beginning." Phillip's look was serious. "Russell and I sailed on ahead to New Orleans and up the river to Kanesville, near Council Bluffs, where Russell went to work building the wagons we would need to haul the machinery here to the valley. I, meanwhile, took $6,000 in gold and began scouring the countryside for the six hundred oxen we estimated it would take to pull the heavy wagons."

John nodded his agreement. "Loren Babbitt, a returning missionary, accompanied the 1,200 pounds of sugar beet seed I shipped ahead of us. In England I continued to round up men who could help ship or manufacture sugar. I ended up with about thirty, including L. John Nuttall, who has now married your sister."

George smiled. "Yes, John has told me how you rounded him up."

"I suppose he has. With our sugar machinery we also shipped the machinery to manufacture fine woolens, which I thought would enhance the Saints' lives. I left Brother Nuttall and Brother Elias Morris in charge of accompanying it to New Orleans while I remained behind to finish some other affairs before following them on the steamship *Niagara*."

"It sounds as though everything was going well."

"We thought so, too," Phillip declared, "until the U.S. Internal Revenue office placed an import duty of over $4,000 on the machinery—more than a third of its original cost. Somehow Brother John paid the amount and then secured several paddlewheel steamers to carry the machinery up the river. When he arrived in St. Louis, unfortunately, I was forced to explain that I hadn't found all the oxen because my wife had been ill.

"Your father, George, recommended an interesting solution; he encouraged me to enter into plural marriage with the French maid who had been serving as my wife's nurse. My wife agreed, as did Marie, and your father performed the sealing. Knowing now that both women would care for each other, I re-embarked on my ox hunt."

"And I went ahead of the machinery to Kanesville," John added, "to check on Russell's progress with the wagons."

"Upriver from St. Louis," Phillip continued, "we experienced our third major disaster. A boiler on one of our paddle-wheels exploded, killing twenty-six of our converts and sinking the vessel and our machinery. It took many days to care for the dead and recover the machinery from the bottom of the Missouri, and we were never certain we had it all."

John shook his head. "They were wonderful people that we lost, some my dear friends. My only solace was in knowing that they had entered in at the correct gate and would be well received beyond the veil. Meanwhile, in Kanesville, I was dismayed to find that Russell—no matter that he was a fine ship builder—had done a pathetically poor job of constructing the wagons. I had built wagons myself in years past, so I knew! He had used green lumber, his workmanship was terribly inferior, the wheels and iron-tires were far too narrow and flimsy for loads such as they would be carrying—they would never do for a journey across the plains and mountains to the valley.

"When I spoke to Russell, however, he flew into a rage, reminding me that he owned more stock than I and was ready to take it all and depart. Seeing no good in a shouting match, I resigned myself to watching the wagons deteriorate on the journey."

"Which they did," Phillip continued. "While Brother John went to Washington to see about getting the import duty reduced—"

"At which I did not succeed," John interjected.

"I was placed in charge of the wagon train. When your father returned from Washington and caught up with us out on the plains, he was dismayed at our slow progress. On our first day, I explained to him that night by the fire, we had made only five miles, yet in that short distance several of the wagons had broken down. Our loads ranged from 5,000 to 9,000 pounds per wagon, and because of the poor construction and green lumber we had many axles break and many, many wheels collapse. Plus we had some wild oxen and green teamsters, and they only added to our delays."

"What did you do?" George asked, feeling both astounded and amused by all he was hearing.

"Do? Why, we finally unloaded the machinery, turned the wagons over to emigrant families with much lighter loads, and returned to Kanesville. There I made a deal with a trader for forty Santa Fe prairie schooners—on credit, I might add—and returned with them to reload the machinery. By then the teamsters had discovered that the flour we had obtained to eat during the journey—on credit, again—had been laced with plaster of paris to add bulk and weight and was no good. Being too late now for another return, we continued, but very quickly found ourselves starving and reduced to eating our own oxen. When the snows first caught us, our remaining oxen ran off into the storm. We spent days then gathering up those we could find, and after one ordeal or mishap after another, we were finally forced to abandon our wagons in the mountains and continue into the valley with the emigrants we had been traveling with. It was November before we were able to retrieve the prairie schooners and machinery and bring them here."

"No wonder you felt there was a concerted opposition," George breathed.

"Yes, but it only got worse." John shook his head. "Russell had arrived in the valley ahead of me, and with Orson Hyde had gone to Brigham with tales that I had misused funds, made false accusations, and so on. The President chose to believe them, and I received a severe tongue lashing.

"I thought it best to remove myself from the conflict, so I ordered the machinery to Provo, intending to set it up there. At that point I was accused of doing all I had done as a way to make money at the hands of the Saints—usury—and so I washed my hands of the whole affair. The President took over, sent 'tithing workers' to replace my carefully selected crew of mechanics and sugar makers, and hauled the machinery back to the Temple lot. There, after a great deal of difficulty, it was assembled and set to work, though it would produce no sugar. Disassembling it once more, President Young had it brought out here to the Church farm, where it sat scattered over two acres with no one certain where to put it or how to put it together properly. It was at that point that I was called to New York to start my paper, *The Mormon.*"

"It was also when Brother Truman Angell was called to build the factory." Phillip smiled sadly. "It took him more than a year to get the building up and all the machinery studied out and installed. None of us were consulted except Mollenhauer and John Vernon, and both of them experienced a curious loss of memory that rendered them of no help whatsoever.

"When, for the second time, a few loads of beets were harvested and the machinery started up to make the sugar, all that was obtained was a black, sticky mess that even the livestock wouldn't eat. That was enough for President Young. He ordered the factory dismantled, the hydraulic presses put to use in the printing office, the vacuum pans used in the paper mill, and other parts used in the

President's woolen mill. Aside from the tremendous effort of your father and others, George, I have heard it estimated that this debacle cost the Church, in cash, about $100,000."

George whistled. "Wow! I'll bet Brother Brigham was upset!"

"And probably still is," John declared.

"So, Father, what do you think happened? Why do you suppose there was so much opposition?"

John smiled. "My boy, there are many answers to that simple question, some of which we may never know. It is possible the cooperative Frenchmen helped us just enough that we couldn't make sugar; after all, it was their industry and they wouldn't want to lose customers. I have now learned that others here in America have failed at the industry after being 'helped' by the French, and so that makes me wonder.

"The bottom of it, however, and this I believe with all my heart, still turns out to be Satan. He despises good works, just as he despises good men, and will raise up everything possible to stop them in their course by using men who have allowed such weaknesses as pride and greed to overrule their natural goodness. When you examine it all carefully, George, you will see that every particle of failure in this great sugar undertaking can be laid at the feet of such men and such weaknesses. For a fact, I believe that failure in any good endeavor ever undertaken by the people of God, individually or as a whole, can be ascribed to this very principle."

"Are you laying pride and greed at the feet of Brigham Young?" George questioned as his eyes sparkled with sly humor.

"No more than I am any other man," John replied.

"But doesn't his attack on your good name make you bitter, Father?"

"Not for a moment, George; and I want you to remember this! I once saw Brother Joseph accuse and humiliate Brigham publicly, and when Brigham, who was innocent, did not rail or fight back,

Joseph wept, embraced him, and told him he had passed the test. On another occasion Joseph told me that I was required to give up your mother, Leonora, to him, to be his plural wife. That was a severe trial, but after praying about it and humbling myself to the earth, George, I told Joseph that if it was the Lord who wished her, that was all right; but if it was only him as a man who was asking, then my answer was no!"

"What did he say to that?"

"Like he had done with Brigham before me, Joseph wept, embraced me, and told me I had passed the test. With this sugar business, Brother Brigham seems to have tested me in like manner. Despite the baseness of the accusations, I have responded to him without anger or argument, and I have every intention of continuing to do so until I have also passed this test.

"Nevertheless, George, you may rest fully assured that despite whatever human frailties Brigham Young may possess, and despite his reasons for accusing me falsely, whatever they may have been, Brigham Young is also the Lord's anointed on the earth at this time—the prophet, seer, revelator, and President of the Church of Jesus Christ in these latter days. He is the Lord's mortal emissary. With all my heart I sustain him in that position and will joyfully do or sacrifice whatsoever I may be asked at his hand—including the giving up of a paltry sugar plant that will not produce sugar!

"Now," John smiled pleasantly, "your mother will have supper prepared, George, and you know how she feels about her table-guests being late—" 1

In the October 1849 general conference, John was called to leave his home and family to serve a mission in France, his assignment to open up that nation to the gospel of Jesus Christ. On the 19TH of October, in company with Lorenzo Snow, Erastus Snow, Franklin D. Richards, and others, he departed the valley and headed east to serve the Lord—a stark contrast to the thousands of men struggling westward toward California in their own self-serving quest for gold.

It was already cold, and the brethren suffered much from the icy winds. There were also Indian troubles at the time, and they encountered a force of warriors that bore down on them in a hostile fashion, though it turned out to be a practical joke the Indians were playing. In Kanesville John tarried for a time with the Saints, then made his way downriver to St. Louis, where he did the same. In St. Louis he also wrote his family:

After a long absence I now sit down to write to you. I have been in this city about three weeks, and stayed in Kanesville about as long. I have been going leisurely along for the purpose of studying French, that I might be the better prepared to enter on my mission on my arrival in France. I have made some progress in the language and hope to be able to speak it on my arrival there. The Saints wherever I go treat me with the greatest kindness and hospitality.

The latter part of our journey over the plains was a cold and dreary one, but the Lord was with us and protected us, and opened out our way before us. The snows fell on our right and left, before and behind, but we never encountered a snow storm until the last day. We arrived safe, however, and all is well.

At Kanesville we were saluted with the firing of guns on our arrival, and the greatest manifestations of rejoicing, and parties, musical entertainments, etc., were gotten up. This has also been the case in St. Louis. Here the Saints have a magnificent hall and a splendid band and do things up in good style.... But these outward tokens of friendship are very little to me, when compared with the heart-felt joy, the kindly feeling, the sympathetic and warm-hearted brotherhood manifested by many of my old friends, hundreds of whom seem anxious in every possible way to promote my happiness, secure my company and have my blessing and friendship. On my arrival both here and in Kanesville the Saints flocked around me like bees; and the greatest trouble I have is that of not being able to fulfill the many engagements that have pressed themselves upon me.

"But," say you, "do you not think of us and home? And do you never think of me...?" This is what I have been wanting to get at for some time, and this long, tedious preface has become wearisome to me—let me tell my feelings if I can. Home! Home! Home! What shall I say? Can I tell it? No, a thousand times no! Your forms, your countenances, your bodies and your spirits are all portrayed before me as in living characters. You are with me in my imaginations, thoughts, dreams, feelings; true our bodies are separated, but there you live—you dwell in my bosom, in my heart and affections, and will remain there forever. Our covenants, our hopes, our joys are all eternal and will live when our bodies moulder in the dust. Oceans, seas, mountains, deserts and plains may separate us—but in my heart you dwell.

Do I see an amiable, lovely woman—my feelings are not there, they fly to my home. Do I see a beautiful infant—hear the prattle of lovely innocents, or the symmetry and intelligence of those more advanced in years? My mind flies to my home—there I gaze upon my wives, there I fondle and kiss my children and revel for a time in this mental delight; but I awake from my reverie and find that it is but a dream, and that mountains, deserts and plains separate us! Do I murmur? No! Do you? I hope not—shall I not say for you, No?

I am engaged in my Master's business; I am a minister of Jehovah to proclaim His will to the nations. I go to unlock the door of life to a mighty nation, to publish to millions the principles of life, light and truth, intelligence and salvation, to burst their fetters, liberate the oppressed, reclaim the wandering, correct their views, improve their morals, save them from degradation, ruin and misery, and lead them to light, life, truth and celestial glory. Do not your spirits co-operate with mine? I know they do. Do you not say, "Go, my husband, go, my father; fulfill your mission, and let God and angels protect you and restore you safe to our bosoms?" I know you do. Well, our feelings are reciprocal, I love my family and they love me; but shall that love be so contracted, so narrow, so earthly and sensual as to prevent my doing the will of my Father in heaven? No, say I, and you echo, No. No! Our thoughts and feelings soar in another atmosphere. We live for time, and we live for eternity; we love here and we will love forever—

> While life or thought or being last,
> Or immortality endures!

Our separations here tend to make us more appreciative of each other's society. A few more separations and trials, a few more tears, a few more afflictions, and the victory will be ours! We'll gain the kingdom, possess the crown, inherit eternal glory, associate with the Gods, soar amidst the intelligences of heaven; and with the noble, the great, the intellectual, the virtuous, the amiable, the holy, possess the reward held in reserve for the righteous, and live and love forever.... May the spirit of peace be and abide with you forever; and when you bow before the Throne of Grace remember your affectionate husband, father and friend.2

In company with Elders Curtis E. Bolton and John Pack, John arrived in Liverpool on the 27TH of May, 1850, and in France on the 18TH of June. After meeting with the mayor of Boulogne-sur-Mer and learning all they could of the local laws, the brethren returned to the seashore in the darkness of night and in prayer gave thanks and asked for divine direction in opening up the work.

John next secured a hall for lectures, just as he had done on the Isle of Man, and wrote a series of letters to the local newspaper concerning the Restoration and the missionaries' purposes in the city. These letters were published both in French and English.

Unfortunately, "the lectures were not very largely attended. The French people," John's biographer reported, "are notoriously indifferent to religion. They are lovers of pleasure more than lovers of God; are gay, volatile, careless, happy, intelligent. Anything, in fact, but religious. Therefore the announcement of these religious lectures did not create much interest." 3

There were, however, exceptions in certain circles. During his first lecture John was confronted by a Protestant minister, whom John refused to debate in the hall because of the strict laws then in place regarding raising a disturbance. The minister—joined by a second, and then a third, in the street—heckled him afterward as he returned to his apartment, and a few days later the three challenged him to a public debate. Once the mayor had approved, John accepted, and the debate was scheduled.

Immediately John was contacted by a Jesuit priest who said to him: "'When they ask about the character of your founders,...just examine into theirs, and I will furnish you all the testimony you want.'" John politely declined his offer, stating: "'I thought if I could not get along without the help of a Jesuit priest, it was a poor case.'" 4

"The debate was to run for three nights, seven to ten, each party having thirty minutes alternately, with three officials of the Church of England as chairmen." 5 "The questions for discussion were stated as follows: First, the late Joseph Smith; his public and pretended religious career. Second, the Book of Mormon; is it a revelation from God? Third, are the ministers of that people [the Mormons] sent of God by direct appointment? The fourth article of the agreement stated that 'Mr. Taylor will have the privilege of discussing the validity of the faith and calling of his opponents.'

"The discussion began on the evening of the 11TH of July.... The first two nights, and one hour of the third evening were taken up on the first three questions, leaving Elder Taylor only an hour in which to enquire into the doctrines and callings of his opponents." 6

The debates were reported in a local newspaper called *The Interpreter.* Some time afterward, John went to England and, using the reports of his opponents' remarks as they had been reported in the paper, at the same time reproducing his own remarks from memory and perhaps hindsight, produced a pamphlet detailing the debate. 7 For years this pamphlet was used rather extensively by other missionaries and was a powerful tool in aiding the work of kingdom building.

One portion of the debate pamphlet worthy of reproduction here is John's testimony regarding the Prophet Joseph Smith. "In discussing the character of Joseph Smith, Elder Taylor's opponents introduced the infamous statements of Doctor Bennett, the Rev. Henry Caswell and others, charging Joseph with a number of crimes and immoralities. Elder Taylor had no documentary evidence to rebut these slanders, but he offered his own testimony to the character of the Prophet: and as Elders Bolton and Pack both knew him personally, he called upon them to testify, which they did. Elder Taylor's own testimony was especially strong. Burning with just indignation at the slanders against his friend, repeated by these priests of a dead theology, he said: I testify that I was acquainted with Joseph Smith for years. I have traveled with him; I have been with him in private and in public; I have associated with him in councils of all kinds; I have listened hundreds of times to his public teachings, and his advice to his friends and associates of a more private nature. I have been at his house and seen his deportment in his family. I have seen him arraigned before the courts of his country, and seen him honorably acquitted, and delivered from the pernicious breath of slander, and the machinations and falsehoods of wicked and corrupt men. I was with him living, and with him when he died; when he was murdered in Carthage jail by a ruthless mob with their faces painted, and headed by a Methodist minister, named Williams—I was there, and was myself wounded. I, at that time, received four balls in my body. I have seen him, then, under these various circumstances, and I testify before God, angels and men, that he was a good, honorable, virtuous man—that his doctrines were good, scriptural and wholesome—that his precepts were such as became a man of God—that his private and public character was unimpeachable—and that he lived and died as a man of God and a gentleman. This is my testimony; if it is disputed bring me a person authorized to receive an affidavit, and I will make one to this effect. 8

When the rather rancorous debates failed to generate any interest in the gospel among the citizens of Boulogne, John and his fellow laborers vacated their apartments and went to Paris. There John engaged in studying French and in teaching whomever would listen the principles of the restored gospel.

Meanwhile, the political situation in France was rapidly

deteriorating. Louis Napoleon, the nephew of the great Napoleon, was in the process of turning his elected office as president of the republic into emperor and ruler of a dictatorship. Unfortunately, when John applied to the government for permission to preach throughout the country, permission was denied. John wrote:

> [T]hey have utterly prohibited us from preaching anywhere throughout the country. I presume they are afraid of excitement for just about the time that the ministry had it [the application] in consideration there was a mob broke out in Denmark that tore down the Saints' meeting house and very much abused many of the Saints. If the French authorities have seen this, which I suppose they have, it would be quite sufficient to deter them from allowing us the privilege of preaching in France. 9

With the entire nation in turmoil and revolution, and having been denied the right to preach, it is surprising that John had any success whatsoever. Yet secret meetings were held in Paris twice a week, and quietly the work spread to Havre, Calais, Boulogne, and elsewhere.

Despite this, John quickly realized that most Frenchmen were not really listening to his message. Rather, they were listening to his words, which they would then argue and debate and discuss almost endlessly. In other words, far too many of the French considered themselves philosophers—men of great intellect who were far too knowledgeable to get caught up in the emotionalism of faith and testimony. John despised this intellectualism, which prevented so many from coming to a knowledge of the truth. He declared:

> [P]hilosophy is about every tenth word they speak.... I was almost buried up in it while I was in Paris. I was walking about one day in the Jardin des Plantes—a splendid

garden. There they had a sort of exceedingly light cake; it was so thin and light that you could blow it away, and you could eat all day of it, and never be satisfied. Somebody asked me what the name of that was. I said, I don't know the proper name, but in the absence of one, I can give you a name — I will call it philosophy, or fried froth. 10

Regarding how he dealt with this philosophy, John declared further:

When they come to see it [the gospel], they rejoice in it, but we do not preach religion much to them, for a great many of them are philosophers, and, of course, we must be philosophers too, and make it appear that our philosophy is better than theirs, and then show them that religion is at the bottom of it.... When they once get interested in the work of God, and get the spirit of God, they rejoice exceedingly in the blessings of the Gospel. 11

On the literary front, while he labored in Paris, John was not only publishing a newspaper — *Etoile Du Deseret, The Star of Deseret* — but he had begun work to see that the Book of Mormon was translated into French. "In the work of translating the Book of Mormon he was greatly assisted by the patient labors of Elder Curtis E. Bolton, Brother Louis Bertrand [Brother Phillip De LaMare] and several highly educated gentlemen whom he baptized in Paris, but whose names unfortunately cannot be obtained.... The translation [was] said to be a very correct one, the original simplicity of the Nephite writers is retained, and it is as literal as the genius and idiom of the French language will admit." 12

In the spring of 1851 John received a letter from Brigham Young encouraging him to find and return with industry suitable for the valley. John "had already been investigating several projects and [was forming] a company 'for the purpose of establishing a large woolen manufactory' he wrote to Brigham in March 13, 1851.

The best machinery will be bought that can be purchased in England & men brought to work it. If fine merino wool can be obtained, as good cloth can be manufactured as in the west of England.... The company will probably bring one or two thousand sheep, merinos...as fine wool is absolutely necessary for broadcloth and fine women's wear. 13

One month earlier he had also been visited by a member wishing to emigrate to Zion, a man who had been involved in the famous sugar manufacturing business in France. Believing that the Lord had directed the man to his doorstep, John immediately went to work, endeavoring to learn what it would take to set up a sugar manufacturing plant in Salt Lake City. Elder Bolton, one of the missionaries who had arrived in France with John, recorded:

I have had to give all my time and attention to the sugar manufacturing of Elder Taylor. He runs me to death. My ankle pains me at night so I can scarcely sleep. I am really ill, not able to go, but go I must. I am too hoarse to speak more than a few words at a time and that only in a whisper. 14

Taking with him his brother-in-law, M. Mollenhauer, and Phillip De LaMare, John visited the Crespel–Delisse sugar refinery at Arras, the oldest beet-sugar refinery in France. The manager, Crespel, "'received [them] with a great deal of kindness and offered to give all the knowledge that he could.' Crespel gave Taylor plans of the machinery at the Arras plant.

De LaMare and Mollenhauer actively joined Taylor in the eight months of investigation, from soil analysis to beet cultivation. The French manufacturers were the soul of affability. Taylor did not have the slightest suspicion that they were holding back vital details of the refining process.

Courtesy of Church Archives, The Church of Jesus Christ of Latter-day Saints. Photo by Marsena Cannon. ©Intellectual Reserve, Inc.

John Taylor   CA. *early 1850s*

In all innocence he had wandered into a ruthless commercial jungle that for centuries had been characterized by power politics, conniving, subterfuge, monopoly, bribery, and war. 15

Unaware that anything might be wrong, John continued to labor, raising capital so he could take back to the valley both the sugar and woolen manufacturing equipment. Meanwhile, "in the latter part of July or about the first of August, 1851, Elder Taylor accompanied by Elder Viet, a German, and a teacher of that language in France, and Elder George P. Dykes, went to the city of Hamburg, Germany. Here, with the aid of Elder Viet, a Mr. Charles Miller, whom [John] baptized shortly after his arrival there, and George P. Dykes, he made arrangements for and supervised the translation of the Book of Mormon into the German language. The work was finally completed and stereotyped; and the text so arranged that the French and German would face each other, each page containing the same matter in the same opening, and thus both could be bound together.

"In Hamburg as in Paris, [John] published a monthly periodical, a royal octavo sheet, which was called Zion's Panier—Zion's Banner. The first number was issued November 1st, 1851. He also preached the gospel and raised up a branch of the Church in Hamburg; after which he returned to Paris, to attend a conference of the French mission appointed to convene there." 16

Because of the oppressive French laws, holding this conference was dangerous for John and the other members of the Church. In spite of heavy police scrutiny they managed it, primarily because John had called the conference on the same day as France's rigged general election. Of the situation, John declared that

"'Liberty,' 'Equality,' 'Fraternity,' were written upon almost every door. You had liberty to speak, but might be put in prison for doing so. You had liberty to print, but they might burn what you had printed, and put you in confinement for it"—such was French liberty! 17

Immediately following the conference, John took his two translations of the Book of Mormon and all else he had gathered together and departed for England—about ten minutes ahead of the French authorities. Apparently having no knowledge of the activities of the gendarmes, who by then had posted officers to apprehend him at every major point of departure, John stopped off for a week in Havre to hold another conference. From there he went to the island of Jersey to hold a third conference, and from there on to England, not once having any idea of the size of the manhunt he was so blithely avoiding.

In England, John finished organizing the Deseret Manufacturing Company, and having brought the death masks of Joseph and Hyrum with him from the valley, as well as numerous descriptions of the dead prophets, John contracted with a British artist, Mr. Gahagan, to produce busts of the two men. He then set about writing a book which would be published under the title *The Government of God*.

> The author defines the kingdom of God to be the government of God, on the earth, or in the heavens; and then in his first two chapters proceeds to place the magnificence, harmony, beauty and strength of the government of God, as seen throughout the universe, in contrast with the meanness, confusion and weakness of the government of men.
>
> It is a bold picture he draws in each case; one displaying the intelligence, the light, the glory, the beneficence and power of God; the other the ignorance, the folly, the littleness and imbecility of man. The great evils, both national and individual which He depicts with such

vividness, the author maintains are beyond the power of human agency to correct. "They are diseases," he remarks, "that have been generating for centuries; that have entered into the vitals of all institutions, religious and political, that have prostrated the powers and energies of all bodies politic, and left the world to groan under them, for they are evils that exist in church and state, at home and abroad; among Jew and Gentile, Christian, Pagan and Mahometan; king, prince, courtier and peasant; like the deadly simoon [*sic*], they have paralyzed the energies, broken the spirits, damped the enterprise, corrupted the morals and crushed the hopes of the world.... No power on this side of heaven can correct this evil. It is a world that is degenerated, and it requires a God to put it right." [18]

Concerning the book, Hubert Howe Bancroft writes: "As a dissertation on a general and abstract subject, it probably has not its equal in point of ability within the whole range of Mormon literature. The style is lofty and clear, and every page betokens the great learning of the author. As a student of ancient and modern history, theologian, and moral philosopher, President Taylor is justly entitled to the front rank; while his proficiency in foreign languages and his knowledge of men and of practical affairs rendered his services no less important as manager abroad than as executive officer at home." [19]

Having turned his manuscript over to his British publisher, John began rounding up the men necessary to install and operate the massive sugar-refining machinery. He chose Elias Morris to go to the valley to build his building; John Vernon, who had helped with the manufacture of the equipment, to go west to install it; Mollenhauer, "'an expert sugar maker and refiner,'" to run the plant, assisted by John Bollwinkel and a Mr. Conner, both of whom had worked in a sugar factory in Liverpool. [20]

In all, John assembled a crew of about thirty men for his projects, including his future secretary and son-in-law, L. John Nuttall. When all was ready the equipment was loaded aboard the sailing ship *Rockaway* at Liverpool. John's cargo included not only the machinery for both the sugar and woolen plants, but three zinc-lined caskets—labeled "machinery"—bearing the bodies of missionaries who had passed away during their labors and which were to be transported back to the valley.

John then spent a little more time in England, obtaining the busts of Joseph and Hyrum from the artist, proofing his typeset manuscript at the publisher's, and putting all else in order. In company with a group of converts he then embarked on the steamship *Niagara* for America. And it was from then on that everything related to the sugar refinery seemed to go downhill—the details of which were outlined at the beginning of this chapter.

After an absence of nearly three years, John arrived in Salt Lake City on the 20TH of August, 1852. Though he had so looked forward to being home after being gone for so long, John instead

> encountered severe criticism instead of praise. Brigham was greatly dissatisfied with the way the DMC had been handled. Orson Hyde, Captain Russell, and John Coward had arrived in the valley ahead of Taylor, claiming he had mishandled affairs and squandered company money. They'd told their story first and...the Church president was inclined to believe [them]. 21

After John decided to build his factory as far away as possible—in Provo—Captain Russell and John Coward turned their shares of DMC stock over to the Church, giving the Church majority ownership and putting Brigham Young in charge.

Immediately the President ordered "tithing hands" to freight all the equipment back to Salt Lake City. Brigham then "placed Orson Hyde in charge of the sugar works, because, he explained,

Courtesy of Church Archives, The Church of Jesus Christ of Latter-day Saints. ©Intellectual Reserve, Inc.

Portrait of Orson Hyde   CA. *early 1840s*

'He is a snug business man,' while 'Brother Taylor will be left out
entirely. He will have no more to do with it.' Only the chief
sugar-maker, Mollenhauer, and John Vernon, the engineer,
remained of the skilled personnel comprising the original crew." 22

Strangely, when beets were grown and the refinery finally put
into operation, things went wrong. "Evidently it took more than
snug business judgment and inspiration to make beet sugar.
The juice turned black, went sour, then fermented. Nothing came
from the vile stuff except foul-smelling molasses that even the
hogs wouldn't eat." 23

After censuring John again at another meeting and totally
removing him from the project, Brigham tried sugar-making again,
once more placing Orson Hyde in charge and putting Truman
Angell to work designing and building a proper factory southeast
of the city—in an area still known as Sugar House.

As Parley P. Pratt had done when he and John had been on the
trail to the valley in 1847 and had met up with Brigham's party that
was returning to Winter Quarters, John made no reply or argument
to the humiliation, but merely submitted, and the next year he
willingly accepted from Brigham Young a mission to New York to
publish a newspaper that would defend and explain the Church.
He had been in New York a full year when the refinery in Sugar
House was ready to try. Even with the previous experience behind
them, and almost two years to have corrected any mistakes, once
again, the factory couldn't make sugar!

By the time John returned to the valley in 1855, the machinery
had been disassembled and the parts scattered to numerous other
projects. Over $100,000 cash had been spent on the failure; the
empty factory remained a haunting memory; sugar continued to be
imported at great cost; and Orson Hyde's vaunted business sense
had not prevailed. It would be twenty-five more years before
a successful sugar refinery would be built in Utah—in Lehi.
Though by then John Taylor would be dead, his son George would

Courtesy of Church Archives, The Church of Jesus Christ of Latter-day Saints. ©Intellectual Reserve, Inc.

Truman Angell, church architect,   *N.D.*
designed the sugar factory at Sugar
House as well as the awe-inspiring
Salt Lake Temple.

be on hand for the successful opening. Again sponsored by the Church, it would become the first unit of the Utah-Idaho Sugar Company.

DOING BATTLE
ON NEWSPAPER ROW

"Margaret seems to be a wonderful young woman, John. Her demeanor is calm and unruffled, her eye clear, and her culinary skills might better be termed a gift. Never have I tasted better plum pudding!"

John Taylor nodded toward his friend and fellow apostle, Parley P. Pratt. "Yes, Parl', she is all I hoped for, and more. Since George A. sealed us as man and wife back in September, I have almost daily discovered new blessings streaming from her person to mine, for which I am constantly thanking the Lord. Many days I feel hard pressed just to remain worthy of her."

"A common feeling, I assure you." For a moment Parley P. Pratt sat silently, gazing into the warm fire. Having been given a mission to preach as led by the Spirit "to the States" by President Young, he had arrived in Philadelphia last week, on December 24TH, 1856, where he had met John Taylor. John was then presiding over the Eastern States Mission and editing *The Mormon,* which Brigham had also asked Parley to write for as part of his mission. Until yesterday—New Year's Eve—Parley had remained in Philadelphia, teaching, conversing, preaching, writing on his history, visiting, and sending articles to John's New York newspaper. Now he was also in New York, seated in the comfortable Brooklyn home

John had rented since his marriage to Margaret Young three months before, sharing with the man and his bride a New Year's feast as well as a few of the struggles he had been having, of late, in the spirit.

"Do you recollect," he abruptly asked John, "how fiercely you resisted my message when I came to you in upper Canada?"

John eyed his burly associate. "What I recall, Parl', is that you looked nothing like I supposed an apostle of the Lord ought to look."

"Yes," Parley sighed, "for some reason the Lord gave me more the shape of a whiskey barrel than of a man."

"Are you certain the Lord deserves all the blame?"

"There, you see?" Parley chuckled. "You have always been forthright with me, John, never afraid to say what was on your mind. You alone could have brought me forth from that dark cloud of doubt back in Kirtland, and with a few short sentences, you did. From that day to this, I have been closer to no other man! You are truly my dearest friend."

"Thank you," John smiled tenderly. "I consider you the same."

"Good. Now I fear I am in a pickle of a different sort, and I could use your counsel."

"It has not been difficult to sense that your heart is troubled." John stopped, knowing he could have said more, for certainly the Holy Spirit had told him more. Instead, though, he felt it best if Elder Pratt were to say it first.

Carefully Parley opened a small daybook he kept in an inner pocket of his vest. "These words, John, I penned last evening before retiring. Oh, how darkness prevails! How ignorant, blind and impenetrable are the minds of men! My Father in Heaven, Thy will be done. As a blank of another year of my life is about to commence to be filled up, I will close the volume of the book I have been writing, commending myself to God and the guardianship of his angels; asking, in the name of Jesus Christ, that my sins and follies, up to this date, may be blotted out, and that my labors and records may be accepted; then I will retire to rest with a conscience void of offense, and with a calm and resigned confidence in my Heavenly Father. If I am privileged to awake in the morning of a new year, I will commence a new book or volume of my life.

"As you see, John, I yet live; though every fiber of my being tells me my days are numbered fewer than I might suppose."

John nodded. "Yes, Parley, the Spirit whispered to me days ago that such was your fear."

"And did the Lord also whisper that my fear is justified?" Parley pleaded, his countenance revealing his anxiety. "You see, John, I do not fear death. You know that, for you carry the same witness of Christ and his work as do I and must surely feel the same. No, I fear only that I may have made a grave mistake, and that my life—my mission before the Lord—will be forfeit because of it!"

"Yes, I too carry that concern."

"I have even gone so far as to write out detailed instructions for my funeral, and I feel a constant panic to see that my history is finished, for the Spirit whispers that it will be an important document for the Church in a coming day. What else, I ask you as a brother, can such feelings mean?"

For a moment John gazed at the floor, thankful that Margaret had been wise enough to remain out of the room. "Perhaps, Parl', you would be willing to share with me what you think this 'mistake' might have been?"

Parley smiled ruefully. "What is Margaret, John? Your fourteenth—no, fifteenth wife?"

"Counting all those I married in order to assist them across the plains and in getting settled in the valley, she is my sixteenth. Of course two left me in Nauvoo; one has divorced me to marry another, for which I gave my most hearty approval; and poor Ann Pitchforth perished at Winter Quarters."

"Yes, I recollect when we learned of her passing and how you grieved. Well, John, my tale involves such a one as Ann Pitchforth. When I returned from my mission to South America I stopped for a time in San Francisco to assist in publishing the *Western Standard*. As I labored among the Saints in that city I became involved in the personal problems of a woman named Elenore McLean. Truly she was one of the most devout members of our congregation, and to look at her, one would suppose she had everything required for happiness. Her husband, Hector, was a customs house official and well respected. She had three beautiful children. And, of course, she had found the gospel.

"Unfortunately, I quickly discovered that her home life was a veritable hell on earth. Each night her husband drank himself into a frenzy, turning himself into a violent brute of a man who took out his rage on Elenore and her children.

"As Elenore and I discussed this from day to day, we grew close. Hector, supposing she had fallen in love with me, shipped the children off to New Orleans to Elenore's father, sending along wild tales of Mormon orgies and other such claptrap to prejudice the minds of her family. He then threatened Elenore that if she attempted to go after or retrieve them, he would have her committed to an insane asylum within twenty-four hours. Of course, I saw no solution but to send her after them anyway, and so using what resources I had available, I set her aboard a ship bound for New Orleans."

"I would likely have done the same."

Parley nodded. "So would any decent man. Shortly thereafter I was summoned by Brigham to return to Utah, and some three months later I was dumfounded to see Elenore come through the door of my home. Through her tears she told of being denied the privilege of seeing or spending even one minute with any of her children, so great was the fear of her family that she might teach them Mormon doctrine or help them escape to Utah.

Having no other choice, therefore, she turned westward alone and made her way to the valley with one of the companies of emigrants then crossing the plains. We spent more time together, planning and discussing how she could get her children back, and before long she had become my twelfth wife."

"Had she divorced Hector by then?" John asked quietly.

Miserably, Parley shook his head. "She had tried, but through further evil on Hector's part had been prevented from accomplishing it. At the time, it seemed as if that could not matter. Surely she had done nothing unrighteous, and I knew that the Lord considered her freed from the villain. That is why we married."

"Unfortunately, Parley, the legal system in this country does not know the Lord. Hector McLean now holds all the cards and can with impunity use you up as he wishes. In fact, you have become the very model of the wife-stealing Mormon polygamist the national papers have been making such a fuss over."

Distraught, Parley nodded his head. "I know, John. I also know that whatever Hector might do, to me or to Elenore, we will be the villains and Hector will be exonerated and vindicated."

"And you fear he will be successful?"

"I don't fear it so much as I feel it. My entire being throbs with the certainty that he will find a way to rob me of my life!"

"Do you intend to do anything about it?"

"Yes, a plan is in place, which if we can bring it off, can return Elenore with her sweet little ones to the safety of the mountains. Elenore has already returned to New Orleans and is putting forth the deception that she is disillusioned with the Church and has abandoned it for good. At the first opportunity she will spirit the children away from there to Houston, where she will remain in hiding with some friends for the winter. For all I know, this has already happened. In the spring she will make her way to Fort Smith, Arkansas, where I will meet her. Together, then, we will join up with a Mormon emigrant company that will be forming in the area."

"And Hector has no knowledge of this plan? He will have followed her to New Orleans, I presume."

"Oh, I'm certain he is there. But the only way he might have knowledge of our plans is if he has had the temerity to rob the United States mail. I doubt even he has those sorts of connections."

"With a customs official," John stated quietly, "one never knows."

As the men walked together to the door, John could not shed the feeling that he was spending his last moments in this life with his dear friend and fellow apostle—the same who had brought Leonora and him into a new life with the glorious message of the gospel of Jesus Christ.

Somehow, he sensed, Hector McLean would be successful—

"Be careful, Brother Parley," John advised as he shook hands good-bye, "and may the Lord go with and protect you." [1]

Parley P. Pratt indeed stayed in touch with John, providing additional articles for *The Mormon* and a poem he had written on his fiftieth birthday, April 12, 1857. This John also published:

> I am fifty years old! I have lived to see
> Seven times seven and a Jubilee....
> I have wandered far, over land and sea,
> To proclaim to the world its destiny—
> To cry to the nations, repent and live,
> And be ready the bridegroom to receive....
> I have lain in a dungeon, bound in chains,
> And been honored in Courts where Justice reigns.
> In a thousand joys, and a thousand fears
> I have struggled on through fifty years.

And now, by the law of God, I am free;
I will seek to enjoy my Jubilee.... 2

"But word from Arkansas made [John] fear that Parley's jubilee might be in the next world, not this. Hector McLean had arrived in the vicinity, searching for his family. At the Fort Smith post office, he obtained letters that Parley had written to Elenore. Parley, meanwhile, had written her at Houston, advising her to come in a Gentile's wagon. He would patrol the Texas road in Indian territory, to meet her before she arrived at Fort Smith." 3

Unable to rid himself of his apprehension over his dear friend's life, John wrote and published in *The Mormon* a somber reply to Parley's poem:

...If a wish from a sincere friendly heart
Can to thee any comfort or joy impart;
If a fervent prayer to God of grace
Could smooth thy path in thy onward race,
That prayer would be, may grace be given
To wend thy onward course to Heaven.
May'st thou abound in corn and wine,
And the blessings of plenty now be thine;
May thy family all be free from care,
And a husband's and father's plenty share;
May thy sun go down with glory rife,
And dying, may'st thou burst into life;
And, when sleeping among the silent dead,
Have the blessings of millions on thy head;
And, living with God, may'st thou be free.
And partake of an endless Jubilee. 4

Short weeks later, as he was preparing with Margaret to depart from New York for his home in Utah (doing his best to get there ahead of an army he had learned had been dispatched by President

Buchanan to do away with the Mormons), John received word from Arkansas that Parley had been murdered by the unrelenting McLean and a few of his family and friends. Truly both Parley's and John's presentiments had been prophetic.

But now back to John's story. Following his precipitous removal from the Church's sugar project, and before he had been given more than a few months to attend to the affairs of his large family, John was called during the April 1853 conference to take up a mission among all the communities of the Saints "'in the valleys of the mountains.'"5 At that same conference he assisted Brigham Young and the other Brethren in dedicating the cornerstones of the Salt Lake Temple.

Though not stated over the pulpit, there is no doubt that the missions to which John and seventy-nine other elders were ultimately called were to counteract the surprise, shock, and even open hostility that had reared its head following the August 29, 1852, announcement of the Church's doctrine of celestial marriage—the plurality of wives.

When it was announced, however, "Taylor felt as if a great burden was taken from his shoulders. At long last, after some twenty years of evasion, denial, and doubletalk, the [principle of plural marriage] was acknowledged as church doctrine. John Taylor wasn't ashamed of the gospel, nor was he afraid to fight for it; but he'd always hated the requirement that he [hide the truth] for it."6

For the next year John traveled throughout a good portion of what is now the western United States, visiting nearly all the settlements of the Saints and encouraging them to greater diligence in their duties and in living their religion—including, if they were called to it, plural marriage. While there was great success among the people of God, among the Gentiles it was a different matter altogether. Parley P. Pratt, serving a mission during this same time period, no doubt echoed John's feelings when he wrote:

Courtesy of Church Archives. The Church of Jesus Christ of Latter-day Saints. ©Intellectual Reserve, Inc.

Parley P. Pratt was one of   *N.D.*
John Taylor's dearest friends

Oh, when will the time come? When shall the veil be rent and the full powers of the apostleship be permitted to be exercised on the earth? It must be before long or no flesh be saved—for the powers of darkness prevail abroad to that degree that it can even be felt physically.

There are none who know the Lord; none who seek after the truth; none who appreciate it when found; none who incline to cease from sin. I had like to have said to be found abroad in the earth. To find one is like lighting a candle and searching diligently for food among the dungeons of darkness, death and famine. 7

Unfortunately:

No sooner was the announcement [of plural marriage] made than misrepresentation distorted this doctrine into everything that was vile and impure. The old stories of licentious practices among the Saints in Nauvoo, fulminated by John C. Bennett and other apostates—but which had no existence except as these same apostates and a few other corrupt men practiced them, and for which they were expelled from the Church—were revived and believed with avidity by a credulous public, until Utah was looked upon as a hot-bed of impurity, and the Mormon religion as a veil under which was hidden all the ungodliness of man's baser and degrading passions. 8

By 1854, sensing that the mood of the country had definitely soured against the Church and feeling that the Church needed its own newspapers and editors in key cities nationwide who would put forth the truth as opposed to the lies and accusations then being published, John was called to New York to start up a paper in that city. Orson Pratt had just started publishing *The Seer* in Washington, D.C.; Erastus Snow and Orson Spencer were to publish a paper in St. Louis; and George Q. Cannon and others were to publish a paper in San Francisco, to which Parley Pratt would ultimately become a contributing editor. But there were also other issues which needed to be addressed.

> The object in starting these publications was to disabuse the public mind, then fast being prejudiced against the Church by the tongue of slander. When the Saints disappeared in the great western wilderness of America there were a variety of opinions as to what would be their fate. Few, however, thought they would survive the terrible ordeal through which they passed in their expulsion from the United States and the subsequent perils and hardships of the great desert. But when the miracle of their preservation was forced upon their attention, and not only their preservation, but the fact, also, that they were more numerous and in possession of more power than when driven from Nauvoo—when it was known that they had laid the foundation of a commonwealth which was soon to be knocking at the gate of the capital for admission into the Union as a sovereign state—when all this was known, their enemies, who flattered themselves that they had seen the last of the hated Mormons, suddenly aroused themselves for a renewal of the suspended conflict. 9

Taking with him Elder Jeter Clinton, Nathanial H. Felt, Alexander Robbins, Angus M. Cannon, and his own eldest son, George J. Taylor, John departed immediately for New York where he intended to throw down the gauntlet of truth before an unbelieving world. But it was a difficult task that he had been given. "Both the pulpit and the press were against him; and there could be no question as to what course political parties would take respecting the question. What the populace condemned, they would condemn. Besides, [John] found himself cramped

George Q. Cannon, tutored
in publishing by his uncle,
John Taylor, at Nauvoo, became
a loyal defender of the Church
as a publisher himself. He founded
George Q. Cannon and Sons in
1866 which later became known
as Deseret Book.

CA. 1850s

financially for such an enterprise. The Church in Utah was unable to furnish the necessary means. The people there were having a severe struggle for existence with the unpropitious elements of the wilderness, and money there was none, or, at least, very little.

"It is true there were many members of the Church in the eastern states at the time, but they were unorganized, and indifferent to the progress or defense of the work of God. Elder Taylor called upon the Saints to come to his assistance in publishing a paper, but it reminded him of a man, he humorously said, in describing the result to President Young, who said, 'I can call spirits from the vasty deep;' 'So can I,' shouted another, 'but they won't come.' Still there were a few who responded, and with what they furnished and the money obtained for the teams and wagons he had brought with him from Utah, and a few hundred dollars which he and those with him could borrow, a paper was started, the first number bearing the date of the 17TH of February, 1855." 10 As John wrote to Brigham Young:

> We commenced our publication,...not because we had means to do it, but because we were determined to fulfill our mission, and either make a spoon or spoil a horn.... How long we shall be able to continue, I don't know. We are doing as well as we can, and shall continue to do so; but I find it one thing to preach the gospel without purse or scrip, and another thing to publish a paper on the same terms. 11

Determined to make no pretense, John called his paper *The Mormon*. His son George designed for him a large and distinctive masthead, occupying a full fourth of the seven-column front page. 12 He then set up shop and began issuing his paper at the corner of Nassau and Ann streets—the very heart of New York's publishing district—with *The Herald* on one side and *The Tribune* on the other.

It was the custom at the time for the newsboys to receive the first edition of any newspaper free and then to sell them for what they pleased. Accordingly, on that date scores of young urchins were soon making the streets of New York echo to the cry, "Mormon! Mormon! Here's yer Mormon!"

Without doubt it was a publishing explosion, for it was in John's nature to hold nothing back when he was defending those principles of truth he held so dear. In that first number, he wrote:

> We are Mormon,...inside and outside; at home or abroad; in public and private—everywhere.... We are such, not because we believe it to be the most popular, lucrative, or honorable (as the world has it); but because we believe it to be true, and...more calculated to promote the happiness and well-being of humanity, in time and throughout eternity, than any other system which we have met with. 13

A short time afterward he declared:

> We have said before and say now, that we defy all the editors and writers in the United States to prove that Mormonism is less moral, scriptural, philosophical; or that there is less patriotism in Utah than in any other part of the United States. We call for proof; bring on your reasons, gentlemen, if you have any; we shrink not from the investigation, and dare you to the encounter. If you don't do it, and you publish any more of your stuff, we shall brand you as poor, mean, cowardly liars; as men publishing falsehoods knowing them to be so, and shrinking from the light of truth and investigation. 14

Whatever the general public thought of John's writing and his position, the editors along "newspaper row" were certainly no converts. The editor of *The New York Mirror* wrote:

> While our public moralists and reformers are making war
> upon the hotels and taverns and private property of our
> citizens, a hideous system—an immoral excrescence—
> is allowed to spring up and overtop the Constitution itself.
> Why are there no public meetings convened in the
> tabernacle to denounce Mormonism? 15

John immediately replied that he was ready to meet the editor
or his reformers in the tabernacle at any time. "*The Herald*
proposed a meeting of ministers at Tammany Hall to expose
the fallacies and abominations of the Saints. When Taylor
welcomed the opportunity of a debate, the ministers backed down,
apparently reluctant to be drawn into a brouhaha with the small
and upstart sect.

"*The Sun* joined the anti-Mormon crusade with vitriolic zeal.
The attack by the entire eastern press was so bitter, in fact,
that when Utah was threatened by famine because of crop
failure caused by drought and another cricket plague...this
desperate plight was hailed as an automatic solution to the
Mormon question—the Saints simply would starve.

"Such attacks brought Mormon support from a most
unexpected source, *The Woman's Advocate*. This paper, devoted
to female rights, might be expected to be the last to rally to
a sect espousing polygamy. However, the *Woman's Advocate* was the
only voice on newspaper row to show compassion:

> We need not be surprised if we learn next spring that
> thousands have perished miserably of starvation....
> But not one word is spoken anywhere [by the press] of
> regret or sympathy; on the contrary there are frequent
> manifestations of satisfaction that the problem of
> Mormonism and its destiny is likely to be settled by the
> grasshoppers. What little comment we have noticed here
> and there has a tone of delighted chuckle that chills the

blood. There is the spirit of murder in it....

"Taylor reprinted the *Advocate* item...[and] published an article [of his own] advocating female rights, deploring the double standard and showing compassion for 'the case of the fallen woman.' Why was it [he editorialized] that:

> when two people commit the same sin, one shall be received into favor again and the other remorselessly driven to destruction?... As the two have sinned alike, punish them both or forgive them both; have for both equal mercy, equal good nature, equal condemnation; above all, equal justice. 16 "

And when it came to begging for charity in behalf of those in Utah who might be starving because of the drought and the grasshoppers, John thundered:

> *The Sun* says there has been no appeal from Utah for help. An appeal for help indeed! They have called for their own, but their rights have been continually withheld, though your statesmen owned their cause was just. And shall they now ask charity of those that robbed and despoiled them of their goods and murdered their best men? We have been robbed of millions and driven from our own firesides into the cold, wintry blasts of the desert, to starve by your charitable institutions, and shall we now crave your paltry sixpences? Talk to us with your hypocritical cant about charity! Pshaw! it's nauseating to everyone not eaten up with your corrupt humbuggery and pharisaical egotism. You forgot you were talking to Americans, born upon the soil of freedom, suckled in liberty, who have inhaled it from their fathers' lips—their ears yet tingling with the tales of a nation's birth—sons of fathers who fought for rights which you, in your bigotry and self-conceit, would

fain wrench from them. Intolerance has thrice driven them from their homes, but the wild burst of liberty of '76, now reverberates through the mountain passes of Utah, bidding defiance to mobocracy and its leaders; and hurling mock charity and pretended patriotism back to the fount of corruption from which it issues. The Mormons neither need your sympathy nor your cankered gold. Your malicious slanders only excite contempt for those base enough to utter them. Your contemptible falsehoods fail to ruffle a feather in our caps.... The God of Jacob in whom the Mormons trust—He who brought up Israel out of Egypt—He it is who sustained the Mormons in their tedious journeyings over the barren deserts and wild mountain passes of this continent. In the dark hour of trial, amid all their distresses, without friends or home— God upheld and sustained them; He sustains them still, and will cause them to shine forth with the bright radiance of eternal truth over the wide world, long after their malicious slanderers shall have sunk to oblivion in the filth of their own corruptions. 17

To no one's surprise, polygamy quickly became a political football which everyone wanted to control and to shout the loudest over. What the Saints had not anticipated, however, was that the major political parties, the Democrats and the Whig Abolitionists (from whom the Republican Party was organized in 1856), would link polygamy to slavery as one of "the twin relics of barbarism." 18

In number after number John fearlessly fought against this attitude, teaching, explaining, cajoling, mocking, ridiculing— doing all within the awesome power of his pen to turn aside the hatred and prejudice of the people of the United States and to show them that plural marriage was in fact a better way. In the first number of the paper, he declared that:

since this doctrine has been promulgated by us as a part of our religious creed, every variety of opinion has been expressed by men in all classes of society. It has been talked about by religious and irreligious, professors and profane. It has been the theme in the legislative hall, the pulpit, the bar-room and the press. Polygamy and the Mormons, Mormons and polygamy have resounded everywhere.... In this our first issue it may be expected that something would be said in relation to this matter. This we undertake as cheerfully as any other task; for we are not ashamed here in this great metropolis of America...to declare that we are polygamists. We are not ashamed to proclaim to this great nation, to rulers and people, to the president, senators, legislators, judges; to high and low, rich and poor, priests and people, that we are firm, conscientious believers in polygamy, and that it is part and parcel of our religious creed. We do this calmly, seriously and understandingly, after due deliberation, careful examination and close investigation of its principles and bearings religiously, socially, morally, physically and politically! We unhesitatingly pronounce our full and implicit faith in the principle as emanating from God, and that under His direction it would be a blessing to the human family....

We are not surprised, [however], that men of reflection and virtue, and having a knowledge of the world should feel indignant at polygamy. They look upon it as something pandering to the brutal passions of man;.... We respect the conscientious feelings of such men; for we know that with their ideas of such things, they must be extremely revolting. But we would respectfully ask such persons if they ever seriously reflected upon the matter? and further: Is it prejudice, education and the corrupt state of society that has led them to these conclusions...or matters of fact deduced from scripture, reason, history or precedence? Did they ever think that Abraham, Jacob, David, Solomon and a host of other good men mentioned in the scriptures were polygamists? That the Twelve Tribes of Israel, to whom belong the covenants and promises, descended from four women, the wives of one man? Did they ever reflect that those men were more virtuous than this generation; and that for such things that are practiced here every day with impunity—adultery—a man would be stoned to death by all Israel? Did they ever reflect that it might be possible for the Lord to be unchangeable? That He had not learned much from man in a few thousand years; and that possibly He was not in error then; and if not then, the same principles might probably be as correct now as they were at that time? It is well for us not to be too hasty....

The Lord's way [plural marriage] as practiced by ancient men of God—the restitution of which has lately taken place—we think will stop [adultery and sexual promiscuity] among us. 19

Week after week John continued the attack, meanwhile responding to any number of plans put forth by one group or another to overthrow the Church. These ranged from flooding Utah with Bibles (John favored this and offered to help ship them there) to plans to flood Utah with ministers who could show Latter-day Saints the error of their ways (John also supported this, assuring his readers that such ministers would be well-treated) to the ultimate in base and evil notions—to send out each three months a detachment of handsome young soldiers who could seduce the girls and women of Utah and carry them off to California, continuing until there was only one wife left for each Utah male.

John countered by contending that the debased continued to clamor against the righteous participants of plural marriage in Utah, demanding that the Saints become exactly like the rest of the nation—all to the end that

> the inhabitants of Utah may...be brought back to the standard Christian regulation of one wife apiece—and as many misses or fast young women as suits our convenience, that a deadly blow may be struck at the virtue of Utah: and that she may be crowded with voluptuaries, and prostitutes like all other good Christian states and cities; that debauchery and corruption may run riot, that we may have our procuresses, pimps, cyprians, hotel accommodations, and houses of assignation; that virtue, chastity and purity may be banished from Utah; that our daughters may be prostituted and our wives debauched; that we may have our Nymphs du Pave,...our infanticides, our maisons d'accouchement, our diseases, doctors and hospitals and all the other appliances of a good Christian community. That when officers, lawyers, judges, soldiers and Gentiles in general go to Utah they can find the same conveniences and accommodations that are to be met with everywhere among the virtuous Gentile monogamous Christians! And all this glory is to be achieved by the gallant officers and soldiers of our army....
>
> What are we to think of a man who is publishing a popular journal, and who publicly and unblushingly advocates seduction, and openly proposes the introduction of debased characters into a Territory for the avowed purpose of seduction, prostitution and infamy, for the purpose of corrupting the Mormons and reducing them to our standard previous to their overthrow? [20]

In the meantime, John also had other duties. Owing to the new "ten pound" plan of the Perpetual Emigration Fund by which converts might travel from Europe to Utah for ten English pounds (approximately fifty dollars), New York was flooded with European emigrants bound for Zion—five thousand of them during John's first year in New York. It became John's responsibility to find housing, food, and even employment for these individuals and then to shepherd them on their way westward as quickly as they could be made ready.

Unfortunately, it was a time of financial turmoil, with 30,000 unemployed in New York City alone. John struggled to find work for the Saints, though in part this problem was solved by sending them to Ebenezer Young, a convert who owned a cotton mill in Westport, Connecticut.

It so happened that Ebenezer also had an attractive, unmarried daughter of twenty, Margaret Young, to whom John was quickly drawn. In *The Mormon* he published her a love letter under the title "The Origin and Destiny of Women."

> Lady, whence comest thou? Thine origin? What art thou doing here? Wither art thou going, and what is thy destiny?… Knowest thou not that eternities ago thy spirit, pure and holy, dwelt in thy Heavenly Father's bosom, and in His presence… surrounded by thy brother and sister spirits of the spirit world, among the Gods? 21

Never one to let it be said that he was preaching what he refused to practice, John approached the much younger Margaret regarding the prospect of her becoming part of his personal family kingdom. Apparently she quite readily agreed. Elder George A. Smith, in the East on a mission to petition the federal government for Utah's admittance as a state, married John to Margaret on September 27, 1856, she becoming John's seventh and final "official" wife. "'Miss Young,' Fanny Stenhouse [wife of writer T. B. H. Stenhouse] reported, made Taylor 'an excellent housekeeper in

Margaret Young Taylor

N.D.

the handsomely furnished house in Brooklyn.'" 22

For two and a half years John kept up his furious pace of writing and presiding, in the meanwhile occasionally visiting Washington and having several interviews with Franklin Pierce, President of the United States. In at least one of these interviews he defended Brigham Young's right to remain governor of Utah; and in all of them he advocated the necessity of Utah being granted statehood as quickly as possible.

During this same time period, events were transpiring in far-off Utah that would have dramatic and long-lasting effects on John's life, ending his mission, closing his paper, and sending him home abruptly. On September 9, 1850, President Millard Fillmore had signed the bill creating the Territory of Utah, and by the 20TH of September the Saints knew that some of the officials appointed by the President were not Latter-day Saints. With the arrival of these officials in Utah in 1851, a rather acrimonious relationship quickly developed between most of them and the good citizens of Utah. These altercations, caused primarily because the federal appointees openly disdained the Saints and even cast aspersions of wickedness and immorality upon them, climaxed when three of them were called to task by Brigham Young. Quickly abandoning their posts, and becoming ever afterward known as Utah's "Runaway Officials," the three with one other Gentile returned to the East early in 1852 and were replaced by four new men who arrived in Utah in the fall. These officials, however, were open, honest men who sought fairness for Saints and Gentiles alike, and so the people of Utah rallied around them.

Chief Justice Reid, in fact, communicated in a letter to the East:

> I have made up my mind that no man has been more grossly misrepresented than Governor Young, and that he is a man that will reciprocate kindness and good intentions

as heartily and freely as anyone, but if abused or crowded hard, I think he may be found exceedingly hard to handle. 23

All would have been well had not two of these men died after a political change had occurred in Washington. In October, 1853, Franklin Pierce, a Democrat, replaced Millard Fillmore, a Whig, as President of the United States. The Democrats by then had pounced on polygamy as one of the twin relics of barbarism, and rumors were soon rife that Pierce intended replacing Brigham Young as governor—thus occasioning John Taylor's visits to lobby for Brigham Young. Then in 1854 came the death of Chief Justice Reid in Utah, followed in June 1855 by the death of Judge Shaver.

President Pierce immediately replaced Associate Justice Shaver with a man named William W. Drummond, who "became more responsible than any other person for the expedition of an army to Utah on grounds that the Mormons were rebelling against the federal government." 24 Of him the historian Hubert H. Bancroft wrote:

> Leaving his wife and family in Illinois without the means of support, [W. W. Drummond] brought [to Utah] with him a harlot whom he had picked up in the streets of Washington, and introducing her as Mrs. Drummond, seated her by his side on the judicial bench. Gambler and bully, he openly avowed that he had come to Utah to make money, and in the presence of the chief justice declared: "Money is my God." When first he appeared in court he insulted the community by mocking at their laws and institutions, and especially at the institution of polygamy. He also declared that he would set aside the finding of the probate courts in all cases other than those which lay strictly within their jurisdiction. Here was a direct issue, and one that was immediately taken up, for as yet

none of the federal judges had declared the powers granted to these courts by the act of 1852 to be of no effect. Nor had any such view of the matter been expressed by the authorities in Washington.

When asking for admission as a state or territory, the Mormons did not suppose that the majesty of the law would be represented by a gamester with a strumpet by his side. 25

And:

That the appointment of Drummond was a disgrace to the administration at Washington is universally admitted by both Mormon and non-Mormon writers.... The non-Mormon Stenhouse remarks: "Plurality of wives was to the Mormons a part of their religion, openly acknowledged to all the world. Drummond's plurality was the outrage of a respectable wife of excellent reputation for the indulgence of a common prostitute and the whole of his conduct was a gross insult to the government which he represented and to the people among whom he was sent to administer the law. For any contempt the Mormons exhibited toward such a man, there is no need of apology." 26

Drummond soon became even more unpopular than had been Judge Brocchus (one of the "runaway officials" who had insulted the Saints from the pulpit during a general conference 27), and after administering justice for a brief term at Fillmore and Carson, fled for home by way of California.

On the day before Christmas, 1856, Parley P. Pratt made contact with John in Philadelphia, where John had gone on Church business. The previous September Elder Pratt had been called on a mission to the States, being instructed both to assist John

Taylor in writing for *The Mormon* and to look after a large group of Saints that had been baptized in Virginia. Periodically over the next few weeks John and Parley engaged in numerous deep conversations which included the topics in the discussion portrayed at the beginning of this chapter. Parley then departed for Virginia—the last time these two dear friends would see each other in the flesh.

Meanwhile:

> In 1856 a number of antipolygamy resolutions first appeared in Congress. That same year Utah made another bid for statehood, but it did not take the Mormon delegates long to discover that this was the wrong time politically. That same year the new Republican party entered its first national campaign and nominated the popular John C. Frémont as its presidential candidate. The party's official platform included a resolution that "it is both the right and the imperative duty of Congress to prohibit in the Territories those twin relics of barbarism—Polygamy and Slavery."
>
> The Republicans lost the election, but the anti-Mormon activities of 1856 had an important effect. Forced to disclaim any partiality for the Saints, the new Democratic president, James Buchanan, felt under obligation to do something to clear both himself and his party from any lingering suspicion that they supported the Mormons in Utah. 28

By early 1857, Buchanan was actively looking for a way to put his administration squarely on the side of those who opposed polygamy—and to do it in a big way! At the same time, ex-judge Drummond was making his way from California back to Washington, where he arrived late in the winter of 1857. On handing in his resignation at that time, Drummond also addressed a letter to the attorney general in which he made numerous groundless accusations against the Church and the people of Utah. Despite its false nature, this letter, written in March 1857, had its desired effect.

When he received and reviewed Drummond's letter, it seemed to President Buchanan that it was exactly what he and others, including Secretary of War John B. Floyd, had been looking for. In it, Drummond "charged that the Mormons looked to Brigham Young, and to him alone, for the law by which they should be governed, and considered no law of Congress binding. Further, he charged, there was a secret, oath-bound organization among all male members of the Church created to resist the laws of the land and acknowledge no law except the priesthood. He further charged the Church with murder, destruction of federal court records, harassment of federal officers, and slandering the federal government. He concluded by urging the president to appoint a governor who was not a member of the Church and to send with him sufficient military aid to enforce his rule." 29

Buchanan admittedly had no information as to Drummond's true character, yet even territorial chief justice John F. Kinney, another non-LDS federal appointee, had "urged Drummond's removal from office because he was immoral and 'entirely unworthy of a place upon the bench.'... Shortly after his inauguration in March 1857, President Buchanan appointed Alfred Cumming of Georgia governor of Utah, to replace Brigham Young. At the same time, in the mistaken belief that the Mormons were in rebellion against the government, Buchanan sent along a large military force to ensure the new governor's acceptance and authority." 30

In May 1857, having learned of the army being sent to Utah, John and Margaret departed from New York for the West, arriving in Salt Lake City on the 7TH of August, 1857. Under Judge Appleby and T. B. H. Stenhouse, *The Mormon* continued publication until September 19, when, owing to the constant clamor over what was then being termed the Utah War, they printed its last number.

15

LION IN A BLOSSOMING VALLEY

It was hot in the open-sided bowery on Temple Square, hot and still, with no movement in the September air. Yet it was nowhere near as muggy as it had been in New York, and John felt great relief over that. Still, this heat was uncommon for the season, and he wished he could take off his coat.

At the moment, Brigham Young was speaking to the four thousand or so assembled Saints, rousing them as only he could do, and John knew that in a few moments it would be his turn at the pulpit to attempt the same thing. Only, for a change he felt no inclination to speak to the Saints. Rather, his entire focus—all his thoughts for the past few moments, in fact—were that he was to direct his remarks, albeit obliquely, to the trim, straight young military officer who sat at his side on the rostrum. Yes, he thought as the spirit of inspiration burned within him, it was to Captain Stewart Van Vliet that the Lord wished him to speak, for it would be the young captain who would carry word of the Saints' cause back to the approaching army.

For nearly a week Van Vliet had been in the valley with his small squad of men, sent by General Harney to purchase forage and lumber for the troops who were marching against the Saints and to assure them that the approaching army meant none of them any harm. The captain was a sincere young man, obviously born and raised a gentleman, and John had no doubt that he believed what he was saying. The problem was that John and the rest of the Brethren knew better. Not only had John himself mingled with a portion of the army while returning to the valley, but the Saints had men in all the camps and knew what was intended. There had been continual boasts among the men and officers, even before they left the Missouri River, of what they intended to do to the "Mormons." The houses were picked out that certain persons were to inhabit; farms, property, and women were to be distributed. "Beauty and Booty" were their watchwords. The Saints were to experience another grand "Mormon" conquest, and their houses, gardens, orchards, vineyards, fields, wives, and daughters were to be the spoils.

In fact, it had already been determined by Brigham and the rest of them that such an army with such objects in view should not enter the Territory, even if this had to be prevented by force of arms. It had further been determined that before their enemies should again revel in the homes which their industry had built, the Saints would burn them to ashes, cut down every fruit tree and shrub, burn the fences, and leave the country behind them a ruined, blackened waste, while they fled again to the wilderness. These, John knew, were bold measures. The "army of Utah," as the invading force was called, marched under the United States flag; it was commanded by United States officers; it had been ordered to Utah by James Buchanan, President of the United States; and to resist it might be construed as rebellion or even treason—which meant hanging to the leaders who opposed it. Yet bold as these measures were, and fraught with such serious consequences to the leaders who had adopted them, they were fearlessly proclaimed and would be promptly executed if occasion demanded.

For a moment John smiled, recalling his own words to the Saints just a day or so after his arrival back in Utah, and again three weeks later. Never one to sidestep or backpedal from what he felt was right, John had stood in this very bowery and thundered: "So far as I am concerned, I say let everything come as God has ordained it. I do not desire trials; I do not desire affliction; I would pray to God to leave me not in temptation. But if the earthquake bellows, the lightnings flash, the thunders roll and the powers of darkness are let loose, and the spirit of evil is permitted to rage and an evil influence is brought to bear on the Saints, and my life with theirs, is put to the test—let it come! I know that President Young and those associated with him are full of the spirit of revelation, and they know what they are doing; I feel to acquiesce and put my shoulder to the work, whatever it is. If it is for peace, let it be peace; if it is for war, let it be to the hilt."

He had meant every word, and from the comments that had followed, he had no doubt others knew it, too. Three weeks later, to put at ease those few who had grown nervous over opposing the United States government, he had added: "There are thousands of you who are Americans, who have been born in this land, whose fathers fought for the liberties we used to enjoy, but have not enjoyed for some years past. There are thousands of such men here who feel the same spirit that used to burn in their father's bosoms—the spirit of liberty and equal rights—the spirit of according to every man that which belongs to him, and of robbing no man of his rights. Your fathers and grandfathers met the tyrant when he sought to put a yoke on their necks; as men and true patriots, they came forward and fought for their rights and in defense of that liberty which we, as their children, ought to enjoy. You feel the same spirit that inspired them; the same blood that coursed through their veins flows in yours; you feel true patriotism and a strong attachment to the Constitution and institutions bought by the blood of your fathers, and bequeathed to you by them as your richest patrimony. There are others of you that have taken the oath of allegiance to the United States;

and some of you not understanding correct principles, may, perhaps, feel qualms of conscience, and think, probably, that if we undertake to resist the powers that are seeking to make aggression upon us, we are doing wrong. No such thing. You let your conscience sleep at ease; let it be quiet; it is not we who are doing wrong; it is others who are committing wrong upon us."

Now it was Sunday, September 13, 1857, and Captain Van Vliet was there, sent by General Harney before he had been relieved of his command by General Albert Sidney Johnston. The Saints wished to believe his assurances of the army's peaceful intentions, but couldn't—not after so much past experience in Kirtland, Missouri, and Nauvoo—and so they refused to sell him anything that might be used by the army—

But Brigham was now finished, and so with a prayer in his heart John arose and stepped to the podium. He began innocuously enough, his every word spoken to the congregation but directed to Captain Van Vliet.

"What was your object in coming here?" he asked the Saints after a few words of introduction. "Was it to rebel against the general government?"

From behind him on the rostrum, Brigham answered loudly: "To get away from Christians."

The bowery burst into laughter, John's included. "Brother Brigham says it was to get away from Christians," he finally continued, "from that unbounded charity which you had experienced amongst them.

"For a fact, however, we came here because we would not help it, and now we have got an idea to stay here because we can help it. This is the feeling I am getting after conversing with a good many of you.

"Why do this people feel so comfortable when an army is approaching? Are you not afraid of being killed? No, not a great deal, you are not. And why is that? Because you have got a principle within you that cannot be conquered in time nor in eternity: you possess the principles of eternal life in your bosoms that cannot be subdued.

"Very well, suppose, after all, that they don't kill us. What would be your feelings if the United States wanted to have the honor of driving us from our homes once again, and bringing us subject to their depraved standard of moral and religious truth? Would you, if necessary, brethren, put the torch to your buildings and lay them in ashes and wander houseless into these mountains? I know what you would say and what you would do."

"Try the vote," Brigham growled from behind him.

John nodded almost imperceptibly. "All you that are willing to set fire to your property and lay it in ashes rather than submit to their military rule and oppression, manifest it by raising your hands."

The congregation, numbering more than four thousand, unanimously raised their hands.

"Thank you," John smiled with satisfaction. "I know what your feelings are. We have been persecuted and robbed long enough; and in the name of Israel's God, we will be free!"

"Amen!" the entire congregation responded with a shout.

"I say amen all the time to that," Brigham declared from behind him.

John nodded with satisfaction, knowing that the young captain was getting the message. "I feel to thank God that I am associated with such men, with such people, where honesty and truth dwell in the heart—where men have a religion that they are not afraid to live by, and that they are not afraid to die by; and I would not give a straw for anything short of that!"

Later, as they stood visiting, it was apparent to John that Captain Van Vliet was little short of astonished. He had not been prepared for such unity of sentiment or purpose. He admired the Saints' courage, he told John, but worried for their safety if things came to a conflict with the government.

"Don't you see, Mr. Taylor?" he urged. "Even if your people should successfully resist the army now on your borders, within another year you will see an overwhelming force sent to suppress and punish you. There will be no way in heaven nor on earth that you can successfully overcome such numbers as will be sent!"

"We know that will be the case," John smiled a little sadly, "but when those troops arrive they will find Utah a desert; every house will be burned to the ground, every tree cut down, and every field laid waste. We have three years' provisions on hand, Captain, which we will cache, and then take to the mountains and bid defiance to all the powers of the government."

"Brother Taylor is right," Brigham declared as he stepped up to the two much taller men. "We have transgressed no law, Captain Van Vliet, and we have no occasion to do so, neither do we intend to. But as for any nation's coming to destroy this people, God Almighty being my helper, they cannot come here! That is my feeling upon that point, and you may report it to your superiors."

Abruptly the stocky President of The Church of Jesus Christ of Latter-day Saints turned and walked away, and without further word John escorted Captain Van Vliet down off the rostrum. Now, he knew, it was all in the hands of the Lord and this naïve young officer— 1

Upon his return from New York on the 7TH of August, 1857, John was no doubt pleased to discover that his writing in *The Mormon* had merited Brigham Young's approval. Two days after his return, he was invited to preach in the bowery on Temple Square. After speaking with great power concerning the state of the eastern press as well as the feelings of the people regarding the Church, he concluded with his own ringing testimony concerning the Church's mission to the world.

Brigham Young spoke next, and he first commended the

labors of the committee, of which John had been a member, who had submitted Utah's most recent petition for statehood to the U.S. government. He then focused his expressions directly to John's labors as editor of the Church's small New York newspaper:

> With regard to the labors of Brother Taylor in editing the paper called *The Mormon,* published in the city of New York, I have heard many remarks concerning the editorials in that paper, not only from the Saints, but from those who do not profess to believe the religion we have embraced; and it is probably one of the strongest edited papers that is now published. I can say, as to its editorials, that it is one of the strongest papers ever published, so far as my information extends; and I have never read one sentence in them but what my heart could bid success to it, and beat a happy response to every sentence that I have read or heard read. Brother Taylor, that is for you; and I believe that these are the feelings and the sentiments of all in this community who have perused that paper. 2

It was nice, John must have thought, to finally have his work appreciated.

It would also have been nice for him to finally have spent a little time with his families on Taylor Row—the line of homes he had built for Leonora and her sister-wives. It would have been wonderful to become reacquainted with his growing children, to introduce all of them to his newest wife, Margaret Young (who was ever after called Maggie), and to spend time working his large family farm in the southwestern part of the valley—already becoming known as Taylorsville. Unfortunately, times in Utah were so critical that he could do little of what he wished—of what would have been nice.

"For several years the crops, through excessive drouth and grasshoppers, had been at least a partial failure; the isolation of the people from manufacturing and commercial centers, with very limited and very slow means of transportation, had left them almost destitute of clothing; an army was *en route* for the Territory, but as to its mission the governor received no definite information, though there was a general and a fairly accurate understanding that its mission was not one of intended peace and good will to the people of Utah." 3

In early September, Captain Stewart Van Vliet was sent with a small detachment of men to see if he could purchase forage and lumber from the Saints—and learned of the Saints' determination to burn their homes rather than be pillaged again, as portrayed at the beginning of this chapter.

The day following Captain Van Vliet's departure for Ham's Fork and the approaching army, Brigham Young declared martial law in Utah. Lieutenant-General Daniel H. Wells went to the front, near Echo Canyon, where he directed the movements of the hundreds of Saints who had rallied against the government forces. He was accompanied by John Taylor and George A. Smith, all of whom remained in the field until mid-December, when it was determined that winter snows, as well as the guerrilla tactics of men such as Major Lot Smith and Colonel R. T. Burton, had successfully stopped the army from approaching any closer to the valley.

Meanwhile, Captain Van Vliet had "returned to the army on Ham's Fork deeply impressed with the seriousness and perhaps with the absurdity of the government's movement against Utah. Moreover he had become the friend of the Mormon people, and his report to the Secretary of War, made at Washington the November following, did much, doubtless, in paving the way for an amicable adjustment of the Utah difficulties." 4

After his return from the front, John attended the state legislature as an elected member from Salt Lake County and was unanimously chosen as Speaker of the House. The primary business of the legislature was to send a memorial to the President and Congress of the United States, reminding them of a previous petition wherein the Saints had requested only the right to be governed by officials duly elected from amongst themselves. They reiterated their petition, at the same time reminding Washington of the numerous wrongs they had suffered and of their status as American citizens who were guaranteed rights, freedoms, and protection—all of which had been stripped from them.

Meanwhile, with winter hard upon them, the situation of the army on the plains of Wyoming was desperate. It took General Johnston

> fifteen days to push thirty-five miles through storms and below-zero weather, cattle died by the hundreds, and the soldiers arrived at the fort [Bridger] only to discover that the Mormons had burned the wooden buildings. The stone walls were intact, however, and provided partial shelter for the winter, and the army had enough cattle and supplies to see it through. A major military engagement would have been impossible. Thus ended the only hostilities of the Utah War....
>
> [I]n the states the difficulties of the army were becoming known, and Buchanan was being severely criticized. He was chided in particular for sending the expedition without first thoroughly investigating the charges and for sending it so late in the season that it could not get through the mountains before snowfall. At this point Thomas L. Kane, a long-time and influential friend of the Saints, offered to go to Utah as a mediator, and his offer was gratefully accepted. It was a near-heroic journey for him. Unable to enter Utah through the mountains because of the heavy winter, he took a ship to Panama, crossed the isthmus, took another ship to southern

California, and went overland through San Bernardino to Salt Lake City, arriving late in February 1858.

After persuading President Young that the Saints should let the new governor enter the territory unmolested, [Kane] traveled eastward through bitterly cold weather to Fort Bridger. [He] persuaded Governor Cumming to return with him to Salt Lake City without a military escort, assuring him that the Saints would accept him peacefully. When Cumming arrived he found that Kane was right, for he was treated with dignity and respect. He administered his office with tact and diplomacy and won the respect and confidence of the people. 5

Nevertheless, the Saints continued to have little trust for the army, which they knew would be marching into the valley as soon as the snows had melted sufficiently for the movement of the troops and wagons. While waiting to learn if Thomas L. Kane would be successful in bringing Governor Cumming into the valley without military escort, John and other Church leaders met in council and decided not to fight, but instead to abandon their homes and retreat southward, leaving men behind to burn everything should the army prove duplicitous. This was a shrewd plan, for the Mormons knew that such a move would be reported nationally and would bring not only public favor upon them, but antipathy for the federal officials who had sent the army in the first place.

Even before Governor Cumming arrived they had begun preparations for a move south. The Saints organized themselves magnificently.... Between the end of March and mid-May some thirty thousand settlers from Utah's northern towns moved south to the vicinity of Provo, leaving behind only enough men to care for fields and crops. If it appeared that the army intended to occupy their homes, these men were to set fire to them. It was an extraordinary operation. As the Saints moved south they cached all the stone cut for the Salt Lake Temple and covered the foundations to make [the site] resemble a plowed field. They boxed and carried with them twenty thousand bushels of tithing grain, as well as machinery, equipment, and all the Church records and books. The sight of thirty thousand people moving south was awesome, and the amazed Governor Cumming did all he could to persuade them to return to their homes. Brigham Young replied that if the troops were withdrawn from the territory, the people would stop moving, but that [they] would rather spend the rest of their lives in the mountains than endure governmental oppression. 6

John's family joined in the massive exodus from Salt Lake City, caching in a gravel bank near Taylor Row such treasures as a piano and other bulky or heavy items beforehand. Two of John's wives, Sophia Whitaker and Mary Ann Oakley, were expecting children at the time of the move, and the wintry conditions they were to endure would make their lives that much more difficult. But hardly more so than for the other wives — Leonora Cannon, who had been through this four times (Kirtland, Missouri, Nauvoo, Winter Quarters); Jane Ballantyne; Harriet Whitaker; Caroline Gilliam; Elizabeth Kaighin; and the newest bride, Maggie Young. And then there were the children, all of whom were either helping or getting in the way of those who did—

It seemed an eternity before [the Taylor family] reached Provo, only forty-five miles south. Most of the refugees were camped on the Bottoms west of town, awaiting directions to the land of milk and honey [where most of the 30,000 refugees expected to be led]. Sophia's heart sank at first sight of "Shanghai," the squalid jumble of tents, dugouts, shelters of log and of mud and willow. Many

Jane Ballantyne in a
photograph taken years
after John Taylor's death

N.D.

people lived in wagon boxes. Brigham and some other officials had temporary housing in the city square.

John was approaching, pushing through the crowd of arrivals. He'd gone ahead to find a place, and by some miracle had located a house in the jam-packed town. It wasn't much, he cautioned as she and Harriet rode with him in the carriage—with springs on it—but anything at all at such a time was a godsend.

The dwelling, belonging to Roger Farrar, was in the back of the lot. It had been used as an outbuilding after a new house was built in front. As she went in, Sophia caught the scent of a chicken coop. The window panes which weren't broken were black with grime. It wasn't much, John said, but they were lucky to find anything.

They lived in the wagon box behind the house; after three days of scrubbing, cleaning, and whitewashing the walls, they moved in. Sophia awoke in the night scratching. The light of a match showed the sheets crawling with bedbugs. They moved back into the wagon. John brought a can of coal oil and everyone worked, going over every crack in floor and walls with rags wet with it. Then John set rocks around the floor and on them put pans smouldering with sulphur, pepper, tar, and horse manure. Two days later they again moved into the house....

The following month, on May 15, Sophia gave birth in the chicken coop to a baby boy, whom the father blessed and christened John Whitaker [Taylor]. 7

On the 26TH of June, the army marched into the quiet and deserted city of the Saints. And though their band played bravely, no Saints were there to hear except those who had been instructed to torch the buildings should the troops try anything. They did not, but marched steadily until they reached the Jordan River, where camp was made for the night. The next day they continued on south and west to Cedar Valley where they erected a permanent camp, ironically named Camp Floyd after the man who was secretly pushing for the South's secession from the Union.

On June 30, believing that the army intended to honor their agreement to leave the Saints alone, Brigham gave the word that the people could return to their homes and then led the procession. "The campaign had taken its toll, and most of the Saints were beset with poverty and frustrated by the confusing chain of circumstances that had interrupted their plans for building Zion." 8

[A] decade and more of achievement and social independence, in the face of hostile nature and hostile humanity, had ended in poverty and disappointment. The picture of 30,000 pioneers trudging back to their hard-won homes, farms, and orchards, with their skimpy and ragged suits and dresses, driving their pigs and family cows, to the accompaniment of jeers from "the cream of the United States Army" would live long in the hearts and minds of the pioneer leaders. None would have dreamed that within three years Babylon itself would be engulfed in a terrible fratricide as the result of which the tables would be reversed: Soldiers would be pulled out of Utah leaving to the Saints the spoils. 9

In February of 1860, "General Johnston left Camp Floyd for Washington, D.C.... General Winfield Scott, not sure of General Johnston's loyalty to the Union after the beginning of the Civil War, relieved him of his command.... In May a number of companies left Camp Floyd for New Mexico. Many of the camp followers, including women and gamblers, left with them, a relief to the people of Utah."10 Soon, with war imminent and then underway, Colonel Cooke, the commanding officer, was given orders to remove the troops and sell anything the army could not take with them at public auction. There, "$4,000,000 worth of property sold for abut $100,000.... Toward the end of July, 1861, the last remnants of the...army that had come to show the power of Uncle Sam and had camped three years in the desert, accomplishing nothing worthwhile, had gone."11

For several years following the Utah War, John labored primarily among the Saints of Utah and the western region, preaching the gospel and usually accompanying Brigham Young on his annual tours of the settlements. "He also attended all conferences and councils, and assisted in a general way all public enterprises.

"He was a member of the Utah Territorial Legislature from 1857 to 1876; and was elected [S]peaker of the House for five successive sessions, beginning in 1857. As the Speaker of the House he won the esteem of the members by his uniform courtesy and fairness. As a member he sought to promote the interests of his constituents and at the same time to legislate for the welfare of the entire Territory.

"In 1868 he was elected Probate Judge of Utah County, and continued in office until the December term of that court in 1870. As the laws of Utah then provided that the probate courts should 'have power to exercise original jurisdiction, both civil and criminal, and as well in chancery as in common law,' the position was one of considerable importance. Especially in those days when the perverseness of Federal judges led them frequently to close the district courts indefinitely....

"During these years, too, he continued to stand up in defense of the rights and liberties of the Saints, missing no opportunity to speak out in his bold, manly style against those who would wrong them."12 One of the most interesting, and far-reaching, of these defenses occurred late in the fall of 1869, when John took to task the Honorable Schuyler Colfax, then Vice President

John Taylor   CA. *1862–72*

of the United States.

Colfax, derisively called "Smiler" because of his often self-righteous attitude, had first visited Utah in 1865, at the close of the Civil War, when he had been Speaker of the House. In company with other men of the eastern establishment, he had spent a week in Utah attending the theater, bathing in the Great Salt Lake, making and listening to speeches, and spending one very informative evening with John at Leonora's home on Taylor Row. Perhaps it was because John knew three of the men, including Colfax, from when he had lived in New York editing *The Mormon* that after dinner, surface politeness had given way to the true feelings of these men regarding the Church.

One of the men, Bowles, "said that the result of the visit was to increase his appreciation of the Mormons' material progress; to evoke congratulations for their order, frugality, morality, and industry; and to excite wonder at the perfection of the church system and enlarge respect for the personal sincerity of its leaders. However, he said frankly, it served on the other hand 'to deepen my disgust at their polygamy and strengthen my convictions of its barbaric and degrading influences.'" [13]

The rest of the visitors quickly joined in, declaring that with the coming of the transcontinental railroad, both Mormonism and polygamy were dead, for such societal anomalies could exist only in perfect isolation. "'The click of the telegraph and the roll of the Overland stage are its death rattle now,'" said Bowles. "'The first whistle of the locomotive will sound its requiem; and the pickaxe of the miner will dig its grave.'" [14] Another even stated his opinion that the Church would vanish so thoroughly that the great Salt Lake Temple, then under construction, might become the transcontinental railroad's new depot.

By 1868, the opinions expressed to John by those powerful men had found their way into print, both newspaper and book, so that the whole country was talking about the forthcoming joining of the railroad and immediate demise of the Mormon Church. This was especially true in Salt Lake City, where Gentile merchants fully expected to reap a veritable harvest through easier shipment of goods combined with the collapse of the Church.

Meanwhile, Latter-day Saint merchants and businessmen—what precious few there were, because Brigham discouraged merchandising for money—were starting to agitate for freer economic intercourse with all classes of people, Mormon and Gentile alike. In other words, they wanted to start making money for themselves, rather than for the people as a whole. Babylon was scratching for a foothold in Zion!

"'There is growing up in our midst a power that menaces us with utter destruction,' declared George Q. Cannon of the First Presidency at October conference, 1868. 'We are told openly and without disguise that when the railroad is completed there will be such a flood of so-called "civilization" brought in here that every vestige of us, our church and institutions, shall be completely obliterated.'" 15

Soon, in a campaign to strengthen the Saints while weakening the power of their adversaries (seen as both the Mormon and Gentile merchants), Church leaders initiated a string of cooperative mercantile establishments throughout the territory. Those few Mormon merchants in Salt Lake City, whether they wished it or not, were merged into one company, Zion's Cooperative Mercantile Institution—ZCMI. From such a strong base giving good prices to all worthy Saints, it was reasoned, none would have reason to trade with Gentiles. From historical perspective, all this accomplished was to unite the Gentiles and free-thinking Mormons of Utah into a united front against Brigham's Saints—a war to the finish for control of Utah.

In the midst of all this, two weeks before Christmas in that year of 1868, Leonora Cannon, John's first love and the true love

Portrait of Leonora Cannon Taylor

N.D.

of his life, died of pneumonia. On top of his grief, there was the wearisome brouhaha surrounding the Mormon boycott of Gentile businesses—as well as the "New Movement"17 of merchants, businessmen, and intellectuals who had grown tired of what they thought of as Brigham's hard-fisted one-man rule—and the economic turmoil it all seemed to be creating. Growing tired of it, John took the opportunity to accompany two other brethren east to Boston the next fall, where they entered into some business negotiations for the Church. It was during this absence, in October 1869, that Schuyler "Smiler" Colfax, now Vice President of the United States under President Ulysses S. Grant, made his second visit to Utah.

Apparently believing that the man who had crushed the Confederacy should now settle the Mormon question "once and for all with the sword," Colfax determined to deliver a major speech to this effect from the steps of his hotel—the Townsend House—in downtown Salt Lake City.

Getting word of this, T. B. H. Stenhouse went to the Vice President and implored him to reconsider his remarks and allow the Mormons to handle their own problems. After all, he reasoned, by their in-fighting they were about to destroy themselves. Why unite them in another war against the government? Colfax ignored his pleadings, and on October 5, 1869, Colfax delivered his speech.

After praising the Saints for all sorts of temporal accomplishments, Colfax swung into an attack on the very heart of the Mormon society.

You have as much right to worship the Creator through... your church organization as I have through the ministers and...creed of mine. But our country is governed by law, and no assumed revelation justifies anyone trampling on the law. If it did, every wrong-doer would use that argument to protect himself in his disobedience to it. 17

His speech was published in its entirety both in Salt Lake City and in the *Springfield Republican,* which John received at his hotel in New York. He read and discussed the speech with his two associates during supper, after which he hurried to his room to begin drafting a reply, which took until breakfast the next morning to complete. It was published in both *The Deseret News* and the *New York Tribune.* Soon there was a counter-reply from Colfax, and then a counter-counter-reply from John—all of it published in the national press and spread across the country. As reported by B. H. Roberts: "Replying to [the first] part of the Vice-President's argument, Elder Taylor commended the magnanimity and even-handed justice of the first paragraph saying that the sentiments did honor to the author of them and that they ought to be engraven on every American heart. To the second paragraph he replied:

> That our country is governed by law all admit; but when it is said that "no assumed revelation justifies any one in trampling on the law," I should respectfully ask, What! not if it interferes with my religious faith, which you state "is a matter between God and myself alone?" Allow me, sir, here to state that the assumed revelation referred to is one of the most vital parts of our religious faith; it emanated from God and cannot be legislated away; it is part of the "Everlasting Covenant" which God has given to man. Our marriages are solemnized by proper authority; a woman is sealed unto a man for time and for eternity, by the power of which Jesus speaks, which "seals on earth and it is sealed in heaven." With us it is "Celestial Marriage"; take this from us and you rob us of our hopes and associations in the resurrection of the just. This not our religion? You do not see things as we do.... I make these remarks to show that it is considered, by us, a part of our religious faith, which I have no doubt, did you understand it as we do, you would

defend, as you state, "with as much zeal as the right of every other denomination throughout the land." Permit me here to say, however, that it was the revelation (I will not say assumed) that Joseph and Mary had, which made them look upon Jesus as the Messiah; which made them flee from the wrath of Herod, who was seeking the young child's life. This they did in contravention of law which was his decree. Did they do wrong in protecting Jesus from the law? But Herod was a tyrant. That makes no difference; it was the law of the land, and I have yet to learn the difference between a tyrannical king and a tyrannical Congress. When we talk of executing law in either case, that means force,—force means an army, and an army means death. Now I am not sufficiently versed in metaphysics to discover the difference in its effects, between the asp of Cleopatra, the dagger of Brutus, the chalice of Lucretia Borgia, or the bullet or sabre of an American soldier.

I have, sir, written the above in consequence of some remarks which follow [John is referring here to the following quote from Colfax]:

"I do not concede that the institution you have established here, and which is condemned by the law, is a question of religion."

Now, with all due deference, I do think that if Mr. Colfax had carefully examined our religious faith he would have arrived at other conclusions. In the absence of this I might ask, who constituted Mr. Colfax a judge of my religious faith? I think he has stated that "The faith of every man is a matter between himself and God alone."

Mr. Colfax has a perfect right to state and feel that he does not believe in the revelation on which my religious faith is based, nor in my faith at all; but has he the right to dictate my religious faith? I think not; he does not consider it religion, but it is nevertheless mine.

If a revelation from God is not a religion, what is?

His not believing it [to be] from God makes no difference; I know it is. The Jews did not believe in Jesus but Mr. Colfax and I do; their unbelief does not alter the revelation.

John further responded to Colfax's arguments that the Saints' marriage practices had "nothing to do with religion" by pointing out that history revealed this as a timeworn excuse used by persecutors throughout the ages to justify their actions:

According to this theory no persons ever were persecuted for their religion.... Could anybody suppose that that erudite, venerable, and profoundly learned body of men,— the great Sanhedrim [sic] of the Jews; or that those holy men, the chief priests, scribes and Pharisees, would persecute anybody for religion? Jesus was put to death,— not for His religion,—but because He was a blasphemer; because He had a devil and cast out devils through Beelzebub the prince of devils; because He, being a carpenter's son, and known among them as such, declared Himself the Son of God. So they said, and they were the then judges. Could anybody be more horrified than those Jews at such pretensions? His disciples were persecuted, proscribed and put to death, not for their religion, but because they "were pestilent fellows and stirrers up of sedition," and because they believed in an "assumed revelation" concerning "one Jesus, who was put to death, and who, they said, had risen again." It was for false pretensions and a lack of religion that they were persecuted. Their religion was not like that of the Jews; ours, not like that of Mr. Colfax.

Loyola did not invent and put into use the faggot, the flame, the sword, the thumbscrews, the rack and gibbet to persecute anybody, it was to purify the Church of heretics, as others would purify Utah. His zeal was for the Holy Mother Church. The Nonconformists of England and Holland, the Huguenots of France and the Scottish non-Covenanters were not persecuted or put to death for their religion; it was for being schismatics, turbulent and unbelievers. All of the above claimed that they were persecuted for their religion. All of the persecutors, as Mr. Colfax said about us, did "not concede that the institution they had established which was condemned by the law, was religion"; or, in other terms, it was an imposture or false religion.

Expanding on his theme of injustices and oppression "perpetrated…in the name of law," John turned again to history and continued in something of a sarcastic vein.

When Jesus was plotted against by Herod and the infants were put of death, who could complain? It was law: we must submit to law. The Lord Jehovah, or Jesus, the Savior of the world, has no right to interfere with law. Jesus was crucified according to law. Who can complain? Daniel was thrown into a den of lions strictly according to law. The king would have saved him, if he could; but he could not resist law. The massacre of St. Bartholomew was in accordance with law. The guillotine of Robespierre, of France, which cut heads off by the thousand, did it according to law. What right had the victims to complain? But these things were done in barbarous ages. Do not let us, then, who boast of our civilization, follow their example; let us be more just, more generous, more forbearing, more magnanimous. We are told that we are living in a more enlightened age. Our morals are more pure, (?) our ideas more refined and enlarged, our institutions more liberal. "Ours," says Mr. Colfax, "is a land of civil and religious liberty, and the faith of every man is a matter between himself and God alone," providing God [doesn't] shock our moral ideas by introducing something we don't believe in. If He does, let Him look out. We won't persecute, very far be that from us; but we will make our platforms, pass Congressional laws and make you submit to them. We may, it is true, have to send out an army, and shed the blood of many; but what of that? It is so much more pleasant to be proscribed and killed according to the laws of the Great Republic, in the "asylum for the oppressed," than to perish ignobly by the decrees of kings, through their miserable minions, in the barbaric ages.

John's reply led to another article by Colfax on "the Mormon question" which was published in the *New York Independent.* In it, B. H. Roberts notes, Colfax repeated the main arguments made in his original speech, made an effort to trace the Mormons' history, and attempted to answer John's arguments. John, of course, replied in an article that was again widely published in the eastern papers. In describing Elder Taylor's reply, Roberts says, with no small hint of admiration: "he corrected [Colfax's] errors, reproved his blunders, answered his arguments, laughed at his folly; now belaboring him with the knotty cudgel of unanswerable argument, and now roasting him before the slow fire of his sarcasm; now honoring him for his zeal, which, however mistaken, had the smack of honesty about it; and now pitying him for being led astray on some historical fact." One passage in particular that led to a little "roasting" from Elder Taylor was Colfax's contention that it was "water," more than the labors of the Saints, that led to the desert's blossoming as a rose. This, B. H. Roberts said, "afforded

Elder Taylor a fine opportunity for one of those poetic flights so frequently to be met with both in his writings and sermons":

> Water! [John exclaimed.] Mirabile dictu! Here I must help Mr. C. out.
>
> This wonderful little water nymph, after playing with the clouds on our mountain tops, frolicking with the snow and rain in our rugged gorges for generations, coquetting with the sun and dancing to the sheen of the moon, about the time the Mormons came here, took upon herself to perform a great miracle, and descending to the valley with a wave of her magic wand and the mysterious words, "hiccory, diccory, dock," cities and streets were laid out, crystal waters flowed in ten thousand rippling streams, fruit trees and shrubbery sprang up, gardens and orchards abounded, cottages and mansions were organized, fruits, flowers and grain in all their elysian glory appeared and the desert blossomed as the rose; and this little frolicking elf, so long confined to the mountains and water courses proved herself far more powerful than Cinderella or Aladdin.... But to be serious, did water tunnel through our mountains, construct dams, canals and ditches, lay out our cities and towns, import and plant choice fruit-trees, shrubs and flowers, cultivate the land and cover it with the cattle on a thousand hills, erect churches, school-houses and factories, and transform a howling wilderness into a fruitful field and a garden?... Unfortunately for Mr. Colfax, it was Mormon polygamists who did it.... What if a stranger on gazing upon the statuary in Washington and our magnificent Capitol, and after rubbing his eyes were to exclaim, "Eureka! it is only rock and mortar and wood!" This discoverer would announce that instead of the development of art, intelligence, industry and enterprise,

its component parts were simply stone, mortar and wood. Mr. Colfax has discovered that our improvements are attributable to water!"

Colfax made another attempt to justify the United States' efforts against polygamy in the face of the Saints' claims that the practice was part of their religion by pointing out the English government's efforts to suppress the suttee, an act they found morally reprehensible, in India. Elder Taylor replied:

> To present Mr. Colfax's argument fairly, it stands thus: The burning of Hindoo [sic] widows was considered a religious rite by the Hindoos. The British were horrified at the practice, and suppressed it. The Mormons believe polygamy to be a religious rite. The American nation consider it a scandal, and that they ought to put it down. Without entering into all the details, I think the above a fair statement of the question. He says "The claim that religious faith commanded it was powerless, and it went down, as a relic of barbarism." He says: "History tells us what a civilized nation, akin to ours, actually did, where they had the power." I wish to treat this argument with candor....
>
> The British suppressed the suttee in India, and therefore we must be equally moral and suppress polygamy in the United States. Hold! not so fast; let us state facts as they are and remove the dust. The British suppressed the suttee, but tolerated eighty-three millions of polygamists in India. The suppression of the suttee and that of polygamy are two very different things. If the British are indeed to be our exemplars, Congress had better wait until polygamy is suppressed in India. But it is absurd to compare the suttee to polygamy; one is murder and the destruction of life, the other is national economy and the

increase and perpetuation of life. Suttee ranks truly with infanticide, both of which are destructive of human life. Polygamy is salvation compared with either, and tends even more than monogamy to increase and perpetuate the human race.

Roberts then says that "Elder Taylor closed the discussion with a vivid exposé of the loathsome immorality and crime that existed in the villages, towns and cities of the East; and called the attention of the Vice-President to the fact that there was work enough for himself, for Congress and also for the moralists and ministers in the United States nearer home, in suppressing the evils by which they were immediately surrounded, without plunging into the isolated valleys of Utah to legislate away the religion of the Mormons, under the specious plea of suppressing crime." 18

> "We have now a territory out of debt;…we have no gambling, no drunkenness, no prostitution, foeticide nor infanticide. We maintain our wives and children, and we have made the 'desert to bloom as the rose.'
>
> "We are here at peace with ourselves, and with all the world. Whom have we injured? Why can we not be let alone?" 19

Here was the Church's "Champion of Rights" at his best! "On returning to Utah [after the first letter] he found himself the lion of the valley. Congratulations showered from all sides. Never, he was told, had the Mormon case been so masterfully presented."20 Neither has history looked upon the exchange with much less fervor. Called by B. H. Roberts, "the most important discussion in the history of the Church," the literary exchange between the two men was thought so highly of, that two thousand copies of it were issued for distribution in Washington and by missionaries throughout the world. At the time it did much to allay the falsehoods and suspicions directed toward the Church and its leaders.

In an interesting twist of fate, three years later, in the summer of 1872, Schuyler Colfax was involved in a scandal of his own making that destroyed his reputation and ended his influence. "Sanctimonious 'Smiler' Colfax, famous for self-righteousness, had while Speaker of the House accepted twenty shares of stock under the counter from the infamous Credit Mobilier, the company organized to build the transcontinental railroad—with millions in government subsidies. A congressional investigation revealed that Colfax had accepted a cash stock dividend from Credit Mobilier, which he lied about under oath; and also was involved in kickbacks from government contracts...

"*The Washington Post* wrote his political obituary: 'A resolution for the impeachment of the bribed and perjured Colfax failed by a majority of three votes.'" 21

John "saw the hand of the Lord in the downfall of Colfax. Once more his faith was vindicated that if the Saints made no compromise with God's laws, the Almighty would smite their enemies hip and thigh." 22

16

THE ESCALATING POGROM AGAINST POLYGAMY

"I'm telling you, Maggie, that is precisely what the man said."
Looking at the note he had made, John read it again. "'While the
case at bar is called The People versus Brigham Young, its other
and real name is Federal Authority versus Polygamous Theocracy.'
It's polygamy they want."

"So," Margaret Young questioned as she bustled about the small
kitchen, "McKean admitted it, then?"

"Yes," John responded as he reached down to lift onto his lap
one of his and Maggie's little ones, a few-months-old baby,
"he admitted that he is a judge on a mission—not for justice, but to
see that plural marriage is overthrown and stamped out."

For a moment Maggie paused, looking at her husband.
Though Elizabeth Kaighin was now John Taylor's senior wife,
he kept his books and study at his most recent wife's home, and she
was pleased to have him there. Maggie also knew that he liked to
rehearse his ideas before her and had once told her she had a mind
like a spring trap. She didn't know about that, but she did know
that she loved this man more all the time and was always a little in
awe of her status as one of his wives.

"John, this could be serious, couldn't it?"

John smiled sadly as he tried burping the baby. "Yes, Maggie,

McKean will do his best to make things hot for us."

"But...how has it come to this? How did the Saints end up with such a sorry popinjay for Chief Justice of the Territory?"

"Popinjay, is it?" John chuckled as he lowered the now contented baby back to the floor. "Well, Maggie, to my way of thinking, it began with Vice President Colfax, who after being drubbed soundly by yours truly, returned east and in a surly mood helped draft the Cullom Bill and then ram it through the House of Representatives. If that had passed, they would have imprisoned all polygamists, confiscated their property, taken their wives and children, and disenfranchised anybody who so much as believed in plural marriage. We would have been compelled to deny an essential of the faith in order to vote. And 40,000 troops would have been sent to Utah to enforce the law."

"I'm thankful it didn't pass," she responded with a shudder.

"So am I. But they weren't finished—and aren't yet. I recall it was while I was laboring with others of the Brethren to draft an official objection to the bill that another of the Colfax coterie and Chaplain of the House, the Reverend Dr. J. P. Newman, delivered a blistering attack against polygamy and the Mormons from his pulpit at the Metropolitan Methodist Church in Washington, D.C., declaring polygamy to be an abomination in the sight of the Lord and prohibited in the Bible. It was no accident that, seated in the congregation, was President U. S. Grant, already an outspoken anti-Mormon."

"I remember when Reverend Newman came here to debate Brother Pratt."

"It was a wonderful show," John smiled mischievously. "They had already battered each other in the national press; then Newman declared he was ready to come here to Salt Lake City to settle the issue in person. Did I tell you that prior to his arrival he had been advised, and I quote: 'If you meet Orson Pratt, you will debate a learned man who knows the Bible well, who is familiar with Greek and Latin, and a man who will stick closely to the Bible text. On the other hand, John Taylor won't leave a grease spot behind.'"

Maggie laughed delightedly. "You do have a reputation, John."

"Yes, I've tried to earn it." Reaching down, John took up the baby again, who once more had started to squall. "I believe I've already burped her, Maggie."

"Yes, you have," Maggie said as she lifted the child from her husband and put her to her breast, "but she's telling you she isn't finished with supper."

"I suppose I'll do better once she learns English." John relaxed once again. "I'll tell you, after those three days, Newman left town a lot more quietly than he had come. While he sincerely believes polygamy to be an abomination, there is no way he could prove it from the Bible."

John sat quietly for a moment, turning through pages in a small day book. "You know, Maggie," he finally spoke while still reading down a page, "the *New York World* speculated that if President Grant had sent those 40,000 troops to Utah if the Cullom Bill had passed, it would mean war. They imagined that the Mormons could give such a force two or three years of fighting at an annual expense to the country of no less than two hundred million dollars. Since the Utah War, I imagine they finally know back East that we should be taken seriously."

"Do you believe that there could have been two or three years of fighting?"

"Oh, we could have given them problems, all right. We still could. The important, thing, Maggie, was that enough others believed it that the Cullom Bill failed to pass the Senate. I must say, I still applaud their next move—giving the vote to women. I suppose they imagined you would all vote yourselves right out of plural marriage—but the women voted exactly as had the men."

"Of course we did. We believe the same."

"And act better," John acknowledged quietly. "So, now that the Cullom Bill and women's suffrage have both failed, we're left with this: President Grant appointing federal officials like Judge McKean to Utah based on their determination to subdue the Saints.

"Did you know, Maggie, that among those offering Grant their services for the post of governor to Utah was the leader of the Josephites back in Nauvoo, and even old Sidney Rigdon, who felt he might do some good in setting the Mormons straight."

"Sidney Rigdon. Wasn't he the Prophet Joseph's counselor at one time?"

"Yes, and a fine Latter-day Saint, until his pride got the better of him," John mused. "Now we've got a Missourian for our governor—fancy that!—and our new chief justice, James B. McKean, along with his rabid Mormon-hating district attorney, Robert N. Baskin. They've already indicted George Q. Cannon and Henry Lawrence for lewd and lascivious cohabitation, and there were other warrants issued on that same charge, or for being implicated in unsolved murders during the Utah War, thirteen years past.

"But it's Brigham Young they have been after all along, and now they've indicted him. He's the big fish in the pond, the one whom, having been taken down, will open the way to giving them the political muscle they think they need."

"And so that is what they are after, do you think? Political power?"

John nodded. "In part, yes, for almost all politicians seek it. But I assure you, Maggie, there is more to this, much more!"

Maggie smiled. "Then I suppose we shall soon see your mighty pen come forth again, as always, in defense of righteousness and truth?"

John's look was a bit sheepish. "Well, I did bring my notes, Maggie, so if you don't mind—"

"What? Senior Apostle John Taylor staying up all night,

his well-worn pen blistering the minions of evil who seem constantly to oppose us?" Maggie chuckled tenderly. "Why, my dear husband, should I mind such a scene as that?" And with a pert toss of her head, Margaret Young carried her now-sleeping baby from the warm and comfortable room. 1

When the Lord raises up his earthly servants, he grants them gifts peculiar to the needs of the generation in which they will serve. Such was obviously the case with John Taylor. At once he was fearless in the face of wrong, supremely confident in his understanding of what was right, and blessed with a masterful command of the English language which flowed with equal power either verbally or through his tireless pen. Add to that his brilliant and constantly inquiring mind; his extremely well-rounded understanding of nations, histories, and governments; his delightful sense of humor; and his rare ability to hear and then follow the whisperings of the Holy Spirit, and it will be seen that he was indeed raised up to remind and reprimand the government of the United States for the folly of its ways in dealing with the Lord's people—the Latter-day Saints.

After he had completed his three-year assignment editing *The Mormon,* and as the nation reeled with the death and horror of the Civil War, John "attributed its cause to a gradual decline of 'national integrity, [an] increase of crime and corruption, and a want of a proper administration of the laws.... Corruption and mob violence began to prevail...[when] the rights of American citizens [the Saints in Missouri] were trampled underfoot, the Constitution and laws desecrated.... Joseph Smith then prophesied that mob law would go forth throughout the land. Mob rule commenced by slow degrees at first, but it gained power until like a mighty avalanche it swept through the land. Since then it has ruled rampant. Shall we join the North to fight against the South? No! Shall we join the South against the North?

As emphatically, No! Why? They have both...brought it upon themselves, and we have had no hand in the matter.'" 2

During that same time period, President Abraham Lincoln signed into law an act of Congress that made plural marriage—polygamy—illegal in the Territories. Though Lincoln was not inclined to prosecute the law, and never did during his administration, John refused to sit idly by waiting for developments. Joseph the Prophet had declared that plural marriage was a divine requirement of all who had the law revealed unto them, it had been so revealed to John and his numerous wives, and he was not about to allow the government to usurp his right to obey God as he chose.

> Whence came this law on our statute books?... Who constituted [the government] our conscience-keepers? Who appointed them the judge of our religious faith, or authorized them to coerce us to transgress a law that is binding and imperative in our conscience? We do not expect that Congress is acquainted with our religious faith; but...we do claim the guarantees of the Constitution and immunity from persecution on merely religious grounds. 3

Six years later John was publicly flailing the "Honorable" Schuyler Colfax, as pointed out in the previous chapter, and scarcely had he finished with that, it seemed, when Utah and the Church were thrown into miserable upheaval by the arrival of new political appointees—specifically one James B. McKean, who was determined to use his new judicial position to bring Brigham Young, and the Church with him, tumbling to the ground. The primary warrior who would stand against the judge and before the people, to the surprise of no one who knew him, would once again be the fiery and eloquent apostle, John Taylor. 4

To Judge Louis Dent, President Ulysses S. Grant's brother-in-law, McKean declared prior to his departure for Utah:

> Judge Dent, the mission which God has called upon me to
> perform in Utah, is as much above the duties of other
> courts and judges as the heavens are above the earth,
> and whenever or wherever I may find the Local or Federal
> laws obstructing or interfering therewith, by God's
> blessing I shall trample them under my feet. 5

In other words, James McKean was a judge with a mission, and he
was utterly reckless in his means and methods of accomplishing it.
"While the Cullom Bill had failed in Congress, the carpetbaggers
acted as if it were in effect. Taylor, as judge of the Utah County
Territorial Court, found himself stripped of authority to preside in
anything but probate and divorce cases, deprived of participation
in the selection of petit or grand juries. McKean's federal courts
took jurisdiction in territorial cases, rejecting the Utah Marshal
and Attorney General in favor of United States appointees;
the U.S. Marshal assumed authority for selecting juries top-heavy
with Gentiles, and took charge of the penitentiary; the U.S.
District Attorney assumed full right to prosecute both territorial
and federal cases; and the U.S. Army stood ready to back up
the arrogant power of the carpetbaggers." 6

"In all this one cannot fail to see that the evident intention
of the group...was to accomplish, without the sanctions of the
law, what the congress of the United States had refused to
authorize." 7

Incensed by this unwarranted usurpation of power, the *Omaha
Herald* called it a conspiracy

> to destroy men and institutions in a territory whose
> civilizing and industrial achievements are the admiration
> of mankind. 8

While the *San Francisco Examiner* editorialized:

> These small fry, popinjay politicians, and would-be

statesmen, know full well that they have no show for promotion until the Mormon power is broken. Hence it is that they seek to create a civil war.... The whole affair is a disgrace to the American name. 9

John, accompanying an English friend to McKean's court to be naturalized, wrote in the *Deseret News:*

> His honor, Chief Justice McKean, informed him that he was now admitted to all the rights of an American citizen.... What are those inestimable rights?—the right to be tried by an imported court before a packed jury of his sworn enemies; the right to the sympathy of the judge while passing sentence of three years hard labor for living with his own wife; the right to have his religion assailed; the right to vote for a legislature to make laws which any political despot can annul at pleasure; the right to pay taxes without representation; the right to be maligned, slandered, and abused; the right to have pimps, whorehouses, gambling saloons, debauchery forced upon us by judicial exertion; the right to live in a satrapy; the right to die and be buried. 10

McKean's next—and biggest step—was to indict Brigham Young, against whom an indictment containing sixteen separate counts was found—each count constituting a separate offense. John and several others of the Twelve and First Presidency pleaded with Brigham not to appear but to go underground. When Brigham explained that he had been promised protection and a fair hearing, John replied, "So was Joseph!... I saw the safe treatment they gave him in jail! I still carry the bullets!" 11

Nevertheless, President Young was determined to go, and did. When he appeared in court to answer these charges, McKean took occasion to declare, as was pointed out in the *vignette* at the beginning of this chapter:

> Courts are bound to take notice of the political and social condition of the country which they judicially rule. It is therefore proper to say, while the case at bar is called "The People versus Brigham Young," its other and real name is "Federal Authority versus Polygamous Theocracy." 12

John, who was in court with Brigham Young when the above declaration was made, was stunned. When word of the judge's dictum got out to the people, "public sentiment was outraged by the high-handed measures of Judge McKean. Popular excitement ran high. For a time there was a threatened collision between the court and the people. It was at this juncture that Elder Taylor published five letters in the *Deseret News,* reviewing the situation in Utah, and denouncing the Territorial government as un-American in principle and oppressive in its operation; but at the same time warn[ing] the people against violent resistance to the court, insolent and oppressive as it was.

"He was in court...when Judge McKean made the statement.... 'A system is on trial in the person of Brigham Young.' This he took for his text in the letters above referred to, and interpreted it to mean,...'Stripped of all its tinsel and wrappings,... it simply resolves itself into this: that the government of the United States is at war with the Church of Jesus Christ of Latter-day Saints.'

"Elder Taylor then proceeds to show that in making war on a system of religion, the great principle of religious liberty itself is threatened, and that such a crusade as that foreshadowed in the declaration of Judge McKean, could but end in disaster to the liberties of the people." 13 The following are portions of these letters:

The whole foundation and superstructure of American

ethics or jurisprudence is based upon the popular will. That its executive, legislative and judicial powers originate with the people, and that the people having granted to the men of their choice, certain powers, agencies and authorities, to act for and in their behalf; limiting all of them by the provisions of the Constitution which all of them take an oath to support, they reserve to themselves, to their state or to "the people," all the remainder.

If indeed the above is a correct exposition of our rights and privileges as American citizens,...how is it that such infamies can transpire as have lately been exhibited in our courts? I may be here met with the statement that we are only a territory; but we are American citizens, and have never abjured our citizenship nor relinquished our Constitutional guarantees.... If the above be true, and the axiom of the declarers of Independence be correct, that governments "derive their just powers from the consent of the governed," what becomes of our federal officers? For not one of our citizens invited them here, or had any vote in their coming, nor was their consent asked. If all just powers are derived from the consent of the governed, then the powers exercised by them [the Territorial officials appointed by the President] must be unjust....

The facts are the people, one hundred thousand American citizens, living in the Territory of Utah, with the full rights of free men, and the protecting guarantees of a written constitution, find in the persons of federal officers "another government" not of the people, and in violation of Constitutional guarantees and authority; claiming to come from the United States, "imperium in imperio," whose policy and practices are in grave particulars at variance with its own; and I ask by what authority it presumes to set itself up against the legitimately constituted authority of the people of the territory or state; by what authority it ignores its laws; by what authority it over-rides and tears down the safeguards of society, fosters in our midst drunkenness, gambling and whoredoms, those infamous adjuncts and institutions of professed civilization; by what authority it repudiates its officers; by what authority it interferes with the religion of the people, with their social, religious, political and moral rights? 14

As much as anything else, though, John intended through his letters to calm the Saints — to help them see that if they restrained themselves from taking the law into their own hands — no matter that they might be justified in doing so — then they would not only give the federal officers no excuses to harm them further, but the Lord would invariably step in and make the Saints' battles His own.

The lamb is drinking below, the wolf is fouling the water above. The big boy is strutting about with a chip on his shoulder, daring you to knock it off. Some pretext is needed. Don't give it to them.... Let the same wisdom that has governed your acts hitherto still be continued. They want a cause of quarrel, that they may rob and pillage according to law. Don't give it to them.... Let them pack juries fresh from houses of ill-fame to try you on virtue. Never mind, it is their virtue that suffers, not yours. Let them try you for living with and protecting your wives and providing for your children; fidelity and virtue are not crimes in the eyes of the Almighty, only in theirs....

"But they are accusing some of our best and most honorable men of murder!" What of that? Who have they subborned [sic] as their accusers? They themselves call them by the mild name of assassins — these are their fellow pirates with whom they hob nob and associate. Be quiet!

"But other aggressions are contemplated; they are bent on provoking a quarrel and mischief." No matter, it takes two to make a quarrel, don't you be one of them.

"They offer themselves to be kicked." Don't do it, have some respect for your boots.

"But they insult us on every hand." What! they insult you! Nature has provided for many animals and insects a certain species of aggression and defense. Some snakes crush their victims in their folds; others carry poison in their teeth; the wasp and scorpion sting you; the ant poisons with its bite; the vampire sucks your blood; while the pole-cat protects itself by its insufferable odor—

"Their power to hurt each little creature feels,
Bulls use their horns and asses use their heels."

Now who would consider himself insulted by the hissing of a snake, the attack of the wasp, or the odor of a skunk? You would simply avoid them. It is not in their power to insult you.

There is no law they can place us under which we cannot obey. We must live above all law, and nothing can harm us if we are "followers of that which is good," so keep quiet!

There is something heroic in being able calmly to view with firm nerves and unblanched cheek the acts of your petty tormentors. Filled with the light of eternal truth, rejoicing in the possession of the favor of God, "having the promise of the life which now is, and that which is to come," standing on a more elevated platform, you can smile with complacency on their feeble attacks, and

"Like Moses' bush ascend the higher,
And flourish unconsumed by fire."

But independent of this, it is our very best policy to be quiet. The court can proceed, yet the sun will rise and set, the earth will roll on its axis, potatoes and corn will grow irrespective of the decrees of courts. Hitherto you have been subject to the misrepresentations and manufactured lies from the small fry of this coterie—little whelps who lick the hands of their master, and vomit their lies by wholesale, to pervert public opinion; but they are found out. They have run their erratic race. You have no fear from them. Your cause is before the public. The eyes of the great American nation are now upon you, and men of honor, probity and position represent your acts. (And to their honor be it spoken the intelligent press, irrespective of party, denounce your persecutors.) This clique are not representatives of American sentiment. The majority of strangers in our midst repudiate them; and there are hundreds of thousands of honest, high-minded, honorable men throughout the land, who despise as much as you do, these infamous acts. We live in the most liberal and enlightened nation in the world; if there are evils, they can be corrected; but the undercurrent, the vital, strong, living sentiment of America is fair play, justice for all, equal rights, liberty, equality and brotherhood; they are opposed to hypocrisy, fraud, injustice and piracy, and will sustain republicanism, democracy, equity and the inalienable rights of man. Men of standing and position are now noting your acts, and they will report them truly and correctly; therefore keep quiet, and do not play into your enemies' hands. For they war, not only against you, but against the liberal, enlightened sentiment of the nation, against the time-honored principles of republicanism and equal rights. 15

When God's "will shall be done on earth as it is done in heaven," the shackles will be knocked from every son and daughter of Adam; there will be proclaimed a universal jubilee, and all mankind will be free, every wrong will be suppressed, and every right maintained. The living, glorious, eternal principles of "doing unto all men as we would they should do unto us," will prevail…"Peace on earth and good will to man," shall be proclaimed to every nation.…Then all hearts shall be made glad, and the voice of mourning and sorrow be banished from the earth;

And every man in every place,

Shall meet a brother and a friend;

and as Parley P. Pratt has it—

Come, ye sons of doubt and wonder,

Indian, Moslem, Greek, or Jew;

All your shackles burst asunder,

Freedom's banner waves for you.

This is what the Latter-day Saints are trying to inaugurate. Judge McKean says it is a system that is on trial. He does not know it, but the above is the system—what he is pleased to call "Polygamic Theocracy." 16

John's letters had their desired effect; there was no popular uprising against Judge McKean. More importantly, as the letters were also carried by the national press, they presented the Latter-day Saint side of the conflict as it had never been presented, listing detail by ugly detail the rape of constitutional rights by Utah's carpetbaggers.

In their arrogance, McKean and his coterie pressed on, indicting Brigham Young for murder based on William Hickman's money-making testimony. 17 When Brigham made his dramatic appearance in court to answer to these charges, he was accompanied by a veritable horde of Saints. Perhaps that was why McKean allowed him to go home afterward instead of to jail, as he had threatened.

John Taylor, master orator
and champion of liberty

CA. 1871

In the new tabernacle a few days later, John declared:

And who are these men they are now prosecuting and persecuting? Why, here is Brigham Young, for instance. I have traveled with him thousands of miles, preaching the Gospel without purse or scrip. What has he done to anybody? Whom has he injured? Can anybody put a finger on it? Not and tell the truth. I know before God they lie. I have been with him in private and public under all circumstances and I know his feelings. I know they are liars when they make these statements, and this people believe it, too.

Well, what shall we do then?... Why—do right!... Don't fight!

We want no vigilant societies here, nor bloodtubs; no "Plug-uglies," nor Ku-Klux, nor John Brown raids, nor Jayhawkers.... We don't want any secret organizations of any kind, nor any infractions of the law.

Let others be breakers of the law, and us the keepers of it. Let others trample underfoot human rights, and us maintain them.... If others want to play the part of tyrants, let them do so, and they will find the tyrant's end....

Now, I would rather be the friend and associate of these men whom they call murderers here than of their most honorable men, and so would this people....

No power in this city nor in these United States, I say—and I will prophesy in the name of Israel's God— shall harm you [John said of the accused].... God will control, direct, and manage all the affairs pertaining to his people, and Israel will rejoice and be triumphant, and the Kingdom of God will be established. 18

The next month a telegram clicked over the wires from Washington, D.C., informing the Saints that "the Supreme Court of the United States [had] decided that the grand and petit jurors summoned by McKean, were both drawn in violation of law, and as 'a legal consequence, all the indictments now pending in the courts of Utah are null and void. Brigham Young and his Mormon brethren must be discharged from confinement, and the records of this judicial conspiracy expunged.'" 19

Unfortunately, McKean was still not through, and since he could not prosecute Mormons as he had planned, he developed a second plan, called by him, "masterly inactivity." In this he hindered or delayed all the business of the courts, hoping meanwhile to get Congress to pass legislation similar to the Cullom Bill. In this he was partially successful, for in 1874 Congress passed the Poland Bill, which in essence abolished courts of the people in the territory and gave the Gentiles—a definite numerical minority in Utah—the right to an equal number of seats on a jury as Mormons.

"The conduct of Judge McKean and the measures introduced into Congress respecting Utah affairs, again brought Elder Taylor out in a series of six letters to the press, in which he made a scathing exposure of federal official corruption in our Territory, and a searching criticism of the various measures pending in Congress, previous to the passage of the Poland Bill. In closing one of these letters that reviewed some of the bills in Congress, he made the following stirring appeal to the national legislators:

With all the reverence and respect due to the rulers of a mighty nation, from the tops of these distant mountains I call upon you to pause in your career, for I also am a teacher, and have a right to be heard. I speak in behalf of one hundred and fifty thousand citizens of Utah. I speak in behalf of forty millions of free American citizens in the United States. I conjure you out of respect for the memory of the dead, as the rightful guardians of the liberties of a vast nation…and in behalf of unborn millions, to pause. I conjure you, in behalf of our honor and integrity, in behalf of republican principles, and the cause of freedom throughout the world. I plead with you in behalf of our common humanity, and the rights of man, to reflect. Would you, to gratify a morbid sentimentality desecrate and tear down one of the most magnificent temples of human liberty, ever erected? Would you wantonly deliver up the sacred principles of liberty, equity and justice, bequeathed by your fathers, to the grim Moloch of party who is crushing, grinding and trampling under foot our God-given rights, and whose sanguinary jaws are extended to gorge and devour the quivering remnants of our feeble, expiring liberty? Have we not had more than enough trouble already…? Can we ever be satisfied? "Let us have peace."…

While our territorial courts, officers and municipal authorities, have been always foremost in punishing crime, whether committed by Mormons or Gentiles, some of the United States officials have shielded and protected criminals, and for this purpose every subterfuge known to the law has been brought into requisition. Thus, by writs of error, injunctions, habeas corpus, pardons, and officious and indecent interference, they have exhibited themselves as the abettors and protectors of crime. They have liberated felons and murderers, encouraged drunkenness and riot, protected and shielded brothel-houses, winked at and sustained gambling, and so clogged the wheels of justice, in both civil and criminal cases, that they have brought the judiciary into such contempt that it has become a stink in the nostrils of honest men.…

I am not writing under the very questionable shelter

of a nom de plume, and have nothing but facts to relate, for which I hold myself responsible. 20

Shortly after John's six letters were published, Judge McKean found Brigham Young in contempt of court and sentenced him to a fine of twenty-five dollars and one day in the penitentiary. While the Church President complied, the rash act finally cost McKean his official head. "No sooner did the country become acquainted with the course he had taken than a storm of public indignation arose, and clamored loudly for his removal from office. Four days afterwards he was dismissed from the bench." 21

The federal officials who replaced the McKean coterie seemed to have far fewer axes to grind, and for some years Utah had a period of peace—a circumstance which vindicated the wisdom of John's counsel to "Be quiet!"

Courtesy of Church Archives, The Church of Jesus Christ of Latter-day Saints. ©Intellectual Reserve, Inc.

John Taylor   CA. *mid-1870s*

17

THE "RUFFIAN" REVELATOR

For a moment John grew silent. It was Sunday, April 9, 1882, another fitful, blustery, and stormy day. It had rained or snowed off and on through the entire general conference, and this, the last day, had been no better. Of course it wasn't cold in the cavernous Tabernacle; the warmth of so many bodies crowded together heated it wonderfully. But he would have appreciated at least a small ray of sunshine—anything to help brighten the spirits of the Saints.

Now, though, as his eyes surveyed the vast, expectant congregation, he felt himself filling with the spirit of prophecy and revelation. It was interesting, he thought, that it felt so much like a pitcher being filled with heated milk—a warm but comfortable sensation that was quickly spreading throughout his entire being.

He had felt it before, of course, even from the time of his childhood; but as President of the Church it seemed to be coming with increasing frequency. Which was good, he thought, for in these troubled times, when all the world seemed arrayed against them, the Saints needed a sense of what was going to happen— of the direction in which their lives would be going.

For that matter, John thought ruefully as he continued to stand in silence, so did he! Now that the Edmunds Bill had been signed into law, now that the Supreme Court had ruled that plural marriage was unlawful cohabitation and therefore a crime against the Constitution—which John knew was untrue but which had nevertheless been determined through the course of law—he had no idea what to tell the Saints so that they could go forward with their lives.

Should he encourage them to continue to preach and practice what they knew was a divine law, or should he, and they, now conform to the constitutional law of the land? It had, John knew, taken many of them a long time to accept the principle of plural marriage in the first place. But now, with this latest attack—

The Reynolds case had not only been a shattering blow to the Saints' confidence in the ultimate protection of the law, but had also stood as evidence that the forces of evil were infecting the highest offices in the land. How could he abandon wives who had already endured so many hardships for the sake of religious principle, and what could he say to his children who would thus seem disowned? Or for that matter, what could he say to the thousands throughout the territory who were in the same terrible position?

Of course he didn't know, but with the Lord's Spirit surging so powerfully through him, John knew it was time to open his mouth and hear what it was that the Lord had to say—

"As a people or community," he listened to himself saying, his voice loud and firm, "we can bide our time; but I will say to you Latter-day Saints, that there is nothing of which you have been despoiled by oppressive acts or mobocratic rule, but that you will again possess, or your children after you.... The Lord has a way of his own in regulating such matters. We are told the wicked shall slay the wicked. He has a way of his own of 'emptying the earth of the inhabitants thereof.' A terrible day of reckoning is approaching the nations of the earth; the Lord is coming out of His hiding place to vex the inhabitants thereof; and the destroyer of the Gentiles, as prophesied of, is already on his way! Already combinations are being entered into which are very ominous for the future prosperity, welfare and happiness of this great republic. The volcanic fires of disordered and anarchial elements are beginning to manifest themselves and exhibit the internal forces that are at work among the turbulent and unthinking masses of the people.

"Congress, I tell you in the name of Israel's God, will soon have something other to do than to prescribe and persecute an innocent, law-abiding and patriotic people. Of all bodies in the world, they can least afford to remove the bulwarks that bind society together in this nation, to recklessly trample upon human freedom and rights, and to rend and destroy that great palladium of human rights — the Constitution of the United States. Ere long they will need all its protecting influence to save this nation from misrule, anarchy and mobocratic influence. They can ill afford to be the foremost in tampering with human rights and human freedom, or in tearing down the bulwarks of safety and protection which that sacred instrument has guaranteed for so many years."

John paused, sweeping his gaze across the silent congregation. "The internal fires of revolution are already smoldering in this nation, and they need but a spark to set them in a flame. Already are agencies at work in the land calculated to subvert and overthrow every principle of rule and government; already is corruption of every kind prevailing in high places and permeating all society; already as a nation, we are departing from our God, and corrupting ourselves with malfeasance, dishonor and a lack of public integrity and good faith; already are licentiousness and debauchery corrupting, undermining and destroying society; already are we interfering with the laws of nature and stopping the functions of life, and have become the slayers of our own offspring, and employ human butchers in the shape of physicians to assist in this diabolical and murderous work."

John stood silently, allowing the Lord's words to sink into the hearts of the Saints. There was a news reporter from the East seated on the front row, and for an instant John thought of him, wondering what he was thinking, feeling—

"The sins of this nation," he continued, his voice ringing, "the licentiousness, the debauchery, the murders are entering into the ears of the Lord of Sabaoth, and I tell you now, you members of Congress, you judges of the various courts of this land, you who have been elected to stand as the executive branch, from the tops of these mountains, as a humble servant of the living God, unless these crimes are stopped, this nation will be overthrown, and its glory, power, dominion and wealth will fade away like the dews of a summer morning!"

John took a deep breath. "I also say to other nations of the earth, that unless they repent of their crimes, their iniquities and abominations, their thrones will be overturned, their kingdoms and governments overthrown, and their lands made desolate.

"This is not only my saying, but it is the saying of those ancient prophets which they themselves profess to believe; for God will speedily have a controversy with the nations of the earth, and, as I stated before, the destroyer of the Gentiles is on his way to overthrow governments, to destroy dynasties, to lay waste thrones, kingdoms and empires, to spread abroad anarchy and desolation, and to cause war, famine and bloodshed to overspread the earth.

"Now, we do not wish to place ourselves in a state of antagonism, nor act defiantly towards this government. We will fulfill the letter, so far as practicable, of that unjust, inhuman, oppressive and unconstitutional law, so far as we can without violating principle; but we cannot sacrifice every principle of human right at the behest of corrupt, unreasoning and unprincipled men; we cannot violate the highest and noblest principles of human nature and make pariahs and outcasts of high-minded, virtuous and honorable women, nor sacrifice at the shrine of popular clamor the highest and noblest principles of humanity!

"We shall abide all constitutional law, as we always have done; but while we are God-fearing and law-abiding, and respect all honorable men and officers, we are no craven serfs, and have not learned to lick the feet of oppressors, nor to bow in base submission to unreasoning clamor. We will contend inch by inch, legally and constitutionally, for our rights as American citizens.... We stand proudly erect in the consciousness of our rights as American citizens, and plant ourselves firmly on the sacred guarantees of the Constitution. We need have no fears, no trembling in our knees about these attempts to deprive us of our God-given and constitutional liberties. God will take care of his people, if we will only do right!"

As his rich, baritone voice thundered throughout the Tabernacle, John felt the change of the Spirit, and he knew it was time to sit down. God had spoken, and now there was just one thing left—

"Our trust is in God," he concluded, his voice for the moment, softer. "You have heard me say before, Hosanna, the Lord God Omnipotent reigneth; and if this congregation feels as I do, we will join together in the same acclaim. Follow me, please." John's rich voice then rose again, abruptly ringing throughout the Tabernacle: "HOSANNA! HOSANNA! HOSANNA TO GOD AND THE LAMB, FOREVER, AND EVER, WORLDS WITHOUT END. AMEN, AMEN, AND AMEN!"

As the echoes of the sacred anthem subsided, the suddenly weakened prophet turned from the pulpit, and with the old wounds from Carthage suddenly throbbing in his body, President John Taylor made his way back to his seat. 1

The news reporter who attended the above conference,

Mr. Phil Robinson of the *New York World,* wrote concerning John's concluding address:

> Acquainted though I am with displays of oriental fanaticism and western revivalism, I set this Mormon enthusiasm on one side, as being altogether of a different character; for it not only astonishes by its fervor, but commands respect by its sincere sobriety. The congregation of the Saints assembled in the Tabernacle, numbering, by my own careful computation, eleven thousand odd, and composed in almost exactly equal parts of the two sexes, reminded me of the Puritan gatherings of the past as I had imagined them, and of my personal experiences of the Transvaal Boers as I knew them. There was no rant, no affectation, no straining after theatrical effect. The very simplicity of this great gathering of country-folk was striking in the extreme, and significant from first to last of a power that should hardly be trifled with by sentimental legislation.... Nor could anything exceed the impressiveness of the response which the people gave instantaneously to the appeal of their President for the support of their voices. The great Tabernacle was filled with waves of sound as the "Amens" of the congregation burst out. The shout of men going into battle was not more stirring than the closing words of this memorable conference, spoken as if by one vast voice. 2

Brigham Young passed away on the afternoon of August 29TH, 1877, having served as President of the Church for thirty-three years. The last words he uttered were, "Joseph! Joseph! Joseph!"3 In that same moment the First Presidency was dissolved, and as per revelation, the Quorum of the Twelve Apostles, equal in authority to the First Presidency, assumed leadership of the Church. 4 And as senior member of the Twelve and President

President Brigham Young   CA. *late-1870s*

of the Quorum, John Taylor became acting Church president. He was sixty-nine years of age.

At Brigham Young's funeral, John declared:

> We are not alone! God is with us, and He will continue with us from this time henceforth and forever. And while we mourn a good and great man dead, I see thousands of staunch and faithful ones around me, and before me, who are for Israel, for God and His kingdom; men who are desirous to see His will done on earth, as angels do it in heaven. 5

Earlier in the year John had been elected as territorial superintendent of district schools and continued for a time in that office even after Church leadership had fallen on his shoulders. In this work, to which he devoted great personal interest because of his belief in and advocacy of formal education, he earned the official praise of Charles Warren, Esq., acting commissioner of education at Washington. 6

In Ephraim, Sanpete County, John prophesied concerning the education of the Saints:

> You will see the day that Zion will be as far ahead of the outside world in everything pertaining to learning of every kind as we are today in regard to religious matters. You mark my words, and write them down, and see if they do not come to pass. 7

And not long after he was sustained as Church president, John was visited by Zina Young Williams, a daughter of Brigham Young who was dean of women at Brigham Young Academy in Provo. Less than a decade old, the Academy was experiencing severe financial difficulties, and Zina had come to John for help.

Taking her by the hand "in a fatherly way," as she put it, he said:

My dear child, I have something of importance to tell you that I know will make you happy. I have been visited by your father. He came to me in the silence of the night clothed in brightness and with a face beaming with love and confidence told me things of great importance and among others that the school being taught by Brother [Karl G.] Maeser was accepted in the heavens and was a part of the great plan of life and salvation; that Church schools should be fostered for the good of Zion's children; that we rejoice to see the awakening among the teachers and the children of our people; for they would need the support of this knowledge and testimony of the Gospel, and there was a bright future in store for the preparing for the children of the covenant for future usefulness in the Kingdom of God, and that Christ himself was directing, and had a care over this school. 8

Sister Williams received the help she sought.

While John was Acting President of the Church, an event occurred that has been a blessing to the Saints through all the years since. In 1879, Bishop John W. Hess of the Farmington (Utah) Ward "asked his members to help him find a way to reach their boys, many of whom were roaming about, undisciplined, and headed for trouble. Aurelia Spencer Rogers suggested forming a children's organization in which boys could be taught useful skills and good behavior. Eliza R. Snow presented the proposal to Elder Taylor, who approved the plan. Sister Rogers then decided that girls ought to be included, and she wrote to Sister Snow for her opinion. Sister Snow agreed, saying, 'I feel assured that the inspiration of heaven is directing you, and that a great and very important movement is being inaugurated for the future of Zion.' President Taylor thereafter directed Sister Snow to assist in organizing the Primary Mutual Association in every ward throughout the Church." 9

Great energy characterized President Taylor's administration of affairs in the Church, both in Zion and abroad. He pushed forward with increased zeal the work on the temples, of which three [Salt Lake, Manti, and Logan] were in course of erection, at the time of his taking control of affairs. He required bishops to hold weekly priesthood meetings in their wards; presidents of stakes to hold general priesthood meetings monthly in their respective stakes; and appointed quarterly conferences in all the stakes of Zion, publishing the dates of holding them for half a year in advance, a custom which has continued until the present.

He personally attended as many of these quarterly conferences as he could, without neglecting the executive branch of his calling, which necessarily occupied much of his time, and kept him at or within easy reach of Salt Lake City. But where he could not go himself, he sent members of his quorum, so that the Saints received much teaching and instruction from the Apostles, more perhaps than at any previous time in the history of the Church. The result was a great spiritual awakening among the Saints.

The work abroad received increased impetus by a greater number of elders being sent to the world. A missionary himself nearly all his life, it was but natural for President Taylor to be interested in the work of preaching the gospel abroad. 10

At the time John followed Brigham Young into Church leadership, there stood in Salt Lake City a home called the Gardo House, which was located on the corner of South Temple and First East. It had been built under the direction of Brigham Young for his wife Amelia—and was called by the *Salt Lake Tribune* (and a good many others) Amelia's Palace. It had reverted, on Brigham's death and the subsequent settlement of his estate, to Church ownership.

Immediately some of the Brethren began encouraging John to take it as his family home, for there was room enough for all his formally recognized wives and children. Time after time he declined. "His habits of life were simple; free from ostentation, as were also those of his family; and had he followed the bent of his own inclination he would have remained in his own humbler home." 11

At the April conference of 1879, however, after a presentation by Elder George Q. Cannon, President Taylor was voted the use of the Gardo House as a family residence. The Gardo at that time was doubtless the largest and finest residence in Salt Lake City— an interesting fact in light of a singular "prophecy made by Elder Heber C. Kimball, who, when President Taylor's circumstances were the poorest, boldly prophesied that he would yet live in the largest and best house in Salt Lake City—a prediction that was fulfilled when President Taylor took possession of the Gardo House as his family residence." 12

It was with considerable reluctance that John accepted the proposition of his brethren, in part because the entire territory was experiencing economic difficulty, and in part because of his own innate sense of modesty. In conference he declared to the assembled Saints:

I will state that I feel very much obliged to my brethren for the generous feeling manifested to myself. Permit me, however, to say with regard to some of these ideas presented to the conference by Brother George Q. Cannon, and which, as he has said, he has frequently presented to me and others of the Twelve, that while I duly appreciate the feelings and views of my brethren, and am not ignorant of the proprieties of life, individually I would not wish to change my position. Personally

Acting President John Taylor   CA. *late-1870s*

I care nothing about the outside show, the glitter and the appearance of men; but I do care about the great and eternal principles associated with the Church and kingdom of God upon the earth. And as stated it was some time before I could make up my mind to accept a proposition of this kind, and I accept it now simply in the capacity of your servant for Christ's sake, for the benefit of the kingdom of God, and that all things may be conducted in a proper manner. 13

On April 6, 1880, the Church celebrated in general conference the fiftieth anniversary of its latter-day organization. Following the pattern established by the Lord in ancient Israel, John designated 1880 to be a Jubilee year and used the occasion "to forgive one-half the debts, $802,000, owed by the worthy poor to the Perpetual Emigration Fund Company. In addition, one thousand cows and five thousand sheep were distributed to indigent members to replace some of the thousands lost in the severe winter of 1879–1880. President Taylor also counseled the affluent to forgive the debts of the poor.

It occurred to me…that we ought to do something, as they did in former times, to relieve those that are oppressed with debt, to assist those that are needy, to break off the yoke of those that may feel themselves crowded upon, and to make it a time of general rejoicing. 14

[You businessmen, bankers, miners and manufacturers,] extend a helping hand. Free the worthy debt-bound brother if you can. Let there be no rich among us from whose tables fall only crumbs to feed a wounded Lazarus. 15

He further counseled the Saints to settle disputes among themselves in order to avoid going to law against a brother and to cease the despicable practice of Church patriarchs competing for fees for the giving of patriarchal blessings as a "'means of obtaining a livelihood.'"16

Finally he directed, with full approval of the Relief Society through a public vote, that the 34,761 bushels of wheat the sisters had obediently put into storage in communities throughout the territory (while the priesthood brethren had stored none, to their chagrin), be loaned out as seed wheat to the most poor of the Latter-day Saints, with the expectation that they would repay it following the next harvest.

> Inasmuch as the brethren...had been careless and slow to heed the counsel of Brigham Young in relation to storing away wheat, he [President Young] requested the sisters to do it, and some of us "lords of creation" thought it a very little thing for our sisters to be engaged in. But we find now they are of some use, and that the "ladies of creation" can do something [better than] we lords.... They have 34,761 bushels of wheat. Who of you men can raise that much? Where's your wheat?17

"The Jubilee year saw a great spiritual awakening among the Society, flowering in the climate of freedom and good will. The gospel became not a Sunday ceremony, but a way of life....

"Taylor's enlightened and liberal administration...made him enormously popular. Where the people had paid great respect to Brigham, the old-timers had loved Joseph, and now the Saints loved John Taylor....

"Even the *Salt Lake Tribune,* though calling Taylor 'The Ruffian,' for his combative temperament, 'The Foreigner' because he was born in England, and 'John the Revelator' for his spirituality, showed him a respect never accorded Brigham.

"An apostate, Josiah F. Gibbs, said, 'John Taylor was an exceptionally able man, and well educated. Mild in his government of the Saints, and "approachable" in his intercourse with them.'"18

To conclude the Jubilee celebration, John bore fervent testimony:

> I testify as my brethren have done, that this is the work of God that has been revealed by the Almighty, and I know it. God will sustain Israel; no power can injure us if we will do what is right. This kingdom will roll on, the purposes of God will progress, Zion will arise and shine, and the glory of God will rest upon her. We will continue to grow and increase, until the kingdoms of this world shall become the kingdoms of our God and His Christ, and He will reign forever and forever. 19

With the apostasy of his friend Edward W. Tullidge, who was publishing books on various aspects of the history of the Church, John could see the need for a history of the Saints written from a more accurate perspective. He began by encouraging the Saints to "'gather up and preserve a history of all the facts pertaining to' the Mormons, copies of documents, journals, personal histories, stories of persecution. 'We are desirous that a truthful record may be had, in convenient form.'

"Shortly thereafter, the prestigious historian, Hubert H. Bancroft, who was engaged in compiling his monumental History of the Pacific States, wrote the church asking for material for his projected History of Utah. Orson Pratt, church historian, offered to supply the history if Bancroft would guarantee to publish it 'without mutilation.' 'This only showed,' Bancroft commented, 'that they were wholly mistaken in the character of my work.' He realized that

> Utah was not the easiest of problems with which to deal historically.... Prejudice against the Mormons was so

strong and universal, and of such long standing, that…[he] well knew that strict impartiality would bring upon [him] the condemnation of both Mormons and Gentiles. If this, then, was the test of truth and fair dealing, [he] must subject [him]self to the censure of both sides;…[he] would not write for the approbation of one side or the other. 20

In council with the other members of the Twelve, John recommended that Bancroft should be given all cooperation and furnished with complete information so that an unbiased history of the Saints might go forth to the world. He then wrote to the historian that he was "pleased to place myself in direct communication with you on this subject…I…take great pleasure in informing you that the Hon. Franklin D. Richards…is one of our leading and respected citizens, and a gentleman who is fully conversant in literary and legal matters…. He is now nearly ready to start for San Francisco [Bancroft's headquarters, at UC Berkeley], and will take with him the historical data." 21

Meanwhile John was also at work on a book of his own. Tired of the old criticism that the Saints were not true Christians, but were more nearly aligned with the faith and customs of ancient Israel, he put together a 200-page doctrinal treatise entitled *An Examination into and an Elucidation of the Great Principle of the Mediation and Atonement of Our Lord and Savior Jesus Christ*. In the book John makes clear "that Latter-day Saints accept Jesus Christ as the divine Son of God and as the Savior and Messiah of the world." 22

At the October conference in 1880, after more than three years of the Church being under the leadership of the Quorum of the Twelve, the First Presidency was formally organized and sustained by the quorums and then the body of the Church, with John Taylor sustained as President, George Q. Cannon

LDS Church First Presidency
(from left): George Q. Cannon,
John Taylor, and Joseph F. Smith

CA. 1880

(John's nephew) as First Counselor, and Joseph F. Smith (son of Hyrum Smith) Second Counselor.

> John Taylor was now invested with the highest office and honors which God gives to man on the earth. He was placed on a par with Melchizedek, Moses, Peter, Joseph and Brigham: for by the action of this conference he was made President of the High Priesthood, whose duty it is to preside over the whole Church, to be like Moses, a seer, a revelator, a translator, a prophet, having all the gifts of God which He bestows upon the head of the Church.
>
> The Lord in describing the power and authority of the Higher or Melchizedek Priesthood, says: It holds the keys of all the spiritual blessings of the Church. It has the privilege of receiving the mysteries of the kingdom of heaven; of having the heavens opened to it; the right to commune with the general assembly and church of the first born; and to enjoy the communion and presence of God the Father, and Jesus the Mediator of the New Covenant.
>
> These are the privileges of the High Priesthood, and John Taylor was called to preside over it, with a right to all the gifts and powers associated therewith. What higher authority can man possess? What honor greater can be given him? [23]

Despite John's being seventy-two when he was set apart by the Twelve as President of the Church, "his form was erect and his step elastic; and he entered upon the performance of his high duties with a zeal and vigor only to be expected of a younger man. He visited the Stakes of Zion in Utah and the surrounding territories, setting them in order, teaching, counseling and encouraging the Saints with all the energy and kindness of his great soul.

"As a sample of his travels and labors among the people…
the following [is a] summary of two of his trips during the year
1881: In the latter part of July, in company with several of the
Apostles and other brethren, he started on a tour to visit some of
the northern Stakes and settlements. He was absent from Salt
Lake City seventeen days, during which time he visited five Stakes
of Zion, viz., Cache, Rich, Summit, Wasatch and Utah, traveling
much of the distance in carriages. Twenty-three meetings were
held by the party. President Taylor attended all but three,
and spoke at the most of them.

"In the latter part of November of the same year, he visited
the southern Stakes and settlements, accompanied by his
Counselor Joseph F. Smith and several of the Twelve Apostles.
This tour occupied five weeks and four days. The party held
sixty-eight meetings; besides many council meetings where advice
and instructions to Presidents of Stakes, Bishops and other
officers of the Church were freely given. Thus he labored
incessantly among the people from his accession to the Presidency
until he was driven into retirement by the judicial crusade waged
against the Saints some years later." 24

During those tours, he taught concerning the divine purpose
behind men holding the priesthood:

These things are given to us for what? To gratify our
ambition? to enable us to ride over and trample under foot
our fellow-creatures? to place power and authority upon
us? No; not for any man's emolument or aggrandizement.
Although there is nothing more honorable, nothing more
dignified, nothing to which a man ought so much to
aspire to as to be a servant of the living God, and to be
commissioned by Him to do His work upon the earth.
And what for? To spread correct principles among men;
to combat priestcraft, statecraft, oppression, fraud and

iniquity of all kinds; and to introduce among men those pure and holy principles by which the Gods are governed in the eternal worlds.

"In addition to these things he taught implicit trust in God, showed the Saints their dependence upon Him, and frequently alluded to the source from whence they derived their knowledge of truth:

> Any intelligence which we may possess,...and which we may be able to impart, is not of ourselves, but of God. It did not originate with Joseph Smith, with Brigham Young, with the Twelve Apostles, nor was it received from any institution of learning, or of science, either religious, political or social. Our philosophy is not the philosophy of the world; but of the earth and the heavens, of time and eternity, and proceeds from God. 25

There was also plenty of office work; visits with dignitaries such as U.S. President Rutherford B. Hayes, with whom John visited during a journey by rail from Ogden to Salt Lake City (in spite of John's efforts, Hayes was not willing to change his anti-Mormon attitude); and a constant stream of letters to answer. John read all of them, then made marginal notes to his secretary and son-in-law, L. John Nuttall, who penned the actual replies. One ordinary day, for instance, might include the following:

> He approved sending a handkerchief to a sick man in Brigham City who had faith it would cure him. Another letter wanted him to arbitrate a bitter feud over water rights. Irrigation was the lifeblood of the desert; the man at the end of the ditch might take his rifle along as well as shovel if the canal was dry when his water turn came. Taylor referred the case to the local ward bishop's court, suggesting appeal to the stake high council if

L. John Nuttall, President Taylor's
secretary and son-in-law

N.D.

necessary. As a policy, he wanted people to settle their own problems, and do it "without going to law against a brother." However, he did intercede in the case of land-jumping on the Portage Indian Farm, advising jumpers that they must decide if the land was worth more than membership in the church....

A long letter from a man in Soledad, California, told of receiving a vision commanding him to seek out John Taylor, the Lord's prophet, and could Taylor advance him train fare to Utah? Taylor scrawled the notation, "Make our usual answer." This, given to all who asked what Mormonism offered them, was that the church could promise nothing except persecution at the hands of the enemies of Christ.

This answer also went to the man who wanted the church to sponsor his invention of a secret cipher, and share the profits.

Sensitive to the need of sympathetic representation in the world press, Taylor approved the sending of contributions—generally of less than $100—for printing and distribution of articles by hardy Gentiles with courage to stand up for a highly unpopular minority.

Plural marriage brought a host of complications. A widow with two children was to become a plural wife. Since she had been sealed for time and eternity as the only wife of her former husband, a good man, should she marry her new husband only "for time," and thus sacrifice the special blessings given plural wives in the hereafter? And should her children be sealed to their father or step-father?

Taylor advised her, and the children, to make their own decision....

A widow of John D. Lee, mother of a dozen children, wanted to be sealed to another husband, not for support nor for love, but because Lee, having been excommunicated, "would not be able to save her" in the hereafter. Taylor advised that things might be adjusted in the realms beyond the grave.

A woman with an abusive husband wanted to be rebaptized, but had been accused of "taking strong medicine to avoid having children" by him. Was she worthy? Taylor approved the baptism, noting that while "these things are unpleasant" they were beyond his control. It was her own business.

He canceled the amount due from a missionary's family who had been unable to pay the rent on the house—which Taylor owned—while the man was in the Lord's vineyard. Another mission problem came from a widow in Philadelphia, who wrote that although her faith was firm, she simply was unable to keep on feeding, clothing, and housing the missionary who had stayed at her home for nine months. Taylor instructed the elder to go elsewhere.

Taylor had called the bishop at Montpelier, Idaho, to take a mission. Eighty-one members of the ward signed a request that he stay at home. Arrival of the railroad had brought a rough class of men; the ward needed the bishop's counsel. Taylor canceled the mission call.

Reports from Lamanite missions indicated that some converts were Indians first and Mormons second. A missionary at Blackfoot, Idaho, took sick and asked an Indian elder to administer by the laying on of hands. The Lamanite refused, saying he wasn't a medicine man.

When a man's wife was seduced while he was away on a mission, the guilty man offered to let the husband kill him. But the husband wasn't vindictive. He just wanted to know if the wife could be forgiven. Yes; and sin no more,

Taylor advised.

A bishop's counselor in Ogden created a scandal by going to an astrologer when sick, who gave him medicine that cured when the laying on of hands hadn't. What to do? Smiling, Taylor made the notation to Nuttall: "A letter to his bishop should be sufficient."...

The mail showed that a surprising number of intellectuals and liberals believed the Mormons should be allowed to practice their religion. Taylor was amused that the Edmunds Law even made converts. Ira C. Hillock wrote from Michigan that ever since the Edmunds Bill started through Congress: "I have been alarmed by a voice sounding in my ears seeming as the loudest thunder (Ira you must be a Mormon) Sometimes in the field— sometimes in the dead of night I leap out of my sleep at this cry (Ira you must be a Mormon)...at last I cried out like Samuel of old (What shall I do to be a Mormon) the answer came at once (Ask President Taylor)."

John Whitaker of Ogden asked a difficult question: "In what year will the son of man make his appearance on the Earth to Reign?"

Taylor's notation in reply was "Matt 24:36." 26

And so it went, day after day, for the third President of The Church of Jesus Christ of Latter-day Saints. Yet he was also prophet, seer, and revelator, and that fact was not lost on the Saints. In October 1892, he extended calls to the apostleship to Heber J. Grant and George Teasdale and called Seymour B. Young as one of the First Seven Presidents of the Seventy.

Much reorganization proceeded. When President Taylor reviewed what he had done and asked the Lord for counsel, the Lord replied: "What ye have written is my will, and is acceptable unto me.... Let not your hearts be troubled, neither be ye concerned about the management and organization of my Church and Priesthood and the accomplishment of my work. Fear me and observe my laws, and I will reveal unto you, from time to time, through the channels that I have appointed, everything that shall be necessary for the future development and perfection of my Church."27

In May, 1884, John traveled to Logan to dedicate the new Logan Temple, the second in the territory to be completed. Before retiring the evening prior to the dedication, as he knelt in supplication concerning the acceptability of the new temple, the Lord responded with some interesting information about the function of temples:

And this house shall be a house of prayer, a house of learning, a house of God, wherein many great principles pertaining to the past, to the present and the future shall be revealed, and my word and my will be made known; and the laws of the Universe, pertaining to this world and other worlds be developed; for in these houses which have been built unto me, and which shall be built, I will reveal the abundance of those things pertaining to the past, the present, and the future, to the life that now is, and the life that is to come, pertaining to law, order, rule, dominion and government, to things affecting this nation and other nations; the laws of the heavenly bodies in their times and seasons, and the principles or laws by which they are governed, and their relation to each other, and whether they be bodies celestial, terrestrial, or telestial, shall be made known, as I will, saith the Lord, for it is my will and my purpose to place my people in closer communion with the heavens, inasmuch as they will purify themselves and observe more diligently my law; for it is in mine heart to greatly bless and exalt my people, and to build up, exalt and beautify my Zion, inasmuch as they shall observe my law. 28

Not many hours later, following the dedication, John performed the sealing ceremonies for two of his sons and their brides—two of the first ordinances performed in the Logan Temple.

As the intense persecution of the early 1870s eased somewhat, the Saints began to breathe a little easier. Part of the reason for the let-up had been what became known as the Reynolds case. Following passage of the Poland Bill, Brigham Young's secretary, George Reynolds, was arrested in 1874 and voluntarily gave evidence against himself—Church leaders feeling that if a "test" case could just get out of Utah and before the Supreme Court, their religious freedoms would be upheld and the crusade against plural marriage would come to a rapid conclusion. For the next five years the case wound upward through the courts until it did reach the Supreme Court, with most people on both sides seeming to pause while awaiting the results. Unfortunately,

> the court turned a deaf ear to all the Saints' arguments and ruled that polygamy constituted an offense against society. On January 6, 1879, therefore, the Anti-Bigamy Act of 1862 was affirmed as the constitutional law of the land.
>
> Needless to say, the decision of the Supreme Court stunned Church leaders.... Should they continue to preach and practice what they believed was a divine law, or should they now conform to the constitutional law of the land? It had taken many of them a long time to accept the principle of plural marriage in the first place.... The Reynolds case was not only a shattering blow to their confidence in the ultimate protection of the law, but was also evidence that the forces of evil were infecting the highest offices in the land. To President John Taylor, his plural family was

based on mutual love and respect as well as religious oblig-
ation. How, then, could he abandon wives who had already
endured so many hardships for the sake of religious principle,
and what could he say to his children who would thus seem
disowned? The seventy-year-old Church leader had fought
too long for the principle to give it up immediately, despite
court decisions. His inward struggle must have been trau-
matic as he considered his options, but the principle
remained the law of God until revoked by God. 29

John "could not advise the Saints to abandon the law of God, for he
had received no revelation authorizing him to do so. He could only
advise them either to hide from law enforcement officers, face
prosecution, or flee to new gathering places outside the United
States. His attitude was boldly expressed to a federal official in
Utah shortly after the Reynolds decision. The United States
Constitution forbade interference with religious affairs, he
declared. 'I do not believe that the Supreme Court of the United
States…has any right to interfere with my religious views, and in
doing it they are violating their most sacred obligations.' Then, in
a powerful response to the common accusation that polygamy was
immoral, he added,

> We acknowledge our children, we acknowledge our wives;
> we have no mistresses. We had no prostitution until it was
> introduced by monogamy, and I am told that these other
> diabolical deeds are following in its train. The courts
> have protected these people in their wicked practices.
> We repudiate all such things, and hence I consider that
> a system that will enable a man to carry out his professions,
> and that will enable him to acknowledge his wife or wives,
> and acknowledge and provide for his children and wives,
> is much more honorable than that principle which violates
> its marital relations, and, whilst hypocritically professing

to be true to its pledges, recklessly violates the same and tramples upon every principle of honor. 30

As the Saints did their best to go on about their business, the crusade against them intensified. John and the others of the Twelve outlined for the Saints what was called the new anti-Mormon campaign against the Church as follows:

> The first proposed point in the new campaign is to prevent the admission of Utah as a state until polygamy is abandoned.
>
> The second is to induce [C]ongress to repeal the law making women in Utah voters.
>
> The third is to induce [C]ongress to disfranchise every man and woman living in polygamous marriage. And if this is not sufficient "to defeat the political views" of the Mormons, "to disfranchise the offspring of all unlawful wives."
>
> The fourth is to rescue the public schools from the control of the Mormons, and to insist upon the establishment of free schools and prohibit the teaching of denominational sentiments in them. 31

They also sent polygamists out as both missionaries and colonists, directing them to places far away from the reaches of the law. For instance, the Salt River Valley in western Wyoming, later called Star Valley, was settled at this time, as were Bunkerville and Mesquite, Nevada. 32 Several groups established settlements in Castle Valley in eastern Utah, and a company of nearly two hundred—mostly young people and small children—under the direction of Platte De Alton Lyman spent the entire winter of 1879–1880 picking and chipping their frigid way east from Cedar City, Utah, down through the amazing Hole-in-the-Rock trail, across the Colorado River, and back up and out across the slickrock deserts of southern and southeastern Utah to establish on April 6, 1880, a new settlement called Bluff on the remote San Juan River. 33 At the same time, more than three thousand Saints were also settling into three main colonies in Mexico— Colonia Juarez, Colonia Dublan, and Colonia Diaz, with more moving in that direction. And only a short time thereafter, "Charles Ora Card, president of the Cache Stake in Logan, Utah, was instructed by John Taylor to seek out a place of 'asylum and justice' in Canada. In September 1886 a small group of explorers went into Canada and identified the vicinity of Cardston, Alberta, as the northern gathering place... and soon settlements spread." 34

On November 7, 1878, a mass meeting of Gentile women in Salt Lake City drafted an appeal to "the Christian Women of the United States," 35 asking them to join the women of Utah in urging Congress to take stronger action against the Saints. "A week later two thousand Latter-day Saint women held a counter demonstration... and passed a resolution endorsing plural marriage as a religious practice." 36

Soon memorials from Latter-day Saint men, women, young men, and young women were wending their way to Congress. Portions from each of these memorials declare:

[From the men] Whatever of polygamy exists among the Mormons, rests solely upon their religious convictions. It is unsupported by any Territorial legislative enactments, and its practice already exposes them to the penalties of Congressional law. And it is better to leave it to the legitimate operations of that law, and the moral influences at work, than to attempt to extirpate it by radically oppressive or revolutionary measures.

[From the women] And moreover, we your petitioners hereby testify that we are happy in our homes, and satisfied with our marriage relations and desire no change....

And we most solemnly aver before God and man that our marital relations are most sacred, that they are divine, enjoining obligations and ties that pertain to time and reach into eternity. Were it not for the sacred and religious character of plural marriage, we should never have entered upon the practice of a principle which is contrary to our early teachings, and in consequence of which our names are cast out as evil by the Christian world.

[From the young men] We deny that the religious institution of plural marriage, as practiced by our parents, and to which many of us owe our existence, debases, pollutes, or in any way degrades those who enter into it. On the contrary, we solemnly affirm, and challenge successful contradiction, that plural marriage is a sacred religious ordinance, and that its practice has given to thousands, honorable names and peaceful homes where Christian precepts and virtuous practices have been uniformly inculcated, and the spirit of human liberty and religious freedom, fostered from the cradle to maturity.

[From the young ladies] We have been taught and conscientiously believe that plural marriage is as much a part of our religion as faith, repentance and baptism.... We solemnly and truthfully declare that neither we nor our mothers are held in bondage, but that we enjoy the greatest possible freedom, socially and religiously; that our homes are happy ones and we are neither low nor degraded; for the principles of purity, virtue, integrity and loyalty to the government of the United States, have been instilled into our minds and hearts since our earliest childhood. 37

"In each memorial the petitioners prayed that Congress would suspend further action on all bills relating to Utah, and send a commission of honorable, intelligent and unprejudiced men and women to enquire into and learn the true state of affairs in said Territory. The signers to the men's petition numbered 16,256; those to the women's, 19,108; young men's, 15,636; young ladies', 14,152; a total of 65,152." 38

Despite such memorials, in 1882 Congress passed the Edmunds Act, which was immediately signed into law by President Chester A. Arthur. That law,

> in addition to defining polygamy and fixing the punishment for it,…also made cohabitation with more than one woman, a misdemeanor, to be punished by a fine of not more than three hundred dollars and six months' imprisonment; it provided that counts for polygamy and unlawful cohabitation might be joined in the same indictment; it made actual polygamists and those who believed in the rightfulness of it, incompetent as jurors in any prosecution for polygamy or unlawful cohabitation; it also made polygamists, or those cohabiting with more than one woman, incompetent to vote or hold office. It vacated all registration and election offices of every description, and placed the registration of voters and the management of elections under a federal returning board, known as the Utah Commission. 39

This was "a five-man board under whose direction test oaths were administered by qualified registrars in political districts throughout the territory. 40

"When the news of the full enactment of this law reached Utah, President Taylor, knowing the vindictive hatred of the conspirators in Salt Lake City who had concocted that law and aroused the popular clamor which induced Congress to enact it; and knowing that they would seek first to entangle him within its meshes because he was President of the Church; and further knowing that such were the nature of his duties to the Church that it was imperative that he have his liberty, that he might watch over the interests of the great people committed to his care—he resolved to make a great personal sacrifice by submitting to this law, unjust, cruel and infamous as it was. He therefore took counsel with his family and it was arranged that his wives return to their former homes, while he continued to reside [alone] at the Gardo House." 41

In the April 1882 general conference, in referring to the passage of the Edmunds Bill and its effect upon the Saints (and perhaps even more pertinent in light of events occurring after the beginning of the twenty-first century), John warned the Saints that a storm was coming and would soon break in fury upon them. "'Let us treat it,' said he, half humorously 'the same as we did this morning in coming through the snow-storm—put up our coat collars…and wait till the storm subsides. After the storm comes sunshine. While the storm lasts it is useless to reason with the world; when it subsides we can talk to them.'

"In the afternoon he again referred to this matter: 'I stated this morning that there was a storm coming—in fact it is raging at present and has been for some little time, and that it would be well for us to keep up our coat collars and protect ourselves as best we could until the storm passed over. There will be a storm in the United States after awhile; and I want our brethren to prepare themselves for it. At the last conference, I think, I advised all who were in debt to take advantage of the prosperous times and pay their debts; so that they might not be in bondage to anyone, and when the storm came they might be prepared to meet it. There will be one of that kind very soon; and I thought I would give you this warning again, and repeat this piece of advice—the wise will understand.'" 42

On April 9TH, the last day of conference, John spoke for over two hours while the congregation listened with rapt attention. "In addition to sketching the rise and progress of the work of the Lord in these last days, he refuted by the most positive testimony the base slanders on which the late agitation against the work was founded. Referring to the assault made upon the Saints under the pretext of suppressing polygamy, he thus defined the position and policy of the Church:

> We covet no man's possessions. But we expect to maintain our own rights. If we are crowded upon by unprincipled men or inimical legislation, we shall not take the course pursued by the lawless, the dissolute and unprincipled. We shall not have recourse to the dynamite of the Russian Nihilists, the secret plans and machinations of the communists, the boycotting and threats of the Fenians, the force and disorder of the Jayhawkers, the regulators or the Molly Maguires, nor any other secret or illegal combination; but we still expect to possess and maintain our rights; but to obtain them in a legal, peaceful and constitutional manner. As American citizens, we shall contend for all our liberties, rights and immunities, guaranteed to us by the Constitution; and no matter what action may be taken by mobocratic influence, by excited and unreasonable men, or by inimical legislation, we shall contend inch by inch for our freedom and rights, as well as the freedom and rights of all American citizens and of all mankind. 43

What John said next is contained in the *vignette* at the beginning of this chapter, concluding with the powerful anthem known as the Hosanna Shout (slightly changed from the way it is rendered today). Again:

> Our trust is in God. You have heard me say before,

Hosanna, the Lord God Omnipotent reigneth; and if this congregation feels as I do, we will join together in the same acclaim. Follow me. HOSANNA! HOSANNA! HOSANNA TO GOD AND THE LAMB, FOREVER, AND EVER, WORLDS WITHOUT END. AMEN, AMEN, AND AMEN! 44

President John Taylor   CA. *mid-1880s*

CHAMPION OF LIBERTY TO THE END

"Pa, wagon coming!"

"All right, Henry. We hear you."

Young Henry Roueche was seated atop the mast of the log hay derrick, not fifty feet away from the open window where his father was working. It was a warm and pleasant June morning, meadowlarks trilling in the fields, two young colts frisking about the pasture where their mothers ate placidly, a flock of young lambs with tails only recently docked doing the same. Altogether, it was a perfect morning for a young fellow like Henry Roueche to be across the field and swimming in the big hole off of Kay's Creek, which marked the boundary of their land. His father had cleared that hole and dug it both wider and deeper, and now it was a fine reservoir for storing water to be used during the late-summer droughts so typical in the area.

For now, though, he could swim in it, raft on it while playing pirates, or even better, fish in it or along the shady creek below, for the fishing was good in the creek all the way to within a hundred yards of where it emptied into the Great Salt Lake.

Still, it wasn't all bad, getting to sit on top of the derrick's high mast. From it he cold see all the way east into Kaysville and up onto the mountains beyond. North and south his views were just as unrestricted, while to the west he could see beyond the marshes and their myriad of wildfowl all the way across the big lake to Antelope Island, which looked beautiful and mysterious all at once! It was a great country, he thought again and again— perfect for the enjoyment of an adventurous young fellow like himself!

Of course his real job was to watch the road and fields for skunks and spotters—dirty infidels who were trying to sniff out the DO of President Taylor and haul him off to the pen. Henry Roueche was disgusted by such men, and he felt highly honored to be able to assist the Lord's prophet in this manner.

Naturally he could just as easily climb on up and out to the end of the beam, he knew, where the cable went around the pulley and dropped to the big old hay fork where it lay on the ground. That would put him another twenty feet higher and make his view that much better. But his ma was having none of that; besides, Henry knew a fall onto the sharp tines of that hay fork would be curtains for a fellow who liked swimming and fishing as much as he did! Besides—

"Pa," he called urgently, keeping his voice as low as possible, "there's a tarp covering the back of the wagon that's coming, and I just saw a hand reach out and pull it taut!"

"That's good enough, Henry." Thomas Roueche's voice was calm, composed. "Scramble on down, now, and get after those lambs. We'll take it from here."

Behind Thomas Roueche in the kitchen, the prophet's bodyguards—Sam Bateman, whose hair and beard had been recently dyed, and Charlie Wilcken, now bearded—calmly rose to their feet, and while Sister Roueche cleared the breakfast table, they emptied their plates into the slop bucket just inside the screened back door. They couldn't see the wagon, but they knew all about it: half a dozen or more deputies hiding under a tarp, two more on the seat, and with a gang of skunks like that, they figured they finally had the President cold. But the great man wasn't about to be captured, the two guards knew—not, at least, on their watch!

"Would you like Jo to slop the hogs?" Sister Roueche asked quietly.

"Sounds good to me, Ma'am. Soon as possible, too, as they're squealing hungry out there."

"Josephine," Sister Roueche called from where she was busy at the kitchen counter, "would you take Grandma out to slop the hogs? Nor have I had time yet to feed the chickens—"

Not taking time to hear any more of her mother's words, twenty-year-old Josephine Elizabeth Roueche—tall, willowy, with dark eyes and hair, and sealed to the prophet the December before so she could, without embarrassment to either of them, serve as his nurse—slipped up the stairs and into the large front bedroom where President Taylor made his office.

"Skunks, Brother Taylor," she said as she moved to the closet.

"I saw the wagon coming about the same time as Henry," John smiled. "I didn't see the tarp move, though, or the hand."

"Henry has sharp eyes." Josephine by now was holding a dress and a sunbonnet she had taken from the closet. As the President of the Church leaned over, pulled off his shoes and socks, and then rolled up the legs of his trousers, Josephine looked on tenderly. She loved this man, she knew—loved him as a wife ought to love her husband—with all her heart and soul. It was such a delight to be around him, to care for him, comfort him, and to help him through this terrible, awful time!

Only, it seemed so unfair that they couldn't have been together when he was twenty or thirty years younger—

"You'll have to help me button this outfit up," the President chuckled as Josephine pulled the baggy old dress down over his clothes. "My fingers aren't too spry this morning."

"It has nothing to do with your fingers, and you know it,"

Josephine teased. "Men never can do up women's buttons. Very well, President, now let me tie this bonnet in place—Good! Grandmother Taylor, you look absolutely ravishing this morning!"

"Thank you, my dear." John made no effort whatsoever to change his voice.

"Would you care to take a walk with me, Granny, whilst I slop the hogs and grain the chickens?"

Chuckling, John followed his young wife/nurse/protector down the stairs and out through the back door. The cool earth under his bony old feet felt good, reminding him of his carefree childhood days on Bridge End Farm in far-off England. Life had seemed so simple then, and so very easy—

Josephine was already dumping the slop into the hog trough when the sound of splintering wood came from the front of the home. The miserable feds had broken down the door! As if a simple knock had somehow gone out of style!

Angry shouting followed, voices and footsteps moved throughout the two-story DO, and two men suddenly appeared from around the sides of the house on the outside, running with pistols drawn. The prophet, now scattering grain to the busy chickens, did not even look up from behind the deep bill of his bonnet. To the two skunks he was just a scrawny, barefoot, likely deaf old crone, not even worth a second glance. But lovely bonnet-less Josephine, on the other hand, her luxurious hair curling in dark cascades over the light print dress covering her delicate shoulders, and who was already giving the two men a shy smile—well, they thought as both lowered their pistols and smiled back, she was worth a more careful examination through any man's eyes!

And pretty Josephine, her dark eyes widening with surprise that the two handsome men had even noticed her, allowed her smile to grow even brighter.

"Take care to feed those chickens proper, Granny," she tossed

Illustration by Robert T. Barrett

over her shoulder as she moved away from the doddering old "woman." "If you should fall I'll be right over here, saying hello to these two nice young men who have come to call—" 1

It didn't take long for the storm predicted by John in the April 1882 general conference to slam with all its satanic fury into the Saints. The first act of the commission appointed by the Edmunds Law to oversee elections in Utah was to

frame a test oath which they required every person to take before he was permitted to register or vote. This practically disfranchised a whole Territory at one fell swoop; and in order to be reinstated as a voter, every man had to take the oath, which required him to swear that he had never simultaneously lived with more than one woman "in the marriage relation"; or if a woman, that she was not the wife of a polygamist, nor had she entered into any relation with any man in violation of the laws of the United States concerning polygamy and bigamy.

By this arrangement it will be seen that those who cohabited with more than one woman in adultery or prostitution, were not affected by its provisions. The roue, the libertine, the strumpet, the brothel-keeper, the adulterer and adulteress could vote. No matter how licentious a man or a woman might be, all but the Mormons were screened and protected in the exercise of the franchise by the ingenious insertion of the clause, "in the marriage relation," a clause which nowhere appears in the Edmunds law. Such broad constructionists were the Commission, that they declared no man or woman who had ever been a member of a family practicing plural marriage, should be permitted to register or vote, no matter what their present status might be. 2

The first to be brought before the courts on the newly construed dual charges of polygamy and unlawful cohabitation was twenty-seven-year-old Rudger Clawson. This young man had first gained prominence among the Saints when, on July 21, 1879, Joseph Standing, presiding elder in the vicinity of Varnell's Station, Georgia, was shot in the face by a mob. They then turned their weapons on Standing's young companion, Rudger Clawson. After folding his arms, then defiantly facing their weapons and telling them to "shoot," which temporarily cowed the murderous mob, Clawson was allowed to leave the scene to secure help in removing his companion.3 A coroner examined Elder Standing's body—which, after Clawson had left for help, had been shot in the head and face more than twenty additional times at close range— and gave a verdict of murder. "Georgia state officials arrested three suspects, but these men were acquitted by the local jury despite the positive identification and eye-witness testimony given by Elder Clawson." 4

Now twenty-seven and married to a plural wife, Clawson's case marked

> the inauguration of as cruel and unjustifiable a judicial crusade as was ever perpetrated against a free people in a professedly free government. He was arraigned both for polygamy and unlawful cohabitation [both misde-meanors], found guilty and sentenced on the 3RD of November, 1884. His sentence on both charges covered a period of four years imprisonment, and eight hundred dollars in fines. 5

After Clawson's conviction but before sentencing, Judge Charles S. Zane, newly appointed federal judge in Utah and the major judicial force in the final battle against plural marriage, allowed the young man to make a statement. Clawson declared: "'Your honor, I very much regret that the laws of my country should come in conflict with the laws of God; but whenever they do, I shall invariably choose the latter. If I did not so express myself, I should feel unworthy of the case I represent.'" 6

Having first been called as a witness in the case, and giving evasive testimony that an unknown number of men could perform plural marriages in an unknown number of places, John was terribly distraught by this obvious miscarriage of justice. Speaking in Ogden a few days after his own appearance at the trial, he declared:

I could not help thinking as I looked upon the scene, that there was no necessity for all this; these parties [Rudger Clawson and his plural wife] need not have placed themselves in this peculiar dilemma. Here was a young man blessed with more than ordinary intelligence, bearing amongst all who know him a most enviable reputation for virtue, honesty, sobriety and all other desirable characteristics that we are in the habit of supposing go to make a man respected and beloved, the civilized world over. He had been trained from early childhood in the nurture and admonition of the Lord...; more than this, some years ago when quite a youth, he had shown his devotion to the faith in which he had been reared, by going forth without purse or scrip to preach in the midst of the unbelieving the doctrines of a most unpopular faith. And as I reached this point in my reflections, my mind instinctively wanders to a monument I gazed at in Salt Lake City cemetery but a few days ago. That monument records in fitting words of respect and admiration the devotion of two young missionaries in a far-off southern state, one of whom had fallen a victim to mob violence, had sealed with his blood the testimony which he bore, the other had stood by him in his hour of sore need, and rescued his mangled body and brought it safely for thousands of miles to the home of his bereaved parents and sorrowing co-religionists.

This heroic young man is the one now arraigned before the courts of his country, for an alleged offense against the morality of the age! Assuming that the reports pertaining to him should prove to be correct, and he really has a plural wife, what then would be the position? He from his earliest recollection, had been taught to reverence the Bible as the word of God, to revere the lives and examples of the ancient worthies whom Jehovah honored by making them His confidants, and revealing unto them the secrets of his divine purposes; he had read of one who was called "the friend of God and the father of the faithful"; of another who was said to be a "man after God's own heart"; of a third who in all things is said to have done the will of heaven, and so on until they could be numbered by the score; yet all these men, the friends, associates and confidants of the great Creator of heaven and earth, were men with more than one wife, some with many wives, yet they still possessed and rejoiced in the love and honor of the great judge of all the world, whose judgments are just, and whose words are all righteousness. This young man is charged with following these worthy examples; it is asserted that he has taken to wife a beautiful and virtuous young lady, belonging, like himself, to one of our most respected families, and who also believes in the Bible, and in the example set her by those holy women of old, such as Rachel, Ruth, Hannah, and others, who honored God's law, and became the mothers of prophets, priests and kings.

And as my cogitations ran, I thought what need had these two to follow such examples of a by-gone age;

why not walk in the way of the world today, unite with our modern Christian civilization, and if passion guide their actions why call each other husband and wife, why hallow their associations by any sacred ceremony—was there any need of such? Why not do as tens of thousands of others do, live in the condition of illicit love? And then if any child should be feared from this unsanctified union, why not still follow our Christian exemplars, remove the foetal incumbrance, call in...the abortionist, male or female that polute [sic] our land? That would have been, sub-rosa, genteel, fashionable, respectable, Christian-like, as Christianity goes in this generation....

And there, in this ignominious position, he stands with every person who might possibly be his friend, excluded from the jury, without the possibility of a fair trial by his peers, not one of the panel being in the least sympathy with himself; by such people this unfortunate young gentleman has to be tried, judged, prosecuted, proscribed and condemned because of his firm and unswerving faith in the God of Abraham, Isaac and Jacob; of David, Solomon, and numerous other God-fearing and honorable men, who, like him, have despised the cant and hypocrisy of an ungodly world, and dared to obey the behests of Jehovah. 7

With additional funds from Washington flowing into the territory, "the storm" increased in fury and in violence. Deputy marshals and their paid minions, called "skunks" by the Saints, multiplied. These "descended on villages in gangs, hunting for 'cohabs.' They broke down doors at midnight for evidence that a man lived with his wife; they grilled children about parents; they arrested pregnant girls, for this was evidence—not of adultery, but of marriage. The skunks didn't bother about arrest warrants.

They raided from hearsay information, gossip, tips from 'spotters'; and spotters, traitors within the ranks, were even lower on the scale than skunks....

"Since skunks were held in such contempt, the ranks were recruited largely from carpetbaggers, apostates, loafers, and malcontents, bitter men who took great glee in hounding men of position and authority. Officials of the church were almost to a man classed as criminals, fair game for the skunks. The prison began filling with the most distinguished citizens of the Territory, until it became known as the most exclusive social club of Utah." 8

> Spotters and spies were employed to betray their neighbors; children were hailed upon the streets and questioned about the affairs of their parents; wives— lawful wives—were dragged into the courts and compelled to testify against their husbands; shamefully indecent questions were put to modest maidens in jury rooms and in open court; juries were packed to convict; a Mormon accused of violation of the anti-polygamy laws stood before a jury of his avowed political and religious enemies; suspicion was equivalent to accusation; accusation to indictment; indictment to conviction; and conviction met almost invariably with the full penalty of the law, unless the victim was so recreant to every sense of honor as to push from him the women he had taken as wives for time and all eternity! 9

John continued as best he could with the affairs of the presidency. Far from being afraid of the more than 50 million Gentiles who were arrayed against his 160,000 Latter-day Saints, John seemed to welcome the conflict. To his counselor George Q. Cannon, he wrote:

If a crisis has got to come, we might as well meet it now as at any other time. Standing on the rock of eternal truth with God for our guide and protection, what have we to fear?...

It is a glorious thing to be on the side of right; it is a glorious thing to battle for truth, virtue, purity, liberty and the rights of man; it is a glorious thing to feel that God is our friend and that we are the friends of God. 10

Nevertheless, as was being done in homes and churches all over the Territory, John had a secret closet built on the third floor of the Gardo House, which he used at least once when marshals were searching the residence. He also supervised the formation of an underground "to protect wanted men and to harbor pregnant [plural wives] until, as time of delivery neared, the girls were spirited outside the Territory to bear [their] babies." 11

Meanwhile, violence against the Saints was also escalating outside of Utah. "The most flagrant act was the 1884 massacre at Cane Creek in Tennessee. There a mob interrupted religious services at the home of James Condor and demanded the surrender of the elders. Shooting ensued, and two missionaries, two investigators, and the leader of the mob were killed and a woman was crippled for life. The mission president had gone to Salt Lake City and had left the mission in charge of B. H. Roberts, soon to become a member of the First Council of the Seventy. Risking his own life, Elder Roberts went to Cane Creek in disguise, secured the bodies of the murdered elders, and sent them to Utah." 12

When the situation in Arizona became even worse than it was in Utah, John wrote to the stake presidents:

There can be no question that there is apparently a concert of action...to push our people to the wall and to destroy our religious liberty and with it our religion itself....

Our brethren are like sheep surrounded by ravening

wolves, and you as shepherds of the flock... must take steps to protect them. 13

John then informed the Brethren that he needed to go to Arizona so that he might counsel the Saints there as the Lord gave him wisdom. With him he took his second counselor, Joseph F. Smith, and also apostles Moses Thatcher and Francis M. Lyman, Bishop John Sharp, and others. They were joined along the way by Elder Erastus Snow.

> The party left Salt Lake City on the 3RD of January, 1885, by the Union Pacific Railway to Denver, thence to Albuquerque, in New Mexico, thence to the settlements of the Saints in Apache County, Arizona, in the vicinity of Winslow.
>
> President Taylor went to St. David, in the extreme south-east corner of Arizona, near Benson, where he met with the Presidents of the four Stakes in that Territory; Jesse N. Smith, Christopher Layton, Alexander F. McDonald and Lot Smith. He found the Saints in a lamentable condition. They had been set upon in the most ruthless manner by their enemies. Nearly all the forms of law had been abandoned in dealing with them, and outrages had been heaped upon them, under the pretext of executing the law, that were well nigh unendurable. Those who had been convicted and sentenced had been shipped off to Detroit, a distance of two thousand miles, notwithstanding there was a good available prison at Yuma, within the Territory. 14

After giving directions and counsel to the presidents of the stakes in Arizona, including the suggestion that a general colonizing effort be made into Mexico, which was begun almost immediately, John and the others journeyed on to the settlements of Saints in

Maricopa County, on the Salt River, and from there they continued westward by rail to Los Angeles and then north to San Francisco. There John and Joseph F. Smith met with Governor Leland Stanford, who willingly advised them concerning financial and other difficulties the Church was experiencing because of the federally sponsored persecution. While there they also attended the theater, visited Chinatown, went to Golden Gate Park to see the acacia in bloom, lunched at the Cliff House overlooking Seal Rocks, and spent some time simply prowling about the city. In that way they found the shack where Parley P. Pratt had lived on Pacific Street; they saw where George Q. Cannon and others, twenty years earlier, had translated the Book of Mormon into Hawaiian and founded the *Western Standard* while John had been in New York publishing *The Mormon*.

> [In San Francisco] Mormons were remembered now primarily through place names. There was Mormon Island on the American River, where one of the richest gold strikes was made by three members of the Mormon Battalion; Mormon Gulch, site of Tuttletown; Mormon Corral, in El Dorado County. And even these names were disappearing. Colonists of [Sam] Brannan's ship gave the name Brooklyn to the city across the bay that was now Oakland. The settlement of New Hope, where the colony grew the first wheat, now was Stanislaus. Mormon Road in Toulumne County had become Slumgullion Road (hardly an improvement); and Mt. Joseph Smith was now Mt. Polomar. 15

John took one afternoon to walk down Valencia Street to call on historian H. H. Bancroft, who happily showed him his library of 60,000 volumes and 100,000 manuscripts. "Taylor saw the busy staff at work, compiling the volumes of [Bancroft's] immense *Works*, of which the *History of Utah* was one. He shook hands with Alfred Bates and

Edward P. Newkirk, the two writers assigned to prepare the history of the Saints for Bancroft's final draft and polish....

"It now had been exactly five years since Taylor had endorsed Bancroft's project, and at last the end was in sight. The historian estimated that the Utah volume would be completed by the end of the year, 1885." 16

Back at his hotel, John learned from a special courier that trouble had developed back in Utah. Deputy Sam Gilson had arrested George Q. Cannon for unlawful cohabitation; he was out on bail and, with L. John Nuttall, was in hiding—in the new barn behind the Church's Tithing Office. Worse, Gilson had warrants for the arrest of John and Joseph F. Smith, and the government was determined to put them all behind bars.

Despite these threats, John determined to return immediately to Salt Lake City. On the other hand, he counseled Joseph F. Smith—who as a precautionary measure was carrying with him the sacred but incriminating Endowment House records—to take an immediate mission to the Sandwich, or Hawaiian, Islands. When they parted, neither man knew they would not see each other again until mere hours before John's death.

Returning immediately to Salt Lake City, John was escorted by two trusted guards, Sam Bateman and Charles Wilcken, to the Tithing Office barn. There he called a secret night session of the Twelve, where all concurred that it was time for him to go underground, just as Joseph had done during the harsh days at Nauvoo prior to his martyrdom.

For the next week John visited at secret rendezvous sites with his various families—Marshal Gilson and his "skunks" meanwhile scouring the valley for him. Then on Sunday afternoon, February 1, 1885, while the Tabernacle was filled to overflowing, John quietly entered and, to the surprised but hushed congregation of Saints, preached his last public sermon.

After relating the wrongs he had witnessed inflicted upon

the Saints in Arizona and the counsel he had given them to disappear from sight or get out of the country, he declared that as the vindictiveness of the courts in Utah had increased, he was giving the Saints in the Tabernacle the same advice.

"He deplored the condition of things in the Territory, not so much on account of the Latter-day Saints, as on the account of the great government of the United States, which had stooped from the proud position it had hitherto boasted as the asylum for the oppressed of all nations, to that of a persecutor of a righteous people for their religion, until they had to find an asylum in an adjoining republic! Referring to the outrages perpetrated both in Arizona and in Utah, he [asked]:

> What would you do? Would you resent these outrages and break the heads of the men engaged in them, and spill their blood? No…avoid them as much as you possibly can—just as you would wolves, or hyenas, or crocodiles, or snakes, or any of these beasts or reptiles…. Get out of their way as much as you can. What! Won't you submit to the dignity of the law? Well, I would if the law would only be a little more dignified. But when we see [that] dignity…bedragged [sic] in the mud and mire, and every principle of justice violated, it behooves men to take care of themselves as best they can…. But no breaking of heads, no bloodshed, rendering evil for evil. Let us try to cultivate the spirit of the gospel, and adhere to the principles of truth…. While other men are seeking to trample the Constitution under foot, we will try to maintain it…. I will tell you what you will see by and by. You will see trouble! trouble! TROUBLE enough in these United States. And as I have said before, I say today—I tell you in the name of God, WOE! to them that fight against Zion, for God will fight against them!" [17]

When John left the Tabernacle that afternoon, it was for the last time. By that night he had vanished into what was called "the underground," and the majority of the Saints, including some in his own family, would never see him again.

His first destination was the Tithing Office barn, where he waited with L. John Nuttall and George Q. Cannon until darkness. Then, escorted by Sam Bateman and big Charles Wilcken, a former Prussian Army veteran who had been decorated with the Iron Cross for bravery, they urged their buggy south to Taylorsville and the home of Bishop Samuel Bennion, where they stayed for the next nine days. Then, because word of John's whereabouts was bound to leak out one way or another, they moved again.

Through the winter John stayed at two residences in Taylorsville, one in Big Cottonwood, and one in Sugar House. These refuges were called by members of the Church "Safe Retreat," "Halfway House," and, most often, the "DO." Those on the underground "were 'on the dodge,' thus, 'DO' in the 'cohab code.'"[18] Always they were just ahead of the deputies, and even when they never ventured from the homes in daylight, spies somehow managed to discover John's whereabouts from time to time and tip the authorities.

It was a suspicious time, a time when conversations were guarded, a time when no one knew which of his friends was in reality his enemy. For all of those forced underground— and certainly for John—it was also a time of terrible loneliness. He dared not spend time with any of his wives or children, for they were just as apt to be imprisoned as he. And so, except for just two brief occasions, he avoided the Gardo House and Taylor Row as he slipped in the dark of night from one safe house to another. Interestingly, while there were many who offered their homes, none who were considered rich ever did so. It was the humble to whose homes he went, and the humble whose homes he blessed. [19]

Meanwhile, "Idaho had passed a Test Oath law, disfranchising all Mormons who believed in plural marriage, on the ground that this made them unpatriotic citizens. The Test Oath resulted in denial of the vote, and the holding of public office, to some 2,000 church members of the Territory. The U.S. Marshal of Idaho was a rabid Mormon-eater, Fred T. Dubois, who relentlessly secured convictions for polygamy and u.c. [unlawful cohabitation], boasting that he could empanel a jury which 'could convict Jesus Christ.'

"Taylor heard that the governor of Idaho, William Bunn, a man with a strict sense of justice, had refused to sign the Test Oath bill; whereupon H. W. ('Kentucky') Smith, who had sponsored the measure, together with another member of the legislature, George Gorton, and Marshal Dubois, called at the governor's office and demanded that Bunn do so. When Bunn said he'd made up his mind to veto it, Kentucky Smith pulled a pistol from his pocket, and said, 'Governor, you will not leave this room alive unless you sign that bill.'

"Fighting fire with fire, Taylor passed the word for Idaho Mormons to 'apostatize' from the Church, in order to meet voting and office-holding requirements, while the Test Oath was being tried in the courts."[20]

With the assistance of his counselors—George Q. Cannon, who was on the dodge with him, and Joseph F. Smith, who did what he could from the Sandwich Islands—John issued a series of general epistles to the Saints, imparting such counsel and instruction as they considered necessary and suited to the several occasions they were made aware of.

These papers are remarkable for their conservative tone and wisdom; for the total absence of anger or vindictiveness, as also for the scope and variety of the subjects they treated upon. They compare favorably with the wisest and best state papers ever issued by kings or presidents, ministers of state or cabinet councils. The flock of Christ, therefore, was not left without the counsel of heaven or the care of the shepherds. 21

In the meantime the legal persecution of the Saints not only continued, but grew worse. Men who at the most were guilty of a misdemeanor, punishable with a maximum sentence of six months imprisonment and three-hundred-dollar fine, were hounded as if they were the very vilest of criminals guilty of the grossest crimes which might endanger the peace and safety of their communities.

"Not satisfied with the penalties affixed to the laws against unlawful cohabitation, the Utah courts determined to increase them by means little short of legislation itself. The trick resorted to was to decree that the time a man had cohabited with more women than one as wives, could be divided up into years, months or weeks, and separate bills of indictment be found for each fragment of time. So ruled the Chief Justice, Charles S. Zane. Judge Orlando W. Powers of the First Judicial District, carried the infamous doctrine still further, and in charging a grand jury, on the 23RD of September, 1885, said: 'An indictment may be found against a man guilty of unlawful cohabitation, for every day, or other distinct interval of time, during which he offends. Each day that a man cohabits with more than one woman, as I have defined the word cohabit, is a distinct and separate violation of the law, and he is liable for punishment for each separate offense.'

"His definition of cohabitation was as follows:

The offense of cohabitation is complete when a man, to all outward appearances, is living or associating with more than one woman as his wife. To constitute the offense it is not necessary that it be shown that the parties indulge in sexual intercourse. The intention of the law-making power, in enacting the law, was to protect monogamous marriage by prohibiting all other marriage, whether evidenced by a ceremony, or by conduct and circumstances alone.

"So held all the courts, and under that ruling such infamies as the following were possible:

> In the case of Solomon Edwards recently accused of this offense—unlawful cohabitation—it was proved by the evidence for the prosecution that the defendant had lived with one wife only since the passage of the Edmunds act, but after having separated from his former plural wife, he called with his legal wife at the former's residence to obtain a child, an agreement having been made that each party should have one of the two children, and the court ruled that this was unlawful cohabitation in the meaning of the law, and defendant was convicted. 22

In all of this, however, John was the polygamist most consistently sought. His own houses, the Church offices, the Gardo House were always watched and regularly searched. "That the place of his concealment was not discovered is little short of the miraculous, since the business to which he continued to give his personal attention was considerable, and required frequent communication with agents who were at liberty to act. He owed his safety, however, more to the promptings of the Holy Spirit than to the cunning of man. More than once, in obedience to its whisperings, and when to all outward appearances there was no danger to be feared, he would leave his place of temporary abode. By frequently changing his place of concealment, while running considerable risk of discovery in moving, he kept his enemies mystified as to his whereabouts.

"Though driven into retirement by a malicious and perverted administration of the Edmunds law, he never allowed it to embitter his thoughts or disturb the calmness and patience of his disposition. No, not even so much as to lead him to speak evil of those who persecuted him. 'God forgive them,' he would say, 'they know not what they do.' 'I pity them, with all my heart.'" 23

As November 1, 1887, John's 79TH birthday, approached, an occasion that would have been celebrated with a large family gathering, John wrote his loved ones as follows:

> As I am prevented from being with you on the present occasion, I desire to send to you my benediction and blessing; and to say unto you: May grace, mercy and peace be extended to you from God our Eternal Father, through our Lord Jesus Christ, who is our Savior, Redeemer and Friend.
>
> I need not say unto you, that it would have afforded me very great pleasure to have been with you on the present occasion.... But, through the dispensation of an All-wise Providence, things are not in a position that we would desire to have them; they are in accordance, however, with the design of our Heavenly Father, who ordains all things in harmony with the dispensation of His providence towards the children of men.
>
> Some people suppose that persecutions and trials are afflictions; but sometimes, and generally, if we are doing the will of the Lord and keeping His commandments, they may be truly said to be blessings in disguise. When our great Redeemer was on earth, He said to His disciples: "Blessed are ye when men shall revile you, and persecute you, and shall say all manner of evil against you falsely, for my sake. Rejoice and be exceeding glad, for great is your reward in heaven, for so persecuted they the prophets which were before you."
>
> Although for the time being, these things may be

painful, yet if properly comprehended and realized, we should look at them in another view, and feel as Paul said to the saints in his day: "For our light affliction, which is but for a moment, worketh for us a far more exceeding and eternal weight of glory; while we look not at the things which are seen, but at the things which are not seen; for the things which are seen are temporal, but the things which are not seen are eternal," and will lead us to reflect in most instances even as John Wesley sang:

"Shall I be carried to the skies,
On flowery beds of ease;
While others fought to win the prize,
And sailed through bloody seas!

"No; I must fight, if I would reign,
Increase my courage, Lord;
I'll bear the toil, endure the pain,
Supported by thy word."

The foregoing are my sentiments, which I express from the bottom of my heart....

...We expect and have faith, that this earth will yet be renovated and purified, the wicked will be rooted out of it, and the righteous inherit it; and we further look forward to the time when there will be a new heaven and a new earth, wherein dwelleth righteousness; and a new Jerusalem, wherein the Lord God and the Lamb will be the light thereof, and you, my wives, and also my children who have come to years of maturity, will have the privilege, if faithful to your covenants, of entering into and partaking of the most exalted, glorious, and eternal blessings, which any men or women on earth have enjoyed in this world, or in the world to come; and will eventually be associated with the Gods in the eternal worlds....

We should be strictly honest, one with another, and with all men; let our word always be as good as our bond; avoid all ostentation of pride and vanity; and be meek, lowly, and humble; be full of integrity and honor; and deal justly and righteously with all men; and have the fear and love of God continually before us, and seek for the comforting influence of the Holy Ghost to dwell with us. Let mothers be loving, kind and considerate with their children, and the children kind and obedient to their mothers, and to their Fathers; and seek always to be governed by good and wise counsel, and so to live every day, and in all our acts, as to keep a conscience void of offense towards God and man. Be kind and courteous to all, seek to promote the welfare of all, be gentlemen and ladies, and treat one another, and all men with proper courtesy, respect and kindness. So shall you be honored by the good and virtuous, enjoy the blessings of a good conscience, and secure the approbation of God, and of the holy angels, in time and throughout all eternity.

The protecting care of the Lord over me and my brethren has been very manifest since my absence from home, for which I feel to bless and praise His holy name. I always am very desirous to acknowledge His hand in all things, and I am very anxious that you should do the same. For to the Lord we are indebted for every blessing which we enjoy, pertaining to this life, and the life which is to come.

While we seek to God our Heavenly Father for His blessings, let us be careful to so live that we can secure and claim them, by our obedience to His laws. Be merciful, and kind, and just, and generous to all. Preserve your bodies and your spirits pure, and free from contamination.

Avoid lasciviousness, and every corrupting influence; that you may be indeed the sons of God without rebuke, in the midst of a crooked and perverse generation.

In regard to my position and that of my brethren who are with me, I am happy to inform you that we now are, and always have been, during our exile, supplied with everything that is necessary to our comfort and convenience. Go where we will, we have good accommodations, plenty of food and the necessaries of life, kind and sympathetic friends, and the best of treatment. I am also happy in the belief that you are comfortably situated. If there is anything that any of you require and you will inform me, I shall be happy to supply it, if within my power. Some of you have written that you "would like to have a peep at me." I heartily reciprocate that feeling, and would like to have a "peep" at you on this occasion; but in my bodily absence my spirit and peace shall be with you.

God bless you all, in time and throughout the eternities to come, is the prayer of your affectionate husband, father and friend in the new and everlasting covenant—

JOHN TAYLOR. 24

Not many months before he wrote the above letter, John's health had begun to fail. Felled as a martyr in Carthage Jail thirty-three years before, he was about to suffer martyrdom for the second time. All his life he had been strong and robust, rarely suffering illness in any form. Now, however, stress caused by the attacks being waged against himself and his people, too little rest because of the constant need to travel at night from one DO to another, too little physical activity because he never dared go out of doors in daylight, no real happiness regarding his home and family life because the government was preventing him from all such associations (including being prevented from attending the funeral of his wife Sophia Whitaker), worry because he knew he was endangering those families who were sheltering himself and those who remained with him—these and other things had begun to take their toll.

"Sustained by his marvelous willpower," however, John "resisted the approach of death with all his characteristic determination. He would neither permit himself nor others to believe that he was seriously ill. But his decreasing inclination to take what little exercise he could under the circumstances; and periods of prostration occurring with increasing frequency, told its own story as to how the battle was going."25

Still, John kept up the fight. When Mormon-hating Utah governor Eli H. Murray began vetoing every bill to pass the legislature, including the appropriations measure and a bill to end discrimination in the territory, John gave his official blessing to a memorial fired off to Congress by the Legislative Assembly. The results were rapid; within days President Cleveland terminated Murray's gubernatorial career.

And when John received reports of Senator Edmunds joining with Senator Tucker to create an even harsher law—one that would plug the few loopholes left to the Saints by the Edmunds Law of 1882—he began actively considering an amendment written by William Scott of Pennsylvania that would give Utah time to draft a state constitution outlawing polygamy. John actively encouraged the writing of such a constitution, which was finished quickly and submitted to Congress.

The Scott amendment failed, however, and though President Cleveland refused to sign the Edmunds-Tucker Law, feeling that it was far too harsh, he did allow it to become law without a signature. When Congress finally rejected the newest Utah application for statehood, even with its polygamy-outlawing proviso, the Edmunds-Tucker Law went into full effect—its aim to "destroy the Church as a political and economic entity." 26 The Church found itself dissolved as a legal entity and all its property in excess of $50,000 escheated to the government, which then rented back such properties as Temple Square and the Historian's Office. At the same time it made all laws against polygamists even harsher and disinherited all children born to plural marriages more than one year after the act was passed.

Brokenhearted by the sufferings of his people, but too ill to don disguises and go out amongst them, John and those with him labored at the DO on another letter of support and encouragement to the beleaguered Saints. He wrote:

> However grievous the wrongs under which we suffer today, there is much to be thankful for. Our land is filled with plenty.... And with these blessings...we have the inestimable blessing of the peace of God.... Let your hearts, therefore, brethren and sisters, be filled with thanksgiving and praise to our God for His goodness and mercy unto us as a people. He has made promises concerning Zion; be assured He will not forget them....
>
> Persecution develops character.... It has strengthened and infused new zeal, courage and determination.... [Remember the Savior's words:] "If ye were of the world, the world would love his own; but because ye are not of the world...therefore the world hateth you."...
>
> Our enemies have designed to destroy the work of God. For this they plot and toil and descend to the depths of infamy.... Instead of crushing the truth, they are advertising it; instead of showing the world how unworthy and contemptible we are, they are unwittingly furnishing us with opportunities to exhibit the heroic qualities we possess; instead of weakening or unsettling the minds of true Latter-day Saints, they are stimulating [our] faith

and supplying [us] with additional proofs of the divinity
of [our] religion....

They would have the world believe that we are low,
sensual, ignorant, and degraded, that our religion is
a system of lust...but thinking people of the world know
that there is no necessity to endure that which the
Latter-day Saints are now enduring, to gratify lustful
appetites or desires....

What does it mean to be like [those who persecute us]?
It means that *E Pluribus Unum* is a fiction; it means that
we tamper with and violate that grand palladium of human
liberty, the Constitution of the United States, and substitute
expediency, anarchy, fanaticism, intolerance, and religious
bigotry for those glorious fundamental principles of liberty,
equality, brotherhood, human freedom, and the rights of
man....

We cannot do it. 27

To the last, then, John championed the rights of his people—
and of free people everywhere—encouraging all who would to
stand boldly for truth in the face of whatever the enemies of truth
might throw at them. It was a magnificent battle John waged,
from the start of his life to the finish, and not once is there any
evidence whatsoever that he flinched!

"The tenth of July marked a crisis in the struggle for life which
alarmed his friends and attendants. The tenth occurred on Sunday.
It had been his custom in these years of exile to hold religious
service on the Sabbath and fast days, the first Thursday of every
month. The brethren who were with him usually took turns
in presiding in these meetings. The service consisted of singing,
prayer, administering the sacrament and such remarks as the
brethren felt inclined to make. On the tenth of July...the meeting
was called as usual and opened, but no one could speak.

President Taylor's illness had taken a turn for the worse and the unpleasant conviction forced itself on those about him least willing to believe it, that he was gradually sinking." 28

The next morning, George Q. Cannon wrote letters to members of the Quorum of the Twelve, informing them of what appeared to be John's rapidly approaching death. After the letters were sent, however, John rallied somewhat, giving all around him renewed hope. Yet the letters had already gone out, and on July 18TH, John's Second Counselor, Joseph F. Smith, arrived from the Sandwich Islands. John "was very weak and low but still conscious; and as he looked up and recognized Brother Joseph, and his attention was called to the fact that the First Presidency were together once more—the first time since December, 1884—he said:

"'I feel to thank the Lord!'

"After this he continued to grow weaker, with only intervals of consciousness, until the evening of the 25TH.

"It was at the house of Thomas F. Roueche, of Kaysville, that President Taylor was fighting out this last battle, with such remarkable determination. On the above named evening, the few friends who were permitted to be with him, among whom were his two Counselors, two of his wives, Mary Oakley Taylor and Maggie Young Taylor, and the Roueche family, were gathered about his bed as he slowly sank under the hand of Death. He was passing away without a struggle, quietly as a child falls asleep. At five minutes to eight o'clock, 'the weary wheels of life stood still'—the great spirit had left its earthly tabernacle." 29

John Taylor, ever courageous defender of truth and right, had triumphantly been called home.

President John Taylor   N.D.

ℰPILOGUE

The following appeared in the Tuesday, July 26, 1887, edition of the *Deseret News*:

Once more the Latter-day Saints are called upon to mourn the death of their leader—the man who has held the keys of the kingdom of God upon earth. President John Taylor departed this life at five minutes to eight o'clock on the evening of Monday, July 25TH, 1887, aged 78 years, 8 months and 25 days.

In communicating this sad intelligence to the Church, over which he has so worthily presided for nearly ten years past, we are filled with emotion too deep for utterance. A faithful, devoted and fearless servant of God, the Church in his death has lost its most conspicuous and experienced leader. Steadfast to and immovable in the truth, few men have ever lived who have manifested such integrity and such unflinching moral and physical courage as our beloved President who has just gone from us. He never knew the feeling of fear connected with the work of God. But in the face of angry mobs, and at other times when in imminent danger of personal violence from those who threatened his life, and upon occasions when the people were menaced with public peril, he never blenched —his knees never trembled, his hand never shook. Every Latter-day Saint always knew beforehand, on occasions when firmness and courage were needed, where President John Taylor would be found and what his tone would be. He met every issue squarely, boldly and in a way to call forth the admiration of all who saw and heard him. Undaunted courage, unyielding firmness were among his most prominent characteristics, giving him distinction among men who were distinguished for the same qualities. With these were combined an intense love of freedom and hatred of oppression. He was a man whom all could trust, and throughout his life he enjoyed, to an extent surpassed by none, the implicit confidence of the Prophets Joseph, Hyrum and Brigham and all the leading men and members of the Church. The title of "Champion of Liberty," which he received at Nauvoo, was always felt to be most appropriate for him to bear. But it was not only in the possession of these qualities that President Taylor was great. His judgment was remarkably sound and clear, and through life he has been noted for the wisdom of his counsels and teachings. His great experience made his suggestions exceedingly valuable; for there has scarcely been a public movement of any kind commenced, carried on, or completed, since he joined the Church in which he has not taken part....

By the miraculous power of God, President John Taylor escaped the death which the assassins of Carthage jail assigned for him. His blood was then mingled with the blood of the martyred Prophet and Patriarch. He has stood since then as a living martyr for the truth. But today he occupies the place of a double martyr. President John Taylor has been killed by the cruelty of officials who have, in this Territory, misrepresented the Government of the United States. There is no room to doubt that if he had been permitted to enjoy the comforts of home, the ministrations of his family, the exercise to which he had been accustomed, but of which he was deprived, he might have lived for many years yet. His blood stains the clothes of the men, who with insensate hate have offered rewards for his arrest and have hounded him to the grave. History will yet call their deeds by their right names; but One greater than the combined voices of all historians will yet pronounce their dreadful sentence....

We feel to say to the Latter-day Saints: Be comforted! The same God who took care of the work when Joseph was martyred, who has watched over and guarded and upheld it through the long years that have since elapsed, and who has guided its destinies since the departure of Brigham, still watches over it and makes it the object of His care. John has gone; but God lives. He has founded Zion. He has given His people a testimony of this. Cherish it in your heart of hearts, and live so each day that when the end of your mortal lives shall come, you may be counted worthy to go where Joseph, Brigham and John have gone, and mingle with that glorious throng whose robes have been washed white in the blood of the Lamb.

This is the earnest prayer for all Saints, and for all the honest in heart, of your unworthy servants in Christ,

GEORGE Q. CANNON
JOSEPH F. SMITH. 1

John's funeral was held in the Tabernacle on Friday, July 29, 1887. During his funeral and afterward, as he was buried in the Salt Lake City cemetery, numerous deputies and "skunks" scanned the crowd. John Taylor might indeed have been beyond their reach, but there were a great many others who deserved to be punished for daring to follow what they truly considered their prophet's inspired counsel—

From the very beginning, plural marriage was a difficult principle for the Saints to live; as public opposition grew into incredibly intense persecution, aided by newly and narrowly defined constitutional law, it turned into a virtual nightmare. It must have been worse than that for President Taylor. Yet never, not one time that we have any knowledge of, did God respond to his pleas with anything other than, "Trust me, my son, and keep going!"

What seems terribly ironic is that after requiring the ultimate sacrifice from President Taylor, exactly three years and two months later, President Wilford Woodruff—John Taylor's successor to the office of President—after having received divine approval from the same Source who had forbidden it of John Taylor, took the opposite tack. Now known simply as the "Manifesto," President Woodruff's document not only initiated the ending of plural marriage within the Church, but inaugurated the cessation of legal persecution against its members.

No matter how this abrupt change in practice and teaching is viewed, questions, particularly concerning the whys of it, remain. Why Wilford Woodruff to stop it? Why not John Taylor? If it was a true and defensible principle and doctrine for the one, why allow it to be abandoned by the other? Why change it at all? The trouble with these sorts of questions is that, ultimately, they can be answered only by God; and thus far, He has said little more than, "Wherefore I, the Lord, command and revoke, as it seemeth me good; and all this to be answered upon the heads of the rebellious, saith the Lord" (Doctrine & Covenants 56:4).

To me, this means simply that God directed each of His prophets, John Taylor and Wilford Woodruff, "as seemeth [Him] good," and my choice is either to sustain them both and be blessed for my faith, or to rebel against one or the other of them, which rebellion will ultimately be "answered upon [my own] head" in whatever manner God chooses.

And why can God apparently reverse courses in such a way? As explained by Elder Hyrum M. Smith and Janne M. Sjodahl:

> The laws of God are immutable. He is the Father of lights, "with whom is no variableness, neither shadow of turning" (James 1:17). "Hath he said, and shall he not do it? Or hath he spoken, and shall he not make it good" (Numbers 23:19)? "The Counsel of the Lord standeth for ever; the thoughts of his heart to all generations" (Psalms 33:11). He is the same yesterday, today, and for ever.
>
> Some take this to mean that the plans of God are never changed, never modified. Here we learn that He commands and revokes, as seemeth Him good; that is, not capriciously, but for good and sufficient reasons. God is a *free agent*. We must not suppose that His immutability deprives Him of free agency. And because He is a free agent, He can command and revoke at will. But those who make it necessary for God, because of rebellion, to revoke laws given for the benefit of His children, will be held responsible. 2

As I finished the story of President John Taylor, I felt overwhelmed with a feeling of sadness intermingled with joy. In every way possible, again and again, President Taylor gave his life for the revealed word of God, and my heart both ached and rejoiced as I read of it. Despite the intense opposition of the world, despite the viciously satanic nature of the attacks he endured personally, and despite his perfectly natural desire for a bit of freedom and peace as he grew older, of him it was required by the Lord to "champion" the freedom of his people all the days of his life. Never was he spared!

Who can guess how many times this kind and gentle soul pleaded with God for the burden of plural marriage to be lifted from himself and his people? Who can imagine how many times his tears wet his pillow because of the pain and suffering he was forced to both endure and to witness? Yet never—no, never—did he waver! In all things he was both submissive and obedient, and I am assured that he will reap the rewards of his obedience forever.

With a sense of awe and wonder I honor him! What courage in the face of terrible adversity he has displayed! What perfect love for his Savior and Redeemer! Yet he was doing nothing more than God has asked of each of us—to follow in the footsteps of our Lord and Master, who in like circumstances to those surrounding President John Taylor, pleaded: "O my Father, if it be possible, let this cup pass from me: nevertheless not as I will, but as thou wilt" (Matthew 26:39).

For whatever reasons (and they must be eternally significant ones), God chose not to give relief at that time, but instead required of President Taylor the ultimate sacrifice. As I come to the conclusion of this great man's story, at least as we have it in mortality, I am more than thankful that he successfully offered it. His courage and determination to obey God and submit to his will in the face of vicious, unrelenting persecution, even unto death, is an incredible example all of us can look to as we face our own trials and tribulations in these tumultuous times—our own persecutions "for righteousness sake."

Because of the courageous, unwavering way he both lived and died, I feel deeply honored to be a part of the Church that God called President John Taylor to lead.

Blaine M. Yorgason

ENDNOTES

CHAPTER 1

1 The material for this historical *vignette* has been adapted from an oral tradition long cherished in the John Taylor family. This was confirmed to the author during a telephone conversation of 4 March 2002 with Dr. Sarah Taylor Weston, of Redwood City, California. Dr. Weston, the daughter of Samuel W. Taylor, is John Taylor's great-granddaughter. The toy horse, still looking ready for a rider after more than an hundred and fifty years, has been returned to Nauvoo by the Taylor family and once again occupies its favored position on the floor of the children's room in the John Taylor home.

2 B. H. Roberts, *The Life of John Taylor* (Salt Lake City: Bookcraft, 1963), p. 449.

3 Ibid.

4 Ibid., pp. 419–420, 423, 433–434.

5 Ibid., p. 414.

CHAPTER 2

1 Material upon which this *vignette* was based was taken from B. H. Roberts, *The Life of John Taylor* (Salt Lake City: Bookcraft, 1963), pp. 23–26; and Samuel W. Taylor, *The Kingdom or Nothing: The Life of John Taylor, Militant Mormon* (New York and London: Macmillan Publishing Co., Inc., 1976), pp. 17–18.

2 Leonard J. Arrington, Susan Arrington Madsen, and Emily Madsen Jones, *Mothers of the Prophets* (Salt Lake City: Bookcraft, 1987, 2001), p. 48.

3   Roberts, *Life of John Taylor,* p. 21.

4   Ibid., p. 21.

5   Ibid., p. 21.

6   Ibid., p. 22.

7   Arrington, Arrington, and Madsen, *Mothers of the Prophets,* p. 48.

8   Ibid., p. 48.

9   Roberts, *Life of John Taylor,* p. 21.

10 Arrington, Arrington, and Madsen, *Mothers of the Prophets,* p. 48.

11 See Roberts, *Life of John Taylor,* pp. 22, 23.

12 Arrington, Arrington, and Madsen, *Mothers of the Prophets,* p. 49. See also Roberts, *Life of John Taylor,* p. 23.

13 Samuel W. Taylor, *The Kingdom or Nothing,* p. 18.

14 Roberts, *Life of John Taylor,* p. 28.

15 Ibid., p. 26.

16 Ibid., p. 27.

17 Samuel W. Taylor, *The Kingdom or Nothing,* p. 19.

18 Roberts, *Life of John Taylor,* p. 27.

19 Samuel W. Taylor, *The Kingdom or Nothing,* p. 19. See also Arrington, Arrington, and Madsen, *Mothers of the Prophets,* pp. 49–50.

20 Arrington, Arrington, and Madsen, *Mothers of the Prophets,* p. 50.

21 Samuel W. Taylor, *The Kingdom or Nothing,* p. 19.

22 Roberts, *Life of John Taylor,* p. 28.

23 Ibid., p. 28–29.

CHAPTER 3

1   Material for this *vignette* was taken from B. H. Roberts, *The Life of John Taylor* (Salt Lake City: Bookcraft, 1963), pp. 29–38; Parley P. Pratt, *Autobiography of Parley P. Pratt,* edited by his son, Parley P. Pratt (Salt Lake City: Deseret Book, 1938, 1985), pp. 110–120; and Samuel W. Taylor, *The Kingdom or Nothing: The Life of John Taylor, Militant Mormon* (New York: Macmillan Publishing Co., Inc., 1976), p. 22–23.

2   Leonard J. Arrington, Susan Arrington Madsen, and Emily Madsen Jones, *Mothers of the Prophets* (Salt Lake City: Bookcraft, 1987, 2001), p. 50.

3   Roberts, *Life of John Taylor,* pp. 29–30.

4   Preston Nibley, *The Presidents of the Church* (Salt Lake City: Deseret Book, 1944), p. 91.

5   Samuel W. Taylor, *The Kingdom or Nothing*, p. 22.

6   Roberts, *Life of John Taylor*, p. 30.

7   Ibid., pp. 30–31.

8   Arrington, Arrington, and Madsen, *Mothers of the Prophets*, pp. 50–51.

9   Leonard J. Arrington, editor, and Paul Thomas Smith, essayist,
     The Presidents of the Church, Biographical Essays (Salt Lake City:
     Deseret Book, 1986), p. 78.

10   Ibid., p. 78.

11   Roberts, *Life of John Taylor*, p. 31.

12   Pratt, *Autobiography*, p. 110.

13   Samuel W. Taylor, *The Kingdom or Nothing*, p. 20.

14   Pratt, *Autobiography*, pp. 114, 116.

15   Ibid., p. 117.

16   Samuel W. Taylor, *The Kingdom or Nothing*, p. 21

17   Ibid., p. 22.

18   Pratt, *Autobiography*, p. 120.

19   Ibid., p. 127.

20   Samuel W. Taylor, *The Kingdom or Nothing*, p. 23.

21   Arrington, Arrington, and Madsen, *Mothers of the Prophets*, p. 51.

22   Samuel W. Taylor, *The Kingdom or Nothing*, p. 23.

23   Arrington and Smith, *Presidents of the Church*, p. 79.

24   Arrington, Arrington, and Madsen, *Mothers of the Prophets*, p. 51.

25   Arrington and Smith, *Presidents of the Church*, p. 79.

CHAPTER 4

1   Material and quotes for this *vignette* have been taken from: Samuel
     W. Taylor, *The Kingdom or Nothing, The Life of John Taylor, Militant
     Mormon* (New York: Macmillan Publishing Co., Inc., 1976), pp. 27–31;
     B. H. Roberts, *The Life of John Taylor* (Salt Lake City: Bookcraft,
     1963), pp. 40–41; B. H. Roberts, *A Comprehensive History of The
     Church of Jesus Christ of Latter-day Saints, Century 1* (Provo, Utah:
     Brigham Young University Press, 1965) 1:404–405. There is some
     disagreement among historians concerning whether or not John
     Taylor was involved in this particular conflict. In writing this *vignette*
     and chapter, the author has followed the lead of John Taylor's
     grandson Samuel W. Taylor.

2   Roberts, *Life of John Taylor*, p. 39.

3   Ibid., p. 39.

4 Samuel W. Taylor, *The Kingdom or Nothing,* p. 28.
5 Ibid., p. 28.
6 Roberts, *Life of John Taylor,* p. 39.
7 Brian H. Stuy, editor, *Collected Discourses* (Burbank, Calif., and Woodland Hills, Utah.: B.H.S. Publishing, 1987–1992) 1.
8 Parley P. Pratt, *Autobiography of Parley P. Pratt,* edited by his son, Parley P. Pratt (Salt Lake City: Deseret Book, 1938, 1985), p.144.
9 Ibid., p. 144.
10 Roberts, *Life of John Taylor,* p. 40.
11 Ibid., p. 40.
12 Mark L. McConkie, *The Father of the Prophet: Stories and Insights from the Life of Joseph Smith Sr.* (Salt Lake City: Bookcraft, 1993), p. 140.
13 Samuel W. Taylor, *The Kingdom or Nothing,* p. 31.
14 See Blaine M. Yorgason, *From Orphaned Boy to Prophet of God, The Story of Joseph F. Smith* (Ogden, Utah: Living Scriptures, 2001).
15 Roberts, *Life of John Taylor,* pp. 42–44. This Dr. Avard was the same man who, two years later in Missouri, took it upon himself to organize a band of men who were called "Danites." In this he once again acted without authority, using secrecy and fearful oaths to bind his followers together, after which they commenced to carry out Avard's scheme of robbery and plunder against the non-Mormons in the area. As soon as Joseph Smith learned of this, Avard was excommunicated and the "Danite" movement was stifled. Unfortunately, rumors of its continued existence plagued the Church for years afterwards.
16 Ibid., p. 46.
17 Ibid., p. 47.
18 Samuel W. Taylor, *The Kingdom or Nothing,* p. 32.
19 See Leonard J. Arrington, Susan Arrington Madsen, and Emily Madsen Jones, *Mothers of the Prophets* (Salt Lake City: Bookcraft, 1987, 2001), p. 51.
20 Roberts, *Life of John Taylor,* p. 48.
21 Ibid., pp. 49–50.
22 Samuel W. Taylor, *The Kingdom or Nothing,* p. 35. Subsequently the temple was used as a recreation hall, while the basement served as a cattle barn. Some forty years after the Mormons left Kirtland, the Reorganized LDS Church obtained title to the building and restored it.

23 Roberts, *Life of John Taylor*, p. 52.

24 Ibid., pp. 52–53. Among those attending these meetings was a gentleman to whom the Prophet Joseph had gone to receive schooling. This man spoke very highly of Joseph as an exemplary, moral young man. He had never investigated the evidences concerning the Book of Mormon, but he knew the Prophet's character was misrepresented by pious frauds, jealous of his influence and the spread of Mormonism.

25 Ibid., pp. 53–55.

26 Samuel W. Taylor, *The Kingdom or Nothing*, p. 38.

27 Roberts, *Life of John Taylor*, p. 56.

28 Ibid., pp. 56–57.

29 Samuel W. Taylor, *The Kingdom or Nothing*, pp. 38–39.

CHAPTER 5

1 Material for this *vignette* has been taken from B. H. Roberts, *The Life of John Taylor* (Salt Lake City: Bookcraft, 1963), pp. 58–64; B. H. Roberts, *A Comprehensive History of The Church of Jesus Christ of Latter-day Saints, Century 1* (Provo, Utah: Brigham Young University Press, 1965) 1:428–493; and Samuel W. Taylor, *The Kingdom or Nothing: The Life of John Taylor, Militant Mormon* (New York: Macmillan Publishing Co., Inc., 1976), pp. 39–51. Whether or not the two hundred riders seen approaching by Joseph Smith and others were Neil Gilliam's forces remains conjectural.

2 Samuel W. Taylor, *The Kingdom or Nothing*, p. 46.

3 Ibid., pp. 39–40.

4 Ibid., p. 40.

5 Roberts, *Life of John Taylor*, p. 62.

6 Samuel W. Taylor, *The Kingdom or Nothing*, p. 40.

7 Roberts, *Life of John Taylor*, p. 63.

8 Samuel W. Taylor, *The Kingdom or Nothing*, p. 52 n. 14. Taylor cites as his source B. H. Roberts, *Missouri Persecutions*, p. 269.

9 Ibid., p. 52. See also Roberts, *Life of John Taylor*, p. 64.

10 Samuel W. Taylor, *The Kingdom or Nothing*, pp. 51–52.

11 Ibid., p. 53.

12 Ibid., p. 54.

13 Roberts, *Life of John Taylor*, p. 65.

14 See Samuel W. Taylor, *The Kingdom or Nothing*, p. 58.

15 Ibid., p. 59.
16 Ibid., p. 59.
17 Roberts, *Life of John Taylor,* p. 67.
18 The hymn's words are "This earth was once a garden place, With all her glories common; And men did live a holy race, And worship Jesus face to face—In Adam-ondi-Ahman. We read that Enoch walked with God, Above the power of mammon; While Zion spread herself abroad, And saints and angels sang aloud—In Adam-ondi-Ahman. Her land was good and greatly blest, Beyond old Israel's Canaan; Her fame was known from east to west, Her peace was great, and pure the rest Of Adam-ondi-Ahman. Hosanna to such days to come—The Savior's second coming, When all the earth in glorious bloom Affords the saints a holy home, Like Adam-ondi-Ahman."
19 Samuel W. Taylor, *The Kingdom or Nothing,* p. 60.
20 Ibid., p. 60.
21 Leonard J. Arrington, Susan Arrington Madsen, and Emily Madsen Jones, *Mothers of the Prophets* (Salt Lake City: Bookcraft, 1987, 2001), pp. 51–52.
22 Roberts, *Life of John Taylor,* pp. 67–68.

Chapter 6

1 Material for this *vignette* was taken from Samuel W. Taylor, *The Kingdom or Nothing: The Life of John Taylor, Militant Mormon* (New York: Macmillan Publishing Co., Inc., 1976), pp. 72–76; and Ann Pitchforth, "Letter to the Saints in the Isle of Man," *Millennial Star* 8 (July 15, 1846). After her baptism and her husband's bitter denunciation of her decision and his subsequent departure for Australia, Ann and her children immigrated to Nauvoo in 1845. With a piano and the allowance her father regularly sent, Ann lived comfortably during her brief time in the city. Her musical talents were appreciated, and she was soon engaged to teach piano to many of the Nauvoo residents. On January 30, 1846, she was sealed to John Taylor as his tenth wife in the Nauvoo Temple.
2 Samuel W. Taylor, *The Kingdom or Nothing,* pp. 60–61.
3 Ibid., p. 61.
4 See Samuel W. Taylor, *The Kingdom or Nothing,* p. 62.
5 Ibid., p. 63.
6 Ibid., pp. 63–64.

7   B. H. Roberts, *The Life of John Taylor* (Salt Lake City: Bookcraft, 1963), pp. 70–71.

8   Ibid., p. 71.

9   Ibid., p. 73.

10 Ibid., p. 74.

11 Samuel W. Taylor, *The Kingdom or Nothing*, p. 65.

12 Joseph Smith, *History of The Church of Jesus Christ of Latter-day Saints* (Salt Lake City: Deseret Book, 1976), 4:111.

13 Ibid., 4:114.

14 Ibid., 4:115.

15 Samuel W. Taylor, *The Kingdom or Nothing*, p. 66.

16 Roberts, *Life of John Taylor*, pp. 77–78.

17 Ibid., p. 78.

18 See Roberts, *Life of John Taylor*, pp. 84–86. Roberts gives the Irishman's name as Mr. Tate.

19 Ibid., p. 82.

20 James B. Allen, Ronald K. Esplin, and David J. Whittaker, *Men with a Mission, 1837–1841: The Quorum of the Twelve Apostles in the British Isles* (Salt Lake City: Deseret Book, 1992), pp. 175–176.

21 Roberts, *Life of John Taylor*, p. 90.

22 Samuel W. Taylor, *The Kingdom or Nothing*, p. 72.

23 Ibid., p. 72.

24 John Taylor to the Editor, February 27, 1841, *Millennial Star* 1 (March 1841): 276–280. See also Roberts, *Life of John Taylor*, pp. 91–93.

25 Allen, Esplin, and Whittaker, *Men with a Mission*, pp. 179–180.

26 Samuel W. Taylor, *The Kingdom or Nothing*, pp. 74–75.

27 Allen, Esplin, and Whittaker, *Men with a Mission*, p. 179.

28 Ibid., pp. 179–180.

29 "Early Church Leaders Visited Isle of Man," *LDS Church News*, 23 August, 1995, p. 10.

30 Samuel W. Taylor, *The Kingdom or Nothing*, p. 76.

31 Preston Nibley, *The Presidents of the Church* (Salt Lake City: Deseret Book, 1941), pp. 95–96.

32 Samuel W. Taylor, *The Kingdom or Nothing*, p. 76.

CHAPTER 7

1 Material for this *vignette* has been taken from B. H. Roberts, *The Life of John Taylor* (Salt Lake City: Bookcraft, 1963), pp. 114–130; B. H. Roberts, *A Comprehensive History of The Church of Jesus Christ of Latter-day Saints, Century 1* (Provo, Utah: Brigham Young University Press, 1965), 2:234–253; Samuel W. Taylor, *The Kingdom or Nothing: The Life of John Taylor, Militant Mormon* (New York: Macmillan Publishing Co., Inc., 1976), pp. 77–97; John Taylor, *Witness to the Martyrdom: John Taylor's Personal Account of the Last Days of the Prophet Joseph Smith,* compiled and edited by Mark Taylor (Salt Lake City: Deseret Book, 1999), pp. 24–66; and Joseph Smith, *History of The Church of Jesus Christ of Latter-day Saints* (Salt Lake City: Deseret Book, 1975), 7:55–87.

2 Preston Nibley, *The Presidents of the Church* (Salt Lake City: Deseret Book, 1941), p. 96.

3 Samuel W. Taylor, *The Kingdom or Nothing,* p. 78.

4 Roberts, *Life of John Taylor,* p. 98.

5 See Samuel W. Taylor, *The Kingdom or Nothing,* p. 78.

6 See Nibley, *Presidents of the Church,* pp. 96–97.

7 Leonard J. Arrington, Susan Arrington Madsen, and Emily Madsen Jones, *Mothers of the Prophets* (Salt Lake City: Bookcraft, 1987, 2001), pp. 52–53.

8 Roberts, *Life of John Taylor,* p. 102.

9 Nibley, *Presidents of the Church,* p. 97.

10 Roberts, *Life of John Taylor,* pp. 98–99.

11 Ibid., pp. 99–101.

12 Samuel W. Taylor, *The Kingdom or Nothing,* pp. 81–82.

13 Ibid. p. 82.

14 Ibid., p. 100, footnote. See also John Taylor, "Notes" on "the lesser known wives of President John Taylor" (Provo, Utah: Brigham Young University, Special Collections). Between 1843 and 1846 when the Saints began to abandon Nauvoo, John took eight additional wives — Jane Ballantyne, Mary Ann Oakley, Mary Amanda Utley, Mercy Rachel Thompson (sealed for time only), Mary Ramsbottom, Sarah Thornton, Lydia Dibble Smith (sealed for time only), and Ann Hughlings Pitchforth. In later years he was also sealed to Ann Ballantyne (who subsequently divorced him), Sophia Whitaker, Harriet Walker, Caroline Hooper Saunders Gilliam, Margaret Young, and Josephine Elizabeth Roueche.

15   John Taylor, *Witness to the Martyrdom,* pp. 24–25.
      See also Smith, *History of the Church,* 7:56–61.

16   John Taylor, *Witness to the Martyrdom,* pp. 24–29.
      See also Smith, *History of the Church,* 7:56–61.

17   Roberts, *Life of John Taylor,* pp. 103–105.

18   John Taylor, *Witness to the Martyrdom,* pp. 30–34.
      See also Smith, *History of the Church,* 7:61–64.

19   John Taylor, *Witness to the Martyrdom,* pp. 37, 38–40.
      See also Smith, *History of the Church,* 7:66, 67–68.

20   John Taylor, *Witness to the Martyrdom,* pp. 43, 45, 47.
      See also Smith, *History of the Church,* 7:71, 73.

21   John Taylor, *Witness to the Martyrdom,* pp. 49–53.
      See also Smith, *History of the Church,* 7:75–79.

22   Roberts, *Life of John Taylor,* pp. 125–126.

23   John Taylor, *Witness to the Martyrdom,* p. 53.
      See also Smith, *History of the Church,* 7:78–79.

24   John Taylor, *Witness to the Martyrdom,* p. 55;
      See also Smith, *History of the Church,* 7:80.

25   John Taylor, *Witness to the Martyrdom,* pp. 57–60.
      See also Smith, *History of the Church,* 7:81–84.

26   John Taylor, *Witness to the Martyrdom,* pp. 63–66.
      See also Smith, *History of the Church,* 7:85–87.

CHAPTER 8

1   The material for this *vignette* has been taken from John Taylor,
      Witness to the Martyrdom: John Taylor's Personal Account of the Last Days
      of the Prophet Joseph Smith, compiled and edited by Mark H. Taylor
      (Salt Lake City: Deseret Book, 1999), pp. 91–93. See also Joseph
      Smith, *History of The Church of Jesus Christ of Latter-day Saints*
      (Salt Lake City: Deseret Book, 1975), 6:621 and 7:101–112.

2   John Taylor, *Witness to the Martyrdom,* p. 67.
      See also Smith, *History of the Church,* 7:88.

3   John Taylor, *Witness to the Martyrdom,* pp. 76–77.
      See also Smith, *History of the Church,* 7:95–96.

4   Smith, *History of the Church,* 6:592.

5   Ibid., 6:592–593.

6   Ibid., 6:595.

7   B. H. Roberts, *The Life of John Taylor* (Salt Lake City: Bookcraft, 1963), p.133.
8   Smith, *History of the Church,* 6:604.
9   Ibid., 6:605.
10   Ibid., 6:607.
11   John Taylor, *Witness to the Martyrdom,* pp. 84, 88–89. See also Smith, *History of the Church,* 7:101–102.
12   John Taylor, *Witness to the Martyrdom,* pp. 88–89.
13   Ibid., pp. 89–92. See also Smith, *History of the Church,* 7:102–105.
14   Smith, *History of the Church,* 6:620–621. This account is given by Willard Richards, who received no wound during the entire attack.
15   John Taylor, *Witness to the Martyrdom,* pp. 93–94. See also Smith, *History of the Church,* 7:106.
16   John Taylor, *Witness to the Martyrdom,* pp. 95–99. See also Smith, *History of the Church,* 7:107–110.
17   John Taylor, *Witness to the Martyrdom,* pp. 100–102, 105. See also Smith, *History of the Church,* 7:110–112.
18   John Taylor, *Witness to the Martyrdom,* pp. 110–111. See also Smith, *History of the Church,* 7:116–117.
19   John Taylor, *Witness to the Martyrdom,* pp. 111–113
20   Ibid., pp. 114–115. See also Smith, *History of the Church,* 7:117–120.

CHAPTER 9

1   Material for this *vignette* was taken from B. H. Roberts, *The Life of John Taylor* (Salt Lake City: Bookcraft, 1963), pp. 157–167. John's powerful statements, slightly edited in this *vignette* for continuity, are as he himself reported making them.
2   Doctrine & Covenants 107:21–24.
3   See George Q. Cannon, *Gospel Truth: Discourses and Writings of President George Q. Cannon,* selected, arranged, and edited by Jerreld L. Newquist (Salt Lake City: Deseret Book Co., 1987), 221. See also Brian H. Stuy, ed., *Collected Discourses of Wilford Woodruff* 5 vols. (Burbank, Calif., and Woodland Hills, Utah: B.H.S. Publishing, 1987–1992), 4:111. Wilford Woodruff described the event by declaring that Joseph Smith "called the Twelve together the last time he spoke to us, and his face shone like amber. And upon our shoulders he rolled the burden of the Kingdom, and he gave us all the keys and powers and gifts to carry on this great and mighty work. He told us

that he had received every key, every power and every gift for the salvation of the living and the dead, and he said: 'Upon the Twelve I seal these gifts and powers and keys from henceforth and forever. No matter what may come to me. And I lay this work upon your shoulders. Take it and bear it off, and if you don't, you'll be damned.'" This is from a discourse delivered at a Temple Workers Excursion, held in the Tabernacle, Salt Lake City, Sunday, June 24, 1894.

4 Roberts, *Life of John Taylor,* p. 158.

5 Ibid., pp. 158–159.

6 Ibid., p. 160.

7 Ivan J. Barrett, *Joseph Smith and the Restoration* (Provo, Utah: Brigham Young University Press, 1967), p. 637.

8 Ibid., pp. 636–637.

9 Joseph Smith, *History of The Church of Jesus Christ of Latter-day Saints* (Salt Lake City: Deseret Book, 1974), 7:422.

10 Barrett, *Joseph Smith and the Restoration,* p. 639.

11 Ibid., p. 634.

12 Ibid., p. 635.

13 Ibid., p. 635.

14 Russell C. Rich, *Ensign to the Nations* (Provo, Utah: Brigham Young University Publications, 1972), p. 3.

15 Roberts, *Life of John Taylor,* p. 160.

16 Ibid., 161–162.

17 Worse for Sheriff Backenstos, the mob now began threatening not only him but his family. He fled for safety to Warsaw, but mobs again came after him, and he turned his horse toward Nauvoo. Still a mob pursued, and when three of their number drew nearer, the sheriff must have thought that all was lost. Abruptly he "came upon Orrin Porter Rockwell and John Redding refreshing their teams at the crossing. He ordered them in the name of the state to protect him. Rockwell assured him he need not fear; they had two fifteen-shooter rifles besides revolvers and fifty rounds of ammunition. As the three mobocrats approached, Backenstos ordered them to stop. They refused, and he ordered Rockwell to shoot. Frank Worrell fell dead from his horse. The mob took the dead body of Worrell and retreated" (Barrett, *Joseph Smith and the Restoration,* p. 641). Worrell, an officer in the Carthage Greys who supervised the guard at the jail on the day of the martyrdom, was thus one of the first of Joseph's and Hyrum's

killers to be brought face to face with his Maker. See James B. Allen and Glen M. Leonard, *The Story of the Latter-day Saints* (Salt Lake City: Deseret Book Company, 1976), p. 225.

18   See Barrett, *Joseph Smith and the Restoration*, p. 641.

19   Roberts, *Life of John Taylor*, pp. 162–163.

20   Ibid., pp. 167–168.

21   Rich, *Ensign to the Nations*, p. 1.

22   Barrett, *Joseph Smith and the Restoration*, pp. 644–645.

23   Leonard J. Arrington, Susan Arrington Madsen, and Emily Madsen Jones, *Mothers of the Prophets* (Salt Lake City: Bookcraft, 1987, 2001), p. 53.

24   Roberts, *Life of John Taylor*, pp. 169–170.

CHAPTER 10

1   Material for this *vignette* was taken from Ann Pitchforth, "Letter to the Saints in the Isle of Man," *The Latter-day Saints Millennial Star*, vol. 8 (July 15, 1846); and Samuel W. Taylor, *The Kingdom or Nothing: The Life of John Taylor, Militant Mormon* (New York: Macmillan Publishing Co., 1976), pp. 110–111, 118–120. Ann Pitchforth Taylor died in a dugout at Winter Quarters on 26 October, 1846.

2   Samuel W. Taylor, *The Kingdom or Nothing*, p. 98.

3   Ibid., p. 98. These women were Elizabeth Kaighin, who was eight months pregnant with his child and who would go west with a later company; Lydia Dibble Granger Smith, fifty-four years of age and a wife of John Taylor only so he could assist with her care; and twenty-four-year-old Mary Amanda Utley and nineteen-year-old Mary Ramsbottom, both of whom were true wives but were firm in their determination not to accompany him westward. Both Elizabeth and Lydia would make their way later.

4   Ibid., pp. 102–103.

5   Russell R. Rich, *Ensign to the Nations* (Provo, Utah: Brigham Young University Publications, 1972), pp. 4–5. Brigham Young called the tobacco squirter "a filthy wicked man." See also Samuel W. Taylor, *The Kingdom or Nothing*, p. 103, for a slightly different retelling of the account.

6   Rich, *Ensign to the Nations*, pp. 7, 8.

7   B. H. Roberts, *The Life of John Taylor* (Salt Lake City: Bookcraft, 1963), p. 170.

8   Ibid., pp. 170–171.

9   Ibid., p. 179–80.

10 Ibid., pp. 180–181.

11 Thomas L. Kane, *The Mormons* (Philadelphia: King and Baird, 1850). See also Taylor, *The Kingdom or Nothing,* pp. 107–108.

12 Hubert Howe Bancroft, *History of Utah* (1890, reprint edition, Salt Lake City: Bookcraft, 1964), pp. 220–221. See also Rich, *Ensign to the Nations,* pp. 11–12.

13 Kane, *The Mormons.* See also Samuel W. Taylor, *The Kingdom or Nothing,* pp. 108–109.

14 Samuel W. Taylor, *The Kingdom or Nothing,* p. 110.

15 Ibid., p. 110.

16 Ibid., pp. 110–111.

17 Roberts, *Life of John Taylor,* pp. 171–172.

18 Ibid., p. 171, footnote.

19 See Rich, *Ensign to the Nations,* pp. 51–63.

20 Roberts, *Life of John Taylor,* pp. 172–173.

21 Ibid., pp. 173–174.

22 Ibid., p. 174.

23 Ibid., pp. 174–175.

24 Kane, *The Mormons.* See also Samuel W. Taylor, *The Kingdom or Nothing,* p. 115.

25 Roberts, *Life of John Taylor,* p. 176.

26 Samuel W. Taylor, *The Kingdom or Nothing,* p. 121.

27 Roberts, *Life of John Taylor,* pp. 177–178.

28 Andrew Jenson, *Encyclopedic History of The Church of Jesus Christ of Latter-day Saints* (Salt Lake City: Deseret News Publishing Co., 1941). Also, Andrew Jenson, *Church Chronology: A Record of Important Events Pertaining to the History of The Church of Jesus Christ of Latter-day Saints* (Salt Lake City: Deseret News, 1914). Samuel and Mary Pitchforth, in company with Samuel's three younger sisters, came to Utah in 1847 in Daniel Spencer's hundred of John Taylor's Company, ultimately settling in Nephi, Juab County, Utah. In 1857 Samuel was called as one of the seven presidents of the 49th Quorum of the Seventy. In 1869 he was called as President of the Levan branch of the Church, where he served until 1872. He died at Nephi on December 21, 1877. His wife Mary served as a member of the General Board of the Relief Society from October 10, 1892, to February 15,

1901, and died at Nephi on November 20, 1907. The author has been unable to learn what happened to the three Pitchforth girls: Mercy, Sarah, and Annie.

29 See Samuel W. Taylor, *The Kingdom or Nothing,* pp. 122–124.

30 John Taylor, *Millennial Star,* in Roberts, *Life of John Taylor,* pp. 182–185.

CHAPTER 11

1 Material for this *vignette* was taken from Samuel W. Taylor, *The Kingdom or Nothing: The Life of John Taylor, Militant Mormon* (New York and London: Macmillan Publishing Co., Inc., 1976), pp. 125–136; Russell R. Rich, *Ensign to the Nations* (Provo, Utah: Brigham Young University Publications, 1972), pp. 162–164, 168–169; and B. H. Roberts, *The Life of John Taylor* (Salt Lake City: Bookcraft, 1963), pp. 186–193.

2 Samuel W. Taylor, *The Kingdom or Nothing,* p. 125.

3 Roberts, *Life of John Taylor,* pp. 186–187.

4 Ibid., pp. 188–189.

5 Ibid., p. 190.

6 Parley P. Pratt, *Autobiography of Parley P. Pratt,* edited by his son, Parley P. Pratt (Salt Lake City: Deseret Book, 1985), pp. 330–331.

7 Roberts, *Life of John Taylor,* pp. 191–192.

8 Pratt, *Autobiography,* p. 331.

CHAPTER 12

1 Material for this *vignette* was taken from Samuel W. Taylor, *The Kingdom or Nothing: The Life of John Taylor, Militant Mormon* (New York and London: Macmillan Publishing Co., Inc., 1976), pp. 137–138; and B. H. Roberts, *The Life of John Taylor* (Salt Lake City: Bookcraft, 1963), pp. 192–193. Concerning the use of mountaintops as temples, Elder Bruce R. McConkie has written: "From the days of Adam to the present, whenever the Lord has had a people on earth, temples and temple ordinances have been a crowning feature of their worship. 'My people are always commanded to build' temples, the Lord says, 'for the glory, honor, and endowment' of all the saints (D&C 124:39–40). These temples have been costly and elaborate buildings whenever the abilities of the people have permitted such; nothing is too good for the Lord, and no sacrifice is too great to

make in his service. *But in the days of poverty, or when the number of true believers has been small, the Lord has used mountains, groves, and wilderness locations for temple purposes. Endowments, for instance, following the latter-day exodus, were first given on Ensign Peak.* (Bruce R. McConkie, *Mormon Doctrine*, second ed. [Salt Lake City: Bookcraft, 1966], p. 780; emphasis mine). See also Joseph Fielding Smith, *Doctrines of Salvation* (Salt Lake City: Bookcraft, 1955), 2:231–257.

2   Samuel W. Taylor, *The Kingdom or Nothing*, pp. 138–139.

3   Ibid., p. 139.

4   Roberts, *Life of John Taylor*, p. 193.

5   Ibid., p. 194.

6   See, Parley P. Pratt, *The Autobiography of Parley P. Pratt*, edited by his son, Parley P. Pratt (Salt Lake City: Deseret Book, 1938, 1985), p. 331.

7   See Roberts, *Life of John Taylor*, p. 200.

8   Pratt, *Autobiography*, pp. 331–332.

9   Roberts, *Life of John Taylor*, pp. 195–196.

10 Pratt, *Autobiography*, p. 335.

11 Roberts, *Life of John Taylor*, p. 202.

CHAPTER 13

1   Material for this *vignette* was taken from Samuel W. Taylor, *The Kingdom or Nothing: the Life of John Taylor, Militant Mormon* (New York and London: Macmillan Publishing Co., Inc., 1976), pp. 146–174; and B. H. Roberts, *The Life of John Taylor* (Salt lake City: Bookcraft, 1963), pp. 209–241.

2   Roberts, *Life of John Taylor*, pp. 206–209.

3   Ibid., p. 211.

4   Samuel W. Taylor, *The Kingdom or Nothing*, p. 149.

5   Ibid., p. 148.

6   Roberts, *Life of John Taylor*, pp. 212–213.

7   Samuel W. Taylor, *The Kingdom or Nothing*, p. 151, footnote. Taylor accuses his ancestor of intentional embellishment, which seems quite harsh considering that nearly all who write reminiscences tend to focus on and go into greater detail concerning their own experiences and thoughts than they do the experiences and thoughts of others.

8   Roberts, *Life of John Taylor*, pp. 213–214.

9   Samuel W. Taylor, *The Kingdom or Nothing,* p. 154.
10 Ibid., p. 155.
11 Ibid., pp. 154–155.
12 Roberts, *Life of John Taylor,* pp. 228, 229–230.
13 Samuel W. Taylor, *The Kingdom or Nothing,* p. 160.
14 Ibid., p. 160.
15 Ibid., p. 161.
16 Roberts, *Life of John Taylor,* pp. 231–232.
17 Ibid., p. 232.
18 Ibid., p. 236–237.
19 Hubert Howe Bancroft, *The Works of Hubert Howe Bancroft, Volume XXVI, History of Utah* (San Francisco: The History Company, Publishers, 1889), p. 433.
20 See Samuel W. Taylor, *The Kingdom or Nothing,* p. 163.
21 Ibid., 167–168. According to Samuel W. Taylor, John Taylor's relations with Hyde were outwardly cordial, but he had little use for the man. Hyde had turned twice against the Prophet and the Saints, once after the banking disaster at Kirtland, again in Missouri. Twice repented and forgiven, Taylor could accept Hyde as one of the Brethren but found it impossible to be his friend. No doubt Hyde sensed this, and it may have been the reason for his joining with Russell in his attack on John Taylor.
22 Ibid., p. 170. Taylor's quotes from Brigham Young are found in Minutes, Sugar Company meeting, March 17, 1853.
23 Ibid., p. 170.

CHAPTER 14
1   Material for this *vignette* is based upon information taken from Parley P. Pratt, *Autobiography of Parley P. Pratt,* edited by his son, Parley P. Pratt (Salt Lake City: Deseret Book, 1938, 1985), pp. 401–403; and Samuel W. Taylor, *The Kingdom or Nothing: The Life of John Taylor, Militant Mormon* (New York and London: Macmillan Publishing Co., Inc., 1976), pp. 187–191
2   Samuel W. Taylor, *The Kingdom or Nothing,* p. 189.
3   Ibid., p. 189.
4   Ibid., pp. 189–190.
5   B. H. Roberts, The Life of John Taylor (Salt Lake City: Bookcraft, 1963), p. 243.

6   Samuel W. Taylor, *The Kingdom or Nothing,* p. 175.

7   Pratt, *Autobiography,* p. 371.

8   Roberts, *Life of John Taylor,* pp. 244–245.

9   Ibid., p. 244.

10   Ibid., 245.

11   Ibid., pp. 245–246.

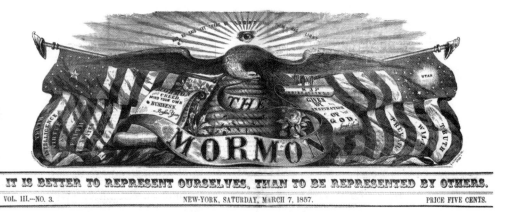

IT IS BETTER TO REPRESENT OURSELVES, THAN TO BE REPRESENTED BY OTHERS.

VOL. III.—NO. 3.   NEW-YORK, SATURDAY, MARCH 7, 1857.   PRICE FIVE CENTS.

12   According to Roberts, the masthead "represented an immense American eagle with out-stretched wings poised defiant above a bee-hive, and two American flags. Above the eagle was an all-seeing eye surrounded by a blaze of glory, and the words: 'Let there be light; and there was light.' On the stripes of the flag on the left was written: 'Truth, Intelligence, Virtue and Faith;' signed, 'John Taylor;' upon those on the right; 'Truth will prevail;' signed, 'H. C. Kimball;' while in the blue fields of one of the flags, the star of Utah shone resplendently. Two scrolls on either side of the eagle bore the following inscriptions: 'Mormon creed—mind your own business,' Brigham Young; and 'Constitution of the United States, given by inspiration of God,' Joseph Smith.

"On the inside, at the head of the editorial column was the American eagle standing on a bee-hive with an American flag on either side. Upon the bee-hive, on one side, leaned the Doctrine and Covenants, Book of Mormon and Bible; on the other a tablet on which was written: 'Peace and good will to man.' The eagle held in its break a scroll on which was written: 'Holiness to the Lord.' "
See Roberts, *Life of John Taylor,* pp. 246–247.

13   Samuel W. Taylor, *The Kingdom or Nothing*, p. 177.

14   Roberts, *Life of John Taylor*, p. 249.

15   Samuel W. Taylor, *The Kingdom or Nothing*, p. 178.

16   Ibid., pp. 178–179. John's comments were published in *The Mormon,*
     October 20, 1855.

17   Roberts, *Life of John Taylor*, pp. 251–252.

18   Ibid., p. 254.

19   Ibid., pp. 255–257.

20   Ibid., pp. 261–262.

21   Samuel W. Taylor, *The Kingdom or Nothing*, p. 183.

22   Ibid., p. 183.

23   Russell R. Rich, *Ensign to the Nations* (Provo, Utah: Brigham Young
     University Publications, 1972), pp. 197–198.

24   Ibid., p. 201.

25   Hubert Howe Bancroft, *The Works of Hubert Howe Bancroft,
     Volume XXVI, History of Utah* (New York, Toronto, London, Sydney:
     McGraw-Hill Book Company, 1889), pp. 490–491.

26   Andrew Love Neff, *History of Utah,* (Salt Lake City: Deseret News
     Press, 1940), pp. 447–448.

27   Rich, *Ensign to the Nations,* pp. 194–195.

28   James B. Allen and Glen M. Leonard, *The Story of the Latter-day
     Saints* (Salt Lake City: Deseret Book, 1976), pp. 297–298.

29   Ibid., pp. 298–299.

30   Ibid., p. 298.

CHAPTER 15

1   Material used in this *vignette* was taken from B. H. Roberts, *The Life
     of John Taylor* (Salt Lake City: Bookcraft, 1963), pp. 273–274, 280–281;
     Samuel W. Taylor, *The Kingdom or Nothing: The Life of John Taylor,
     Militant Mormon* (New York and London: Macmillan Publishing
     Co., Inc., 1976), pp. 192–194; and Russell R. Rich, *Ensign to the
     Nations* (Provo, Utah: Brigham Young University Publications, 1972),
     pp. 245–248.

2   Roberts, *Life of John Taylor*, p. 271.

3   Ibid., p. 271.

4   Ibid., p. 281.

5   James B. Allen and Glen M. Leonard, *The Story of the Latter-day
     Saints* (Salt Lake City: Deseret Book, 1976), p. 307.

6   Ibid., p. 308.

7   Samuel W. Taylor, *The Kingdom or Nothing*, pp. 204–205. John Whitaker Taylor was the father of Samuel W. Taylor, author of this brief account. John Taylor "was to have a total of thirty-four children by his seven acknowledged wives, plus an adopted daughter. There is no available record of his progeny by his 'little-known' wives" (See Taylor, p. 206, footnote).

8   Allen and Leonard, *Story of the Latter-day Saints,* p. 309.

9   Leonard J. Arrington, *Great Basin Kingdom* (Cambridge: Harvard University Press, 1958), p. 194.

10   Rich, *Ensign to the Nations,* p. 286.

11   Ibid., pp. 286, 287.

12   Roberts, *Life of John Taylor,* pp. 299–300.

13   Samuel W. Taylor, *The Kingdom or Nothing,* p. 225.

14   Ibid., p. 225.

15   Ibid., p. 228.

16   This movement of merchants and free thinkers, spearheaded by William S. Godbe and Elias L. T. Harrison, and supported by numerous other intellectuals including John's friend T. B. H. Stenhouse, gradually coalesced into what became known as the Godbeite Movement—a mostly peaceful and primarily economic protest against the Church's cooperative stores, its ban on mining, and so forth. The movement started a newspaper called the *Mormon Tribune,* which in short order fell into Gentile hands and became the *Salt Lake Tribune*—which became without question the greatest single enemy of the Church, blocking statehood for Utah and "bringing the Church to the brink of destruction over the issue of polygamy." Though Samuel W. Taylor calls these people merely "ahead of their time," approximately 5,000 individuals apostatized from the Church because of this movement, and most of its leaders were excommunicated. (*The Kingdom or Nothing,* p. 231.)

17   Samuel W. Taylor, *The Kingdom or Nothing,* p. 232; and Roberts, *Life of John Taylor,* p. 301.

18   Roberts, *Life of John Taylor,* pp. 301–309.

19   Samuel W. Taylor, *The Kingdom or Nothing,* p. 238.

20   Ibid., p. 235.

21   Ibid., pp. 253–254.

22   Ibid., p. 254.

Chapter 16

1   Material for this *vignette* is taken from Samuel W. Taylor, *The Kingdom or Nothing: The Life of John Taylor, Militant Mormon* (New York and London: Macmillan Publishing Co., Inc., 1976), pp. 239–243; see also p. 240, footnote, which is taken from "Reminiscences of Prest John Taylor," a talk delivered by Matthias F. Cowley, October 4, 1925.

2   Leonard J. Arrington, editor, and Paul Thomas Smith, essayist, *The Presidents of the Church* (Salt Lake City: Deseret Book, 1986), pp. 103–104.

3   Ibid., p. 104.

4   B. H. Roberts, *The Life of John Taylor* (Salt Lake City: Bookcraft, 1963), p. 311.

5   Edward W. Tullidge, *Life of Brigham Young* (New York: n.p., 1876), pp. 420–421.

6   Samuel W. Taylor, *The Kingdom or Nothing*, p. 244.

7   B. H. Roberts, *A Comprehensive History of The Church of Jesus Christ of Latter-day Saints, Century 1* (Provo, Utah: Brigham Young University Press, 1965), 5:391.

8   Samuel W. Taylor, *The Kingdom or Nothing*, p. 244.

9   Ibid., p. 244.

10   Ibid., pp. 244–245.

11   Ibid., p. 246.

12   Roberts, *Life of John Taylor*, p. 313.

13   Ibid., pp. 313–314.

14   Ibid., pp. 314–315.

15   Ibid., pp. 315–318.

16   Samuel W. Taylor, *The Kingdom or Nothing*, p. 250.

17   Hickman's "confessions," made in Fort Douglas to a news reporter and writer named Beadle, were subsequently published as one of Beadle's books, entitled *Brigham's Destroying Angel*.

18   Samuel W. Taylor, *The Kingdom or Nothing*, p. 19. See also Roberts, *Life of John Taylor*, p. 318.

20   Ibid., pp. 320–321.

21   Ibid., p. 322.

CHAPTER 17

1   The material used in this *vignette* was taken from B. H. Roberts, *The Life of John Taylor* (Salt Lake City: Bookcraft, 1963), pp. 360–365; and James B. Allen and Glen M. Leonard, *The Story of the Latter-day Saints* (Salt Lake City: Deseret Book, 1976), pp. 358, 390–391.

2   Roberts, *Life of John Taylor,* p. 366.

3   Allen and Leonard, *Story of the Latter-day Saints,* p. 375.

4   See Doctrine & Covenants 107:22–24.

5   Roberts, *Life of John Taylor,* p. 325.

6   Ibid., pp. 323–324.

7   Leonard J. Arrington, editor, and Paul Thomas Smith, essayist, *The Presidents of the Church* (Salt Lake City: Deseret Book, 1986), p. 109.

8   Ibid., p. 109.

9   Ibid., pp. 107–108.

10   Roberts, *Life of John Taylor,* pp. 329–330.

11   Ibid., p. 331.

12   Ibid., p. 331.

13   Ibid., pp. 331–332.

14   Arrington and Smith, *Presidents of the Church,* p. 108.

15   Samuel W. Taylor, *The Kingdom or Nothing: The Life of John Taylor, Militant Mormon* (New York and London: Macmillan Publishing Co., Inc., 1976), p. 280.

16   Ibid., p. 280.

17   Roberts, *Life of John Taylor,* p. 335.

18   Samuel W. Taylor, *The Kingdom or Nothing,* p. 280–281, incl. footnotes.

19   Roberts, *Life of John Taylor,* p. 338.

20   Samuel W. Taylor, *The Kingdom or Nothing,* p. 276.

21   Ibid., pp. 277–288. Taylor adds in a footnote: "Bancroft was the first outsider to receive full church cooperation—and the last. It is difficult to overestimate the importance of his *History of Utah* as a framework for subsequent scholars and historians.... His collection of materials, housed in the Bancroft Library, University of California at Berkeley, is still being mined by researchers.... [His book's] value...simply cannot be questioned."

22   Arrington and Smith, *Presidents of the Church,* p. 109. See also Taylor, *The Kingdom or Nothing,* p. 278, for interesting, if perhaps speculative, details.

23 Roberts, *Life of John Taylor,* pp. 341–342.
See also Doctrine & Covenants 107:18, 19, 91, 92.

24 Ibid., pp. 346–347.

25 Ibid., p. 348.

26 Taylor, *The Kingdom or Nothing,* pp. 312–315. The scriptural passage suggested by John Taylor reads: "But of that day and hour knoweth no man…"

27 Arrington and Smith, *Presidents of the Church,* p. 110.

28 Ibid., pp. 110–111.

29 Allen and Leonard, *Story of the Latter-day Saints,* pp. 358, 390–391.

30 Ibid., p. 392.

31 Russell R. Rich, *Ensign to the Nations* (Provo, Utah: Brigham Young University Publications, 1972), pp. 401–402.

32 Allen and Leonard, *Story of the Latter-day Saints,* p. 385.

33 For a historically accurate, but fictionalized account, of this incredible pioneering experience, see Blaine M. Yorgason, *Hearts Afire,* Books One, Two, and Three (Salt Lake City: Shadow Mountain, 1997, 1998, 1999).

34 Allen and Leonard, *Story of the Latter-day Saints,* pp. 387–388.

35 Ibid., p. 392.

36 Ibid., p. 392.

37 Roberts, *Life of John Taylor,* pp. 356–358.

38 Ibid., p. 358.

39 Ibid., pp. 358–359.

40 Arrington and Smith, *Presidents of the Church,* p. 111.

41 Roberts, *Life of John Taylor,* p. 359.

42 Ibid., pp. 360–361.

43 Ibid., pp. 361–365.

44 Ibid., p. 365.

CHAPTER 18

1   Material for this *vignette* was taken from Samuel W. Taylor, *The Kingdom or Nothing: The Life of John Taylor, Militant Mormon* (New York and London: Macmillan Publishing Co., Inc., 1976), pp. 372–375; B. H. Roberts, *The Life of John Taylor* (Salt Lake City: Bookcraft, 1963), p. 409; and John Taylor, "Notes" on "the lesser known wives of President John Taylor" (Provo, Utah: Brigham Young University Special Collections).

2   Roberts, *Life of John Taylor,* pp. 369–370.

3   See Russell R. Rich, *Ensign to the Nations* (Provo, Utah: Brigham Young University Publications, 1972), pp. 403–404.

4   James B. Allen and Glen M. Leonard, *The Story of the Latter-day Saints* (Salt Lake City: Deseret Book, 1976), p. 390. See also Rich, *Ensign to the Nations,* p. 404.

5   Roberts, *Life of John Taylor,* p. 371.

6   Allen and Leonard, *Story of the Latter-day Saints,* pp. 395–396.

7   Roberts, *Life of John Taylor,* pp. 372–376. See also Rich, *Ensign to the Nations,* p. 405: Rudger Clawson, who was released a year early when his parents appealed to the President of the United States for clemency for their son, "was ordained an apostle on October 10, 1898, and became president of the Council of the Twelve. He died at the age of eighty-six on June 21, 1943."

8   Taylor, *The Kingdom or Nothing,* p. 325.

9   Roberts, *Life of John Taylor,* p. 378.

10   Samuel W. Taylor, *The Kingdom or Nothing,* pp. 323–324.

11   Ibid., p. 325.

12   Allen and Leonard, *Story of the Latter-day Saints,* p. 390.

13   Samuel W. Taylor, *The Kingdom or Nothing,* p. 327.

14   Roberts, *Life of John Taylor,* p. 381.

15   Samuel W. Taylor, *The Kingdom or Nothing,* p. 332.

16   Ibid., pp. 332–333. Samuel Taylor notes that the Utah manuscript "was finished late in 1885, edited for printing the following year, and published 1889."

17   Roberts, *Life of John Taylor,* pp. 383–384. It is remarkable—considering the arrogance and cruelty of many of the skunks, sneaks, spies, and federal officials—that no U.S. deputy was ever injured by the Saints (see Taylor, *The Kingdom or Nothing,* p. 335, footnote).

18   See Samuel W. Taylor, *The Kingdom or Nothing,* p. 336, footnote.

19 It is interesting to wonder how many times President Taylor had to remind himself of his mother's lifelong joy at having for three weeks hidden the Prophet Joseph Smith; and to realize that he was providing families of willing Saints the same choice blessing.

20 Samuel W. Taylor, *The Kingdom or Nothing*, pp. 339–340. "As a reward for his untiring efforts, Dubois subsequently became Idaho's delegate to Congress, and the state's first senator. He was prominent in the Smoot investigation of 1904–7, which was the final attempt of the U.S. government to smash the Mormon Church" (p. 339, footnote 4).

21 Roberts, *Life of John Taylor*, pp. 384–385.

22 Ibid., pp. 388–390.

23 Ibid., pp. 390–391.

24 Ibid., pp. 391–398.

25 Ibid., p. 407.

26 See Allen and Leonard, *Story of the Latter-day Saints*, p. 406.

27 See Samuel W. Taylor, *The Kingdom or Nothing*, pp. 359–361.

28 Roberts, *Life of John Taylor*, pp. 407–108.

29 Ibid., p. 409.

EPILOGUE

1 B. H. Roberts, *The Life of John Taylor* (Salt Lake City: Bookcraft, 1963), pp. 410–416.

2 Hyrum M. Smith and Janne M. Sjodahl, *Doctrine and Covenants Commentary* (Salt Lake City, Deseret Book Company, 1976), p. 322.

BIBLIOGRAPHY

Allen, James B., Ronald K. Esplin, and David J. Whittaker. *Men with a Mission, 1837-1841: The Quorum of the Twelve Apostles in the British Isles* (Salt Lake City: Deseret Book, 1992).

Allen, James B., and Glen M. Leonard. *The Story of the Latter-day Saints* (Salt Lake City: Deseret Book, 1976).

Arrington, Leonard J. *Great Basin Kingdom* (Cambridge: Harvard University Press, 1958).

Arrington, Leonard J., Susan Arrington Madsen, and Emily Madsen Jones. *Mothers of the Prophets* (Salt Lake City: Bookcraft, 1987, 2001).

Arrington, Leonard J., editor, and Paul Thomas Smith, essayist. *The Presidents of the Church, Biographical Essays* (Salt Lake City: Deseret Book, 1986).

Bancroft, Hubert Howe. *History of Utah* (1890, reprint edition, Salt Lake City: Bookcraft, 1964).

——. *The Works of Hubert Howe Bancroft, Volume XXVI, History of Utah* (San Francisco: The History Company, Publishers, 1889).

Barrett, Ivan J. *Joseph Smith and the Restoration* (Provo, Utah: Brigham Young University Press, 1967).

Cannon, George Q. *Gospel Truth: Discourses and Writings of President George Q. Cannon.* Selected, arranged, and edited by Jerreld L. Newquist (Salt Lake City: Deseret Book, 1987).

"Early Church Leaders Visited Isle of Man." *LDS Church News,* 23 August, 1995.

Jenson, Andrew. *Church Chronology: A Record of Important Events Pertaining to the History of The Church of Jesus Christ of Latter-day Saints* (Salt Lake City: Deseret News, 1914).

——. *Encyclopedic History of The Church of Jesus Christ of Latter-day Saints* (Salt Lake City: Deseret News Publishing Co., 1941).

Kane, Thomas L. *The Mormons* (Philadelphia: King and Baird, 1850).

McConkie, Bruce R. *Mormon Doctrine,* second ed. (Salt Lake City: Bookcraft, 1966).

McConkie, Mark L. *The Father of the Prophet: Stories and Insights from the Life of Joseph Smith Sr.* (Salt Lake City: Bookcraft, 1993).

Neff, Andrew Love. *History of Utah* (Salt Lake City: Deseret News Press, 1940).

Nibley, Preston. *The Presidents of the Church* (Salt Lake City: Deseret Book, 1944).

Pitchforth, Ann. "Letter to the Saints in the Isle of Man," *The Latter-day Saints Millennial Star* vol. 8. July 15, 1846.

Pratt, Parley P. *Autobiography of Parley P. Pratt.* Edited by his son, Parley P. Pratt (Salt Lake City: Deseret Book, 1938, 1985).

Rich, Russell R. *Ensign to the Nations: A History of the LDS Church from 1846 to 1972* (Provo, Utah: Brigham Young University Publications, 1972).

Roberts, B. H. *A Comprehensive History of The Church of Jesus Christ of Latter-day Saints, Century 1.* 6 vols. (Provo, Utah: Brigham Young University Press, 1965).

——. *The Life of John Taylor* (Salt Lake City: Bookcraft, Inc., 1963).

Smith, Hyrum M., and Janne M. Sjodahl. *Doctrine and Covenants Commentary* (Salt Lake City: Deseret Book, 1976).

Smith, Joseph. *History of The Church of Jesus Christ of Latter-day Saints.* 7 vols. (Salt Lake City: Deseret Book, 1974).

Smith, Joseph Fielding. *Doctrines of Salvation.* 3 vols. (Salt Lake City: Bookcraft, 1955).

Stuy, Brian H., ed. *Collected Discourses of Wilford Woodruff.* 5 vols. (Burbank, California and Woodland Hills, Utah: B.H.S. Publishing, 1987–1992).

Taylor, John. To the Editor, February 27, 1841, *Millennial Star* vol. 1. March 1841.

——. "Notes" on "the lesser known wives of President John Taylor." (Provo, Utah: Brigham Young University, Special Collections).

——. *Witness to the Martyrdom, John Taylor's Personal Account of the Last Days of the Prophet Joseph Smith.* Compiled and edited by Mark Taylor (Salt Lake City: Deseret Book, 1999).

Taylor, Samuel W. *The Kingdom or Nothing: The Life of John Taylor,*
    Militant Mormon (New York and London: Macmillan Publishing Co.,
    Inc., 1976).
Tullidge, Edward W. *Life of Brigham Young* (New York: n. p., 1876).
Yorgason, Blaine M. *Hearts Afire.* Books one, two, and three
    (Salt Lake City: Shadow Mountain, 1997, 1998, 1999).
——. *From Orphaned Boy to Prophet of God, The Story of Joseph F. Smith*
    (Ogden, Utah: Living Scriptures, 2001).

TOPICAL INDEX